Robert Ernest Hubbard

Robert Ernest Hubbard is an associate professor at Albertus Magnus College in New Haven, Connecticut, and the director of the college's Computer Information Systems Program. For 12 years he has been webmaster of major Web sites on American Revolutionary War General Israel Putnam and entertainers Phil Silvers and William Boyd.

Additional contributors:
Jeff Bahr is the author of *Amazing and Unusual USA* and the co-author of seven volumes in the Armchair Reader series.

J. K. Kelley has a B.A. in history from the University of Washington in Seattle. He has contributed to numerous Armchair Reader books.

David Morrow has been a writer and editor for 20 years. His recent work includes co-authoring *Florida on Film* and contributing to the reference guide *Disasters, Accidents, and Crises in American History.*

Cover credits:
Archive Holdings Inc. (bottom left); **© Corbis** (top left); **INTERFOTO Pressebildagentur/Alamy** (top right); **Touchstone/Jerry Bruckheimer Inc./The Kobal Collection/Andrew Cooper** (bottom right)

Contributing Illustrators: Robert Schoolcraft, Erin Burke, and Shavan R. Spears

Factual Verification by: Chris Smith and Marci McGrath

Armchair Reader is a trademark of Publications International, Ltd.

West Side Publishing is a division of Publications International, Ltd.

Louis Weber, CEO
Publications International, Ltd.
7373 North Cicero Avenue
Lincolnwood, Illinois 60712

ISBN-13: 978-1-4127-9819-8
ISBN-10: 1-4127-9819-1

Manufactured in U.S.A.

8 7 6 5 4 3 2 1

Contents

Last Person Standing

❑ ❑ ❑ ❑

We all know the saying "Living well is the best revenge." A corollary to that could be "Living well and living longer is the best revenge." We all want to live well and to a ripe old age, and that is the theme of *Armchair Reader*™: *The Last Survivors.* It is a cosmic version of the kids' contest of who can hold their breath the longest.

As we compiled the stories for this book, we were fascinated with the many examples of courage, tenacity, and humor. Here is just a sampling of what you will find in this volume:

- On May 8, 1902, Mount Pelée erupted, destroying the city of St. Pierre and killing more than 30,000 people. The only person to survive—**Ludger Sylbaris**—was found severely burned in the town jail's underground cell. He was later pardoned and told his story on tours with the Barnum and Bailey Circus.
- A fire killed 146 workers at the Triangle Shirtwaist Factory in New York City in 1911. Last survivor **Rose Rosenfeld** escaped as the company executives did, by hopping a freight elevator to the roof. She retold her story throughout her life to promote reform.
- The last surviving speaker of the 1963 March on Washington (at which Reverend Martin Luther King Jr. gave his "I Have a Dream" speech) is **John Lewis,** who is now a U.S. congressman.

As you've noticed from the above examples, the names of the last survivors jump off the page because they are bigger, bolder, and underlined—which, in our opinion, is the next best thing to seeing your name in lights. We strove to tell as wide a variety of stories as we could find. Our goal was to entertain and inform, concentrating on the personal stories of those involved while unearthing all the enticing particulars. As with all the books in the Armchair Reader™ series, we've designed this book to be enjoyed no matter where you open it. So sit back in your armchair, or find another comfortable spot, and peruse at will.

P.S. If you have any questions, concerns, or ideas pertaining to this book, or you would like more information about other West Side titles, please contact us at: **www.armchairreader.com.**

Disasters

❑ ❑ ❑ ❑

What does it really *take to be a survivor? The following people who lived through volcanoes, shipwrecks, fires, and hurricanes could give us a few pointers.*

The Galveston Hurricane

In the early evening of September 8, 1900, a hurricane came in from the Gulf of Mexico, hitting Galveston Island and Galveston, Texas. In a few hours, more than 8,000 people were killed. It was the highest death toll for any natural disaster in U.S. history. Initially a tropical storm over Cuba, the hurricane devastated the Texas coast, then lost intensity as it traveled up to the Great Lakes, on to Eastern Canada, and out to the North Atlantic Ocean. Galveston resident **Maude Conic** was the last survivor of the hurricane. She may have been as old as 116 when she died in 2001.

• •

The Unique Journey of the *Roma*

When the Galveston hurricane made landfall, ships moored in the harbor were tossed about like children's toys. Nobody discovered this quicker than Captain William Storm, who commanded the steamer SS *Roma*.

The ship and crew fought an epic battle to remain secured to Galveston's Pier 15, but it proved an exercise in futility. At 7:15 P.M., the storm pulled the vessel free of its chains, and the *Roma* was carried broadside up the channel.

The *Roma*'s first contact came when it struck the steamship *Kendal Castle*, loosening its moorings. The *Roma* then smashed broadside through three railroad bridges before finally holding fast against a fourth situated beside a wagon bridge.

When the storm subsided, the vessel rested miles from its starting point. The *Roma* sustained considerable damage to its starboard side, but not one of its crew members was injured. Considering that bizarre journey, it was a genuine miracle.

• •

* * * *

When the Galveston hurricane's storm surge struck, most people ran for their lives. Not so Joseph Corthell. Repeatedly maneuvering his rowboat into danger's path, Corthell and his three brothers scanned the roiling waters in search of survivors. The brave team is credited with saving some 200 lives.

* * * *

After the hurricane, Galveston erected a 17-foot seawall.

* * * *

Galveston was again flooded in 2008, when the eye of Hurricane Ike made landfall as a Category 2 storm.

* * * *

The Saga of the *Boston*

As a new, fully green crew member aboard the American trading ship *Boston* in 1803, Englishman **John Jewitt** was coping with the difficulties of sea life. In addition to having to learn just about everything connected with sailing, Jewitt, an armorer (weapons maker) who had apprenticed under his father, was trying his best to head off repeated bouts of seasickness. Although he couldn't possibly know it, stomach distress was soon to become the least of his problems.

Everything centered on an outburst the ship's captain had in front of Chief Maquina, a Nootka tribal leader, while docked at Nootka Sound, Vancouver Island. When Chief Maquina returned a broken firearm and told the captain that the gun was *peshak* (bad), the captain launched into a volley of insults and slurs, calling the chief a liar. Since he was speaking English, a language that the chief supposedly didn't understand, the captain thought he could do this with impunity. He was wrong. The powerful chief knew only too well what some of the key words meant and silently declared war on the *Boston*.

The day before the ship was to go out to sea, Maquina and his men attacked the *Boston*. The attack came swiftly, while Jewitt was below deck. He heard a commotion and ascended, only to be struck a glancing blow by an ax. Maquina saved Jewitt from further injury because he knew Jewitt's weapon-making skills would be useful. All but one of his crewmates were brutally massacred. (The other survivor, John Thompson, was found hours later; Jewitt was able to convince Maquina to spare Thompson's life by falsely claiming that Thompson was his father.)

From that point on, Jewitt and Thompson were slaves. When they arrived at the chief's village on Friendly Cove, however, the villagers greeted Jewitt with an outpouring of unexpected affection. Even the chief now showed a genuine affinity for his captive.

At one point, Maquina arranged a marriage between Jewitt and one of the women in his tribe (though she eventually went back to live with her family). Despite such unexpected treatment, it was understood that should Jewitt or Thompson try to escape, "daggers would come." Clearly, however, this wasn't a typical master/slave relationship.

This situation would continue until 1805, when the ship *Lydia* rescued the captives. During his time in captivity, Jewitt kept a journal. In 1815, he recounted his bizarre tale in *A Narrative of the Adventures and Sufferings of John R. Jewitt*. The book brought Jewitt a measure of notoriety, and he lived out his days playing the captive in plays and singing his signature song, "The Poor Armourer Boy." Jewitt spent the latter part of his life in New England and died in Hartford, Connecticut, on January 7, 1821.

The Quarrel

On the 19th, the king [Maquina] came again on board... He had much conversation with Captain Salter, and informed him that there were plenty of wild ducks and geese near Friendly Cove, on which the Captain made him a present of a double-barrelled fowling piece.... The next day Maquina came on board with nine pair of wild ducks, as a present, at the same time he brought with him the gun, one of the locks of which he had broken, telling the Captain that it was *peshak*, that is bad. Captain Salter was very much offended... considering it as a mark of contempt for his present, he called the king a liar, adding other opprobrious terms... Maquina knew a number of English words, and unfortunately understood but too well the meaning of the reproachful terms that the Captain addressed to him. He said not a word in reply, but his countenance sufficiently expressed the rage he felt, though he exerted himself to suppress it, and I observed him . . . repeatedly put his hand to his throat, and rub it upon his bosom, which he afterwards told me was to keep down his heart, which was rising into his throat and choking him.

—Excerpt from *A Narrative of the Adventures and Sufferings of John R. Jewitt*

The Sinking of the *Duncan Dunbar*

When the clipper ship *Duncan Dunbar* slammed against a reef off Australia in August 1857, a heavy toll was exacted from Sydney. In a few short hours, 63 passengers and 58 crew members making the journey there from London were committed to a watery grave.

Thousands of the living would begin their grieving process, for the ship was not full of strangers—it was full of Sydney locals returning after visiting friends and family in England. Word of the wreck quickly spread, and the townspeople hurried to the shore to inquire about loved ones. When they came upon the wreckage and saw the bodies floating in the water, they were heartbroken. The only survivor of the disaster was seaman **James Johnson,** who was rescued more than a day later from the ledge of a cliff.

Newtown's St. Steven's Cemetery staged a mass funeral for the victims and later erected a monument in their honor. During the September 24 ceremony, 20,000 mourners lined George Street to view the seven hearses and more than 100 carriages that held the victims. In deference to the tragedy, scores of bankers and shopkeepers closed their businesses, bringing commerce in the city to a virtual halt.

Today, the Hornby Lighthouse is situated near the fated site at the tip of South Head. It stands as a brick-and-mortar reminder of the perilous hazards found just beneath the waves, and as a final legacy to those doomed souls aboard the *Duncan Dunbar*.

In later years, James Johnson became a lighthouse keeper at the entrance to Newcastle Harbor, where on July 12, 1866, he helped rescue Frederick Hedges, the lone survivor of the 60 men and women on the *Cawarra* when it sank. On April 13, 1915, Johnson died in Sydney at age 78.

The Peshtigo Fire

On October 8, 1871, North America's worst forest fire occurred in northeastern Wisconsin and Michigan's Upper Peninsula. About 1,500 people died, including 800 of the 2,500 residents of Peshtigo, Wisconsin. The city was totally destroyed in an hour, leaving the nearby Peshtigo River as the only place of safety. Poor logging practices and an exceptionally dry summer were blamed for the fire. **Augusta Wegner Bruce** was the last living survivor of the conflagration. She died on February 10, 1974, at age 104.

Coincidentally, the "Great Chicago Fire" erupted the very same evening as the conflagration at Peshtigo. Although the Chicago fire was smaller and its death toll a mere fraction of the Peshtigo tragedy, the brouhaha made over the Chicago blaze would serve to obscure the worst forest fire in North American history. It's not too surprising.

The Chicago fire took place in a highly populated, major American city. This ensured reams of newspaper coverage featuring hair-raising, first-person accounts. Since Chicago was a major player in national and world commerce, this too factored into the fire's notoriety.

Perhaps the greatest reason for the Chicago fire's fame was the story about "Mrs. O'Leary's Cow." Blamed for kicking over a lantern and starting the Chicago blaze, the controversial tale was long regarded as factual. Today, it's considered dubious at best. Because of such sensationalism, the Peshtigo fire has been dubbed the "forgotten fire." Too bad Peshtigo didn't have its own cow story to tell.

What Caused the Flames?

Like many great conflagrations, the cause of North America's worst forest fire is open to conjecture. Factors such as a prolonged and widespread drought provide reasons for the epic disaster but stop short of pinpointing its origin. What is certain is that the enormous fire (which was 10 miles wide and 40 miles long) burned for two days and claimed the lives of approximately 1,500 people. When the fire reached the waters of Green Bay, it lost its fuel source, and its stormlike winds diminished. A rainstorm delivered the blaze its final deathblow. A poem published in the *Marinette Eagle* captures the tragedy's essence:

> On swept the tornado, with maddening rush,
> Uprooting the trees o'er the plain, thro' the brush,
> And the sky-leaping flames, with hot, scorching breath,
> Gathered parents and children to the harvest of death.
> As years roll along and the ages have sped
> O'er the charred, blackened bones of the Peshtigo dead,
> And the story is told by the pen of the sage,
> In letters immortal on history's page,
> No fancy can compass the horror and fright,
> The anguish and woe of that terrible night.

The Johnstown Flood

On May 31, 1889, a catastrophic breach of Western Pennsylvania's South Fork Dam delivered unimaginable destruction to gritty Johnstown, a steel company town in a valley 14 miles below. With 2,209 deaths attributable to the dam break, the tragedy ranks among the worst in American history. As if such loss of life weren't unsettling enough, subsequent reports of improper dam maintenance and outright neglect led to a startling conclusion: The Johnstown Flood could have been avoided.

During the Gilded Era (1845–1916), the South Fork Fishing and Hunting Club membership roster read like a veritable "Who's Who" of wealthy industrialists. Such magnates as Andrew Carnegie and Henry Clay Frick would summer at the fishing and boating oasis at

Lake Conemaugh, conveniently located just a short train ride from Pittsburgh.

But there was a problem brewing beneath the lake's surface. Since the club had acquired the property, dam maintenance had gone by the wayside. Worse still, members had lowered the dam's height and installed fish traps in the spillway to prevent stocked fish from escaping. These screens would at times collect debris and render the spillway almost useless. In addition, critical discharge pipes had been removed and never replaced. Despite warnings and recommendations from dam inspector Daniel Morrell, the members maintained this dangerous status quo. The stage was set.

A Spectacular Downpour

When the rains came on May 31, 1889, they came with a vengeance. The U.S. Army Signal Corps estimated that six to ten inches of rain fell over the region in a 24-hour period. Just after 4:00 P.M., things turned ominous at the South Fork Dam. A "whooshing" noise signaled the dam's unceremonious end, and untold horrors were about to unfold.

A 36-foot wall of water and debris slammed into Johnstown with a roar. It lifted all objects in its path, even freight cars. In an instant, entire families were obliterated and others were fractured, leaving large numbers of widows and orphans.

In the flood's aftermath, lawsuits against the wealthy club members went nowhere because the court viewed the catastrophe as an "act of God." With this, the tragic episode was committed to history, and life in the flood-prone valley went on.

An infant just three months old when the tragedy occurred, last survivor **Frank Shomo** lived until the ripe old age of 108.

* * * *

On June 5, Clara Barton and the Red Cross arrived in Johnstown. They got to work building hotels and distributing furniture and supplies. This mission helped establish the agency's reputation.

* * * *

The *Sindia* Runs Aground at Ocean City

The *Sindia* was a four-masted steel-hulled British ship on its last leg from Japan to New York City. On December 15, 1901, it was hit by a major storm and became lodged in the sands near Ocean City, New Jersey. It slowly started sinking. All of the ship's crew were removed safely. Still under water and sand today, parts of the ship continue to break loose and wash up on the beach at Ocean City. The last survivor of the *Sindia* crew, **David Jackson,** died in 1970 at age 90.

What Was Onboard the *Sindia*?

Interest in *Sindia*'s sandy sarcophagus goes beyond *fin de siècle* artifact-hunting. Word spread that it carried Boxer Rebellion loot from China: gold and jade from ransacked temples. If so, why didn't the captain fish out the "temple spoils" before *Sindia* broke up? Salvagers soon rescued much of the ship's cargo; why not the "manganese"? Why no record of crew members collaborating with salvagers? Because bamboo matting and dishes weren't worth it, and that's all that really remained. Moreover, *Sindia*'s Chinese port of call, Shanghai, didn't experience much of the post-Boxer looting. That occurred mainly in Peking/Beijing.

For years, *Sindia*'s rusty corpse tantalized salvagers and beach-goers. Humans can keep a buried treasure legend alive for centuries: The secret word is *gold.* After the early years, seeping water and sand sank efforts to plunder *Sindia*'s tomb. Each year *Sindia* sinks a bit deeper. If full salvage were easy, someone would have succeeded by now.

* * * *

Sindia *set sail from New York in 1900 with kerosene for Shanghai. The ship called next at Japan, where it loaded silk and porcelain. Captain McKenzie planned to unload the goods in New York in time for the Christmas shopping season. Instead, salvagers unloaded them in New Jersey.*

* * * *

Mount Pelée Unleashes Its Fury

On May 8, 1902, the Mount Pelée volcano on the Caribbean island of Martinique erupted after a half century of inactivity. Even though there were definite signs of an impending disaster, the population of the town actually increased during the week of the tragedy because of an upcoming election.

When the volcano unleashed its full fury, lava, hot ash, and hot gas destroyed the city of St. Pierre in minutes. More than 30,000 people were killed, a larger number than in any other single volcanic eruption of the 20th century. Only one person survived—a 25-year-old prisoner named **Ludger Sylbaris.** Four days after the eruption, he was found severely burned in the town jail's underground cell. Later, he was pardoned and told his story on tours with the Barnum & Bailey Circus. Sylbaris died in 1929 at age 55.

Eyewitness Accounts

Most of the ships in St. Pierre's harbor perished as well. The crew of the doomed British steamer SS *Roraima* saw the eruption unfold. *Roraima*'s assistant purser wrote: "I saw St. Pierre destroyed. The city was blotted out by one great flash of fire. Of eighteen vessels lying in the road, only the British steamship *Roddam* escaped, and she lost more than half of those on board."

Another *Roraima* officer described it eloquently: "My first thought was that it was the end of the world. It would have been said that all that there is of dynamite in the universe had just made jump the mountain."

Soon *Roraima* itself burned and sank. One young nurse lamented: "When we could see each other's faces they were covered with black lava, the baby was dying, Rita, the older girl, was in great agony and every part of my body was paining me."

* * * *

When animals flee, so should people. The deadly pit vipers and foot-long centipedes of Mount Pelée were no joke, and in the days leading up to the eruption, the intensifying heat and ash drove the venomous critters down into St. Pierre en masse. Some 50 people (mostly children) and 200 animals died of snakebite.

* * * *

The Wreck of the Old 97

On September 27, 1903, the Old 97—a mail express train known for its speed—had left the station late and was trying to make up some time. As it neared Danville, Virginia, it came upon a sharp curve and jumped the track. The train fell into a ravine 75 feet below, killing 11 people. A ballad about it, "The Wreck of the Old 97," became famous. Eight-year-old **Herman Lester** was walking along the tracks when the accident occurred and witnessed the tragedy. Lester lived to be more than 100 years old and was the last to survive among the wreck's witnesses.

* * * *

The engineer's body was found outside the cab, not inside "with his hand on the throttle" as the song goes.

* * * *

Vernon Dalhart's 1924 recording of "Wreck of the Old 97" became one of America's first million-sellers. It also inspired the first big music copyright lawsuit (1927), which proved an inconclusive sinkhole for legal fees. We still aren't sure who wrote the original. Johnny Cash, Woody Guthrie, Boxcar Willie, The Seekers, Hank Williams III, and Shel Silverstein (to name a few) have all covered it.

* * * *

The *General Slocum*

As the sidewheel steamer *General Slocum* cast off into New York's East River on the morning of June 15, 1904, the band played "A Mighty Fortress Is Our God." A local Lutheran congregation had chartered *Slocum* for its annual Sunday School picnic on Long Island. Some 1,330 people, mainly immigrant German women and children from the Lower East Side, bubbled with anticipation.

Any parishioner who knew *Slocum*'s history was demonstrating serene faith. In 13 years of paddling about New York, the ship had racked up several vessel collisions and numerous groundings. Corrupt federal inspectors had recently certified its life preservers (the life preservers proved to be useless—if not lethal—which gives an indication of how inept the inspectors were). The same inspectors did not even bother to check the lifeboats and fire hose.

A Voyage Through Hell Gate

Slocum's course lay through a stony, swirly shoal called Hell Gate. Approximately forty minutes into the trip, as Captain William H. Van Schaick focused on navigating the hazard, a boy yelled up to the pilothouse: "Hey, Mister! The ship's on fire!" Presuming a bad practical joke, Van Schaick swore, "Get the hell out of here!"

Crew members soon echoed the warning. Van Schaick looked outside and saw two causes for concern: flames consuming the steamer's port side and passengers leaping overboard. The crew deployed the fire hose; it fell apart, rotten. Passengers clawed for life preservers, many of which disintegrated into useless rags and cork dust. The crew was not trained in fire procedures and had never dislodged a lifeboat. Nor could they have on this journey, for the *Slocum*'s boats were wired and painted to the deck.

Van Schaick didn't like his chances on the nearby shore because of the rocks and the lumberyards and oil tanks beyond, so he gritted his teeth and floored it for North Brother Island, a mile away. *Slocum* left a wake of drowning and burnt passengers as the rapid passage fanned the flames. The ship shoaled just short of North Brother. Numerous swimmers and small craft hurried to the rescue, often risking their own lives.

Appalling contemporary photos show dozens of corpses washed ashore. The grim human accounting was 1,031 dead, including two of the crew of 30. Van Schaick suffered burns and a broken ankle. Officials blamed the fire on crew carelessness in the lamp room. Only Van Schaick paid a legal penalty, doing three-and-a-half years in Sing Sing Prison before his pardon by President William Howard Taft.

The public outcry had a lasting effect, as every excursion boat in New York underwent inspection in earnest. Many failed as badly as *Slocum* should have. Many well-dressed rear ends were chewed, the U.S. Steamboat Inspection Service swabbed its decks, and higher safety standards came in force. Many survivors moved away from their Lower East Side neighborhood, where they felt haunted by memories of the friends they had lost in the fire.

Adele Liebenow was the youngest survivor of the *Slocum* disaster. Six months old when the *Slocum* caught fire, she lost two sisters, two cousins, and an aunt that day. Her parents survived with serious burns. On the disaster's first anniversary, toddler Adella (name changed by her parents to sound more English) had the sad honor of unveiling the *Slocum* victims' memorial. In no way could the sweet little girl imagine that she would outlive every other survivor.

Adella Wotherspoon (née Liebenow) died at Roseland, New Jersey, on January 26, 2004, one century old—the last of the survivors of the *General Slocum.*

The Trials

When a thousand people die, someone must pay. *Slocum* owner Frank Barnaby did everything possible to avoid being that someone. He hurried to counterfeit safety records, then blamed the whole mess on corrupt federal inspectors (fair) and panicked passengers (ridiculous).

A grand jury saw it otherwise, indicting Van Schaick, Barnaby, the inspector, and eight others for manslaughter by criminal negligence. When three hung juries failed to convict the inspector, thus sinking most of the other indictments (including Barnaby's), prosecutors decided to try only Van Schaick. By tradition and law, a vessel's master is responsible for the safety of the passengers and crew. Van Schaick made the easiest scapegoat, and the jury faulted him for ultimate negligence. Under the Seaman's Manslaughter Act of 1838, he got the maximum sentence: ten years.

* * * *

Up until September 11, 2001, the Slocum *tragedy ranked as New York City's deadliest disaster.*

* * * *

The Slocum *tragedy was mentioned in James Joyce's novel* Ulysses. *Why? The* Ulysses *story is set on June 16, 1904—the day after the real-life catastrophe.*

* * * *

San Francisco's 1906 Quake

Of the handful of people alive in the 21st century who survived 1906's San Francisco earthquake, the most famous was **Charles Lane.** Born Charles Levison, he was just a year-old tot when the house started rocking. In young adulthood, he decided acting was more enjoyable than selling insurance (thus demonstrating good instincts). As Charles Lane, he became a full-time thespian and a founding member of the Screen Actors Guild in 1933.

Lane would act for more than 70 years. Hollywood soon typecast him to always play an obstacle or nemesis: the cranky businessman, the collection agent, the stodgy banker. This led to few leading roles, but it ensured that TV and movie buffs would recognize his respectable "Establishment" face (if not his name). For example, when Lucy had a baby boy on *I Love Lucy,* Lane portrayed another expectant father waiting with Lucy's husband, Ricky. He is perhaps best remembered for his recurring role as railroad penny-pincher Homer Bedloe on the *Petticoat Junction* TV series (from 1963 to 1970). A witty, warm man who was the living opposite of his typecasting, Lane passed away at age 102 in 2007.

The Fire

The quake was bad—but not catastrophic by itself. The serious devastation began when the tremors upended numerous oil lamps, igniting dozens of fires. Matters got even worse when the gas mains ruptured. Even this might have been contained, but the water mains also broke. To complete the melancholy recipe, the initial quake mortally injured the fire chief—a devastating loss of leadership.

The blaze quickly overwhelmed firefighting efforts in the downtown core. Fire caused about 90 percent of the total destruction. Short of water, desperate firefighters dynamited buildings to create firebreaks. Had experts done this, it might have helped; done by relative amateurs, it more often started new fires. So did property owners: Many were insured against fire but not earthquake damage. A little timely arson assured eventual payment.

Inadequate as the dynamite method may have been, it did eventually halt the spreading flames—more than 500 incinerated city blocks later.

* * * *

In the hours after the quake, San Francisco Mayor Eugene Schmitz issued a shoot-to-kill order, which authorized law-enforcement officers to kill anyone caught looting or committing any other crime.

* * * *

Famed tenor Enrico Caruso, caught in the quake, vowed never again to visit San Francisco. He kept that vow.

* * * *

Dix and *Jeanie* Cross Paths

On November 18, 1906, a clear and calm day in Washington State's Puget Sound, Captain Percy Lermond of the passenger ferry *Dix* went below to collect fares. He left unlicensed First Officer Charles Dennison at the helm.

Dix's path soon converged with that of the freight schooner SS *Jeanie*, which reversed props and tried to avoid the ferry. Dennison became confused and steered *Dix* directly into her path. *Jeanie* T-boned *Dix,* rolling the ferry hard to port. Ballast shifted and seawater gushed in, sinking *Dix* within five minutes.

Of the 77 people aboard, 42 were lost, including Dennison. *Jeanie* rescued the other 35, one of whom was Captain Lermond. He was faulted for failing to provide a lookout before he went to collect fares, and his license was revoked. It was later reinstated, and he again worked as a ship's captain, but his work was restricted to cargo ships. *Dix* remains under 600 feet of water in Puget Sound.

The *Dix*'s last survivor was **Alice Simpson Bassett,** who was 13 at the time of the incident. A nonswimmer, she may have stayed afloat because of air collected in her skirt. In 1973, Bassett attended a ceremony to place a commemorative marker on the shoreline.

* * * *

Jeanie *later became a casualty in her own right, running aground off British Columbia in 1913.*

* * * *

The Triangle Shirtwaist Fire

On a Saturday afternoon in March 1911, workers at the Triangle Shirtwaist Factory in New York City were getting ready to go home after a long day. They were tidying up their workspaces and brushing fabric scraps off the tables and into large bins. Someone on the eighth floor carelessly threw a match or cigarette butt into one of those bins, and within minutes, flames took over the factory floors. Panicked workers rushed to evacuate, and many on the ninth floor became trapped. There were two exit doors on that floor, but one was blocked by fire and the other was locked—a precaution owners deemed necessary to prevent thefts by workers. The terrified people on that floor were faced with two choices: wait for rescue (and likely die in the fire) or jump from the windows. Many chose to jump. Overall, 146 workers died in the tragedy.

Austrian Jewish immigrant **Rose Rosenfeld** survived by figuring out how the executives were handling the situation. Rose hopped a freight elevator to the roof, where she was rescued by firefighters. When the bosses tried to bribe her to testify that the doors hadn't been locked, Rose refused. Her anger at the needless death lasted a very long lifetime.

Rose married Harry Freedman in 1927. Two of their three children had polio; Rose helped them regain the ability to walk. Rose Freedman promoted reform by retelling her story throughout her life. She was a diehard L.A. Lakers basketball fan, and her numerous friends knew never to phone during games. Rose died February 15, 2001, age 107, the last survivor of the Triangle Shirtwaist fire.

* * * *

A shirtwaist *was what we call a* blouse *today.*

* * * *

A Horrible Sound

I was walking through Washington Square when a puff of smoke issuing from the factory building caught my eye.... I saw every feature of the tragedy visible from outside the building. I learned a new sound—a more horrible sound than description can picture. It was the thud of a speeding, living body on a stone sidewalk.

The first ten... shocked me. I looked up—saw that there were scores of girls at the windows....

"Call the firemen," they screamed.... They were all as alive and whole and sound as were we who stood on the sidewalk.... We heard the siren of a fire engine in the distance....

"Here they come," we yelled. "Don't jump; stay there."

The firemen began to raise a ladder. Others took out a life net and, while they were rushing to the sidewalk with it, two more girls shot down.... It seemed to me that the thuds were so loud that they might have been heard all over the city....

I remembered these girls were the shirtwaist makers. I remembered their great strike of last year in which these same girls had demanded more sanitary conditions and more safety precautions in the shops. These dead bodies were the answer.

—William Shepherd, United Press International reporter and eyewitness to the fire

* * * *

When even Tammany Hall joined in the call for better standards, you knew the situation was bad. After the Triangle Shirtwaist tragedy, the garment workers' union, local politicians, and crusading reformers joined forces for a common cause, beginning a workplace safety reform cascade that would continue through the New Deal of the 1930s—a tide not even greedy corporations could avoid.

* * * *

The *Titanic*

In the most famous ship disaster in history, on April 15, 1912, the RMS *Titanic* struck an iceberg in the North Atlantic and sank in less than three hours. Of the 2,227 passengers and crew, only 705 survived. Of these, Britain's **Millvina Dean**—the youngest passenger on the ship at about ten weeks old—was the last survivor. Dean lost her father in the sinking. In 2009, actors Leonardo DiCaprio and Kate Winslet made generous donations to a fund to cover Dean's mounting nursing home expenses. Dean passed away on May 31, 2009, at age 97.

The Journey of an Iceberg

Most North Atlantic icebergs *calve* (detach) from the Greenland ice sheets. From the Greenland coast, the Labrador Current carries them south, where they may calve *growlers* (mini-icebergs) and *bergy bits* (big ice chunks). When they hit the Gulf Stream (roughly New Jersey's latitude), they melt.

In a typical year in the early 1900s, six to eight ships would hit icebergs. Most collisions occurred off Newfoundland's rugged coast, far north of *Titanic*'s path. The luxury liner was right along the southern edge of the danger zone, and maritime scuttlebutt had it that the 'bergs were further south than usual.

The disaster inspired the foundation of the International Ice Patrol (IIP), which first experimented with naval gunfire to destroy the icebergs. When the targets proved indestructible, the IIP did a far more practical thing: find and track icebergs, keeping mariners apprised by "Marconigram" (radio).

• •

* * * *

Titanic *nearly collided with another vessel, the* New York, *while pulling out of the dock at Southampton.*

* * * *

Could someone raise the Titanic's *halves from her two-mile-deep tomb? It would be monstrously expensive. Since the halves would likely disintegrate in the process, salvagers wouldn't get a second chance. Some complain that deep-sea gawkers are already accelerating* Titanic's *deterioration. Since the ship is an inadvertent mass grave, many object to raising it on moral grounds. Bottom line: It ain't happening.*

* * * *

Male *Titanic* Survivors

French passenger **Michel Navratil** was only three years old when the *Titanic* sank. His few memories of the event involved his father waking him and dressing him. He also remembered being happy to be in the lifeboat. He went on to work as a professor of philosophy in Montpellier, France. When he died in 2001 at age 92, he left four women to share the distinction as *Titanic*'s last survivors. Michel's father (also named Michel) was one of the 1,522 fatalities on *Titanic*, but there's far more to little Michel's tale.

Navratil *père* had abducted his sons Michel and Edmond from a collapsing marriage. The concealed pistol found on his body implies that he would have resorted to force rather than surrender his sons. Their mother, Marcelle, who must have been frantic, had no idea what had become of them. Navratil *père* skedaddled from France to Southampton, where he bought three second-class tickets aboard *Titanic* under assumed names. He meant to start a new life in America, beyond his ex-wife's legal reach.

As we all know by now, that plan foundered. Navratil *père* handed his sons through the women-and-children-only cordon and bade them farewell as *Titanic* lowered lifeboats. They never saw Papa again.

Little Michel and Edmond survived, and their plight as the "*Titanic* Orphans" stood out in print even above the post-sinking media din. The Children's Aid Society fostered them at the New York home of fellow survivor Margaret Hays, who had looked after the boys on the lifeboat. Soon word came from Europe: Marcelle had recognized them from news stories and would be on the next ship to reunite with them and bring them back to France. On *Titanic,* even the few happy conclusions bore tragic tinges.

* * * *

The body of Navratil père *was recovered, and he was buried in Halifax, Nova Scotia (150 bodies recovered from the* Titanic *were buried in Halifax because it was the closest city with rail access). Although Navratil was Catholic, he was buried in the Jewish cemetery. Because the ticket found on his body carried the name Louis Hoffman (Navratil's assumed name), rescuers thought he was Jewish. The error was not discovered until after Navratil had been buried.*

* * * *

The Mystery Ship

Several passengers and crew members aboard the *Titanic* reported seeing the lights of another ship on the horizon as the *Titanic* was foundering. Modern *Titanic* buffs feud over this "mystery ship." What is known:

- The British freighter SS *Californian* was in the vicinity.
- *Titanic* survivors reported some sort of nearby ship sighting.
- *Californian* witnesses recall seeing white rockets at the right time to be *Titanic*'s distress signals.

Solved? Not quite. Some doubt that the mystery ship was the *Californian.* Discrepancies in *Titanic* and *Californian* witnesses' testimony raise reasonable doubt. It's hard to say whether the differences mean something, or if they resulted from simple stress and distraction.

By the time *Californian* steamed over to help *Carpathia* fish out survivors, no more remained. *Californian*'s captain later came under cold scrutiny for the tardy response. The question of his culpability can boil enthusiasts' blood to this day.

The Rescue Operation

After the *Titanic* hit the fatal iceberg, the RMS *Carpathia* came to its aid. Unlike the "mystery ship," *Carpathia* was helpful. *Carpathia*'s alert radio operator relayed *Titanic*'s distress call to Captain Arthur Rostron, who twice clarified the message because he was shocked to receive such a call from the *Titanic.* Now he would learn just what sort of ship and crew he had. Defying the obvious risk of an iceberg strike, the *Carpathia* raced to the site of *Titanic*'s last bearings while the crew readied everything from hot drinks to blankets to rescue gear. In forlorn optimism (they expected to find *Titanic* afloat), they prepared to load baggage and mail.

When the ship arrived, there was no *Titanic. Carpathia*'s crew began a five-hour operation, retrieving lifeboats and comforting stricken survivors. If it hadn't been for these rescuers, most might have died of hypothermia. Rostron later received plentiful well-deserved accolades, including induction as a Knight Commander of the Order of the British Empire and a U.S. Congressional Gold Medal.

The last survivor of the rescue operation was 15-year-old apprentice **Herbert Johnston.** He helped pull survivors onto the *Carpathia.* Johnston later served in both world wars and died in South Africa in 2002 at age 104.

* * * *

The International Ice Patrol was merely one of the safety strides brought on by Titanic's *loss. Passenger ships would now monitor the radio 24/7. Ships increased their lifeboat complements. New liners reflected design lessons gleaned from the disaster: longer rudders (for improved maneuvering), double hulls, and improved riveting (icy waters had made* Titanic's *rivets brittle).*

* * * *

Titanic's Last Surviving Officer

In his testimony at the inquiry into the *Titanic* disaster, Fourth Officer **Joseph Groves Boxhall,** the last surviving officer of the *Titanic,* recalled hearing the three bells from the crow's nest, signaling an iceberg had been spotted. Boxhall was sent to inspect the front of the ship; he found no damage, but a passenger did hand him a piece of ice that had fallen onto the deck. Boxhall later took the bearings (41°46' N 50°14' W) dispatched in the distress call. Boxhall was detailed to command one of the half-full lifeboats, and it was his green flare that guided *Carpathia* to the rescue.

He served in World War I, then in the merchant marines until retirement. A quiet man by nature, Boxhall rarely discussed April 15, 1912, until very late in life. In 1958, he agreed to give technical consultation for the movie *A Night to Remember,* and he later gave a BBC interview about *Titanic.*

Boxhall died in 1967 at age 83. In accordance with his request, his ashes were scattered at *Titanic*'s last coordinates.

Male Survivors

Was it really women and children first? Mostly. Some first- and second-class women passengers refused to be parted from their husbands. Until the end was near, most people who stayed didn't expect to die. The *Titanic* was unsinkable, as any fool knew, so why panic?

Dividing up the *Titanic*'s souls, first- and second-class children had the highest survival rate: 83 percent. Third-class women (46.1 percent) and children (34.2 percent) out-survived first-class men (32.6 percent). Lowest was second-class men (8.3 percent), then third-class men (16.2 percent), then male crew (21.7 percent).

Why did some men survive? Someone had to row and steer the lifeboats. Trained sailors historically do that better than society matrons, though many of these acquitted themselves admirably. At the end, there were a few emergency boats left when the captain gave the *sauve qui peut* (every man for himself) order. A number of crew members survived aboard these emergency boats.

* * * *

Only three of Titanic*'s 23 female crew members perished.*

* * * *

One of Titanic*'s most famous passengers, hereditary multimillionaire John Jacob Astor IV, reportedly asked to join wife Madeleine in a lifeboat due to her "delicate condition" (pregnancy). Denied permission, he died with the ship. Madeleine survived to give birth to JJA VI in August. This* in utero Titanic *survivor died in 1992.*

* * * *

The *Empress of Ireland*

In the wee hours of May 29, 1914, the Canadian steamship *Empress of Ireland* sank in the St. Lawrence River after a collision with the Norwegian collier *Storstad.* The two ships had crossed paths just east of Rimouski, Quebec, on a narrow stretch of the river. Of the nearly 1,500 people aboard the *Empress*, more than 1,000 died. After the tragedy, questions would come with rapid-fire succession. Why did the liner sink just 15 minutes after the collision? Why were so few of its lifeboats launched? How could the *Storstad* emerge from such a violent collision virtually unscathed?

History would list fog as the principal cause for the disaster, but it wasn't the only culprit. In an ironic twist, *Empress's* Captain Henry Kendall made a bad situation worse when he ordered an evasive turn to starboard. Instead of striking the *Storstad* a glancing blow as he had hoped, reports suggest that the *Storstad's* bow pierced the "liner's steel ribs as smoothly as an assassin's knife." With the super-hardy *Storstad* (specifically fortified to break through ice) doing the piercing, there was little doubt which ship would come out on top.

With a sudden list to starboard that prevented the launch of most of her lifeboats, the *Empress* gave up the ghost. The last living survivor was **Grace Martyn,** who passed away in 1995. She was eight years old at the time of the sinking.

Today the *Empress of Ireland* rests approximately 130 feet below the surface of the St. Lawrence River. Despite its relatively shallow depth, extremely cold temperatures and severe tidal currents make reaching the craft a dicey proposition. But even with such hazards acting as a natural shield, unscrupulous divers have found their way to the wreck. Since the 1980s, underwater marauders have caused much damage at the site, including the removal of skeletal remains.

The Impact of the Sinking of the *Empress*

The passenger liner *Empress of Ireland* was owned and operated by the Canadian Pacific Steamship Company and was responsible for that firm's regular Liverpool to Quebec City run. Although not as large or ostentatious as some of her contemporaries (the *Titanic* measured in at a whopping 882 feet versus the *Empress*'s 548 feet), the *Empress* provided a critical link with Canadian Pacific's transcontinental railroad and drew her fair share of notable passengers.

In addition to human cargo that included a steady flow of European immigrants, the liner was also responsible for transporting mail. During these times the ship was known as the RMS *Empress of Ireland*, an official title bestowed upon the ship by the British government.

When it collided with the *Storstad* and dragged more than 1,000 people down with it, the *Empress of Ireland* ensured that it would be remembered: To this day, the shipwreck is considered the worst in Canadian maritime history.

• •

Last *Lusitania* Survivor

On May 7, 1915, during the height of World War I, a German U-boat torpedoed the luxury liner RMS *Lusitania* as it steamed across the Atlantic toward Liverpool, England. The vessel sank with alarming haste, taking almost 1,200 people along with it.

Just one week before the fateful journey, Germany issued a warning to "vessels flying the flag of Great Britain, or any of her allies" planning voyages through waters adjacent to the British Isles. Since a number of British merchant ships had already been destroyed by German U-boats, *Lusitania*'s Captain William Turner understood full well that these Teutonic forces meant business.

Despite such dangers, the *Lusitania* departed New York Harbor on May 1, 1915, bound for Liverpool with approximately 2,000 passengers on board. In theory, the captain's avoidance strategy should have been straightforward. He would use the *Lusitania*'s superior speed to sidestep enemy attacks while adhering to a set of evasive directives prescribed by the British Admiralty. In reality, he did neither. For reasons still shrouded in mystery, the *Lusitania* actually slowed when it reached enemy waters, sailing close enough to shore to present a tempting target. When a lurking U-boat fired its torpedoes, the resulting explosion sealed *Lusitania*'s fate. A second blast, now believed to have come from disturbed coal dust (Germany would later claim this as being onboard munitions) completed the job.

Audrey Lawson-Johnston (née Pearl) of Bedfordshire, England, is the last survivor of the sinking. Still living in 2009 at age 94, she was a mere infant at the time of the tragedy. She went on to marry Hugh Lawson-Johnston, whose grandfather had developed the beef-extract product Bovril. The last survivor who claimed to remember the sinking was American Barbara McDermott of Connecticut. She was 95 when she passed away in April 2008.

Rescue Efforts

Although the *Lusitania* sank less than 15 miles off the shores of southwestern Ireland, rescue steamers and tugs needed some two hours to reach the ship. In a scenario where every minute counted, the nearby fishing vessel *Wanderer* rushed to *Lusitania*'s aid after seeing the liner suddenly list. "Go for her, be British!" came the urgent cry from the *Wanderer*'s captain as the tiny vessel made its way to the floundering liner and set about the business of rescuing its survivors.

The *Wanderer*, strained with a heavy payload of humanity, rendezvoused with the tug *Flying Fish* some two miles off the coast of Kinsale, Ireland. The tug's captain, Thomas Brierly, organized a shuttle system with the *Wanderer* that would transport survivors from the site of the tragedy to Queenstown (now Cobh), Ireland. Making several such perilous journeys, the team is credited with saving some 200 people.

* * * *

Alfred Vanderbilt, son of railroad magnate Cornelius Vanderbilt, was on board the Lusitania. *When the ship began to sink, he offered his life jacket to a young mother. Since Vanderbilt couldn't swim, this selfless act cost him his life.*

* * * *

Chicago's Deadliest Disaster

Never in the annals of maritime catastrophes has salvation been so agonizingly close, yet so far away. The excursion steamer *Eastland* presented a heartbreaking scenario when it rolled over while moored to a busy Chicago River dock. Before the day was through, hundreds had perished in a mind-boggling tragedy.

Chartered for a Western Electric company picnic on July 24, 1915, the 269-foot vessel was scheduled to carry employees across Lake Michigan to Michigan City, Indiana, for the day's festivities. But it was not to be. The *Eastland* never left port.

Survivors and onlookers described a topsy-turvy effect that seemed to increase as more travelers were added. When the passengers crowded to one side of the vessel to wave to family and friends on the dock, the side-to-side motions escalated. It was during these undulations that the 2,000-ton steamer reached an apex from which it could not recover. In the span of a few moments, the *Eastland* capsized.

Despite being so close to the scene, there was little that would-be rescuers could do; much of the drama was playing out beneath the vessel, out of reach. Passengers who were on the upper deck when the steamer tipped fell into the water had a decent chance of survival. Most of the passengers below deck (inside the ship), however, became trapped or were crushed when the ship tipped over. In the end, more than 800 people lost their lives on Chicago's deadliest day.

After the tragedy, some heroes did stand out. One was Charles R. E. Bowles, a 17-year-old volunteer diver whom the veterans nicknamed "The Human Frog." Bowles bravely ventured into the most remote parts of the *Eastland* and worked tirelessly—from the early morning and into the night. He was credited with recovering 40 bodies.

Libby Hruby, the last known survivor of the *Eastland* tragedy, died on November 6, 2004, at age 99. Only ten years old at the time of the incident, she survived the sinking with the help of her sister and a fellow passenger.

* * * *

To improve safety and qualify for an increase in passenger capacity, modifications—including the addition of lifeboats—were completed just weeks before the tragedy. Ironically, these measures may have increased the ship's top-heaviness, playing a prominent role in its demise.

* * * *

Restless Spirits

There are numerous stories of hauntings related to the *Eastland* disaster, but none more famous than the phenomena experienced at Oprah Winfrey's Harpo Studios. Oprah's workplace stands on the site of the old Second Regiment Armory Building, which served as a temporary morgue at the time of the *Eastland* disaster. Some Oprah employees have heard various odd sounds, such as children's laughter, old-time music, clinking glasses, whispering voices, footsteps, slamming doors, sobbing, and muffled screams. Do the employees merely have active imaginations? Or could they be hearing the eternal pleas and sufferings of *Eastland* victims? You decide.

The *Britannic*

During World War I, commercial ships were regularly pressed into war service. These consisted mostly of smaller vessels, which, after refitting, would serve as troop transports and armed merchant cruisers. Redefining the genre, the *Britannic*—the 1914 sister ship of the ill-fated *Titanic* and the largest liner afloat—would be commissioned as a hospital ship in 1915 before it ever had a chance to carry a civilian passenger.

The converted liner, resplendent in bright white paint festooned with three large red crosses (two additional crosses were lit at night), featured everything one might expect from a typical hospital. Fancy fitments gave way to medical wards on the ship's upper decks, while dining and reception areas became operating rooms. Nurses and orderlies occupied cabins originally intended for the under-classes. Despite the ship's utilitarian changes, nods to the *Britannic*'s luxurious role were found in its first-class swimming pool and elegant first-class staterooms. Not surprisingly, the latter housed the upper echelon: the ship's doctors, nursing matron, and medical corps officers.

On November 21, 1916, the rechristened HMHS *Britannic* struck a mine in the Kea Channel in the Aegean Sea. The ship suffered a mortal wound and sank with blisteringly fast speed. As a testament to efficient rescue procedures, only 30 of the ship's more than 1,000 passengers perished. The last survivor of the tragedy was **George Perman,** who was just 15 years old at the time of the sinking. He passed away in 2000 at age 99.

One Lucky Lady

"Three strikes and you're out" apparently didn't apply to Violet Jessop. The lucky Englishwoman would serve aboard the infamous trio of White Star ships (*Olympic*, *Titanic*, *Britannic*) when accidents befell them—and would live to tell the tale each time.

In 1911, Jessop was working as a first-class attendant on the *Olympic*. While sailing off the Isle of Wight, the British warship HMS *Hawke* collided with her vessel. Both ships sustained heavy damage, but they managed to stay afloat and no lives were lost. Strike one.

In 1912, Jessop was working aboard the luxury steamer *Titanic*. After the ship struck an iceberg, Jessop was ordered into a lifeboat. There, in relative safety, she watched the enormous ship plunge into infamy in the icy waters of the North Atlantic. Strike two.

Jessop's most harrowing moment came in 1916 while serving as a nurse aboard the doomed HMHS *Britannic*. Jessop was forced to abandon the swiftly sinking vessel after it had hit a mine. "I leapt into the water but was sucked under the ship's keel which struck my head," said Jessop. Somehow, she managed to survive. Strike three.

At this point an "out" would normally be called. But not for this plucky lass. She continued to sail and even served on the *Olympic* once again before retiring from sea duty. The unlikely tale of Violet Jessop, thrice saved by the fickle hand of fate, seems nothing short of miraculous.

• •

* * * *

When the Britannic *struck an underwater mine, its trip to the bottom of the Aegean Sea was extraordinarily swift. Contributing to such speed were scores of open portholes on the vessel's lower decks. Left open as a way to ventilate the ship's hospital wards, they allowed additional water to pour in when the vessel began to list. The ship slid beneath the waves less than an hour after the explosion.*

* * * *

Evidence suggests that Britannic *wasn't the name originally intended for the third ship of the Olympic-class trio. After the* Titanic *disaster, owners of the White Star Line were faced with a decision: Should they name their final ship* Gigantic, *as they had planned? Or, considering the circumstances, should they go for a more mundane tag? In the end,* Britannic *was the name bestowed upon the craft, which was struck down despite its humble name.*

* * * *

Ocean Liner Captains

Of the captains of the ships on our list, *Empress of Ireland* **Captain Henry Kendall** was the last to survive. He passed away in a London nursing home in 1965 at age 91. Major ocean liner disasters and the fates of the ship captains follow:

- *Titanic*: Its captain, 62-year-old Edward John Smith, went down with the ship on April 15, 1912.

- *Lusitania*: Captain William Thomas Turner died at his home in Great Crosby, United Kingdom, in 1933 at age 76.
- *Britannic*: Captain Charles Bartlett died in 1945 in his late 70s.
- *Empress of Ireland*: Captain Henry Kendall died in 1965 at age 91.

* * * *

"You have sunk my ship!"

—Captain Henry Kendall, after being pulled aboard the Storstad

* * * *

Not on My Ship!

Four years before the *Empress of Ireland* sank, Captain Henry Kendall was working as a skipper aboard the SS *Montrose*. Fancying himself an amateur detective, the captain would often "size up" his passengers, deciding which ones were on the straight and narrow and which ones weren't.

During a voyage from Antwerp to Quebec City, Kendall read a *Daily Mail* article that outlined the tale of Dr. Hawley Harvey Crippen and his girlfriend Ethel Le Neve. Scotland Yard was seeking the fugitive Crippen in connection with the murder of his wife, and Le Neve was believed to be traveling with him.

With the intriguing story in the back of his mind, Kendall noticed that one of his passengers bore a strong resemblance to Dr. Crippen. His suspicions mounted when he saw that the passenger, a Mr. Robinson, was traveling with a peculiar man of slight build whom he referred to as his son.

While observing the pair from a stealthy distance, Kendall saw the two "men" embrace in a romantic manner. Convinced he had identified Crippen and his girlfriend, Kendall contacted Scotland Yard by wireless.

When authorities boarded the *Montrose* in Canada, a positive identification would be made. Kendall's sleuthing had proven correct. Ethel Le Neve would be acquitted of any wrongdoing, but Dr. Crippen wasn't quite so fortunate. He would be convicted of murdering his wife and was hanged on November 28, 1910. The incident marked the first time that a fugitive had been tracked down via wireless telegraph.

The Steamboat *Columbia*

On July 5, 1918, the South Side Athletic Club of Pekin, Illinois, chartered the steamboat *Columbia* for an evening cruise along the Illinois River. The destination was the upriver Al Fresco Amusement Park in Peoria, an agreeable spot where partiers could escape their troubles and enjoy a fun-filled evening. As the club's largest annual event, the cruise drew some 500 people, mostly from the towns of Pekin and neighboring Kingston Mines, Illinois.

On its return voyage *Columbia* suddenly found itself mired in fog. While moving uncertainly through the murky conditions, the vessel wandered too close to shore and struck a submerged tree stump. The resulting wound proved fatal. Due to the river's shallow depth, however, the ship would only partially sink. Despite such luck, 87 people would die as a result of a ceiling collapse triggered by the forceful collision.

The tragedy ranked as one of the worst inland water accidents in U.S. history. The last living survivor of the *Columbia* was **Lucille Adcock.** Only 19 years old at the time of the mishap, Adcock survived by clutching a flagpole until she was rescued. On August 13, 2006, at the ripe age of 106, she expired. At her death, the grand dame of the *Columbia* disaster left 45 great-grandchildren and 48 great-great-grandchildren.

Al Fresco Amusement Park

Flinging open its gates on June 10, 1905, Al Fresco Amusement Park brought an era of fun and frivolity to Peoria. Situated along a stretch of the Illinois River where the waterway's gentle breezes and agreeable scenery acted as an inviting backdrop, the park offered amusements that ran from the benign and mild to the thrilling and frightfully wild.

In a colorful nod to the latter, motorcycle jumpers, high divers, and wire-walkers could often be found cheating death at the park. Such daredevilry coexisted beside more gentle amusements, which included Dewey Beach—a place where visitors could swim or fish—and the Japanese Garden, a multitiered pavilion that featured name acts such as escape artist Harry Houdini and Wild West cowboy Buffalo Bill. A figure-eight roller coaster and 65-foot-tall Ferris wheel rounded out the amusements.

Al Fresco Amusement Park flourished until the late 1920s when rising river levels delivered its death knell. After its rides became damaged by recurring floods, they were dismantled or left to rot, and a colorful piece of Illinois history drew to a close.

A Seven-Destroyer Pileup

Shortly after nightfall on September 8, 1923, seven of fourteen ships of the U.S. Navy's Destroyer Squadron 11 ran aground near Santa Barbara, California. The accident would claim the lives of 20 sailors from the USS *Young* and three more from the flagship USS *Delphy*. Its occurrence is representative of the crude navigation methods that prevailed during the era.

At the time of the incident, Captain Edward H. Watson was piloting the *Delphy*. After checking his charts against bearings supplied by a radio direction finding (RDF) station at Point Arquello, the captain was satisfied that he was at the Santa Barbara Channel and initiated his turn into the waterway. He was dead wrong. In reality, the *Delphy*—and by extension all of Squadron 11—was at Honda Point, several miles north and further east than Watson believed. When a sickening crunch indicated his ship had run aground, the captain realized his error and sounded the ship's siren.

In short order, six more ships from the squadron ran aground, but none more devastatingly than the USS *Young*. After ripping its hull open on submerged rocks, the vessel rolled over onto its starboard side.

Earlier that day, the mail steamship *Cuba* had also run aground off Honda Point. It was surmised that this grounding and the ones that followed may have resulted from unusual currents produced by a recent earthquake in Toyko. This theory was never proven, however.

Last survivor **Gene Bruce** was 16 years old when he was aboard the *Chauncey.* He experienced the grounding of his own ship, which was cut open by the propellor of the USS *Young*. Bruce served in the navy for six more years after the tragedy. During the 1930s, he helped paint the dangerous upper sections of San Francisco's Golden Gate Bridge. Few workers were willing to climb that high, and Bruce earned $2.00 an hour, which was good money during the Great Depression. In 1998, Bruce was a participant in the a ceremony that marked the 75th anniversary of the Honda Point incident. Bruce lived some 82 years beyond the tragedy, to the advanced age of 98.

A Jump into Treacherous Waters

When the armada of ships grounded one by one, the USS *Young* took the mightiest hit. As the ship foundered on its starboard side in a turbulent, rock-strewn sea, a number of valiant acts ensured the survival of most of its crew.

Due to the *Young*'s extreme list, its lifeboats could not be deployed. Understanding this, commanding officer William L. Calhoun ordered his crew to the port side of the vessel to await rescue. When the USS *Chauncey* grounded upright just 75 yards from the *Young*, a stepping-stone to salvation was created. Without hesitation, Chief Boatswain's Mate Arthur Peterson dove into the churning sea to join the two ships with a line. Once accomplished, a series of raft shuttles delivered all 70 of the *Young*'s surviving sailors to safety aboard the *Chauncey.*

For such efforts, well-deserved commendations were made. Lieutenant Commander Calhoun was cited for "coolness, intelligence, and seamanlike ability" directly responsible for the tragedy's "greatly reduced loss of life." Chief Boatswain's Mate Peterson would be commended for "extraordinary heroism" for his courageous swim.

Other players aboard the *Young* would also receive mention. These included a Lieutenant E. C. Herzinger for "especially meritorious conduct," and Fireman First Class J. T. Scott, for his heroic attempt to close down the ship's master oil valve to stave off an explosion.

* * * *

Captain Watson of the Delphy *received a court martial for his navigational blunder, but he wasn't the only one held responsible. Varying degrees of blame were placed on those commanders who had also grounded their vessels. With this move, the Navy was following a tradition that holds captains responsible for the safety of their ships, even when they are sailing in formation.*

* * * *

Navigational methods have greatly improved since Honda Point. Breakthroughs such as the global positioning system (GPS) and enhanced radar/sonar have rendered manual plotting methods such as "dead reckoning" nearly obsolete. A ship's crew can now pinpoint its position down to a few feet and can "see" underwater protrusions that may cause it harm. Although solid-state navigation has taken the luster off of manual plotting, many captains believe that the safest setup involves knowledge of both methods. Electronics can and do fail, after all.

* * * *

Nome Diphtheria Epidemic

Dr. Curtis Welch served as a Public Health Service physician in Nome, Alaska. In January 1925, a severe illness began spreading among Nome's children. When fatalities began, Welch realized it was diphtheria—a highly infectious disease battled with antitoxin (also called *serum*).

Nome's supply of diphtheria serum was small and stale. If fresh serum didn't arrive within two weeks, Welch would need to order child-size coffins instead. Welch radioed a plea for help.

There were no roads to Nome in the wintertime. Serum could travel by rail as far north as Nenana, but it would have to go the last 674 miles by the dogsled mail route, which usually took 25 days. A team of 20 (mostly native; some Russian and Scandinavian) mushers with 150 dogs positioned their sleds to relay the serum through the mid-winter snow and −50°F cold.

The first sled left Nenana on January 27. On February 2 an exhausted Norwegian banged on Welch's door carrying the precious package. Several mushers sustained severe frostbite en route, and many dogs gave their lives. Not one vial was broken, however. Thanks to the serum, only a handful of Nome's people died. Today, the world-famous annual Iditarod race commemorates this event.

Jirdes Baxter, who was 11 months old at the time of the epidemic, is the last survivor alive as of 2009.

What Is Diphtheria?

As late as the 1920s, the United States had more than 100,000 diphtheria cases annually, with a mortality rate near 10 percent (heavily concentrated in children). Diphtheria is now rare in the industrialized world. In developing nations, however, the disease is more common.

Diphtheria symptoms usually begin with a sore throat, fatigue, and fever. The bacteria attack the upper respiratory tract, producing a potentially lethal toxin. Because the toxin phase comes very swiftly, every minute counts when starting treatment.

Antitoxins combat illness, whereas vaccines prevent them. The serum sent to Nome in such valiant haste functioned by neutralizing the bacteria's deadly toxin, much like snake antivenin. The first diphtheria vaccine was developed in 1913, but the diphtheria toxoid-containing vaccine (invented 1929), ranks alongside the polio and smallpox vaccines as one of history's great public health strides. Where vaccine is unavailable, diphtheria outbreaks still take lives.

The *Italia*

In 1928, Italian aviation pioneer Umberto Nobile planned several airship flights to the Arctic. He hoped to base his airship *Italia* at the Norwegian island of Spitzbergen, supported by an Italian merchant vessel. If he could moor an airship at the North Pole and bring back valuable scientific information, he could prove the value of dirigibles while burnishing his reputation.

In the past, he had explored (and feuded) with renowned Norwegian explorer Roald Amundsen. The churlish Norseman wasn't invited this time.

En route from the North Pole back to Spitzbergen on May 25, 1928, *Italia* crashed on the icepack. The impact mashed the cabin, ejecting ten crew members (one fatally). Six others floated helplessly away in *Italia*'s remaining portion and were never seen again. The nine remaining crew members and Nobile's dog (happily unhurt) camped on the ice, radioing in vain for help while surviving on emergency supplies and a polar bear they had killed.

When the icepack broke up, setting them adrift on a disintegrating floe, the survivors' situation became even worse. Five days after the crash, Italian naval officers Filipo Zappi and Alberto Mariano, with Swedish scientist Finn Malmgren, set out to seek help. The despondent Swede faded and died; the Italians survived until rescue.

A Russian ship finally detected the party's SOS on June 3. Smelling good propaganda, the Soviets sent icebreakers and aircraft to join the international search effort.

A Swedish pilot landed near Nobile's party on June 23 but could bring out only one person. Nobile was both light and injured, so the Swede chose him and his dog. The aging Soviet icebreaker *Krassin* eventually rescued most of the survivors on July 12.

The last survivor of the *Italia* rescue effort was **Giulio Bich,** one of an elite Alpini (mountain troops) rescue team arranged by Nobile in advance. Bich died in 2003 in Cervinia, Italy, at age 95.

Amundsen's Rescue Mission

By 1928, Roald Amundsen was a world-famous polar explorer, with good reason: He was the first to reach the South Pole, the first to visit both poles, and the first to traverse the Northwest Passage. Before *Italia*, Amundsen had engaged Nobile to build the dirigible *Norge* for an Arctic crossing. After a successful North Pole passage in 1926, Amundsen and Nobile bickered over credit for the expedition, with each naturally advancing his own role.

Amundsen was eager to fly north and join the search for *Italia*—though perhaps not with great altruism. He may have partly wanted to be the Seasoned Nordic Expert rescuing the Inept Mediterranean Hired Pilot. In any event, Amundsen's aircraft stopped transmitting three hours out of Tromsø, Norway. He was never found, but a pontoon from his floatplane washed up off Tromsø. Even if he survived the apparent plane crash at sea, he surely died in the aftermath.

Tragedy at the Millfield Mine

The Millfield disaster of November 5, 1930, was Ohio's worst mining accident, killing 82 at the Sunday Creek Coal Company's #6 mine. At 11:45 A.M. a rockfall at the back of #6 ruptured a cable, arcing electricity into a pocket of *firedamp* (mostly methane). *Whoosh!* The blast twisted I beams like pipe cleaners, made instant kindling of shoring timbers, mangled rail cars into instant train wrecks, tore up 760 feet of track, and scorched equipment more than 1,500 feet from the blast. To worsen matters, the explosion filled the mine with afterdamp: lethal concentrations of carbon monoxide (CO) mixed with carbon dioxide and nitrogen.

When it was over, 138 miners had survived the disaster. Some escaped early; others described forlorn, desperate searches for safe air and a clear path out. Many could only sit tight and await rescue. Fatalities included Sunday Creek Coal's president, four other executives, and four visitors. Sad but ironic: They were inspecting such recent safety improvements as steel I beam supports, brick-work, electric lighting, and a new ventilation shaft to vent flammable or toxic gases.

The son of a Hungarian immigrant who also worked in #6, young **Sigmund Kozma** toiled in the mine hooking up coal cars. Shortly after they felt the explosion, he recalls his dad hurrying to rig a barrier with brattice cloth, protecting their room from the deadly afterdamp. They waited three hours before heading for the exit, with Sigmund Jr. carrying a wounded man to safety. Kozma died in 2009 at age 97.

An Heroic Effort

Alert Sunday Creek Coal supervisor John Dean saved himself and 18 others with timely action. After the explosion, Dean instructed his miners to brattice themselves into a room, lest the afterdamp get them.

Two disregarded his suggestion and made a run for the entrance, then cried out for help. Dean went after them, but he found them overcome by afterdamp. Too weakened to carry them, he dragged himself back to the bratticed room. Once inside, he collapsed. Dean was one mine boss who barely survived his own valor.

The Gresford Disaster

Few places know the dangers of coal mining better than Wales, United Kingdom. On September 22, 1934, an explosion rocked the Dennis Section of Gresford Colliery in Wales.

Rescue and firefighting teams spent two days trying to battle their way in, ringed by the miners' wives and children. Only a few got good news: Six miners managed to crawl out through an air passage. Three rescuers died exploring another vent.

After two days of desperate work, authorities doubted that anyone inside could still be alive. Rather than risk more lives, they sealed up the pit while the fire still raged below. Nearly all of the 266 miners who died remain entombed there today. Investigators never learned the exact cause, but modern researchers suspect that sparks from a miner's pick ignited methane.

Lamp-boy **Albert Rowlands** was 14 at the time. His father, John, a decorated World War I vet, had gotten him the job. John and Albert were biking to work when Dad admonished his boy to pedal ahead; tardiness was a big no-no for lamp-boys, whose job was to hand out the mining lamps. John picked up his lamp at another window, so Albert missed that last possible sight of his father.

As Albert describes it, people who heard a loud noise and shaking earth were imagining things: The explosion was neither heard nor felt above ground. A foreman sent Albert to fetch an ambulance, and some other workers went home to spread word, bringing the authorities in great haste. As of 2008, Albert was alive at age 88—Gresford's last survivor. He has never been down in a mine since the tragedy.

The Inquiry

The Gresford disaster had potential criminal implications for the mine owners, so both sides brought heavy legal artillery to the inquiry. Labour Party Member of Parliament Sir Stafford Cripps, an odd but capable legislator, represented the miners; star barrister Hartley Shawcross defended management. The greatest obstacle to an investigation—much less prosecution—was the absence of physical evidence or witnesses, all of same being conveniently inaccessible and/or deceased.

The board compelled not one shareholder or owner to testify. While Cripps's questioning laid bare a variety of shoddy safety practices at Gresford, the investigators couldn't agree who was to blame. Issuing a vague, guarded statement, they faulted everyone: miners, inspectors, foremen, and management. No one paid a legal or financial consequence. Safety didn't improve in British coal mining until the 1954 Mines & Quarries Act.

The rest of Gresford Colliery continued operations until 1973. Those who perished received a memorial, but not until 1982.

* * * *

Barrister Hartley Shawcross was a rising star in British legal circles when he agreed to defend the Gresford mine owners. That none were convicted speaks to his talents. When Nazi leaders went on trial at Nuremberg 12 years later, Shawcross served as the Crown's chief prosecutor.

* * * *

Some of the slain miners had double-shifted in hopes of attending a soccer game the next day.

* * * *

The *Hindenburg*

On May 6, 1937, German zeppelin LZ-129, immortalized in history as the *Hindenburg*, caught fire during mooring at Lakehurst Naval Air Station, New Jersey. More than thirty people died in the incident.

Today, a hydrogen gasbag sounds like a scary way to fly. In the 1930s, it was expensive but swift, part of the great novelty of passenger air travel. In 1936, the *Hindenburg* made ten round-trips to New York and seven to Brazil. It could cross the Atlantic in two days for $400 (one-way; which would be roughly $6,000 today). The fastest ocean liners took approximately four days.

The paying customer enjoyed opulent comfort, fine dining—even a cocktail lounge. A 200-foot promenade deck featured aerial views few people had ever enjoyed. Barf bags were unnecessary; no one got airsick because passengers could feel very little movement. Some passengers enjoyed watching the luxury liners poke along far below.

The *Hindenburg* was the largest airship ever made—an immense symbol in a political culture where immensity was vitally important. It flew over the 1936 Berlin Olympics, Nazi swastikas on its fins, trailing the Olympic flag from its gondola. The *Hindenburg* served as a trans-Atlantic billboard for the resurgent Germanic pride embodied in Nazism. In those tense prewar years, the *Hindenburg*'s Lakehurst arrival was a major media event.

The last surviving crew member as of 2009 was 14-year-old cabin attendant **Werner Franz.** A water tank above him ruptured at just the right time to soak him, thus helping him resist the fire. The last surviving passenger, **Werner Doehner,** was eight when the great airship caught fire. His mother (also a survivor) threw him out the window. He awoke in the hospital to learn that his father and sister had perished. He rarely spoke about the disaster, but in more recent years he has been interviewed for documentaries.

What Caused the Disaster?

Why did the *Hindenburg* use flammable hydrogen rather than inert helium? For one thing, helium airships could still burn—the fuel and skin remained fire risks. For another, the United States had a world helium monopoly, and refused to sell it to Germany for strategic reasons. What torched the *Hindenburg?* In order of reasonable probability, theories include:

- Static electricity: The airship could have built up a static charge from stormy local weather, which may have discharged when it tried to dock. It may have first ignited the highly flammable doping on the ship's surface.
- Foul play/sabotage: Adolf Hitler had abundant enemies in Germany. *Hindenburg* Commander Max Pruss, who survived, strongly suspected an anti-Nazi saboteur.
- Engine sparks: One member of the ground crew later recalled a shower of sparks from an engine as the airship maneuvered.
- Lightning: It's possible that a small lightning crackle set the fire.

Neither the American nor the German governments wanted to ask too many questions, so both publicly endorsed the static-electricity theory.

* * * *

"Oh, the humanity!" Radio reporter Herb Morrison's shaken, agonized narration of the tragedy is legendary. Most modern playbacks mislead: They play his voice too fast (making him sound more rattled than he was). They also suggest it was broadcast live (it wasn't) and combined with video (nope). The episode vaulted him into a very successful broadcasting career.

* * * *

The Hindenburg *incident was by no means the only major airship catastrophe; it was simply the highest-profile one. Airships were proving too fragile for passenger use, even as early passenger airlines were gaining the dominant role they hold today. Today numerous countries and firms (famously, Goodyear) operate airships for advertising or observation purposes—especially at football games.*

* * * *

The Empire State Building was completed in 1931. The builders had envisioned zeppelins mooring at its peak. The 86th floor was to house the ticket office and lounge. Travelers were to embark and disembark on the 102nd floor. In the end, skyscraper-side updrafts and ground crew platform issues doomed the concept.

* * * *

Smoking was permitted aboard the Hindenburg, *but only in a specially pressurized smoking room.*

* * * *

The Sinking of the *Glorious*

In June 1940, the British were in full evacuation from Norway after an Allied defeat. The aircraft carrier HMS *Glorious,* having evacuated two RAF squadrons, broke away from a larger convoy and steamed for Scapa Flow, Scotland, with its escorting destroyers HMS *Acasta* and HMS *Ardent.*

None had radar. *Glorious* had no topside lookout, nor any combat air patrol airborne. Historians still struggle to explain how decorated World War I naval veteran Captain Guy D'Oyly-Hughes could allow this.

About 4:00 P.M. on June 8, 1940, *Ardent* moved off to identify two bogeys to the west and found the worst possible scenario: the speedy, powerful German battlecruisers *Scharnhorst* and *Gneisenau.* In such a case, the overwhelmed destroyers could only distract and delay, hoping to buy the more valuable carrier's survival.

Despite smokescreens and suicidal valor, the *Ardent* was finished off by 5:30 P.M. *Glorious,* whose flight deck was disabled early by 283mm shell hits, never got an aircraft launched. *Glorious* sank at 6:00 P.M.

Acasta's skipper, Commander C. E. Glasfurd, then wrote a valiant chapter in Royal Navy history. As *Glorious* went down, Glasfurd brought *Acasta* through the smokescreen to torpedo *Scharnhorst* (rather seriously, it turned out)—and paid dearly for it. *Acasta*'s only survivor, Leading Seaman Nick Carter, fired the torpedo that scored the big hit. Carter later described how Glasfurd stayed aboard to tend the wounded, then lit a smoke on the bridge and waved his sailors farewell. As *Acasta* sank at 6:20, *Gneisenau*'s skipper drew its flag to half-mast and stood his crew to attention to honor their gallant adversary, and then ran for port. Absent that mauling, the German ships might have caused considerable damage to the main evacuation fleet.

About 800 of the 1,558 sailors survived the initial sinking of the *Glorious* and the two destroyers. Due to poor communication, it took four days for rescuers to reach them; many sailors died as they awaited rescue. As of 2006, the last survivor was 84-year-old **Fred Thornton.** He recalled those four terrible days, when frostbitten survivors gave up one by one until only 39 (38 from the *Glorious* and one—Nick Carter—from the *Acasta*) remained alive for a Norwegian fishing vessel to haul aboard. (Six more became POWs when rescued by Germans.) After the war, Fred worked in a pub until retirement.

Why the Delay?

Glorious radioed several distress calls, but the nearby cruiser HMS *Devonshire* dared not reply, much less assist; it was transporting the Norwegian royal family, government, and gold reserves to rally Norway from exile. Should the ship have radioed for help, thus possibly betraying its position? Most likely its officers assumed others would respond. In chilly strategic terms, *Devonshire*'s cargo was indeed more valuable than a thousand lives... except that the next day the ship broke radio silence concerning an escort rendezvous, so the silence excuse dissolves.

Didn't any other British ship hear the distress call? Someone should have; there were plenty in the area. Couldn't the Royal Navy spare a destroyer for survivors? The German reports of the sinking were intercepted; were they disbelieved? Hello? Anyone?

The kindest answer is the general confusion of a major evacuation. Human lapses and bungling surely factored. We won't know for sure until the locked Admiralty records finally creak open in 2040.

* * * *

The last of Gneisenau's *280mm turrets, salvaged from its later scuttling, survives today in a coastal defense museum outside Trondheim, Norway.*

* * * *

Guess who built Glorious? *Harland and Wolff of Belfast. H&W also built RMS* Titanic.

* * * *

The Assault on the USS *Peary*

On February 19, 1942, Navy destroyer USS *Peary* was vigorously attacked by Japanese dive bombers. The aerial assault sank the ship and extinguished the lives of some 91 sailors.

The attack occurred when the *Peary* was anchored at Port Darwin, the capital city of Australia's Northern Territory. The destroyer had been operating out of Darwin since mid-January, taking part in Allied escort missions and antisubmarine patrols, and was anchored for the purpose of refueling. Ironically, this steel tether would prove the ship's undoing.

When a series of Japanese bombers shelled the vessel in a mid-morning surprise attack, the *Peary* was little more than a sitting duck. Unable to slip her anchor in time to stage a retreat, the vessel suffered five direct hits. Nevertheless, the *Peary* mounted a formidable defense. Even as the ship sank, personnel continued to fire upon the attackers until all planes had departed.

Pipe Fitter Third-Class **Dallas Widick** was the man responsible for taking in the ship's anchor. Paddling ashore in one of its rowboats, Widick was one of only 30 crew members to survive the disaster. Widick was also the last living survivor, dying in 2008. His family scattered his ashes over the spot where the *Peary* went down.

The Memorial

Long after crew members of the USS *Peary* slipped free their earthly bonds, a memorial honoring their sacrifice was erected at Darwin's Bicentennial Park. The monument, constructed by the Royal Australian Navy (RAN), features a four-inch gun retrieved from the sunken destroyer by diver Carl Atkinson. Beside it rests a plaque that lists the names of all hands lost. The gun points to the ship's final resting place.

Dedicated on January 29, 1992, the ceremony was overseen by Northern Territory Chief Minister Marshall Peron. USS *Peary* survivors Dallas Widick and Melvin Duke were present for the unveiling.

On May 3, 2001, Widick, the final remaining survivor, was again on hand when the RAN commemorated the 59th anniversary of the sinking.

"I'm honored to be here among friends, both Australian and American," proclaimed the long-retired sailor. "It makes my heart proud that after almost 60 years since many of my shipmates fell here, that there are still these ceremonies to remember their honor and bravery."

• •

No Mercy for Those Aboard the *Ceramic*

On December 6, 1942, the British liner SS *Ceramic* was torpedoed by a German U-boat as it moved through the Azores. The Australia-bound craft, transporting soldiers and civilians, met its fate at the hands of submarine *U-515* commanded by Werner Henke. The sub picked up only one survivor, leaving the rest to die.

Three months before the *Ceramic*'s ill-fated voyage, the German *U-156* torpedoed and sank the ocean liner RMS *Laconia*. When the U-boat approached the sinking liner to search for senior military personnel among the survivors in the water, *U-156* Lieutenant Commander Werner Hartenstein realized many of the survivors were civilians and Italian prisoners of war. At that point, *U-156* and three other submarines plucked survivors from the sea and, in some cases, draped Red Cross flags on their decks to indicate nonthreatening cargo. During the rescue operation, a U.S. Army B-24 Liberator spotted the U-boat and received orders to attack. The U-boats, now under full attack from the American bomber, would escape only after cutting tow lines to lifeboats containing rescued survivors. Because of the incident, the German Navy handed down the "*Laconia* Order," which would halt all rescue efforts associated with sunken vessels and would directly affect the future sinking of the SS *Ceramic*.

Observing the new orders, sub *U-515* was no longer interested in lifesaving measures. After it launched its torpedoes, it watched the *Ceramic* slip beneath the waves, moving toward the ship hours later only in hopes of rescuing its captain for interrogation. When stormy seas precluded an in-depth search of the site, the *U-515* fished out the closest survivor. Royal Engineer **Eric Munday** would be vigorously interrogated but lived to tell the tale.

The disaster would commit more than 650 people to an early grave and land Munday in a prisoner of war camp, where he remained until war's end. The book *SS* Ceramic: *The Untold Story* would later document Munday's harrowing experience.

Henke's Fate

When *U-515* Commander Werner Henke refused to rescue survivors from the SS *Ceramic*, he invited retaliatory measures. Allied propaganda reports declared Henke a war criminal and claimed Henke had "machine-gunned" helpless survivors of the *Ceramic*. "Authorities" threatened to bring Henke to trial at war's end and hang him for "crimes against humanity." Henke caught wind of some of these broadcasts, though in his mind the threats against him came specifically from Britain, rather than from the Allies in general.

Although Henke was following orders when he fled the scene of the *Ceramic* sinking, it was later reported that Henke felt haunted for abandoning survivors during the *Ceramic* incident. Perhaps because of this, the commander later defied the *Laconia* Order and rescued survivors from the SS *California Star* and SS *Phemius* after sinking them in 1943. Nevertheless, the supposed British threats loomed very real in the back of Henke's mind.

On April 19, 1944, a group of U.S. ships—the USS *Guadalcanal* among them—left Casablanca with a specific mission to find and sink U-boats. The American ships were equipped with sophisticated detection equipment that enabled them to locate *U-515*. After a dramatic chase, *U-515* was sunk by the American forces.

Henke survived the sinking and was held in the United States as a prisoner of war. In June 1944, he was transferred to Canada. Knowing that Canada held strong British ties, Henke believed his execution was a certainty. The commander decided to deny his captors their chance. On June 15, Henke scaled a prison fence. After disobeying repeated shouts of "Halt," the German U-boat commander was shot dead. Henke is buried at Ft. Meade, Maryland.

The Loss of the *Escanaba*

On June 13, 1943, the Coast Guard cutter USS *Escanaba* was performing submarine sweeps on its Greenland to Newfoundland North Atlantic run. While escorting a flotilla of seven ships, the *Escanaba* suddenly exploded. The blast and subsequent sinking, thought to be the result of a German torpedo attack or mine hit, killed 101 of the 103 sailors aboard.

The high death toll resulted from a number of factors. These included the powerful blast itself; the early morning timing of the attack, which caught many hands fast asleep; the absurdly fast three-minute sinking time; and the frigid 39-degree water temperature that snuffed out crew members' lives with alarming speed.

When the tug *Raritan* moved in to pick up survivors, two, **Raymond F. O'Malley** and Melvin A. Baldwin, were found alive but passed out. O'Malley later told of being pulled down with the *Escanaba* when it sank but of somehow fighting his way back to the surface.

Such pluckiness would lend itself well to O'Malley's future vocation as a Chicago police officer. He would live until 2007, when he passed away at age 86.

Escanaba's Past Rescues

Known primarily as a "U-boat killer," the cutter USS *Escanaba* also took part in its share of marine rescues. In 1940 alone, the vessel was credited with saving the lives of 11 people and safeguarding some 20 ships. But it was far from done.

In June 1942, the *Escanaba* came to the aid of the torpedoed passenger ship SS *Cherokee*. Though 89 went down with the craft, the *Escanaba* managed to pluck 22 survivors from the sea.

Continuing in its lifesaving efforts and expanding on its *Cherokee* rescue, the *Escanaba* broke new ground in February 1943 when it assisted the mortally wounded SS *Dorchester*. Employing rescue swimmers for the very first time, the vessel rescued 132 sailors from the icy North Atlantic. In an ironic twist, medals would be posthumously awarded to *Escanaba's* Lieutenant Commander Carl Peterson, Lieutenant Robert Prause, and Ensign Richard Arrighi after the *Escanaba* itself sank in June.

* * * *

Designed for light ice-breaking in the Great Lakes, the 165-foot Escanaba *served in that capacity for eight years. A call to duty during World War II saw the vessel refitted with sounding gear and depth charges—necessary equipment for its new role as a sub chaser. The craft was deployed as an escort ship in the ice-choked North Atlantic, where it saved many vessels and lives.*

* * * *

The Sad Story of the *Valleyfield*

When the Canadian frigate HMCS *Valleyfield* was sunk by a German U-boat on the night of May 6, 1944, hopeful crewmates awaited rescue from nearby convoy vessels. As it turned out, their faith was misplaced. Scores perished in a frigid 32-degree sea, not as a direct result of the sinking, but rather as the victims of an official Navy practice that delayed their rescue.

Heading for Cape Race, Newfoundland, with 168 crew members aboard, the *Valleyfield* zigzagged across the North Atlantic. This evasive maneuver was standard practice to help elude German U-boat attack. At a point 50 miles off the coast, *Valleyfield* encountered icebergs, a condition that forced the vessel to sail a straighter course. This proved to be a fatal mistake. The German submarine *U-548* drew a direct bead on the frigate and pressed its launch button.

When the torpedo pierced the *Valleyfield's* port side, the resulting explosion snapped the ship in two. As the frigate went down, panicked crew members clung to floating debris and awaited rescue. With the HMCS *Giffard* cruising just a few miles behind the now-sunken craft, their chances of survival looked good.

But such perceptions were deceiving. When the *Giffard* realized that the *Valleyfield* was missing, the ship followed a Navy protocol that ordered a search for the U-boat *before* a rescue attempt was made. With a critical amount of time eaten up this way, the *Giffard* found only 43 of the crew alive (and five of whom would later die) when it came to the ship's aid. Many victims had succumbed to prolonged exposure in the freezing waters.

Last survivor **Jake Warren** pursued a career in politics. He was appointed deputy minister of industry, trade, and commerce (1968–71); high commissioner to the United Kingdom (1971–75); and ambassador to the United States (1975–77). He passed away in 2008 at 87 years of age.

The 1946 Elko, Nevada, Crash

On September 5, 1946, a San Francisco-bound Douglas DC-3 crashed while attempting to land at the Elko, Nevada, airport. Descending in foggy conditions, the Trans-Luxury Airlines charter flying out of New York hit a small hill some two miles from the airport. The fiery crash killed twenty-one passengers and crew. Remarkably, one person managed to escape harm.

The sole survivor was four-year-old **Peter Link** of Brooklyn, New York. The boy, traveling with his parents and baby sister, was found conscious in a sitting position approximately 100 feet from the wreckage. Miraculously, he had suffered only minor injuries.

The *Truculent*

On the night of January 12, 1950, the 270-foot-long submarine HMS *Truculent* was moving along the surface through England's Thames Estuary. As it made its way through a particularly narrow portion of the channel, the vessel encountered the Swedish ship *Divina,* which had reinforced bows to help it navigate through Baltic ice. The *Divina* rammed the *Truculent,* and the *Truculent* began to sink. Unfortunately, the *Divina*'s ship-to-shore radio was inoperative at the time—a condition that exacerbated an already tragic situation.

Five of the *Truculent*'s crew were immediately thrown overboard by the impact, and seventy-five others went down with the submarine. Amazingly, all but one were alive when they reached the bottom some 70 feet below. With carbon monoxide building up in the cabins, an agonizing decision was reached. The sailors would brave a piercing cold swim to the surface and await rescue. It seemed their only chance.

According to eyewitness accounts, nearly all hands survived the long swim to the top. Unfortunately, the majority of these would be swept out to sea with the current or killed by the effects of hypothermia.

After the accident, the *Divina* searched fruitlessly for survivors, then continued on its course. A half-hour after impact, the Dutch *Almdyck* heard shouts coming from the water and rescued the five sailors who had been thrown overboard. After *Almdyck* sent a "Subsmash" (coded SOS) signal, *Divina* soon rejoined the search. But the damage had already been done. *Divina* fished ten more survivors from the bone-chilling waters, but the double whammy of strong current and severe cold ensured that there would be no others.

In the end, 65 sailors perished, mostly due to the bitter cold. Immersion suits, which have now become standard issue, were only then being tested. If they had been available, they undoubtedly would have saved many lives.

In 2008, the last survivor of the *Truculent,* 84-year-old **Fred Henley,** attended the submarine's 58th annual memorial service. Henley was one of the original five sailors thrown off the sub when it was first struck on that fateful winter evening.

The New Orient Coal Mine Explosion

On December 21, 1951, a massive explosion occurred at the New Orient Coal Mine in West Frankfort, Illinois. Some 120 workers were inside the mine at the time of the explosion, but only one would live to tell of it.

With 12 miles of tunnels, the New Orient Mine was considered the biggest shaft coal mine in the world. It had suffered its share of small explosions—which are nearly unavoidable in coal mining—but never anything as sizable as this blast.

Sole survivor **Cecil Sanders** managed to live through the horror for 60 hours before being rescued. "We tried to put up canvas curtains so the gas would go around us," said Sanders in describing the plight of his group, "but the gas current was so strong it caught us between two air courses. We knew the only thing to do was find a hole and hope the gas would go over us." Sanders eventually lost consciousness, coming to only after a rescuer's flashlight jarred him back to reality.

Although the cause of the explosion was never confirmed, the mine had a dismal safety record with 21 safety code violations cited at a previous inspection. In 1952, Congress amended and strengthened the Coal Mine Health and Safety Act. It gave federal mine inspectors the power to close any mine that they deemed unsafe.

The Magsaysay Plane Crash

On March 17, 1957, an airplane carrying Filipino President Ramón Magsaysay and 25 others crashed in the Philippines. Reporter **Néstor Mata** was the sole survivor. Thrown from the plane, he was found several hours after the crash suffering from severe burns. He was still alive in 2008 at age 82.

The *Carl D. Bradley*

On November 18, 1958, the 623-foot freighter *Carl D. Bradley* cruised on Lake Michigan, toward its home base of Rogers City, Michigan, for reloading. The vessel was returning from Gary, Indiana, where it had dropped off a load of limestone. While the vessel was en route, the temperature dropped about 20 degrees; gale winds were forecast, and the crew prepared the vessel for severe weather. That night the vessel was caught by a gale packing 65-mph winds that churned up enormous waves. The storm snapped the

Bradley's hull in two, and the ship went down near Gull Island. More than thirty crew members perished outright. Four others clung to a life raft and prayed for deliverance. Only two survived.

Deck watchman **Frank Mays** and first mate Elmer Flemming fought for life through brutal conditions. With the air temperature hovering around the 40-degree mark and water temperature some four degrees colder than that, the duo managed to hang on after two other crewmates lost their grip. The pair battled through 30-foot waves, watched their raft capsize three times, and endured 15 agonizing hours of exposure before being rescued by the U.S. Coast Guard cutter *Sundew* the following morning.

As of 2008, 76-year-old Mays is the last living survivor of the tragedy. He recounted his survival story in the book *If We Make It 'Til Daylight*, which was published in 2003.

The Dag Hammarskjöld Crash

On the night of September 17, 1961, United Nations Secretary-General Dag Hammarskjöld of Sweden and 15 others took off from an airport in Leopoldville (former Belgian Congo). Their airplane crashed just before reaching its landing point in Northern Rhodesia.

After learning that violence had erupted between troops in the Katanga province of the Congo and noncombatant forces of the United Nations, Hammarskjöld had arranged for a conference with President Moise Tshombe of Katanga. Any hopes of brokering peace were instantly dashed when the Secretary-General's DC-6 violently crashed through a stand of trees and disintegrated.

The craft had been under orders to fly only at night to avert risks posed by Katangan jet fighters. After the crash, investigators suspected foul play and advanced their investigations accordingly. In the end, no evidence of anything other than a "controlled crash into terrain" was ever uncovered, but conspiracy theories persisted. The most popular of these involved onboard bombs and surface-to-air missile attack. Burmese diplomat U Thant was chosen to succeed Hammarskjöld as Secretary-General, and the official crash investigation drew to a close. The only survivor of the tragedy, American security officer **Harold Julian,** died several days later from injuries sustained in the crash.

Dag Hammarskjöld

To call Secretary-General Dag Hammarskjöld (1905–61) an effective diplomat is a gross understatement. Upon Hammarskjöld's death, President John F. Kennedy remarked, "I realize now that in comparison to him, I am a small man. He was the greatest statesman of our century."

The son of Swedish prime minister Hjalmar Hammarskjöld, Dag Hammarskjöld was immersed in the political life at a young age. In a 1953 radio address, Hammarskjöld said, "From generations of soldiers and government officials on my father's side I inherited a belief that no life was more satisfactory than one of selfless service to your country or humanity."

After earning two degrees from Uppsala University, Hammarskjöld added a law degree and a doctoral degree in economics. The true embodiment of a Renaissance person, Hammarskjöld was well versed in the arts, literature, and history, and equally competent in physical pursuits such as gymnastics and skiing.

In 1930, Hammarskjöld entered public life in Sweden as a secretary to a governmental commission on unemployment. He rose through the ranks to become Sweden's UN delegate in 1949. In 1953, he was elected Secretary-General of the United Nations, a position to which he would be reelected in 1957.

Hammarskjöld received the Nobel Peace Prize posthumously in 1961 for a body of work that included the release of 15 American flyers held by the Chinese in 1955, efforts in the 1956 Middle East crisis between Egypt and Israel, and his final attempt at uniting warring factions in the Congo.

The *Thresher*

Only two hours before the nuclear submarine USS *Thresher* departed on its last fateful run, reactor control officer **Raymond McCoole** received notice that his wife had sustained an eye injury. Released from duty to be by her side, McCoole inadvertently sidestepped a disaster that would see the loss of 129 less fortunate souls.

Dubbed the *Thresher*'s "luckiest man," the sole surviving sailor would have strong feelings about the incident and would often wonder if his presence could have prevented the tragedy.

The unthinkable occurred during postoverhaul sea trials 220 miles off Boston on April 10, 1963. As the *Thresher* was nearing its scheduled test depth (5,500 feet), the vessel suddenly began to fill with seawater. The last recorded communications with the support ship USS *Skylark* feature the ominous sounds of compartments collapsing. The *Thresher,* at sea for barely three years, was no more.

Investigations would point to a weld failure in the vessel's saltwater piping system. McCoole maintained that his experience level could have affected the outcome since he would know when *not* to follow procedure; particularly in regard to the full shutdown of the *Thresher*'s engines. "I would have drawn the steam, not shut it down," said McCoole after the tragedy. Ultimately, he would blame the U.S. Navy for allowing the sub to go to sea with "glaring deficiencies," criticizing them for rotating personnel immediately prior to the ship's sea trials.

McCoole retired as a lieutenant commander after serving 24 years in the Navy's Submarine Service. He received multiple commendations, including a Presidential Citation and the National Defense Medal of Honor. He passed away in 2005 at age 75.

In Search of the *Titanic*—or the *Thresher*?

In a tale that smacks of deception and intrigue, Bob Ballard, the famous oceanographer responsible for locating the RMS *Titanic* in 1985, admitted in June 2008 that his discovery was partly a cover-up for the real task of locating the USS *Thresher* and USS *Scorpion* submarines. The Navy wanted to know if the nuclear reactors aboard the subs were intact (they were), and it also wanted to prove or disprove the theory that the *Scorpion* had been torpedoed by the Soviets (it wasn't).

According to Ballard, his top-secret search was a necessary tradeoff with the U.S. Navy. "I couldn't tell anybody," explained Ballard, who needed the Navy's funding for his *Titanic* search. "There was a lot of pressure on me. It was a secret mission. I felt it was a fair exchange for getting a chance to look for the *Titanic*."

The Loss of the *Morrell*

On November 26, 1966, the ore freighter SS *Daniel J. Morrell* set out from Buffalo, New York. Accompanied by the freighter *Townsend,* the *Morrell* was headed to Taconite, Minnesota, for the last trip of the season. Three days out, the ships found themselves battling a brutal storm with 60-mile-an-hour winds and 30-foot waves. As they made their way up the eastern coast of Michigan, the *Townsend* took refuge in the relative safety of St. Mary's River; the *Morrell* remained trapped by the roiling waters of Lake Huron.

At 2:00 A.M. on November 30—when the ship was about 20 miles north of Harbor Beach—the storm ripped the *Morrell* in two. Of the crew of 29, only four were able to make their way to a raft. The ship had gone down so fast, no one could send a distress signal; rescue operations were not mounted until the ship was reported overdue at its destination at noon the next day. When the raft was spotted near Port Hope, Michigan, only Watchman **Dennis Hale** remained alive, semiconscious and suffering from exposure after 38 hours.

Hale remained haunted by the tragedy for the next 16 years. He could not go near any large body of water, and during heavy storms he would hide in his basement. Then in 1982, he was invited to give a talk about the incident at the Great Lakes Shipwreck Museum in Sault Ste. Marie, Michigan. Hale reluctantly agreed, intending to say only a few words about how grateful he was to be alive. He instead spoke for an hour, offering the audience an emotional outpouring about the terror he experienced, the guilt he felt over surviving, and the deep bond he had always felt for his fellow crew members. Hale found that by talking through the experience with the attentive crowd at Sault Ste. Marie, he was finally able to come to terms with his experience. He has spoken at many shipwreck conferences since, and he has even been out on a boat on Lake Huron again.

* * * *

Investigators attributed the disaster to the type of steel that was used to make the Morrell. *It was prone to crack and break in cold weather.*

* * * *

Flight 255

In August 1987, a Northwest Airlines jet crashed into a highway after takeoff from Detroit Metropolitan Airport. The flaps were not correctly set for takeoff, and the plane stalled shortly afterward.

Of the 154 people aboard, all died except **Cecelia Cichan,** then four years old. Cecelia's parents and six-year-old brother were killed in the crash. Understandably, Cecelia experienced an outpouring of attention after the tragedy, but some child psychologists speculated that her newfound celebrity might hinder the little girl's ability to recover from the trauma she had experienced. At the request of her extended family, the judge overseeing the civil suit for the accident sealed her records to protect her privacy. A maternal aunt and uncle from Birmingham, Alabama, accepted custody of young Cecelia and carefully shielded her throughout her childhood. Cecelia graduated from college and got married, and the firefighter who discovered her in the wreckage attended her wedding. She remains an intensely private person, though she occasionally posts updates and comments through a Web site that has been set up as a memorial to the victims of the crash of Flight 255 (www.flight255memorial.com).

Pilot Error or System Malfunction?

Witnesses say that at takeoff, Flight 255 struggled to get off the ground and began to dip sharply from side to side once it became airborne. About half a mile from the runway, the left wing struck a light pole and the plane plummeted downward, bursting into flames as it skidded across the ground.

Investigators suspected that the plane's wing flaps, which provide stability and lift, had not been properly set for takeoff. Flight data recorders and analysis of the wreckage confirmed the theory. The National Transportation Safety Board determined that the pilot had not properly set the flaps and that an electrical short prevented an onboard alarm system from warning of the error. The plane's manufacturer now recommends that the alarm system be tested before every takeoff, but investigators of a similar crash of a Spanish airliner in 2008 found that that plane's alarm system had failed as well.

• •

The Thredbo Landslide

On the night of Wednesday, July 30, 1997, a landslide roared down an embankment near the village of Thredbo in New South Wales, Australia. It first swept away the Brindabella Ski Club's lodge, Carinya, and then followed with a parking garage. The massive wall of earth, rock, concrete, and vehicles continued down the slope, finally slamming into the staff quarters of the Bimbadeen ski lodge, completely destroying that four-story structure.

Although this happened at the height of the area's ski season, only one person was in the Carinya lodge that night, and 18 people were in the Bimbadeen staff quarters. Rescue workers shortly arrived on the scene, but operations were hampered by cold weather, the unstable arrangement of the rubble, and the threat of a leaking gas main. They recovered one body on Thursday and three more on Friday; by Friday night, rescuers had given up any real hope of finding any survivors.

A Cause for Hope

Early on Saturday morning, however, they discovered ski instructor **Stuart Diver** pinned beneath three slabs of concrete next to the lifeless body of his wife. The couple had been in their first-floor bedroom of the Bimbadeen lodge at the time of the disaster, and the entire building had collapsed upon them. Rescuers rigged a system to deliver liquid nourishment to Diver and to blow warm air over him, hoping to curb the effects of malnourishment and exposure to the frigid winter air. After ten hours of careful digging, they pulled Diver, suffering from lacerations and mild hypothermia, from the rubble.

Investigators later determined that a leaking water main had eroded the embankment of a mountain road above the lodges, and caused the landslide. The government agencies responsible for maintaining infrastructure in the area were held accountable and paid some $40 million in settlements. Diver later opened his own bed-and-breakfast hotel in the Thredbo area and remarried in 2002.

The Sago Mine

Coal mining has long been a dangerous and thankless profession, and in many ways it is defined by the conflict between the working-class laborers who toil underground and the huge companies that pay them to do so. No incident in recent memory has better illustrated that history than the Sago mine disaster of January 2, 2006, in Upshur County, West Virginia.

In the early morning of January 2, 2006, two work crews entered the Sago mine about 15 minutes apart. Shortly thereafter, a pocket of methane gas in an abandoned area of the mine exploded, rupturing the seals that divided it from active mining areas and flooding the mine with smoke and carbon monoxide.

One of the 13 workers in the first crew was killed in the explosion and the other 12 were trapped more than 250 feet below ground. Sixteen other workers who had been stationed above the point of the explosion immediately made their way toward the trapped miners but were forced back to the surface due to dangerous levels of toxic gas.

Mass Confusion and Miscommunication

Amid a blizzard of media coverage, rescue workers spent the next day and a half working to reach the trapped workers, whose families waited anxiously in a nearby church. Just after midnight on January 4, word came from the rescue command center that all but one of them had been found alive. The families celebrated their seeming good fortune as various media outlets trumpeted the miraculous news. But three hours later, to the outrage of the families, a mining company spokesman revealed that there had been a tragic miscommunication. Only one miner—**Randal McCloy Jr.**—had actually survived.

Investigators determined that the trapped laborers had attempted to clear the wreckage blocking their escape but were driven back by smoke and fumes. Following standard procedure, they retreated to an area of relatively clean air deeper in the mine and constructed a makeshift barrier to keep the deadly carbon monoxide out. Each person had been equipped with an emergency breathing apparatus, but they were forced to share their limited supplies of oxygen when four of the emergency breathing apparatuses failed to work.

Eventually, their refuge was flooded with toxic gas and 11 of those trapped perished. McCloy was likely only minutes from death when rescuers reached him 44 hours after the explosion. He suffered from carbon monoxide poisoning, a collapsed lung, brain hemorrhaging, and limited heart function. He remained in a coma for three weeks and was unable to speak for several days after regaining consciousness.

Following months of treatment and intensive therapy, the lucky miner was released from the hospital and returned to his home on a street renamed Miracle Road in his honor. McCloy made a full recovery, and in 2008, he celebrated his 29th birthday with his wife and three children.

The Grieving Continues

Various groups conducted investigations into the tragedy, including labor organizations, state and federal agencies, and both houses of the U.S. Congress. Many were outraged to learn that the mine's owner, International Coal Group, had received more than 200 violation notices from state and federal regulators in the year before the disaster, though most of them were for minor infractions not directly related to safety. The cause of the explosion was never definitively determined, but most investigators attributed it to a lightning strike that occurred near the entrance to the mine.

Within weeks of the disaster, new state and federal laws aimed at improving mining safety were passed. The new regulations required better communication systems for both miners and rescuers, as well as additional survival equipment for miners. Many felt it was too little, too late. Months after the disaster, the tragedy claimed more victims. Two workers who had been in the mine the day of the explosion committed suicide in 2006—one in August, and one in October.

Explorers

❑ ❑ ❑ ❑

Did Ludwig Leichhardt make it across Australia in 1848?
Who published the first comprehensive classification of Native American languages?
What types of mineral wealth does the Congo have?
This chapter answers these questions and more!

Spanish Explorers

- Vasco Núñez de Balboa (1475–1519) was the first European to reach the eastern coast of the Pacific Ocean.
- Juan Ponce de León (1460–1521) colonized Puerto Rico and led the first European expedition to Florida in search of the Fountain of Youth.
- Lucas Vasquez de Ayllon (ca. 1475–1526) was a colonial judge who established a settlement in South Carolina in 1526.
- Pánfilo de Narváez (ca. 1478–1528) led an inland expedition of Florida in 1528. The ill-fated venture was plagued by desertion, hurricanes, lost supplies, and hostile encounters with natives.
- With the aid of his brothers, Francisco Pizarro (ca. 1475–1541) conquered the Incan Empire of South America.
- Hernando de Soto (ca. 1500–42) led an expedition across southeastern North America. De Soto was the first European to see the Mississippi River.
- Juan Rodríguez Cabrillo (?–1543), who was Portugese, was involved in the Spanish conquest of Central America and went on to explore and claim the California region.
- The first Spaniard to explore the Amazon River, Francisco de Orellana (ca. 1500–46) told tales of native groups led by fierce warrior women.
- Hernán Cortés (1485–1547) established Spanish dominion over Mexico, relying on equal parts military force and political maneuvering among native groups to gain control of the Aztec Empire.

- A Spanish governor of Mexico, Francisco Vásquez de Coronado (ca. 1510–54) explored the American Southwest in search of a fabled city of gold. He was the first European to encounter the Pueblo and to see the Grand Canyon.
- Álvar Núñez Cabeza de Vaca (ca. 1490–1560) survived Pánfilo de Narváez's disastrous expedition and led three other survivors on an eight-year odyssey across the American Southeast and back to Mexico.
- Pedro Menéndez de Avilés (1519–74) established a Spanish settlement in St. Augustine, Florida. It became the oldest continuously inhabited city in North America.
- Gonzalo Jiménez de Quesada (ca. 1495–1579) led a Spanish expedition into the central plains of modern-day Columbia.
- Luis Vaez de Torres (?–1613?) was the first European to travel through the Torres Straight (between Australia and New Guinea).
- The last of the great Spanish explorers was **Juan de Oñate** (ca. 1550–1630), who led the exploration of New Mexico. In 1601, Oñate sent an exploring party into present-day Kansas. He died in 1630 at about 75 years of age, the last of the Spanish explorers.

The Pizarro Brothers

In the 16th century, Francisco Pizarro and his three half-brothers ruled Peru. The Pizarro brothers were

- Juan Pizarro (1505–36)
- Francisco Pizarro (ca. 1475–1541)
- Gonzalo Pizarro (ca. 1502–48)
- **Hernando Pizarro** (ca. 1475–1578)

The Pizarro brothers were born in Trujillo, a vibrant commercial city in western Spain. Their father was an army captain. Only Hernando was his legitimate son; the other brothers were products of various affairs.

In 1502, Francisco sailed to the West Indies and established himself as a successful explorer. From 1519 to 1523, Francisco lived in the new town of Panama and served as the mayor. He went on to lead an expedition down the west coast of South America in 1523, and it was on this journey that he heard rumors of a wealthy native civilization in Peru. Wanting to see this civilization for himself, Francisco sent to Panama for reinforcements. When his request was denied, Francisco traveled to Spain to appeal to King Charles V. He won the monarch over, and Francisco, his brothers, and 180 others set sail for Peru in January 1531.

When they arrived in Peru, they were greeted by the Incas. Though he at first presented himself in friendship, Francisco soon kidnapped and executed the Incan ruler, Atahualpa. The Pizarro brothers assumed control of the region, and they proved to be particularly brutal overlords, using torture and execution to solidify power, amass vast personal wealth, and put down frequent rebellions.

Francisco, Gonzalo, and Juan all died violently in Peru. When Hernando, the remaining Pizarro brother, returned to Spain, he did not receive a warm welcome. Many Spaniards were angry at him over his role in the execution of Diego de Almagro, a Spanish soldier who was one of the leaders of the conquest of Peru. Hernando was imprisoned for 20 years.

While he was in pirson, Hernando married his niece (his brother Francisco's daughter). Through this marriage, Hernando accumulated great wealth, which allowed him to live comfortably until his death in 1578 at around 103 years of age.

Portuguese Explorers

- A Portuguese nobleman who sponsored numerous voyages to West Africa, Henry the Navigator (1394–1460) is noted for fostering exploration, commerce, and the development of new ship designs and navigational techniques.
- Bartolomeu Dias (ca. 1450–1500) was the first European to sail around Africa's Cape of Good Hope, laying the way for Vasco da Gama's voyage to India.
- The first European to sail to Brazil, Pedro Álvares Cabral (ca. 1467–1520) claimed the huge landmass for Portugal, greatly increasing the nation's wealth and influence in the New World.

- Ferdinand Magellan (ca. 1480–1521) sailed from Spain around the southern tip of South America and on to the Philippines, where he died. His expedition continued westward back to Spain and was the first to circumnavigate the globe.
- **Vasco da Gama** (ca. 1469–1524) was the first to sail directly from Europe to India via the Cape of Good Hope at Africa's southern tip. Leaving Lisbon in 1497, he arrived in India the following year and returned home in 1499. The last of the Portuguese explorers, he died in 1524.

Italian Explorers

- Marco Polo (1254–1324) spent 25 years traveling with relatives through the Middle East and Asia, much of that time serving the Mongol emperor Kublai Khan. His exploits became famous with the publication of *The Travels of Marco Polo (Il milione)*.
- Though Italian, John Cabot (ca. 1461–99) sailed to the New World under the British flag. He landed along the eastern coast of Canada and claimed the region for England.
- Undoubtedly the most famous explorer of his era, Christopher Columbus (1451–1506) captained the first voyage to the Americas that led to further exploration and conquest for Spain.

- Amerigo Vespucci (1454–1512) made several voyages along the eastern coast of South America and was among the first to recognize that the New World was in fact a new world, and not Asia.
- Sailing for France, Giovanni da Verrazano (ca. 1485–1528) was the first European to explore New York Harbor.
- **Father Eusebio Francisco Kino** (1645–1711), missionary and explorer, was the last of the Italian explorers. He explored regions of present-day Mexico, California, and southern Arizona.

He introduced wheat, cattle, and sheep to the area and proved that Baja, California, is a peninsula (not an island, as was previously thought).

The Leichhardt Expeditions

Ludwig Leichhardt, a Prussian linguist and naturalist, traveled to Australia in his late 20s in search of knowledge and adventure. He spent two years collecting and studying geological and botanical samples in the area around Sydney. In August 1844, he embarked upon a privately funded expedition of the northeast coast of the continent. Since his party of ten had long been given up for dead, they were hailed as heroes when they arrived in Port Essington on December 17, 1845.

Leichhardt next planned a government-sponsored expedition to traverse the entire continent from east to west. Setting out in December 1846, the group struggled against heavy rains, bouts of malaria, and a lack of food. They returned seven months later, having covered only 500 miles. Undaunted, Leichhardt mounted another attempt to cross the continent in March 1848. The party stopped briefly at an outpost known as McPherson's Station in April and then continued on their way. They were never heard from again.

The Discovery of a Mysterious Nameplate

Over the next ten years, several attempts to find Leichhardt were made, but little evidence was found. The fate of the expedition has remained one of the great mysteries of Australian exploration. Around 1900, a brass strip bearing Leichhardt's name and the date 1848 was discovered by an Aborigine named Jackie. The strip was attached to a burnt-out firearm. Jackie gave the gun to his boss, prospector Charles Harding, who threw the gun away but treasured the nameplate. Harding kept the plate hidden but would occasionally show it to friends.

Around 1917, Harding gave the plate to his friend Reginald Bristow-Smith. Bristow-Smith loaned the plate to the South Australian Museum in 1920 and to explorer Larry Wells in 1934. Wells let the Royal Geographical Society of Australia study the plate, and in 1937, the society declared the plate genuine. Government agencies then lost track of the plate, and it was not returned to Bristow-Smith until 1964. Historian Dr. Darrell Lewis helped the National Museum of Australia get in contact with the Bristow-Smith family in 2005, and the museum purchased the plate in 2006. Because Jackie discovered the plate in western Australia, the name-plate shows that some members of the expedition likely made it at least two-thirds of the way to their destination.

The last survivor of the Leichhardt expeditions was **John Mann,** who died in 1907 at about age 88. An experienced surveyor, Mann had served as second in command on Leichhardt's second journey. He was highly critical of Leichhardt's skills and blamed the failure of the expedition on his indecisiveness, poor planning, and bad judgment.

The Dr. Kane Rescue Expedition

Former U.S. Navy surgeon Elisha Kane commanded the small ship *Advance*. As part of a research expedition, Kane and his crew spent the winters of 1853 and 1854 in the Arctic. They became trapped and were rescued by a government ship in 1855. The last survivor of the rescuers was gunner's mate **George D'Vys.** After the expedition, D'Vys served with the Union Army in the Civil War and worked as a businessman in Boston. He died in 1900 at age 68.

Burke and Wills

In 1860, Robert O'Hara Burke and William John Wills led the first expedition of Europeans to cross the Australian continent from south to north. The expedition was not charged with any scientific or cultural inquiry; its goal was simply to be the first to complete the south-north journey.

In order to save time, Burke repeatedly divided the group, moving ahead with small advance parties with limited provisions. In this fashion, he, Wills, **John King,** and Charles Grey completed the journey to the Gulf of Carpentaria in the north. Grey died of dysentery as the four returned to meet up with the main expedition, and the others stopped for a day to bury him. Exhausted and dangerously low on provisions, they arrived at the rendezvous a half day after the main party decided to give up on them and head for a nearby settlement. Burke and Wills both died, but King managed to survive with the aid of Aborigines.

King never fully recovered from the ravages of the journey, and he died in 1872 at age 31. He has generally been hailed as a hero, though some historians believe he may actually have murdered Burke in the wilderness.

The Powell Expedition

In 1869, geologist John Wesley Powell (1834–1902) explored the Green and Colorado River canyons. In 1871, he journeyed down the Colorado River and mapped the area. Of the ten explorers who joined Powell on the 1871 expedition, the last survivor was **Frederick Dellenbaugh.** Just eighteen years old at the time, Dellenbaugh served as both a mapmaker and the expedition's artist. He died in 1935 at age 82.

John Wesley Powell

During the American Civil War, John Wesley Powell served as commander of a Union artillery unit. He left the service with the rank of major but without his right arm, which was amputated after it was shattered by a musket ball at the Battle of Shiloh. Powell became a professor of geology, first at Illinois Wesleyan University and then in the state university system. He headed several expeditions in the Rocky Mountain region, and in the 1870s, he oversaw federal surveys of public lands in the American West. Powell published several important works in geology and conservation. He also earned respect among anthropologists when he published the first comprehensive classification of Native American languages; this classification system is still in use today. Later in life, Powell headed the Smithsonian Institution Bureau of Ethnology and served as director of the U.S. Geologic Survey. He died in his home in Maine at age 68.

Stanley and Livingstone

Dr. David Livingstone first went to Africa from Scotland to win Christian converts. Finding little success, Livingstone reinvented himself as an explorer. Although an intrepid seeker of knowledge, he proved a lousy expedition chief. After his 1858 Zambezi Expedition flopped, Livingstone had a difficult time finding donors willing to fund his expeditions. Regardless, he set out in search of the Holy Grail of 1800s African exploration—the Nile River's source.

Livingstone never did find the source of the Nile, though he did discover the source of the Congo River. In 1866, Livingstone took sick in the wilds of south-central Africa and lost touch with civilization for nearly six years. As a publicity stunt, the *New York Herald* newspaper sent journalist **Henry Morton Stanley** on a Livingstone hunt. In 1871, Stanley found Livingstone near Lake Tanganyika and (supposedly) greeted him with the famous question, "Dr. Livingstone, I presume?" They became colleagues and friends.

Stanley (1841–1904) outlived Livingstone (1813–73) by 30 years. One of Stanley's last wishes was to be buried next to Livingstone in London's Westminster Abbey, but the British government refused permission.

Stanley and the Congo

Don't expect the Congolese to build Stanley any monuments—he helped midwife the so-called "Congo Free State" (today the Democratic Republic of the Congo, which is not the same as the Republic of the Congo). The Congo Free State became the poster child for bad colonialism.

Stanley got a lot of press when he found Dr. Livingstone. This attracted interest from Belgium's King Leopold II, who contracted Stanley to explore, build roads, and make deals with native leaders. Leopold thus established a personal fief in the Congo, and from 1877 to 1885 he secured access to rubber and copper—materials that were vital to

European industry. Leopold's thugs wrung forth every ounce of both, infamously severing the hands of any Congolese who failed to meet the rubber quota.

No one can know how many Congolese died under Leopold, but estimates run to millions. The Congo achieved independence from Belgium in 1960, but this naturally wealthy nation has endured despotic kleptocracies ever since.

* * * *

The Congo is rich in diamonds, gold, copper, cobalt, manganese, and zinc. Foreign speculators have taken notice and invested heavily in mining efforts. Despite this cash infusion, poverty remains rife and corruption runs rampant. According to Human Rights Watch, a New York–based organization that tracks human-rights abuses, tens of thousands of civilians have been killed or run off their land by greedy rebels.

* * * *

"We went into the heart of Africa self-invited; therein lies our fault."

—Henry Morton Stanley

* * * *

The Lady Franklin Bay Arctic Expedition

The 1800s were years of exploration and experimentation. The Lady Franklin Bay Expedition (LFBE) fit into a grand plan called "First International Polar Year." This was not really a time period—it was a multinational project to share scientific data from 13 diverse Arctic stations. The LFBE would install a colony on eastern Ellesmere Island, Canada's northernmost territory, to gather data and test the feasibility of Arctic colonies.

After a postponement in 1880, in which crooked organizer Henry Howgate embezzled a good portion of the funding, the LFBE tried again the following year. On July 11, 1881, under command of Army Lieutenant Adolphus Greely, the 25-strong expedition called their new Ellesmere camp "Fort Conger."

Stranded Near the Top of the World

Ellesmere Island is no paradise. With an area nearly as large as Minnesota, its population today is fewer than 150 people. That may be because Ellesmere's winters make Minnesota look like Bora-Bora. No matter how inhospitable Duluth may get come January, it's never isolated from all supply as Ellesmere can be. Operating before the advent of aircraft and nuclear-powered icebreakers, Greely's soldiers learned the hard way that ice movements could prevent resupply at Lady Franklin Bay for years at a time.

When ice and weather defeated several efforts to relieve the LFBE in 1882–83, things got nasty at Fort Conger. Even making allowances for the uncomfortable situation, by all accounts Greely's leadership was arrogant and insensitive. After much bickering, Greely decided to take his sick, mutinous, starving outfit southward in small boats. They got as far south as Cape Sabine, Pim Island (barely halfway down Ellesmere), before ice and weakness forced them ashore. Dissension, starvation, and cold began claiming lives. By the time rescuers reached Pim Island, only Greely and six others were alive, surrounded by gnawed shoe leather and partly eaten companions.

Indian Wars veteran **David L. Brainard** outlived the other six survivors, dying in 1946 at age 89. Following his rescue, he was stationed in the Philippines during the Spanish-American War and was military attaché in Portugal during World War I.

The National Geographic Society

Ah, for the days when knowledge was hip. On January 13, 1888, an impressive group of people met in Washington, D.C., to consider a new project. Pooling their curiosity about the world and its peoples, they launched an organization devoted to advancing geographical knowledge: the National Geographic Society.

You might recognize the names of some of those founders, especially telephone inventor Alexander Graham Bell. If you read the previous page, you'd spot Adolphus Greely—now a general commanding the Army Signal Corps. Looks like his Lady Franklin Bay debacle wasn't a career wrecker.

About six months after its founding, the society started a semi-scholarly journal. Anyone who's ever waited in a dentist's office has seen *National Geographic* magazine. Vol. I, #1 contained a message from the society president, geographic and geological studies, notes on a recent storm, and the society by-laws. Judging by the first issue's membership list, most early members worked for the U.S. Geological Survey or the U.S. Coast & Geodetic Survey.

Today the society is one of the most visible nonprofit research organizations in the world, a font of captivating photography and geographic journalism. The youngest founder was 23-year-old geologist **Robert Muldrow II.** A decade later, he would become the first to measure Mount McKinley's altitude by instrument. The last surviving founding member of the National Geographic Society, he died July 28, 1950, age 86.

Peary's Journey to the Pole

Robert E. Peary (1856–1920) led an expedition toward the North Pole in 1909. Joining him on the final leg were African American Matthew Henson (1867–1955) and four Inuit: **Uutaaq,** Sigluk, Iggiannguaq, and Ukkujaaq.

Why did Peary bring Henson and the Inuit? He had to. Peary was 53, with lots of missing toes, and he mostly rode a dogsled. Whether he reached the Pole or not (and there's reasonable doubt), he couldn't even have attempted the trip without loyal assistance from Henson and the Inuit.

Henson was the ideal polar explorer: self-educated, skilled in dog mushing, fluent in Inuktitut. At one point Henson slipped off an ice floe into the Arctic water, whereupon Uutaaq quickly hauled him out and helped him into dry clothes, saving his life.

Anyone who guesses that Peary got all the credit while the others were ignored wins a slab of *muktuk* (whale blubber). Not until old age did Henson gain some of the recognition he deserved. Though Henson died in 1955, his remains were not interred in Arlington National Cemetery until 1988. Uutaaq passed away a few years after Henson, making Uutaaq the last survivor of the six who at least got near the Pole.

* * * *

As the ice cap retreats, Russia, Canada, and Denmark are all concerned with Arctic sovereignty. Russia argues that the Lomonosov Ridge, an undersea uplift that halves the Pole, is an extension of its continental shelf. At stake are an estimated 10 billion metric tons of oil and gas—once problematic to extract, but increasingly less so now.

* * * *

In 1894, Peary brought Ahnighito, *a 31-ton meteorite, back from Greenland. Explorers had long wondered where Greenland Inuit got iron; mystery solved. The meteorite seems to be a chunk of a crumbled planet's iron-nickel core and is particularly interesting to geophysicists, who can't visit Earth's core. Ahnighito can be seen at the American Museum of Natural History in New York.*

* * * *

An Eskimo Orphaned in New York

In 1897—to fulfill a request made by American Museum of Natural History curator Franz Boas—Robert Peary brought six Greenland Inuit to New York for study. One young widower, Qisuk, brought his little son, Minik. The four adults soon caught tuberculosis and died, and a young adult named Uisaakassak went home, leaving Minik alone.

The orphaned Minik wanted to give his dad a proper Inuit funeral. The problem was that scientists wanted the bones for a display, so they substituted a covered dummy. Poor Minik later found out about the sham and demanded the real body. The museum claimed to know nothing about the remains. In 1909, Minik gave up and asked Peary to bring him back to Greenland.

Minik had a difficult time readjusting to Inuit life, and he returned to America in 1916. He found work as a lumberjack in New Hampshire and became good friends with another lumberjack, Afton Hall. Hall's family welcomed Minik, and it seemed that he had finally found a place where he felt at home. But when the 1918 flu epidemic reached New Hampshire, Minik succumbed to the illness. He died that year and was buried near the lumberjack camp.

In 1993, the remains of Minik's father and the other Eskimos who died in New York were returned to their native land. They are buried in a church cemetery with a plaque above them that reads: "They have come home."

• •

The Sourdough Expedition

In 1910, four miners set out to conquer Mount McKinley, the highest mountain in North America. The four adventurers, **Charles McGonagall,** Peter Anderson, William Taylor, and Thomas Lloyd, brought along a 14-foot spruce pole to plant on the mountain for people back in Fairbanks to see. Anderson and Taylor made it to the top. When they returned, they found the pole wasn't visible and they were not believed. Three years later, another expedition climbed the higher South Peak of McKinley and saw the pole on the North Peak. The last survivor of the four miners was McGonagall.

Amundsen Sets His Sights on the South Pole

On October 19, 1911, Roald Amundsen's South Pole quest began at the Ross Ice Shelf of Antarctica with 5 assistants, 4 sleds, and 52 dogs. International bragging rights were on the line, as Briton Robert F. Scott was also heading for the Pole.

Amundsen had originally planned to go for the North Pole but quietly changed plans after hearing of the recent North Pole expeditions by Frederick Cook and Robert Peary. Only en route did he send Scott a terse heads-up.

Scott lost the race by five weeks. Deflated, his party turned for home but never made it. One key reason they failed was that Amundsen's party handled their sled dogs better. Scott's crew did the majority of the work themselves and were less efficient. A 1912 search party found Scott's final, tragic camp with the bodies and diaries of his expedition.

Olav Bjaaland played a key role on Amundsen's team. His savvy reengineering reduced the sleds' weight by 75 percent—an important factor in Amundsen's success. A ski champion in his native Norway (a modern U.S. comparison would be a Super Bowl MVP quarterback), the high-spirited trail-breaker was excited to join the race.

Bjaaland was also the last survivor of the expedition. He died at age 88 in 1961.

* * * *

Antarctica is glacial wasteland, one and a half times the area of Canada. In 1959, a dozen nations signed the Antarctic Treaty demilitarizing Antarctica, declaring it a nuclear-free zone, and suspending all formal territorial claims. If it becomes possible to extract resources from Antarctica, we may learn the treaty's true worth.

* * * *

* * * *

Sled dogs are now banned from Antarctica because they were spreading the canine distemper virus to the continent's seals.

* * * *

Global Warming and the Polar Ice Sheets

Both polar ice caps fluctuate annually, but lately they've been retreating. This process builds on itself because it changes Earth's surface reflectivity: less white ice (heat reflective) replaced by more blue ocean (heat absorbent) means we slurp up more solar energy, accelerating the melting.

A total Antarctic melt would raise the seas by more than 200 feet—enough to swamp several island nations and nearly every coastal city on Earth. Most doubt the melting will reach that extreme, however. The topic pushes hot buttons because fossil fuels are believed to accelerate global warming as their by-products trap atmospheric heat.

It is not certain how much the seas will ultimately rise. Given the potential global consequences, humanity can hardly dismiss the question out of hand.

First Team to Fly Nonstop Across the Atlantic

In 1927, Charles Lindbergh was the first person to fly solo nonstop across the Atlantic Ocean. Dozens of aviators had flown it before—just not alone. The first team to fly an aircraft nonstop across the Atlantic Ocean was John Alcock and **Arthur Whitten-Brown.** On June 14, 1919, these two British men flew 1,950 miles from Newfoundland to Ireland in a little more than 16 hours. Sir Arthur Whitten-Brown, who died in 1948, was the last living of this pair of aviators. Alcock died only six months after the record-breaking flight when he crashed while delivering a plane to a Paris aircraft exhibition.

Byrd's First Antarctic Expedition

U.S. Navy Rear Admiral Richard E. Byrd's 1928 Antarctic Expedition broke a rather long U.S. Antarctic exploration dry spell (88 years, since the last trip had been in 1840). Byrd was the first to integrate aerial photography, snowmobiles, and advanced radio communication into Antarctic study. With two ships, three airplanes, 83 assistants, lots of dogs, and a large heap of radio gear, Byrd set up a camp on the Ross Ice Shelf called Little America.

The expedition spent all of 1929 and January 1930 in Antarctica, making a flight over the South Pole and exploring Antarctic topography while recording a full year on the icy continent. Its tremendous success made Byrd famous.

Norman Vaughan, Byrd's chief dog musher, dropped out of Harvard and became the first American to drive sled dogs in the Antarctic. Byrd gave his MVP lasting credit by naming a 10,302-foot Antarctic mountain and a nearby glacier after him. (A few days before turning 89, Vaughan became Mount Vaughan's first ascender!)

At the 1932 Winter Olympics at Lake Placid, New York, Vaughan competed in dog mushing as a demonstration sport. Serving in the army in World War II, he became a colonel in charge of Greenland dogsled training and rescue. In one famed exploit, he rescued 26 downed airmen, then returned alone to recover the Norden bombsight, a top-secret device that was able to pinpoint targets using infrared radiation.

Born in 1905, Vaughan passed away on December 23, 2005, at age 100. He was the expedition's last living member.

* * * *

*After Vaughan rescued the airmen in 1942, the planes that were left behind became known as the Lost Squadron. One of the planes—*Glacier Girl*—was recovered in 1992 and is now on display at a Kentucky air museum.*

* * * *

The Mawson Antarctic Expeditions

Sir Douglas Mawson, veteran of the first Australian Antarctic expedition, went back to the icy continent in 1929–31 to lay formal British (later Australian) claim to a large chunk of Antarctica. He also planned a great deal of research, especially in the field of marine biology. The resulting discoveries made Mawson one of Australia's most honored scientists. Considering his terrible ordeal during the 1911–14 Australian expedition, in which he narrowly escaped death in a crevasse, it took considerable courage for him to venture to the area for a second time.

Alf Howard, 103 years old in 2009, is the only remaining survivor of the 1929–31 expeditions. He was just 23 when he signed on with Mawson as a chemist and hydrologist. Mawson praised Howard's work, making special note of the difficult conditions on board the ship. Howard went on to a remarkable 50-year career at the University of Queensland (UQ), teaching and researching in Human Movement Studies (kinesiology). After retirement, this living Australian legend continued to donate his time to UQ as a research fellow.

* * * *

When glacial ice flows over uneven terrain, it sometimes breaks apart. The resulting gap is called a crevasse*—one of Antarctic travel's direst perils. Snow tends to camouflage crevasses, so it's easy to miss them until one falls in. Antarctic travelers must know crevasse recovery skills because Antarctica doesn't give many second chances.*

* * * *

The Nautilus Expedition

In 1931, Australian explorer and aviator Sir Hubert Wilkins (1888–1958) attempted to pass under the North Pole in *Nautilus*, an ice-cutting submarine. Although the mission was unsuccessful, scientific information was obtained, and the expedition proved that submarines could pass beneath the Arctic ice. The last survivor of the 25 sailors who participated in the voyage was Assistant Engineer **Raymond W. Drakio.** Alive in 2008 at age 97, he survived being washed overboard during the Atlantic crossing and was one of 14 participants who completed the entire mission.

Byrd's Second Antarctic Expedition

Buoyed by popular interest and yet-unanswered questions, Admiral Byrd took a second expedition to Antarctica in 1933. Much of Antarctica remained unmapped; the full nature of the vast Ross Ice Shelf was of great interest, and there remained vast knowledge gaps in the continent's ecology. Even the weather was not yet well understood (beyond "really freaking cold").

Little America II arose from the snow on January 17, 1934. This expedition used generators to drive power tools, an Antarctic first. Byrd wanted to absorb the full Antarctic experience and planned to spend several months alone at a weather hut. Memo to future explorers: Vent your generator's exhaust properly! Carbon monoxide slowly began to poison Byrd; fortunately, he realized what was happening and requested rescue before succumbing.

American biologist **Alton A. Lindsey** is believed to be the last living scientist from Little America II. Byrd could hardly have made a better choice than the curious, easygoing Lindsey, who spent his entire career adding to our biological and ecological knowledge. During his time in Antarctica, Lindsey studied the continent's seals and penguins. In 1960 Admiral Byrd asked that 12 coastal Antarctic islands be named the Lindsey Islands in his honor.

Aside from his work in the Antarctic, Lindsey helped preserve the Indiana shore of Lake Michigan, which eventually became the Indiana Dunes National Lakeshore. And because of Lindsey's work studying volcanic vegetation in New Mexico, the oldest dated wood in the American Southwest is also named after him (Lindsey Ancient Tree Site). Lindsey died in December 1999 at age 92.

The First Successful Mount Everest Expedition

On May 29, 1953, New Zealander **Edmund Hillary** and Nepalese Sherpa Tenzing Norgay reached the summit of Mount Everest, the world's tallest mountain. Norgay died in 1986, leaving Hillary as the last survivor of the two climbers. Hillary passed away in 2008 at age 88.

Project Mercury

In 1959, the National Aeronautics and Space Administration (NASA) selected 110 pilots to be tested for the new Mercury space program. The following finalists became the Mercury Seven: **Scott Carpenter,** Gordon Cooper, **John Glenn,** Virgil "Gus" Grissom, Walter Schirra, Alan Shepard, and Donald "Deke" Slayton.

The Mercury missions were NASA's first efforts at sending humans into space and then recovering them. The first two missions lasted only about 15 minutes and demonstrated that the method worked (mainly, that nothing blew up and you could get the astronaut back alive). On the third, U.S. Marine John Glenn earned fame by becoming the first American to orbit Earth. On the sixth and last, Gordon Cooper stayed up for 34 hours and made 22 orbits.

The orbital and suborbital flights revealed important information about how humans handle space travel. The astronauts were guinea pigs, returning home to every medical test, poke, and prod one can imagine. The project's success represented an important Cold War boost for U.S. prestige and national morale during the tense Cuban Missile Crisis years, and its lessons proved essential for the 1969–72 Apollo lunar landings. The Mercury Seven, who shared a bond like no other, remained close for the rest of their lives.

As of 2008, only 86-year-old John Glenn and 82-year-old Scott Carpenter remain alive. After leaving NASA, Carpenter pursued his interest in oceanography and became a novelist; Glenn served as a U.S. senator for 24 years.

Music

❑ ❑ ❑ ❑

Who wrote "Animal Crackers in My Soup"?
Which musician turned to yoga to heal his back pain?
Who wrote "God Only Knows," a favorite song of Paul McCartney?
Read this chapter to find out.

Last Personal Friend of Beethoven

Young **Gerhard von Breuning** held the honor of being Ludwig van Beethoven's last earthly friend. When Gerhard was 12 years old, he lived just across a Vienna square from the great composer. He became acquainted with Beethoven through his father, Stephan, a man Beethoven had befriended while living in Bonn, Germany. Gerhard visited Beethoven nearly every day and became a dear friend to the composer.

Gerhard would recount their close relationship some 47 years later in the book *Aus dem Schwarzspanierhaus (Memories of Beethoven: From the House of the Black-Robed Spaniards)*. In Beethoven—a man whose musical compositions would form the core of orchestral and chamber music heard throughout the world—Gerhard found much inspiration. In his book, Gerhard discusses his idolization of the icon, as well as Beethoven's playfulness, generosity, and idiosyncrasies; Gerhard is able to detail elements of a personal life that few others witnessed. Gerhard also describes some darker times, including quarrels Beethoven waged with Stephan von Breuning and how the friendship survived. Gerhard remained close to Beethoven up until the composer's death in 1827. Gerhard went on to become a physician, and he died in 1892.

Italian Opera Composers

- Gaetano Donizetti (1797–1848) composed 75 operas, including *Lucia di Lammermoor.*
- Gioacchino Rossini (1792–1868) was a master of opera buffa. His most famous works are *The Barber of Seville, La Cenerentola,* and *William Tell.*
- Giuseppe Verdi (1813–1901) is considered by many to be the greatest Italian opera composer of the 19th century. His works include *Aida, La Traviata, Rigoletto,* and *Otello.*
- After studying at the Milan Conservatory, **Giacomo Puccini** (1858–1924) wrote mostly tragic operas, including *La Boheme, Tosca, Madama Butterfly,* and *Turandot.* He was the last of the greatest masters of Italian opera to die, passing away in 1924 at age 65.

* * * *

What comic "shorts" were to movie intermissions, opera buffa *was to 19th-century opera. This operatic farce provided levity to an art form that was often drop-dead serious. First showing up in the mid-1700s during* Intermezzi *(intermission), opera buffa generally featured a comic group of characters and a pair of lovers. All dialogue was sung, but the discourse was recited. Opera buffa was immensely popular and eventually morphed into its own brand of full-length entertainment. Components of the art form eventually found their way into serious opera.*

* * * *

Children of Enrico Caruso

Gloria Caruso Murray was the last living child of tenor Enrico Caruso when she passed away on December 5, 1999, at age 79. Murray was not even two years old when her father died in 1921, and her own talents fell in the area of visual art rather than music. This fact disappointed many of her father's fans. Caruso himself had high performance hopes for his daughter: Just after her birth he declared, "Ah, she has the vocal cords, just like her daddy!" Murray specialized in portraits and landscapes, but in contrast to her famous father, she pursued her art in relative anonymity. She spent the last years of her life in Jacksonville, Florida.

Enrico Caruso

Enrico Caruso (1873–1921) grew up in Naples, Italy. His family was poor, and his father was an alcoholic. To earn money, Caruso sang street serenades. He went on to sing opera on the South Italian circuit, then auditioned for the great composer Giacomo Puccini in 1897. Puccini was blown away by the range and tonal quality of Caruso's magnificent voice. He remarked, "Who sent you to me—God himself?"

Soon, all the world would hear the great gifts bestowed upon Caruso. A 1903 debut at New York's Metropolitan Opera led to 18 seasons of performances—a span that included 607 appearances in 37 separate productions. Gramophone recordings of the tenor's voice sold in the millions and paved the way for the modern record industry. His premature death at age 48 shocked the world and elevated Caruso to legendary status.

The Russian Five

The "Russian Five," aka "The Mighty Handful," was a breakout musical force formed by five Russian composers in the 1860s. The artists came together in an attempt to escape the then-prevalent influence of Italian opera and other western European music. They hoped to promote their own form of Russian composition. Stylistic elements setting the composers apart included passages lifted from Cossack and Caucasian dances and lyrical bits taken from peasant songs.

The Russian Five were:

- Modest Mussorgsky (1839–81)
- Aleksandr Borodin (1833–87)

- Nikolay Rimsky-Korsakov (1844–1908)
- Mily Balakirev (1837–1910)
- **César Cui** (1835–1918)

César Cui, the last surviving member of the five, was a creator of piano music, operas, and songs. He also worked as a military engineer and professor with an expertise in fortifications. Perhaps the least known of the five, Cui died in 1918 at age 83.

Les Six

French composers Georges Auric, Louis Durey, Arthur Honneger, Darius Milhaud, Francis Poulenc, and **Germaine Tailleferre** were members of a musical movement known as "Les Six." Their compositions stood as a simplified and jazzily rhythmic alternative to the weighty German Romanticism practiced by composers such as Strauss and Wagner. The style of Les Six incorporated key tonal elements of the Russian Five. In fact, French critic Henri Collet dubbed the composers "Les Six" as a way to associate them with the Russian Five. The last survivor was Tailleferre, the only female member of the sextet. She passed away in 1983. The musical legacy of Les Six lives on through the group's surviving descendants and associates, thus ensuring a unique stylistic niche for French musical composition.

Children of Francis Scott Key

In 1814, Francis Scott Key (1780–1843) wrote "The Star Spangled Banner" to celebrate a victory over the British in the War of 1812. In 1931, it was made the U.S. national anthem. Key's last surviving child, daughter **Elizabeth Howard,** died in 1897 at age 93.

Composers of Major U.S. Patriotic Songs

Irving Berlin, considered one of the greatest popular songwriters of all time, wrote the classic "God Bless America." He died at age 101 in 1989, long after the other major patriotic songwriters.

The following are other U.S. patriotic songs and their composers:

- Francis Scott Key (1779–1843), "The Star-Spangled Banner"
- Samuel Francis Smith (1808–95), "America" ("My Country 'Tis of Thee")
- Julia Ward Howe (1819–1910), "Battle Hymn of the Republic"
- Katharine Lee Bates (1859–1929), "America, the Beautiful"
- John Philip Sousa (1854–1932), "Stars and Stripes Forever"
- George M. Cohan (1878–1942), "You're a Grand Old Flag"
- Woody Guthrie (1912–67), "This Land Is Your Land"

Tin Pan Alley

"Tin Pan Alley" is a block of row houses on West 28th Street in Manhattan. The buildings were put up for sale in the fall of 2008, but the Historic Districts Council wants the buildings to have landmark status. From the 1880s to the 1950s, this area produced the most famous songs in American pop music. During these years, passersby could hear music coming from these buildings; one journalist claimed the music sounded like someone pounding on tin pans, and the area has been called Tin Pan Alley ever since.

Irving Caesar

Renowned lyricists from the era read like a veritable who's who of American music: Clarence Williams, Irving Berlin, Hoagy Carmichael, Cole Porter, and **Irving Caesar** merely scrape the surface of talent falling under the Tin Pan Alley banner. In the days when a song's popularity was determined by how many copies of sheet music it sold, immensely popular songs such as Al

Jolson's "Swanee" and Shirley Temple's "Animal Crackers in My Soup" (lyrics for both were penned by Caesar) ensured that the new art form would not only survive, but thrive. When Caesar died in 1996 at the advanced age of 101, his passing marked the end of the original group of Tin Pan Alley lyricists. Nevertheless, the musical style lives on—a fact evidenced famously (if rather bizarrely) in 1985 with rocker David Lee Roth's cover of Caesar's "Just a Gigolo."

The Ink Spots

From the 1930s to the 1950s, the Ink Spots, a singing group comprised of four African American men, accomplished the near impossible: During a time of strict racial segregation in the United States, Deek Watson, Charles Fuqua, Orville Jones, and **Jerry Daniels** won mainstream acceptance and applause. With such well-crafted songs as "If I Didn't Care," "I'll Never Smile Again," and "Java Jive," it's small wonder.

During the 1940s, the Ink Spots performed for American troops and collaborated with such esteemed artists as Ella Fitzgerald, Count Basie, Dinah Washington, Nat King Cole, Cab Calloway, and Lena Horne. Pushing further into the mainstream, the musicians teamed up with comedians Bud Abbott and Lou Costello for the 1942 movie *Pardon My Sarong*. It was an experience the Ink Spots heartily enjoyed.

In 1989, the breakthrough quartet was inducted into the Rock and Roll Hall of Fame. Their musical influence has fostered many copycat splinter groups—the ultimate form of recognition. Jerry Butler, founding member of the Impressions, summed up the group's accomplishments in one simple sentence: "The Ink Spots were the heavyweight champions of quartet singing." The last survivor of the original Ink Spots was Jerry Daniels, who passed away in 1995 at age 79. Though all of the original members have now died, there is a current version of the group that still does performances.

The Carter Family

Founded by singer/fiddler Alvin Pleasant (A. P.) Carter, singer **Sara Carter** (A. P.'s wife), and guitarist Maybelle Carter (A. P.'s sister-in-law) in the 1920s, the members of The Carter Family became superstars of bluegrass and country music.

In 1928, the group signed a contract with Victor records. With an emphasis on vocals over standard hillbilly instrumentals—and Maybelle's unique guitar style, which would come to be known as "Carter Scratch" (the combination of rhythm and lead)—the group recorded such hit songs as "Wildwood Flower" and "Keep on the Sunny Side." The Carter Family was moving country music in a new, exciting direction.

Bob Dylan and Johnny Cash would list The Carter Family as huge influences in their respective careers. The group was inducted into the Country Music Hall of Fame in 1970. The last survivor of the original Carter Family was Sara, who passed away in 1979.

* * * *

The Carter Family experienced its share of fame, but many believe the trio's star could have risen higher had fate not intervened. Only four days before The Carter Family was to be featured in Life *magazine, Japanese forces attacked Pearl Harbor. The earth-shattering event preempted the feature, thus robbing the band of national exposure. The Carter Family disbanded two years later.*

* * * *

Ellington's Orchestra

Jazz composer and bandleader Duke Ellington was born in 1899 and died in 1974 at age 75. Regarded as one of the most influential figures in jazz, the "Duke"—who was responsible for such hits as "Take the 'A' Train," "Sophisticated Lady," and "Passion Flower"—dubbed his musical style "American Music" because he didn't want to be limited to jazz. Ellington received a prodigious number of awards, including the Grammy Lifetime Achievement Award in

1966 (in addition to 13 previous Grammys), the Presidential Medal of Freedom in 1969, and the French Legion of Honor award in 1969. More than 12,000 people attended his New York funeral. During the service, singer Ella Fitzgerald exclaimed, "It's a very sad day. . . . A genius has passed."

Duke Ellington

Herb Jeffries, who turned 97 in 2008, is the last original member of Duke Ellington's orchestra. The singer of "Flamingo" and "Satin Doll," Jeffries had previously worked as singing cowboy "Bronze Buckaroo" in all-black Western films. Of mixed heritage (his great-grandmother was Ethiopian, his parents European), Jeffries worked hard to erase the racial stereotypes that prevailed during his day.

Born and raised in Detroit, Michigan, Jeffries was troubled by the fact that American Westerns featured white cowboys only. In a proactive move, he raised money to produce his own Western. He starred as cowboy "Bob Blake," who was fearless and advised viewers to shoot only in self-defense and to never drink alcohol or smoke cigarettes. After completing a series of such films, Jeffries joined Duke Ellington's band.

Healing Through Yoga

The fact that singer Herb Jeffries is closing in on the century mark is even more of a miracle than it may first appear. In 1948, the musician nearly died when his plane crashed while flying from Las Vegas to the San Fernando Valley. He and his pilot survived the crash, but Jeffries came away with three herniated discs in his back. Jeffries was in tremendous pain and doctors recommended surgery—a solution that Jeffries soundly rejected. Instead, Jeffries turned to Yogi Paramahansa Yogananda for help. The nontraditional treatments took some eight months, but afterward X-rays showed that Jeffries's back had healed. Jeffries continued to practice yoga even after his complete recovery because he felt that the discipline helped him feel youthful and fit.

Ellington at the Cotton Club

The Cotton Club, a nightclub that operated in Harlem in the 1920s and 1930s, featured the great African American performers of the day. The last survivor to perform with the great Duke Ellington at the famous club was guitarist **Lawrence Lucie,** who celebrated his 101st birthday on December 18, 2008.

Lucie, the son of a jazz musician, began playing during childhood. He mastered the mandolin, banjo, and violin before finally taking on the guitar. Lucie worked as a barber by day and at night studied banjo at the Brooklyn Conservatory of Music. He would make the switch to guitar when he entered the professional ranks. After subbing for Duke Ellington's guitarist at the Cotton Club in 1931, doors sprang open. Lucie would go on to work with such noted musicians as Coleman Hawkins, Fletcher Henderson, Jelly Roll Morton, and Billie Holiday.

Big Band Leaders

- Chick Webb (1909–39) became one of the giants of the big band era. "A-tisket, A-tasket" signifies his biggest hit.
- With mega-hits including "In the Mood," "Chattanooga Choo Choo," and "Moonlight Serenade," Iowan Glenn Miller (1904–44) achieved big-band supremacy.
- One-half of the famed Dorsey Brothers, younger brother Tommy Dorsey (1905–56) found shared success with such songs as "I Get a Kick out of You" and "Lullaby of Broadway." He later broke off on his own and scored again with "I'm Getting Sentimental over You" and "I'll Never Smile Again."
- The older half of the Dorsey Brothers, Jimmy Dorsey (1904–57) was content to remain with the band while his brother took the lead role. Top-ten hits including "What a Difference a Day Made" and "I Believe in Miracles" stand as testament to the fruitful pairing.
- Paul Whiteman (1890–1967) was progressive in his musical outlook. He proclaimed jazz "the folk music of the industrial age." Fittingly, this bandleader was a well-oiled machine when it came

to churning out hits. “Let’s Fall in Love,” “Together,” and “Rhapsody in Blue” kept his “factory” hummin.’

- Gene Krupa (1909–73) is considered one of the most influential drummers of the 20th century. He invented the pairing of drums that would come to be known as the standard “kit” and raised drum solos to an art form.
- “It Don’t Mean a Thing if It Ain’t Got that Swing” was one of his most famous numbers, and swing Duke Ellington (1899–1974) certainly did. “Don’t You Know I Care (Or Don’t You Care to Know)” and “Perdido” continued such hip, “to and fro” swaying.
- A onetime contortionist from a traveling circus, Harry James (1916–83) twisted himself into a successful bandleader. His swinging version of “You Made Me Love You” turned appreciative teens into quivering masses of flesh.

- Count Basie (1904–84) was bestowed with the honor of “Count” beside the regal likes of fellow bandleaders Benny “The King of Swing” Goodman and Edward “Duke” Ellington. Basie’s band featured energetic ensemble work and generous soloing. “One O’ Clock Jump” and “Jumpin’ at the Woodside” kept toes a-tappin.’

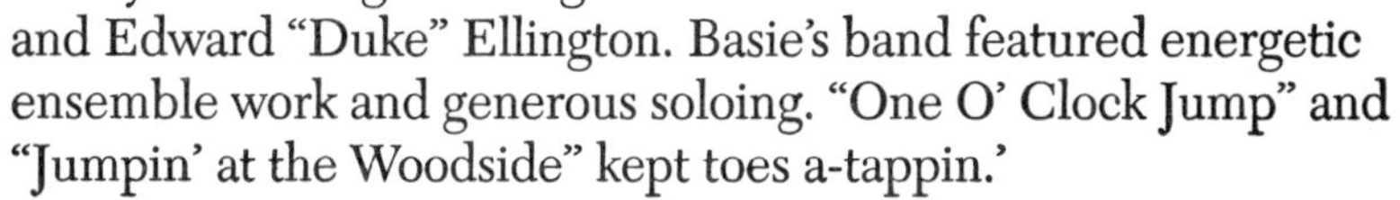

- Benny Goodman (1909–86), the “King of Swing,” scored more than 100 hits during his career. “Sing, Sing, Sing,” “Blue Moon,” “Moonglow,” and “Jersey Bounce” were among them.
- Considered by many to be the greatest drummer to ever pick up sticks, Buddy Rich (1917–87) had a career that spanned seven decades. His caustic humor, as finely honed as his precision drum licks, made him a talk-show favorite.
- John Birks “Dizzy” Gillespie (1917–93) was known for his comical antics—hence his nickname—in addition to his world-class trumpeting. With his trademark upturned horn, Gillespie ushered in the bebop era.

- Responsible for such ditties as “Hi-De-Ho” and “Minnie the Moocher,” former law school student **Cab Calloway** (1907–94) was known for his energetic “scat” singing and frequent appearances at the Cotton Club.
- Known as “King of the Vibes,” percussionist/bandleader **Lionel Hampton** (1908–2002) elevated the vibraphone to first-class status. “On the Sunny Side of the Street” and “Hot Mallets” rank as two of his most popular songs.
- Born Arthur Arshawsky, **Artie Shaw** (1910–2004) was noted for such hits as “Begin the Beguine” and “Everything’s Jumping.” He was equally noted for his eight marriages. Actresses Lana Turner and Ava Gardner were but two “victims” who famously took the plunge with Shaw. The last living great big band leader, Artie Shaw died at age 94 on December 30, 2004.

The Glenn Miller Orchestra

The Glenn Miller Orchestra made considerable contributions during the swing era. It dazzled audiences with such hits as “(I’ve Got a Gal in) Kalamazoo” and “Tuxedo Junction” and became a musical tour de force. In the year 1940, the Glenn Miller Orchestra recorded 45 songs that reached the top-seller charts—this is still a record today.

After the United States entered World War II, Glenn Miller volunteered to join the army and serve his country by entertaining Allied troops around the world. On December 15, 1944, Miller boarded a plane in London that was to take him to Paris; he was planning to make arrangements to bring his band to Paris later in the month to perform a Christmas concert. Sadly, Miller’s plane never arrived at its destination and is assumed to have crashed into the English Channel. Miller was declared dead; he was just 40 years old.

Trumpet-playing “hired gun” **Les Beigel** was the last surviving member of Glenn Miller’s original band. In 1937, Beigel was regarded so highly, Miller himself hired him sight unseen via telegram. But Beigel’s ascension to the highest ranks hadn’t come easy. The hardworking musician spent many years on the road honing his craft before the fairy-tale note from Miller arrived.

Music was a major part of Beigel's life; the trumpeter blew through his mouthpiece well into his 80s. "Les Beigel, Music for All Occasions," read the master's modest business cards. He delivered his final performance in 1997 and passed away in 2004 at age 95.

The Crooners

- The first African American man to attain mainstream acceptance as a pop singer, Nat King Cole (1919–65) made his breakthrough with the haunting "Mona Lisa." His much heralded "Christmas Song" has become synonymous with the Yuletide season.
- The most electronically recorded human voice in history, the iconic Bing Crosby (1903–77) may be best known for his rendition of "White Christmas."
- Dean Martin (1917–95) burst onto the scene as part of the Martin and Lewis comedy team. The part-time singer, full-time drinker (at least in image) was the personification of "cool." "That's Amore" seized the charts while the crooner's role in the 1960s Rat Pack cemented his legend.
- Arguably the most famous crooner of all time, Frank Sinatra (1915–98) electrified fans with such runaway hits as "My Way" and "Strangers in the Night." A successful acting career helped turn this boy from Hoboken, New Jersey, into a household name, and his carousing with the Rat Pack kept his name in the papers.
- Less flashy than many crooners, Mel Torme (1925–99) did a slow, jazzy burn into people's hearts. "That's All" and "I Wished on the Moon" reveal his "Hep Cat" style.
- **Perry Como** (1912–2001) sold more than 100 million records in a 60-year career and was one of the most popular American singers of the 20th century. This former barber from Pennsylvania cut the pop charts down to size with such hits as "It's Impossible" and "I Wonder Who's Kissing Her Now." His fame spread through

performances on radio and television, leading to a lifetime total of 27 gold records. When he passed away in 2001, he was the last living of the 1940s male vocalists who were dubbed the "crooners."

The Mills Brothers

One of the most popular African American vocal groups, the Mills Brothers began as "Four Boys and a Guitar" in 1930. With an uncanny ability to imitate musical instruments using voices only, and intricate harmonies that rendered their sound as smooth as glass, John Jr., Herbert, Harry, and Donald sounded more like a Dixieland instrumental combo than a singing group.

The Mills Brothers, who learned their trade by singing along with a barbershop quartet, went on to collaborate with such heavy hitters as Louis Armstrong and Ella Fitzgerald. The brothers were also the first African Americans to give a command performance before the British monarchy.

Hit songs recorded under the Mills Brothers banner include "You Always Hurt the One You Love," "Paper Doll," and "Tiger Rag." The band was inducted into the Vocal Group Hall of Fame in 1998 and continues on with the help of a renewed cast today. **Donald Mills,** the last survivor of the original foursome, died at age 84 in 1999.

The Andrews Sisters

One of the most popular singing groups of the 1940s, the Andrews Sisters (Laverne, Maxene, and Patty) occasionally sang with Bing Crosby but were most famous for their USO work during World War II. Their hits included "Boogie-Woogie Bugle Boy" and "Don't Sit Under the Apple Tree." The Andrews Sisters also appeared in several Hollywood movies. **Patty Andrews,** the last surviving Andrews Sister, was still alive in 2009 at age 91.

Rodgers and Hammerstein

Richard Rodgers (1902–79) and Oscar Hammerstein II (1895–1960) formed one of the most creative teams in the history of musical theater. During their 17-year partnership, their productions included *Oklahoma!, The King and I, South Pacific,* and *The Sound of Music.* They accumulated 35 Tonys and 15 Oscars. Rodgers was the last survivor of the pair, dying in 1979 at age 77.

The Jordanaires

Starting in the late 1940s as a gospel group, the Jordanaires have backed up some of the biggest stars in the business. The original group, formed by brothers Bill and Monty Matthews, included Culley Holt, **Bob Hubbard,** and Bob Money. By 1958, this original grouping gave way to Gordon Stoker, Neal Matthews Jr., Ray Walker, and Hoyt Hawkins. The four would prove to be the most enduring Jordanaires ensemble.

As key contributors to the "Nashville Sound," a style that featured "crooning" leads and "smooth" background vocals, the Jordanaires became a favorite with Elvis Presley, who used them on his records and films for more than a dozen years. Songs including "Surrender," "Follow That Dream," and "Can't Help Falling in Love" merely scrape the surface of popular songs produced through the famous collaboration. Patsy Cline, Rick Nelson, Loretta Lynn, and a host of other greats helped keep the band busy through the 1960s and 1970s, the singers' golden era.

Today, a current version of the group (Louis Nunley, Gordon Stoker, Ray Walker, and Curtis Young) continues the legacy. The Jordanaires were inducted into the Country Music Hall of Fame in 2001. Of the five original members, only Bob Hubbard was alive in 2008, when he celebrated his 80th birthday.

The First Grammys

The Grammy Awards were first awarded in 1958. **Perry Como** (1912–2001) was the last surviving of the four people who received awards at that year's ceremony. Como won the award for

Best Male Vocal Performance, for his performance of "Catch a Falling Star."

The following artists also won Grammy Awards that year:

- Record of the Year and Song of the Year: Domenico Modugno (1928–94), for "Nel Blu Dipinto di Blu" (Volare)
- Album of the Year: Henry Mancini (1924–94), for "The Music from Peter Gunn"
- Best Female Vocal Performance: Ella Fitzgerald (1917–96), for "Ella Fitzgerald Sings the Irving Berlin Songbook"

The Coasters

Formed in 1955 by **Carl Gardner,** the Coasters were a great rhythm & blues/rock group of the late 1950s. The combination of a top-notch African American vocal group with songs written by two Jewish songwriters, Jerry Leiber and Mike Stoller, led to a series of hit records. In 1987, the Coasters were inducted into the Rock and Roll Hall of Fame. In 2008, lead singer Carl Gardner—the only one of the original group still alive—celebrated his 80th birthday.

Bill Haley and His Comets

Often considered the first rock 'n' roll band, Bill Haley and His Comets was founded in 1952. The original members of this group were Bill Haley, accordion player Johnny Grande, and guitarists Billy Williamson and **Marshall Lytle.** Their song "Rock Around the Clock" came to be a symbol for rock music itself. As of 2008, Lytle, at age 74, is the last of the original members still alive.

The Beatles

In the early 1960s, four working-class men from Liverpool shook the world of rock music in Britain. In 1964, their fame and their music spread to the United States and around the world. John Lennon and **Paul McCartney** wrote most of the group's songs. The other two members were guitarist George Harrison and drummer **Ringo Starr.** With songs such as "She Loves You," "Yesterday," "Penny

Lane," "Hey Jude," and "Let It Be," The Beatles became the most popular group in music history. As of 2008, only two Beatles remain—McCartney at age 66 and Starr at 68. John Lennon was murdered at age 40 in 1980, and George Harrison succumbed to throat cancer in 2001 at age 58.

The Mamas and the Papas

One of the greatest folk-pop groups of the '60s, The Mamas and the Papas offered a melodic alternative to "statement" songs and hard-edged rock 'n' roll. Hits such as "California Dreamin'" and "Monday, Monday" spoke more to shared experiences than to turbulent times.

Singer **Michelle Phillips** outlived all other band members (she celebrated her 64th birthday in 2008) and found further expression in the acting world. She spent decades on such television shows as *Knots Landing, Matt Houston,* and *The Love Boat.* Daughter Chynna Phillips inherited her mother's musical talent and fronted Wilson Phillips, a pop group that included Carnie and Wendy Wilson, daughters of The Beach Boys' Brian Wilson.

The following were the other members of The Mamas and the Papas:

- Cass Elliot (1941–74)
- John Phillips (1935–2001)
- Denny Doherty (1940–2007)

The Wilson Brothers of The Beach Boys

The Beach Boys, a 1960s rock 'n' roll group featuring Al Jardine, Mike Love, and the three Wilson brothers (Brian, Carl, and Dennis), were noted for their rich harmonies and thoughtful lyrics. Virtually inventing California rock (a genre that celebrated surfing, dating, and driving), The Beach Boys helped change the landscape of modern rock 'n' roll.

Brian Wilson wrote and composed such hit songs as "Little Deuce Coupe," "Fun, Fun, Fun," and "I Get Around," which captivated a new generation. The group's playful fare made every day seem like a romp in the surf. In later years, The Beach Boys' sound would evolve. Brian would write deeper, more sophisticated ballads such as "Wouldn't It Be Nice" and "God Only Knows."

The band played on into the mid-1980s but would ultimately suffer insurmountable blows. Dennis Wilson's death by drowning in 1983 was presumed to have been caused by his excessive drinking. Carl Wilson succumbed to lung cancer in 1998, leaving Brian Wilson, Al Jardine, and Mike Love to carry on. Eventually, infighting and legal battles split the band apart. Brian Wilson was plagued with mental health issues and drug addictions that would nearly kill him. Al Jardine moved into the production end of the business, but rejoined Brian Wilson for a 2006 tour that celebrated the album *Pet Sounds,* which was originally released in 1966. Mike Love eventually formed a new version of The Beach Boys without Jardine and Wilson. The Beach Boys were inducted into the Rock and Roll Hall of Fame in 1988.

Brian Wilson, the eternal teenager always in search of the next big wave, reached age 66 in 2008 and officially became a senior citizen. He continues to write music and tour, and he keeps in touch with fans through brianwilson.com.

* * * *

Looking back on the 1960s during a recorded interview, Brian Wilson spoke of his "Beatles-envy." Wilson incorporated elements of The Beatles' style into his own compositions. With Pet Sounds, *Wilson hoped to surpass The Beatles'* Rubber Soul. *Proving that envy often runs both ways, The Beatles paid The Beach Boys the ultimate compliment when they patterned* Sgt. Pepper's Lonely Hearts Club Band *after* Pet Sounds. *Paul McCartney considered the song "God Only Knows" a personal favorite.*

* * * *

Of all The Beach Boys, Dennis was the only one who actually surfed.

* * * *

World Events

❑ ❑ ❑ ❑

How did Cleopatra and Caesar first meet?
Who are the American Bonapartes?
Did Gandhi ever win the Nobel Peace Prize?
Read on and find out.

Rome's First Triumverate

In 60 B.C., the alliance of **Julius Caesar** (100–44 B.C.), Pompey the Great (106–48 B.C.), and Marcus Crassus (115–53 B.C.) was known as the First Triumvirate. Caesar was the last survivor of the three. One of the greatest generals in history, Caesar triumphed in the Gallic Wars (58–50 B.C.) and defeated Pompey at Pharsalus (48 B.C.). He was assassinated in 44 B.C. by a coalition of 60 Roman senators who opposed his rule for various political and philosophical reasons. Members of the group lured Caesar to a back room of the senate offices under the guise of presenting a petition to him; they then stabbed him repeatedly.

Caesar and Brutus

Marcus Junius Brutus was an influential political and military figure in the Roman Empire. As Caesar consolidated his power during the Roman civil wars, Brutus fought against him but was later pardoned after being defeated. A fierce supporter of democracy, Brutus then allied with Caesar and became a close friend and counsel as the famous leader worked to bring order and peace to the empire. When Caesar had himself declared sole ruler for life, Brutus saw his dreams of a Roman republic shattered, and he became one of the leading figures in the conspiracy to assassinate the new dictator. Caesar was surprised by the betrayal of his longtime ally and is said to have asked, "Et tu, Brute?" ("You too, Brutus?") at the time of his murder. In the power struggles that ensued after Caesar's death, Brutus was defeated in battle by Marc Anthony and Octavian in 42 B.C. To avoid being captured, he killed himself with his sword.

* * * *

Caesar entered Egypt with his armies as the young Queen Cleopatra struggled with her younger brother over the throne. Both sought Caesar's support to secure power. The night before the scheduled meeting, Cleopatra smuggled herself into his headquarters rolled up in a carpet that was presented to him as a gift. Enamored with the beautiful and clever woman, Caesar helped her gain sole control of Egypt.

* * * *

Successors to Alexander the Great

Macedonian king Alexander the Great is considered one of the greatest generals in history. He conquered most of the land between Greece, Egypt, and India. When Alexander died in 323 B.C. at age 32, his half-brother Philip III became king and Alexander's generals became rulers of their respective territories. Three generals ultimately ruled the major pieces of Alexander's empire: **Seleucus,** Antigonus, and Ptolemy. The last survivor was Seleucus, the ruler of Babylon, who was killed in 281 B.C. at age 77.

Napoleon

Napoleon was born in 1769 on the Mediterranean island of Corsica, which had recently fallen under the control of France. As a young man, he excelled in science and mathematics. He joined the French armed forces and studied military history and theory during the tumultuous years of the French Revolution. When members of the royal family threatened to restore the monarchy, Napoleon took advantage of the popularity he had earned through successful military campaigns to take control of the government as part of a three-person council. He quickly pushed out the other two leaders and built a French Empire that redefined the national boundaries of Europe. Other nations formed coalitions to challenge Napoleon on the battlefield, but all crumbled before the great general. A man of simple tastes but great ego, he died in 1821 while exiled on the island of St. Helena, six years after being forced from power.

Napoleon's Ministers

Napoleon was Emperor of France from 1804 through 1814 and part of 1815. **Étienne-Denis Pasquier** was born two years before Napoleon on April 21, 1767, and was the last remaining of Emperor Napoleon's ministers. Pasquier served the emperor as councilor of state and prefect of police. After Napoleon's defeat, Pasquier continued to play important roles in the French government, becoming chancellor of France in 1837. Pasquier died in 1862 at age 95.

The French Government Under Napoleon

The French Revolution of 1789 replaced the authority of the nation's monarchy with promises of democracy and equality, but a decade of squabbling among social and political groups left the country with no stable government. When Napoleon stepped into the void, he spoke of the liberal ideals of the revolution but established a far stronger dictatorship than most French kings ever enjoyed. He allowed elections for local government, but these offices were all answerable to the authority of prefects appointed to each region by the emperor. He also established the Napoleonic Code, which granted some civil rights and allowed for the rise of a true middle class, but also favored business interests and protected the property rights of the wealthy. After Napoleon's defeat at Waterloo, the nation lurched from one form of government to another for more than 50 years—a restored but weakened monarchy, a short-lived republic, and another empire headed by Napoleon's nephew—before establishing a modern democracy in 1870. Many of the institutions established by Napoleon, such as the prefects, survived it all and remain part of French government today.

Waterloo

On June 18, 1815, Napoleon Bonaparte was defeated at the Battle of Waterloo, and his power was ended forever. One of his soldiers, **Victor Baillot,** was wounded in the battle but survived for another 82 years. Baillot died in the small village of Carisey in Bourgogne, France, on February 3, 1898. He was 104 years old and the last living veteran of the Battle of Waterloo.

The Significance of Waterloo

The Battle of Waterloo occurred near Brussels between French forces under Napoleon and combined British, Belgian, Dutch, German, and Prussian armies led by the British Duke of Wellington. The day began with Wellington and Napoleon facing each other across the field of battle after a night of heavy rain. The French leader delayed his attack until noon to allow the field to dry so that his artillery and cavalry could move more freely. French forces unsuccessfully attacked Wellington's center throughout the afternoon. Their early evening attack broke their opponent's center, but by then Prussian forces had assaulted the French flank, drawing critical resources away from the main fight. Wellington regrouped, drove the French back, and then advanced forcefully. Beset on two sides, the once-feared French army retreated. Over the preceding 20 years, Napoleon had established himself as one of the most powerful rulers and most successful military strategists since the days of the Roman Empire. His defeat at Waterloo ended once and for all his rule of France and his great influence over the affairs of Europe.

Napoleon's Marshals

Auguste Frederic Louis Viesse de Marmont, duke of Ragusa (1774–1852), was the last survivor of Napoleon's marshals. De Marmont entered the artillery in 1792, fought for Napoleon at Marengo in 1800, and served as governor of Dalmatia and later of Illyria. Napoleon made him a marshal of France in 1809. In 1813, de Marmont fought with distinction at Lutzen, Bautzen, and Dresden, but in 1814, he surrendered Paris, joined the Allied forces, and was reviled as a traitor by the Bonapartists. At the restoration of the monarchy, he was made a peer of France by King Louis XVIII. He wrote his memoirs during the last years of his life, in exile outside of France. De Marmont died in Venice in 1852.

* * * *

The military rank of marshal is comparable to the rank of general in the U.S armed forces and has been used by various countries over the last thousand years. The rank was eliminated in France after the Revolution because of its association with the old monarchy, but Napoleon reinstated it and gave his 18 marshals significant autonomy in using the forces under their command.

* * * *

Napoleon's Siblings

French Emperor Napoleon I had nothing against nepotism. That was good news for his little brother and last surviving sibling, **Jérôme Bonaparte,** whom Napoleon made king of Westphalia in 1807. Good at decorating but a mediocre ruler and a bungling general, Jérôme lasted only until the French military lost Westphalia. Deposed in 1813, he rallied to Napoleon at Waterloo and promptly hurt his brother's fortunes with further soldiering blunders.

Jérôme moved to Italy after the war, and his fortunes again picked up in 1848, when his nephew, Louis Napoleon, became

Napoleon III of France. Jérôme was made a marshal and also became commander of Les Invalides, a residence for retired soldiers. Jérôme died in 1860 at age 75, and his remains lie at Les Invalides.

The American Bonapartes

Before becoming a king, Jérôme established family roots in America. His first wife was Betsy Patterson, a Baltimore merchant's daughter. Napoleon disapproved of the union and actually barred Betsy (who was pregnant at the time) from coming ashore in France. Betsy returned to the United States, and the perpetually unfaithful Jérôme more or less pretended their marriage and child hadn't occurred. An astute investor, Betsy died very wealthy in 1879.

Betsy and Jérôme's grandson, Charles Joseph Bonaparte (1851–1921), was a distinguished American and bane of corruption who, as attorney general under Theodore Roosevelt, helped create a special group of agents that would later be called the FBI. He served as secretary of the Navy (1905–06) and attorney general (1906–09).

The First Nobel Prize Winners

- Sully Prudhomme (1839–1907) won the first Nobel Prize in Literature. He was a French poet and leader of the Parnassian movement, which advocated a traditional and formal style of verse.
- Henry Dunant (1828–1910) and Frédéric Passy (1822–1912) shared the first Nobel Peace Prize. In 1863, Dunant founded the organization that would become the International Red Cross. Passy was a French economist who championed free trade as a way to bring nations together. He was one of the founders of the Inter-Parliamentary Union, an organization that today continues to advocate open discourse between nations to prevent the escalation of conflicts. Passy served as a negotiator in several volatile international disputes.

- Jacobus H. van 't Hoff (1852–1911) won the first Nobel Prize in Chemistry. Hoff was a Dutch chemist who taught at a veterinary school. His work on mathematical models for describing chemical solutions helped found the field of physical chemistry.
- Emil von Behring (1854–1917) was awarded the first Nobel Prize in Physiology or Medicine for developing a serum against diphtheria.
- **Wilhelm Conrad Röntgen** (1845–1923) was awarded the 1901 Nobel Prize in Physics because of his discovery of X-rays, which he accidentally discovered while performing experiments with electricity. He named them "X"-rays because they were unknown. When others sought to rename them "Röntgen rays," he objected. He also refused to apply for patents on his discovery because he did not want to interfere with people obtaining benefit from it. When Röntgen died in 1923, he was the last survivor of the first Nobel recipients.

The *Potemkin*

Discontent with czarist rule grew throughout Russia after the turn of the 20th century. It was fueled by poverty among the working class and peasants, greed and excess by the aristocracy, and the mismanagement of the Russo-Japanese War.

The first sign that discontent would lead to the Russian Revolution of 1917 occurred aboard the battleship *Potemkin* in 1905. When a crew member named Vakulinchuk complained to an officer that the crew was being served spoiled meat, the officer shot Vakulinchuk. The crew promptly revolted. Seven officers were killed, and the crew took control of the ship. They sailed to the Ukrainian town of Odessa and inspired soldiers and citizens there to overthrow local rule.

The Black Sea Fleet arrived to put down the uprising, but sailors in the fleet refused to fire on their comrades aboard the *Potemkin*. The mutineers unsuccessfully sought fuel and supplies at several ports, then sailed to Romania and turned the ship over to authorities there. Some returned to Russia to complete their service or face trial, but others scattered across the globe.

Ivan Beshoff, the last survivor of the *Potemkin* mutiny, was born near Odessa. He worked in the engine room of the *Potemkin* and was one of the escapees. After the mutiny, Beshoff traveled widely; he journeyed through Turkey and on to England, eventually settling in Ireland in 1913 because that was where he had felt the most free. He worked for an oil distribution company and was twice arrested because he was suspected of being a Soviet spy. He eventually married, raised a family, opened a fish-and-chips restaurant, and became a respected member of the Dublin community. Beshoff died on October 25, 1987, at age 104. His family continues to operate his restaurant on Upper O'Connell Street.

Capturing the Story on Film

After the Russian Revolution of 1917, Soviet leaders struggled with the task of uniting a nation of 160 million people who were largely illiterate and spoke 100 different languages. The leaders embraced cinema as a way to reach across these boundaries and spread Marxist ideology.

In the 1920s, the government agency that oversaw film production ordered a young director named Sergei Eisenstein to shoot a film about the *Potemkin* mutiny; they directed him to emphasize the brutality of the czarist regime and the strength of a united proletariat. Eisenstein applied his theories of montage editing—juxtaposing two unrelated images to create a powerful new idea in the mind of the viewer—and created *Battleship Potemkin* (1925), one of the greatest works in film history.

The film's most famous sequence depicts czarist soldiers massacring civilians on the steps of a public square in Odessa. Though no such massacre ever occurred, the techniques used by Eisenstein for this scene became standard in the film industry. Many films have included references to the Odessa Steps sequence, including Francis Ford Coppola's *The Godfather,* Brian De Palma's *The Untouchables,* George Lucas's *Star Wars Episode III: Revenge of the Sith,* and Woody Allen's *Love and Death.*

The Panama Canal

The notion of a canal across Central America connecting the Atlantic and Pacific oceans had been dreamed of for centuries, as it would avoid the dangers of South America's Cape Horn and shorten sea voyages by several months and thousands of miles. However, such a huge feat couldn't be seriously considered until the advances of the Industrial Revolution in the 1800s.

Ferdinand de Lesseps, a French entrepreneur who had overseen construction of the Suez Canal, first made an attempt in 1881. Heavy rain, intense heat, difficult terrain, and tropical diseases stymied de Lesseps's sea-level plan. Whenever the crews made progress, flooding would quickly wash all their work away. When only 11 miles of the required 50 had been dug after seven years of work, almost $300 million, and the loss of 20,000 lives, de Lesseps gave up.

In 1901, newly elected American President Theodore Roosevelt committed to building a canal, citing the need to join the U.S. Atlantic and Pacific fleets as a matter of national security. When negotiations with the government of Colombia (which owned the area considered most suitable for a canal) broke down, the United States supported a group of local residents and businesspeople in seceding from Colombia and forming the nation of Panama. The new nation promptly granted the U.S. the rights to build the canal.

Construction began in 1904, and the canal opened in 1914. Key to the success of the American effort was a more organized, practical "lake and lock" plan by chief engineer John Franks Stevens. In addition, a successful public health campaign led by Dr. William Gorgas greatly reduced the scourge of malaria and yellow fever.

Alexander Bernard Heron was born in 1894 and started working at the Panama Canal's construction site at age 14. He ultimately spent a total of 48 years of his life working at the canal. When he died at age 105 in early 2000, he was the last of the Panama Canal builders.

* * * *

Canal locks allow ships to travel from areas of higher elevation to lower elevation, and vice versa. Huge gates divide the canal into sections of differing elevations. As a ship enters a section, the gate behind it closes, and then sluices open in the gate in front of it, allowing the water level to even out between the section the ship is in and the section it is traveling toward. The gates in front of the ship then open, and the ship can move ahead to the next section, where the process is repeated.

* * * *

The Panama Canal Expansion

The treaty granting the United States the right to build the Panama Canal also gave the U.S. complete control over the canal's operation; over the years Panamanian citizens began to resent this arrangement. After decades of negotiations, the canal was finally given over to Panamanian control in 1999 (although the United States reserved the right of military intervention if the waterway's security was ever threatened). Since then the canal has been ably managed by the Panama Canal Authority (PCA), which has increased traffic and reduced both accidents and the average transit time for ships.

Seeking to further improve the canal's usefulness to world trade, the PCA has begun an ambitious expansion plan to allow the canal to handle more traffic and larger ships. Analysts estimate that by 2011, nearly 40 percent of ships will be too large to fit through the Panama Canal. These so called "post-Panamax" ships (a ship that just fits through the canal is called a "Panamax" ship) currently dock at West Coast ports; cargo is carried to the East Coast via truck or rail. The expansion is scheduled to be completed by 2015.

* * * *

Before the Panama Canal, ships had to travel around Cape Horn at the southern tip of South America to go from the Atlantic to the Pacific. The great distance posed one obstacle, but the treacherous waters around the Horn were the real threat. Heavy storms, ever-changing and violent winds, limited visibility, and the threat of icebergs make this one of the most feared routes on the high seas.

* * * *

Gallipoli

Early in World War I, Allied forces mounted an invasion of the Ottoman Empire on the Gallipoli Peninsula in modern-day Turkey. Three different landings were made simultaneously—one by British/Irish troops, another by the French, and a third by a small contingent of the Australian and New Zealand Army Corps (ANZAC).

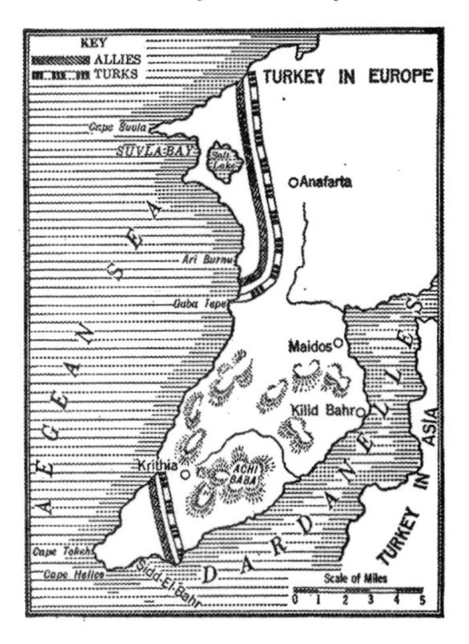

The invaders met fierce resistance; for several months they were able to do little more than hold their landing zones. The ANZAC position was burdened by particularly difficult terrain and bouts of dysentery and typhoid, but they still managed to inflict heavy losses on the enemy day in and day out. After being bolstered by 20,000 reinforcements, the ANZAC forces waged a fierce assault and finally captured the high ground. The effort left them exhausted and disorganized, however, and they were soon driven back by a withering counteroffensive.

Though the campaign ended in defeat, the heroism and tenacity of the ANZAC soldiers became a point of national pride for the newly formed nation of Australia. ANZAC Day (April 25) is one of the country's most important national holidays. **Alec Campbell** served as a water carrier during the battle and was the last survivor of the ANZAC forces at Gallipoli. He died on May 16, 2002, at age 103. The prime minister of Australia left an official visit to China to attend his state funeral.

* * * *

In 1981, Australian director Peter Weir released the film Gallipoli, *a coming-of-age story set during the famous failed invasion. An immediate international success, the evocative, hauntingly beautiful film vaulted Weir, lead actor Mel Gibson, and the entire Australian film industry onto the world stage.*

* * * *

Easter Rising

The people of Ireland had begrudgingly lived under English rule for centuries. Notions of rebellion perpetually swirled throughout the culture, but the first concrete steps toward independence occurred on Easter Monday (April 21) of 1916.

Against the wishes of their leadership, about 1,800 breakaway members of the Irish Volunteers led by **Eamon de Valera** and 15 others took control of Dublin and proclaimed an Irish Republic. The small band of ill-equipped rebels never had any real hope of victory, and British forces put the rebellion down after only eight days. But the bold effort of the Irish, coupled with the harsh reprisals of the British, prompted many in the country to more actively pursue independence in the years that followed.

All the leaders of the Easter Rising except de Valera were executed within a few weeks. De Valera was spared in part because he was a U.S. citizen. (De Valera was born in New York City in 1882 to a Spanish father and an Irish mother. Because he was just a toddler when his father died, the boy was sent to live with his mother's family in Ireland.)

De Valera, who was released from jail after a few years, remained a major figure of the Irish independence movement. From 1919 to 1920, he toured the United States to raise funds and seek support for an independent Ireland. When the Irish Free State was finally declared in 1921, de Valera became a leading political figure and eventually served as president of Ireland for several decades. At his death on August 30, 1975, he was the last surviving leader of the pivotal Easter Rising.

The First Dáil

The first meeting of the Irish revolutionary parliament known as the First Dáil occurred in 1919. It included famous Irish leaders Michael Collins, Eamon de Valera, Countess Constance Markievicz, and Arthur Griffith. The last surviving member was **Sean MacEntee,** who passed away in 1984 at age 94.

Russia's Provisional Government

Contrary to what many people believe, the Bolsheviks did not overthrow Czar Nicholas II. Between the czar's abdication and the establishment of Lenin's communism, a provisional government—a form of democracy—came to Russia for a period of eight months. The last survivor of this provisional government was **Alexander Kerensky,** who was appointed the government's premier in July 1917. Kerensky fled soon after the Bolshevik revolution began in November of that same year. He lived in England for a while, then ran a newspaper in France; he finally settled as a teacher in the United States. He died in New York City in 1970 at age 89.

* * * *

Czar Nicholas II was a cousin of King George V, but the British king refused to grant Nicholas asylum. On July 17, 1918, the Bolsheviks executed Czar Nicholas II and his family.

* * * *

The Russian Revolution

Vyacheslav Molotov, who joined the Bolshevik party in Russia in 1906 at age 16, probably deserves the title "survivor" more than anyone in the history of Russian communism. Molotov gained favor with Lenin, and then served Stalin when the notoriously suspicious Communist leader was purging almost all people of power. Molotov, who became Soviet foreign minister during World War II, fell out of favor with Khrushchev in the 1950s. He was appointed a delegate to the International Atomic Energy Agency in 1960, was expelled from the Communist party in 1962, and was accepted back into the party in 1984. Molotov died in 1986 at age 96.

* * * *

The term "Molotov cocktail" was coined to insult Molotov, who made the absurd claim that Soviet planes were dropping food, not bombs, on the Finnish people when the Soviets invaded Finland in 1939.

* * * *

The Paris Peace Conference

In 1914, Archduke Franz Ferdinand of the Austro-Hungarian Empire was assassinated in a Serbian plot, pushing a long-simmering feud in the Balkans to all-out war. Unfortunately for the rest of Europe, a network of treaties and alliances between the combatants and their neighbors drew virtually all other major powers on the continent into the conflict. World War I had begun.

The conflict involved the greatest mobilization of soldiers and war machinery the world had yet seen, but the next several years were spent fighting to a draw at the cost of millions of lives. Both the Allied Powers and Central Powers struggled to win the support of other nations. Italy and the United States were eventually lured into the conflict on the side of Britain, France, and the other Allies, sealing the fate of Germany, Austria-Hungary, and the Central Powers.

The tide clearly turned in 1918, and during 1919, leaders of the Allied nations spent months at the palace of Versailles in France planning their new vision for war-ravaged Europe. Given their great economic and military power, the "Big Four" countries—the United States, France, Great Britain, and Italy—dominated the discussions.

American President Woodrow Wilson pushed hard for measures that would ensure stability in Europe, including a new body called the League of Nations that would endeavor to resolve international disputes in a peaceful fashion. Bowing to popular pressure at home for some benefit to come from the terrible war, the other leaders focused more on financial and territorial gains for their nations. **Vittorio Orlando** (1860–1952), Italy's prime minister, stormed out of the conference after his bid for control of Balkan lands was rejected by the other leaders. Eventually, however, the meetings produced the Treaty of Versailles and brought an official end to the war.

Orlando resigned as prime minister of Italy before the treaty was signed. He occasionally reemerged as a significant figure in Italian politics during the next 25 years and helped establish democracy in his country in the years following World War II. He died in 1952, the last of the Versailles Treaty's "Big Four" leaders.

The following were the other major participants in the Versailles Treaty at the end of World War I:

- Woodrow Wilson (1856–1924), U.S. president
- Georges Clemenceau (1841–1929), French premier
- David Lloyd George (1863–1945), British prime minister

Rejecting the Treaty

For Woodrow Wilson, the League of Nations was the single most important objective of the peace negotiations at Versailles. Though he came to the conference with many other goals, the League was the only significant one that survived the negotiations because the other victorious leaders refused to see the war end without some practical gains for their long-suffering nations.

When the treaty was sent to the U.S. Senate for approval, it faced stiff opposition. Some objected to the many concessions it allowed to European nations; others feared that the United States would lose autonomy over its own affairs to the League of Nations. Though physically exhausted from presiding over both the war and the peace talks, Wilson went on a grueling tour of the country, hoping to raise enough popular support to force the Senate to accept the treaty. He collapsed during the tour, then suffered a stroke and nearly died.

The treaty was rejected by the Senate, and America remained technically at war until 1921, when Congress passed a resolution that declared an end to hostilities.

Turkey's War of Independence

As a result of World War I, the Ottoman Empire lost a great deal of Turkish territory to the Allied Powers. In response to this, a nationalist movement was started by Turkish military leader Mustafa Kemal (1881–1938), later known as Kemal Ataturk. In 1922, his troops forced the removal of Greek troops from Turkish territory, negotiated a new treaty with the Allies, and founded the Republic of Turkey. The last survivor of the Turkish War of Independence was soldier and World War I veteran **Yakup Satar.** He was 110 when he died on April 2, 2008.

Children of Charles Darwin

Charles Darwin, the grandson of Wedgwood china founder Josiah Wedgwood, developed the theory of evolution, and—through his book *The Origin of Species*—distributed it to a wide audience. Charles and Emma Darwin had ten children. The last of these, scientist and former soldier **Leonard Darwin,** died in 1943 at age 93.

The Scopes Trial

In 1925, Tennessee passed a law banning the teaching of evolution in public schools. The American Civil Liberties Union sought to challenge this law and recruited science teacher **John Scopes.** Scopes defied the law by teaching evolution to his class and was promptly arrested. His trial, which pitted top defense attorney Clarence Darrow against prosecutor William Jennings Bryan, turned into a media circus. Scopes was found guilty and fined, but the evolution versus creationism debate rages on.

John Scopes was the last surviving major participant in the Scopes trial. After the trial, Scopes quit teaching and earned a master's degree in geology from the University of Chicago. He then took a job in Venezuela as a petroleum engineer. Scopes died in 1970.

German Legislators Who Voted Against the Nazis

In 1933, the German Parliament (the *Reichstag*) passed the Enabling Act, which dissolved Parliament and gave Adolf Hitler's cabinet complete control. The last of the legislators who voted against the Enabling Act was **Josef Felder.** After Parliament was dissolved, Felder escaped to Austria. From there he went to Czechoslovakia, but he soon returned to Germany because he was unable to get his family out of the country. Felder was imprisoned at Dachau for nearly two years.

After World War II, Felder ran a newspaper, then served in the West German Parliament from 1957 until 1969. After the reunification of Germany in 1989, he attended the opening session of the new Parliament—the only member of the pre-war Parliament to do so. Felder died in Munich in 2000, two months after his 100th birthday.

The Abraham Lincoln Brigade

A group of American volunteer warriors formed a battalion called the Abraham Lincoln Brigade to aid the Republican (socialist) side against General Francisco Franco's Nationalists (fascists) in the

Spanish Civil War of the 1930s. Many people around the world faced a question in those days: Would human governments move toward fascism or socialism? In the 1930s, socialism was mostly a pro-labor and pro-poor movement with a wide following in the United States. Mainly labor activists and left-wing idealists, the Lincolns felt it was their duty to play a part in the ideological battle.

The Brigade's first eight commanders became casualties; the ninth, 22-year-old **Milton Wolff,** survived the war. The Abraham Lincoln Brigade's last living commander, he died on January 14, 2008, at age 92.

Scottish Veterans of the Spanish Civil War

Approximately 500 Scottish men fought in the Republican Army's International Brigade against the Nationalist forces of General Franco. The last of these was **Stephen Fullarton,** who died in 2008 at age 88. Fullarton volunteered for the brigade in 1938; he had to lie about his age in order to begin training (he was only 18 at the time, and the Communist party required recruits to be at least 21 years of age).

Fullarton traveled to Spain via Paris in April 1938. He had to be smuggled over the Pyrenees Mountains into Spain because the border with France was officially closed. Fullarton's active duty ended when he was shot and seriously wounded. He went on to serve with the British Royal Air Force in South Africa during World War II. After that war, Fullarton returned to his engineering work in Edinburgh.

Heads of State from World War II

King Michael I (in exile) of Romania is the last surviving pre-World War II head of state. Born in 1921, Michael became heir apparent in 1925 when his father, Carol II, went into exile with his mistress. Michael became king in 1927 upon the death of Ferdinand I. In 1930, with the approval of Romania's Parliament, Carol II came back and brushed Michael aside. Michael became king once again in 1940, under Ion Antonescu's pro-German regime. Michael tossed Antonescu out in 1944 and declared war on Germany.

The Communists forced Michael into exile in 1948. That year, U.S. President Truman awarded Michael the Legion of Merit for his anti-Nazi revolt. Michael got married and settled in Switzerland as a commercial pilot. He didn't go back to Romania until 1992, after Nicolae Ceaucescu's regime was finally dead and buried. His rapturous reception scared the post-Communist government so badly that they told him to stay away for five years. Age 86 as of 2008, Michael has expressed willingness to reign again if Romania wants him, but it is highly unlikely.

The Cambridge Five

John Cairncross was long suspected of being the "Fifth Man" of the Cambridge Five Soviet spy ring that also included Guy Burgess (d. 1963), Kim Philby (d. 1988), Donald Maclean (d. 1983), and Anthony Blunt (d. 1983). All were young Communists at Cambridge in the 1930s, recruited by NKVD (Soviet secret police and forerunner of the KGB) agent Samuel Cahan.

Working in the British Bletchley Park code-breaking operation during World War II, Cairncross sent the Soviets piles of western Allied cipher material, plus any German intel the British decoded. In 1951, Burgess (a sloppy alcoholic) defected. Unfortunately for Cairncross, Blunt didn't get all the incriminating material out of Burgess's apartment before British counterintelligence arrived. Cairncross confessed; he was not prosecuted but was ordered to leave Britain. He got a job with the UN in Italy, then he retired in France.

Doubt remained about Cairncross's complicity until 1991, when his former Soviet overseer Yuri Modin ratted him out. Cairncross died in 1995 at age 82, the last survivor of the Cambridge Five.

Cuba's 1940 Constitution

After four centuries of Spanish domination, Cuba got its first heady breeze of independence in 1902, with the U.S. victory in the Spanish-American War. In 1940, Cuban leaders enacted a progressive constitution providing for a minimum wage, land reform, public education, and governmental checks and balances. Modern Cuban Americans still revere the promise of this document, which was suspended after a 1952 coup by General Fulgencio Batista, who set himself up as dictator. He promised to retain the constitution's essence, but he did not.

Fidel Castro's Communists made a lot of noise about restoring the 1940 Constitution, but they instead repealed the document. In fairness, however, they followed some of its mandates more faithfully than Batista ever did.

Emilio Ochoa, the last living signatory to Cuba's 1940 constitution, died in Miami in 2007. He had been a senator in Cuba, but he left after Castro seized power. He worked as a taxi driver in Miami.

Children of Mohandas Gandhi

Mohandas Gandhi was born October 2, 1869, in Western India. After college, he studied law in London. He returned to India in 1891, then traveled to South Africa. While living there, he fought against the country's racist policies.

When he returned to India, he was already well-known for his work on behalf of Indians in South Africa, and he quickly rose to power in the Indian National Congress. In 1919, Britain began to intern people suspected of promoting insurrection, and this caused Gandhi to more actively protest British policies in India. He became an advocate of peaceful noncooperation with the British (boycotting British goods, for example).

In 1922, Gandhi was sentenced to six years in prison. When he was released after two years, he devoted himself to improving relations between Muslims and Hindus. When, in 1947, negotiations with the British resulted in the division of India into Hindu India and Muslim Pakistan, Gandhi felt dejected. He fasted in an attempt to promote reconciliation. On January 30, 1948, Gandhi was assassinated by a Hindu fanatic who accused Gandhi of allowing Muslims to steal a part of India.

Son **Ramdas Gandhi** (1897–1969) was the last survivor of Mohandas Gandhi's children. First arrested for political protests in South Africa at age 14, Ramdas Gandhi took an active role in supporting his father's nonviolent struggles.

* * * *

Mohandas Gandhi was afraid of the dark; he kept a light on by his bed as he slept.

* * * *

Mohandas Gandhi was nominated several times, but he never won the Nobel Peace Prize.

* * * *

The Declaration of the State of Israel

As World War II drew to a close, tens of thousands of Jews were fleeing Europe and heading for Palestine. Britain, which controlled the territory at the time, was focusing on recovering from the effects of the war and was not up to the task of enforcing peace between Arabs and Jews in Palestine. All British personnel were pulled out of the area, and the territory was turned over to the UN.

Palestinian Jews sought full independence—something the Soviet Union supported but their newly independent Arab neighbors opposed. The United States proposed a truce in the ongoing guerrilla war, but that didn't satisfy Palestine's Jews. When Britain's mandate expired on May 14, 1948, the Israeli Provisional State Council met to declare the State of Israel.

Meir Vilner immigrated to Jerusalem from Poland in 1938. An implacable foe of Britain before independence, as an Israeli, he supported fair treatment for Palestinian Arabs. He later served as secretary general of Israel's (mostly Arab) Communist party from 1965 to 1988. Vilner passed away in 2003 at age 84, the last living signer of the Declaration of the State of Israel.

The 1948 Arab-Israeli War

The 1948 Arab-Israeli War began when five Arab nations (Egypt, Syria, Transjordan, Lebanon, and Iraq)—invaded after Israel declared the state of Israel. Hundreds of thousands of Palestinian Arabs left Israeli territory—whether the Arabs or Jews pressured them out or whether they fled a combat zone remains a central issue. After the 1949 cease-fire, refugees were supposed to receive either the right to return or compensation for lost property. They got neither.

In 1947, British-born **Monty (Mordechai) Green,** a former officer with the Indian Army during World War II, volunteered to help the Jews create a professional army. When war broke out, he became a major general with the Israel Defense Forces. Green was the last surviving major general from the 1948 Arab-Israeli War when he died in 1998 at age 84.

Stalin's Successors

On March 5, 1953, Joseph Stalin died after serving as absolute dictator of the Soviet Union for 30 years. A power struggle ensued between **Georgi Malenkov,** who succeeded Stalin as premier; Nikita Khrushchev, first secretary of the Central Committee of the Communist Party; and Nikolay Bulganin, who replaced Malenkov as premier in 1955. In 1958, when Khrushchev became premier as well as Communist party chief, it was obvious to the world that he had obtained control of the country. The last survivor of these three men, Georgi Malenkov, died in 1988, during Mikhail Gorbachev's rule.

Khrushchev Denounces Stalin

At the 1956 Soviet Communist Party Congress (held in a secret session), Soviet Premier Nikita Khrushchev denounced former dictator Joseph Stalin for turning the Soviet Union into a place of terror and repression. Although Khrushchev was correct, one notes that he only dared say it over Stalin's embalmed cadaver.

The last living witness to the speech was **Nikolai Konstantinovich Baibakov,** a longtime Soviet oil commissar and industrial planner. In 1942—showing his traditional gentle subtlety—Stalin told Baibakov that he would be shot if the USSR lost the Caucasus oil fields to the Germans. He also threatened to shoot him again if they did not produce immediately once liberated. For decades, Baibakov headed Gosplan (the Soviet central planning apparatus) with mixed success: good on oil production, not so good on agriculture and the ruinous arms race spending. Seeking fresh ideas, Mikhail Gorbachev pushed Baibakov aside in 1985. Baibakov died March 31, 2008, at age 97.

Children of Joseph Stalin

As of 2008, only one of Soviet dictator Joseph Stalin's children was still alive. **Svetlana Alliluyeva** was born in 1926. She graduated from Moscow University in 1949 and stayed on to teach Soviet literature and English. In 1965, Svetlana began working at a publishing house, translating Russian literature into English. She defected to the United States in 1967. She was happy there at first; she was a celebrity of sorts and gained recognition for her memoirs, *Twenty Letters to a Friend.* She married architect Wes Peters, and they had a daughter, Olga.

Svetlana was rumored to be temperamental and unpredictable. She and her husband divorced, and Svetlana moved to England in 1982, hoping to enroll Olga at a regimented boarding school. Svetlana became disenchanted with England and returned to the Soviet Union in 1984. Unhappy there as well, Svetlana spent much of the 1990s in England and later moved to a retirement home in the United States.

The Stalin Peace Prize

Novelist **Howard Fast** was born in 1914 and grew up poor in Manhattan. His mother died when he was still a small child, and his father held various jobs, from ironworker to cable-car conductor to garment worker. Because of the difficulties Fast encountered growing up, he was always a champion of the rights of the poor.

Fast sold his first story to a magazine when he was just 17 years old, and he sold his first novel a year later. His most noteworthy works include *Conceived in Liberty* (1939), *Citizen Tom Paine* (1943), *Freedom Road* (1944), *Spartacus* (1951), *The Immigrants* (1977), *The Last Frontier* (1997), and *Greenwich* (2000). He also wrote numerous detective novels under the pseudonym E. V. Cunningham.

Fast became a Communist in 1943. He served jail time for refusing to cooperate with the House Committee on Un-American Activities and was later blacklisted. In 1953, Fast won a Stalin Peace Prize. With the de-Stalinization of the USSR after 1956, the award was renamed the "Lenin Peace Prize." Disillusioned by Stalinism and increasingly influenced by Zen Buddhism, Fast quit the party in 1956. The last living American winner of the Stalin Peace Prize, Fast died in March 2003 at age 88.

The 1956 Hungarian Revolution

The 1956 popular uprising against the Hungarian Communist government started on October 23, when police fired on a student demonstration in support of Polish autonomy from the USSR. Hungarian Communist party head Ernö Gerö called for Soviet intervention on October 24, and Soviet forces took up positions in Budapest. In the following week, Imre Nagy became prime minister of a new Hungarian government and prepared to repudiate the Warsaw Pact.

Soviet troops had garrisoned Hungary since World War II, though they mostly stayed out of sight. Now more divisions moved in. On November 4, Marshal Ivan Konev's tanks struck, crushing the rebels in a week and killing several thousand people. Nagy and other rebel leaders were executed.

The revolution's last surviving leader was **General Béla Király,** who commanded the revolutionary militia in 1956. For a few days he was also acting minister of defense of the Nagy government. He later escaped to the West, settling in the United States and becoming a professor of history at the Brooklyn College of the City University of New York. In 1990, in his late 70s, Király returned to his native land and became a member of the Hungarian Parliament. As of 2008, he was still alive at age 95.

The Warsaw Pact

In 1955, West Germany joined the NATO alliance, prompting the Soviet Union to form the Treaty of Friendship, Cooperation, and Mutual Assistance. Better known to history as the Warsaw Pact, this treaty integrated all member militaries under the aegis of the Soviet Ministry of Defense. The Soviet Union, Albania, Bulgaria, Czechoslovakia, East Germany, Hungary, Poland, and Romania were all Warsaw Pact countries.

In addition to the 1956 Hungarian Revolution, Pact forces crushed the Czechoslovakian uprising in 1968. That year, Soviet Premier Leonid Brezhnev announced the "Brezhnev Doctrine." The short version: "All Pact countries must remain Communist, and none can withdraw."

U.S. Secretaries of State Who Have Won the Nobel Peace Prize

Henry Kissinger, who was secretary of state from 1973 to 1977, was born in Germany on May 27, 1923. He came to the United States in 1938 and served in the U.S. Army during World War II. Later, as a national security adviser to Richard Nixon and secretary of state, he was instrumental in shaping U.S. policies on China, Russia, and Vietnam. Kissinger was alive as of 2009. He received the Nobel Peace Prize in 1973, making him the last U.S. secretary of state to win the prize.

The following are other U.S. secretaries of state who have won the Nobel Peace Prize:

- Elihu Root (1845–1937) won the prize in 1912 for his work coordinating Latin American peace conferences.
- Frank B. Kellogg (1856–1937) was awarded the prize in 1929 for his role in authoring a treaty to outlaw war.
- Cordell Hull (1871–1955) was awarded the 1945 prize for his role in the establishment of the UN.

Children of Albert Schweitzer

Born in 1875 in Alsace (which was then part of Germany), Albert Schweitzer was a man of many talents and accomplishments. He earned a licentiate in theology and doctorates in medicine and philosophy, wrote the book *The Quest for the Historical Jesus,* and was an internationally known concert pianist and an authority on Bach. After he turned 30, however, Schweitzer devoted his life to humanitarian causes and to serving the people of Africa. He opened a hospital in French Equatorial Africa (now Gabon) in 1913.

Daughter **Rhena Schweitzer Miller,** who died in 2009 at age 90, was the last living child of Dr. Albert Schweitzer. After her father's death in 1965, Rhena took over the administration of the hospital, which still exists today.

Children of Haile Selassie

Emperor Haile Selassie ruled Ethiopia from 1930 until 1974. Many believe he was a direct descendant of King Solomon and the Queen of Sheba. Selassie was overthrown by Marxist dictator Mengistu Haile Mariam in 1974 and was kept prisoner at the palace for a year afterward. He died in 1975—the official cause of death was listed as complications from a prostrate operation, but many suspected foul play.

Selassie's last surviving child was **Princess Tenagne Worq,** who was also held captive after her father was overthrown. She was imprisoned for 15 years. After her release, she lived in Britain and also the United States for a time, but she spent the last several years of her life in Ethiopia. She died in 2003 at age 91.

* * * *

Rastafarianism, which draws its name from "Ras Tafari," Haile Selassie I's name before he took the Ethiopian throne, is a religious movement that considers Selassie a biblical messiah on par with Jesus of Nazareth.

* * * *

General Secretaries of the Soviet Communist Party

Dictator Joseph Stalin created and occupied the position of General Secretary of the Communist Party of the Soviet Union. After his death, whoever acquired the title was assumed to have control of the country. In 1991, the position disappeared with the dissolution of the USSR. **Mikhail Gorbachev** was the last living person to hold this position.

Gorbachev was born to a peasant family near Stavropol in the Caucasus region on March 2, 1931; his father was an agricultural mechanic on a collective farm. Gorbachev earned a law degree from Moscow State University in 1953. During the 1960s, Gorbachev was the head of the agricultural department for the Stavropol region, and it was during these years that he began to notice the shortcomings inherent in the Soviet system.

Gorbachev joined the Central Committee in 1971 and became a full Politburo member in 1980. He rose to the leadership role in 1985 and began working on reforms. His goals were openness (*glasnost*) and restructure (*perestroika*). He desired an end to the arms race that was devouring Soviet funds. However, it was difficult for Gorbachev to find a balance between the hardliners (who felt threatened by his reforms) and the reformers (who felt he wasn't going far enough).

The hardliners staged a coup in 1991, as they kidnapped Gorbachev while he was on vacation in the Crimea. The coup was not successful—many civilians protested it, and it did not have the support of the military—but Gorbachev never regained the confidence of the people. He resigned as the Soviet Union fell to pieces. He ran for reelection again in 1996 but received only 1 percent of the vote. He celebrated his 78th birthday in 2009 and currently serves as president of the Gorbachev Foundation, a think tank in Moscow.

* * * *

Mikhail Gorbachev won the Nobel Peace Prize in 1990.

* * * *

Art

How did a group of painters come to be called "Impressionists"?
What became of van Gogh's "Yellow House"?
Which group of artists was dubbed "The Ashcan School"?
Read on to find out.

The Impressionists

Heads will nod in synchronous unison when you comment on a painting's Impressionistic aspects. Impressionism began in France in the mid-1800s. A group of artists, including **Claude Monet** and Pierre-Auguste Renoir, joined together after their works were repeatedly rejected for exhibition at the prestigious Salon in Paris. The artists staged their own exhibition in 1874.

Impression: Sunrise, a painting of Monet's that was exhibited at the separate exhibition, garnered particular scorn from critics; they derided its "unfinished" appearance. The artists were gratified by this scorn because they felt that what they were doing was new, different, and exciting. They began to call themselves "Impressionists" (after the Monet painting) to show that they were going to continue to innovate rather than give in to the critics.

Instead of describing a scene precisely, Impressionists tended to focus on the sensation the scene conveyed. In short, Impressionists broke all the rules of the day. Some instructors of Impressionistic painting teach the acronym ELBOW:

- **E:** Everyday life—no contrived or ornate scenes
- **L:** Light—specifically, sunlight
- **B:** Brushstrokes—small and subtle, in primary colors
- **O:** Outdoor—Impressionists painted outside to capture L and W
- **W:** Weather and atmosphere—these elements create the overall *impression,* hence the name

The last living Impressionist was Claude Monet, who died on December 5, 1926, outliving Mary Cassatt by fewer than six months.

The following artists are also considered major Impressionists:

- Edouard Manet (1832–83)
- Berthe Morisot (1841–95)
- Alfred Sisley (1839–99)
- Camille Pissarro (1830–1903)
- Edgar Degas (1834–1917)
- Pierre-Auguste Renoir (1841–1919)
- Mary Cassatt (1844–1926)
- Claude Monet (1840–1926)

Claude Monet

19th-Century British Landscape Painters

The last surviving 19th-century British landscape painter was **Joseph M. W. Turner** (1775–1851). His only possible equal, John Constable, died in 1837. At his death at age 76, Turner left a large amount of money to be used to help struggling artists. He also left hundreds of paintings and thousands of his watercolors and drawings to the British nation.

The following artists were also contemporaries of Turner:

- Thomas Girtin (1775–1802)
- Philip James de Loutherbourg (1740–1812)
- Richard Parkes Bonington (1802–28)
- Peter De Wint (1784–1849)

Last Person to Have Personally Known Vincent van Gogh

To put it charitably, Vincent van Gogh was quite the character. Influenced by Impressionism, the Dutch artist developed his post-Impressionist style in the "Yellow House" of Arles, France, during 1888–89. It was in Arles that van Gogh, after a dispute with friend Paul Gauguin, is reputed to have severed part of his own ear. The Arlésiens eventually circulated a petition to get the "crazy redhead" out of town. The police closed his house, and he went to an insane asylum. Sadly, a 1944 bombing raid demolished the Yellow House.

Jeanne Calment of Arles, who waited on van Gogh as a teen in her uncle's shop, was the last living person who knew him. Young Jeanne found the artist to be a complete jerk—dirty, ugly, rude, and (worst of all) ill-dressed. She had a comfortable life: Married to a wealthy merchant, Calment had leisure to pursue musical and athletic hobbies. At 85, she took up fencing. As van Gogh's Arles centennial approached, Calment naturally got a lot of attention.

When Calment died on August 4, 1997, she was 122 years, 5 months, and 14 days old—the oldest person ever recorded and confirmed in modern times. She attributed her longevity to olive oil, port wine, and chocolate.

* * * *

*Van Gogh was a prolific artist, but not a profitable one. Many believe he sold only one painting during his lifetime—*Red Vineyard at Arles, *which can be seen at the Pushkin Museum in Moscow.*

* * * *

The Eight

In 1908, a group of painters often called "The Eight" chose to display their work at New York's Macbeth Gallery rather than put up with the National Academy of Design's snooty jury system. Dubbed "The Ashcan School" by a snide art critic, these artistic rebels depicted gritty New York realities, showing scenes that high society didn't want to see: crummy streets, tenements, bums, fights, poverty, prostitution. The Eight seemed to revel in defying critics and dunking unsuspecting viewers in urban mud puddles.

The Eight were Arthur Bowen Davies, Robert Henri, William Glackens, Ernest Lawson, George Luks, Maurice Prendergast, **Everett Shinn,** and John Sloan. Shinn, the youngest, was the last survivor. He got his start as a news artist, sketching such disaster scenes as fires and train wrecks. He went on to create pastel drawings that ran in *Harper's Weekly.* Shinn passed on in 1953 at age 76.

The Generation of '27

The Generation of '27 was a cultural movement of 1920s Spanish poets and artists. Their common goal was to use vivid language and imagery to connect Spain's rich cultural roots with the European avant-garde of the day. They left us an uncommonly diverse and interesting snapshot of their nation and era.

Although Spain was neutral in both world wars, Spaniards were quite partisan in their bloody, bitter civil war (1936–39). The cataclysm blew the Generation of '27 apart, just as it shattered their interwar optimism. Some died; others went into exile. Generation of '27 members included painter Salvador Dalí (1904–89), writer Pedro Salinas y Serrano (1891–1951), poet Federico García Lorca (1898–1936), and film director Luis Bunuel (1900–83). The last survivor was **José Bello,** who died in January 2008 at age 103.

California Style

The California Style of watercolor painting, popular from the 1920s through the 1950s, featured brightly colored everyday scenes from California life. It drew on the many ingredients of the great California ethno-cultural mix: Okies fleeing the Dust Bowl, Hispanics new and old, the rise of Hollywood, dizzying urbanization, and Asian influence.

Prominent California Style artists included Millard Sheets and Dong Kingman. The genre's last surviving major artist was **Milford Zornes.** Zornes first learned about art from his mother, who was a schoolteacher. After high school, Zornes hitchhiked across the country, then traveled to Europe. He took art classes after returning to California, and in the 1930s he began working for the Public Works of Art Project. This program produced works of art that would be displayed in post offices and other public buildings. After viewing a work by Zornes at the Corcoran Gallery of Art in Washington, D.C., President and Mrs. Franklin D. Roosevelt selected it for display in the White House.

Zornes was drafted in 1943 and worked for the army as an artist in Burma, China, and India. He spent his later years as a watercolor painting instructor, and he died in February 2008 at age 100.

Native Americans

❑ ❑ ❑ ❑

How many Cherokee died along the Trail of Tears?
How many languages are spoken in Alaska?
How many buffalo are there in the United States?
This chapter has all the answers!

Squanto and the Patuxet People

In 1614, **Squanto**—the last survivor of the Patuxet people—was captured by English Lieutenant Thomas Hunt, a subordinate of Captain John Smith. Smith had left Hunt behind when he left New England because he wanted Hunt to establish a settlement in the area. After Smith left, Hunt lured Squanto and several other Native Americans aboard his ship, then took them to Málaga, Spain, and tried to sell them as slaves. He was able to sell only a few of the captives, however, before local priests seized the rest. Squanto convinced the priests to allow him to return home, and he managed to get to London, where he met John Slany, the treasurer of the Newfoundland Company. Squanto lived with Slany for a year or so and became fluent in English during this time. Slany arranged for Squanto's passage back to North America. When Squanto returned home, he was devastated when he found that the entire Patuxet village had perished (likely from viral hepatitis). He then visited the neighboring Wampanoag village and eventually settled there.

In a few months, Squanto and the Wampanoag people realized that English emigrants had settled in Patuxet. After observing the English settlers for some time, the Wampanoag people, who had lost many of their own members to disease, decided to try to ally with the newcomers against the stronger, hostile Narragansett people. Because he was fluent in English, Squanto served as the translator in discussions between the settlers and the Wampanoag during the spring of 1621.

The Wampanoag began helping the English establish their settlement (which the English named Plymouth). They taught them everything from the best fishing spots to how to plant corn and squash to how to draw maple syrup from trees. The Wampanoag also helped the settlers establish fur-trading posts. By the fall of 1621, the settlers were confident their food supply would last through the winter, and they invited the Wampanoag to feast with them. Together, they celebrated the first Thanksgiving.

The following spring, Squanto suddenly became ill while guiding Plymouth governor William Bradford around Cape Cod. After a few days, the last of the Patuxet died. He was approximately 37 years old.

* * * *

The English settlers had brought wheat with them, but it did not thrive in the rocky New England soil.

* * * *

What was on the menu for the first Thanksgiving? Beans, berries, squash, corn soup, corn bread, deer, duck, goose, swan, and turkey.

* * * *

The Trail of Tears

In 1830, the U.S. Congress passed the Indian Removal Act, which forced the resettlement of most Cherokee from their homes in the southeastern United States to land west of the Mississippi River. Those Cherokee who refused to go were arrested by the U.S. Army between 1838 and 1839 and sent to an area that was then called "Indian Territory" (now Oklahoma). Of the 15,000 Cherokee who set out on the journey, more than 4,000 died along the way. **Edward Wilkerson Bushyhead** was seven years old when he moved with his family. Later in his life he traveled to California, where he became a sheriff, then served as chief of police, and eventually owned a newspaper. When he died at age 75 in 1907, he was believed to be the last survivor of the Trail of Tears.

The Great Native American Leaders of the 19th Century

Lakota Sioux chief **Red Cloud,** the last of the great 19th-century Native American leaders, was born in 1822 in what is now North Platte, Nebraska. Red Cloud is most noted for his successful resistance against the U.S. development of the Bozeman Trail during the 1860s. The trail ran through Lakota hunting grounds, but the U.S. Army had begun constructing forts along the trail. Red Cloud's assaults against the forts were so successful that the U.S. government was forced to sign the Fort Laramie Treaty, which stipulated that the United States would abandon those forts. Red Cloud's success was short-lived, however. By the end of the 1870s, there were no longer any Indian nations independent of the American government. Red Cloud died December 10, 1909, on a reservation in North Dakota.

The following were also great Native American leaders of the 19th century:

- Tecumseh (ca. 1768–October 5,1813) was the Shawnee chief who was defeated by General William Henry Harrison at Tippecanoe.
- Osceola (ca. 1804–38) led the Seminoles during the Second Seminole War.
- Cochise (ca. 1815–74) was the Chiricahua Apache chief who staged many successful guerrilla attacks against the U.S. Army.
- Crazy Horse (ca. 1849–77) was the Lakota war chief at the Battle of the Rosebud.
- Sitting Bull (ca. 1831–90) led his band of Sioux to Canada after the Battle of Little Bighorn.

Sitting Bull

- Chief Joseph (1840–1904) led the Nez Percé in their battles against U.S. troops in the Wallowa Valley.
- Geronimo (1829–1909) led Chiricahua warriors in battles against U.S. troops in Arizona and New Mexico.

* * * *

"When I was young I walked all over this country, east and west, and saw no other people than the Apaches. After many summers I walked again and found another race of people had come to take it."

—*Cochise*

* * * *

Geronimo's Surrender

On September 4, 1886, Geronimo, the last Apache chief still fighting the U.S. Army, surrendered to General Nelson Miles in Skeleton Canyon near the Arizona–New Mexico border. Most of Geronimo's people went into captivity, first in Florida and then in the Southwest.

The last surviving witness to Geronimo's bitter surrender was **Jasper Kanseah,** Geronimo's nephew and the band's youngest warrior (he was 11 years old at the time). Kanseah was born on the Chiricahua reservation; his father died before his birth. Just a small child when the Chiricahua reservation was closed and the Chiricahua were forced to move to the San Carlos reservation in 1876, Kanseah was left with only his grandmother after his mother died during the journey. Kanseah had trouble keeping up along the way, and his grandmother carried him at times.

Kanseah was about 11 years old when Geronimo came to San Carlos. Geronimo took Kanseah with him when he left and trained him as a warrior. After Geronimo's surrender, American authorities sent Kanseah to Carlisle Indian School, which he was lucky to survive—many Apache students died there of disease.

After nine years of schooling, Kanseah returned to captivity. Finally freed in 1913, Jasper Kanseah did several stints as a cavalry scout and was honorably discharged each time. He died in 1959, approximately 86 years old.

* * * *

Jasper Kanseah's grandson Berle became an important leader and language preservationist among the Chiricahua Apache—and took the knowledge to Hollywood. In 2003, Berle Kanseah served as a technical adviser in the Ron Howard thriller The Missing, *helping the actors articulate the Chiricahua language properly. When Berle Kanseah passed away in 2004, his people lost a living library.*

* * * *

The Battle of Sugar Point

The Battle of Sugar Point occurred on October 5, 1898, on the shore of Leech Lake in northern Minnesota. About one hundred U.S. Third Infantry soldiers were sent to the American Indian reservation to arrest one man from the Leech Lake band of the Ojibwe (Chippewa) who was accused of bootlegging. After a soldier accidentally fired his weapon, a fight ensued between the soldiers and Native Americans that left seven soldiers dead and ten wounded. None of the Ojibwe were wounded. This battle was the last substantial military engagement between the U.S. Army and Native Americans.

The last surviving person present was **Emma Bear,** who was just a baby at the time. Her father served as a negotiator during the battle. When he tried to stop the fighting, he was arrested. Emma Bear passed away in 2001 at age 103. She had two daughters and one son, and she worked various jobs to provide for her family's needs, from beadwork to rug braiding to waitressing.

The Buffalo Nickel

The Native American profile on the front side of 1913–38 buffalo nickels was created by designer James Earle Fraser and is a composite of three Native American chiefs. The last living of these chiefs was **Big Tree,** who died in the 1920s. The other two Native American chiefs used as models for the buffalo nickel were Iron Tail (ca. 1850–1916) and Two Moons (1847–1917).

The End of the Trail

James Earle Fraser, whose father helped recover the bodies of the Seventh Cavalry from Little Bighorn, once worked as an assistant to Augustus Saint-Gaudens. Fraser later became a renowned sculptor in his own right. Shortly after designing the buffalo nickel, Fraser completed his masterwork for the 1915 Panama-Pacific International Exposition: *End of the Trail,* an evocative plaster sculpture of a dejected American Indian lancer on an equally despairing mount.

World War I metal shortages unfortunately preempted a bronze casting, and the sculpture started deteriorating. It has since been restored and is on display at the National Cowboy & Western Heritage Museum in Oklahoma City.

* * * *

Most Americans refer to the species Bison bison *(the American bison) as a buffalo. With regrets to the University of Colorado, it is not a buffalo—it's a bison. The European bison,* Bison bonasus, *is the only other surviving member of the genus. Both are distant cousins of the world's two true buffalo: the Asian water buffalo and the African (Cape) buffalo.*

* * * *

Comanche Code Talkers

Most people associate code talkers with World War II, but the system was actually first used in World War I. While soldiers from the 142nd Infantry Regiment were fighting with the French Army against the Germans in northern France in 1918, Allied leaders had become suspicious that the Germans were intercepting their communications; the leaders were frustrated and trying to come up with a solution to this vexing problem. When one American captain overheard two of his soldiers having a discussion in their native Choctaw language, he thought of a plan. Allied forces began experimenting with a new code based on the Choctaw language, and it was wonderfully successful—the Germans never broke it.

Inspired by Choctaw code talkers' successes in World War I, the U.S. military again used Native American languages for battlefield communication during World War II. Fourteen Comanche speakers landed at Utah Beach at Normandy on D-Day, and eight Meskwaki from Iowa became code talkers in North Africa.

The Marines ran the largest code talker program, utilizing some 400 Diné (Navajo) speakers in the Pacific. Marine code talkers didn't simply speak Diné, they used a Diné-based code that only a Diné speaker could learn. None of the codes were ever broken. Non–code talking Diné POWs could tell that the words were Diné but couldn't tell what the messages meant.

The last surviving Comanche code talker, **Charles Chibitty,** died July 20, 2005, at age 83. Chibitty was born Near Medicine Park, Oklahoma, in 1921. He enlisted in 1941 and trained at Fort Benning in Georgia. At a 2002 meeting with Pentagon officials, Chibitty gave some examples of how certain words and phrases would be translated: A tank was a "turtle," and a machine gun was a "sewing machine." In a touch of sagacious comedy, Adolf Hitler was *posah-tai-vo* ("crazy white man").

* * * *

In 2002, Nicolas Cage starred in Windtalkers, *a World War II action movie depicting two Navajo code talkers. Unfortunately, Hollywood chose to focus mainly on big-budget star Cage, with the code talkers as minor participants. The film lost money, much to the delight of its many critics.*

* * * *

Meskwaki Code Talkers

The last survivor of the Meskwaki code talkers who served in North Africa was **Frank Sanache,** who died in 2004 at age 86. Twenty-seven Meskwaki men enlisted as a group about a year before Pearl Harbor, and eight became code talkers. Since there were so few of them, they worked 24-hour shifts. The code talkers scouted up to two miles ahead of the main force and communicated via walkie-talkies; their duties posed above-average risk of death or capture.

Sanache was captured by the German *Afrika Korps* in Tunisia and spent more than two years at a POW camp in Hammerstein, Poland. Each day he ate a cup of soup, two potatoes, a glass of water, and a slice of bread, and he unloaded lime from train cars. The lime left him with chronic lung damage, but he enjoyed much respect from his people for the way his service had represented them. After the war, he worked in a paper mill until retirement.

For many years, few non-Meskwaki knew of the code talkers. That changed when Senator Tom Harkin of Iowa read about them in a magazine. His legislation to honor the Meskwaki code talkers with medals passed the U.S. Senate in September 2008—too late for Frank Sanache, holder of three Bronze Stars, to enjoy it.

The Eyak Language

The Eyak people lived in southern Alaska, and Eyak was one of about 20 native languages spoken in the state. The last native speaker of the Eyak language (and the last full-blooded Eyak) was **Marie Smith-Jones** of Anchorage. Her Eyak birth name was Udach' Kuqax*a'a'ch, which means "a sound that calls people from afar."

Her father worked in the fishing industry, and Smith-Jones started working in a cannery at age 12. In 1948, she married William F. Smith, a fisher from Oregon, and—like most parents in Alaska at the time—she did not pass her native language on to her children. Most Alaskan children were taught English and were punished if they were overheard speaking native languages on school grounds. When her sister died in 1992, Smith-Jones was left as the last native speaker of Eyak. She became concerned that the language would die with her, so (in collaboration with the University of Alaska) she compiled an Eyak dictionary. Smith-Jones passed away in 2008 at age 89.

Alaskan Languages

Alaska's 20 native languages fall into four linguistic groups: Eskimo-Aleut, Athabascan-Eyak-Tlingit, Haida, and Tsimshian. Scientists remain in debate over the family trees of many native languages, but genetic evidence suggests that their speakers arrived in mass migrations before 10,000 B.C.

Why so many languages in four groups? Alaska is big, and the land bridge that connected Asia and Alaska during the Ice Age was 1,000 miles wide and existed for thousands of years.

Think of Romance language evolution since Julius Caesar (about 2,000 years). Despite shorter distances and larger-scale transportation, Latin fell into disuse, but it spawned Spanish, French, and Italian. Now consider more than 10,000 years of evolution, and you can imagine how far apart languages could diverge.

* * * *

Marie Smith-Jones became an international symbol for language extinction, speaking twice before a United Nations forum on indigenous peoples' rights to preserve their languages and cultures. She lived long enough to learn that the General Assembly passed the Declaration on the Rights of Indigenous Peoples—and to know that she influenced its evolution.

* * * *

When the Exxon Valdez *ran aground in 1989, it spilled 240,000 barrels of oil into the traditional fishing grounds of the Eyak people.*

* * * *

The Cherokee Nation Treaty of 1866

The Cherokee Nation is one of the largest Native American groups in the history of the United States. Many members now live in poverty, but at one time it was a wealthy nation.

Before the Civil War, some Cherokee had Southern plantations that held as many as 100 African slaves. When the Civil War began, the Cherokee officially sided with the Confederacy (though thousands fled and fought with the Union Army); this made all previous treaties between the Cherokee and the U.S. government null and void.

After the war, new treaties were drawn up. As part of the Cherokee Nation Treaty of 1866, the Cherokee guaranteed newly freed slaves citizenship in the Cherokee Nation. However, few African American freedmen were embraced by the Cherokee, and even today many of their descendants struggle for full acceptance.

The last surviving Native American signatory to the Treaty of 1866 was **Chief Samuel Houston Benge.** Benge fought for the Union during the Civil War and achieved the rank of lieutenant. He died at his farm on October 23, 1902, at age 70. He is buried at Fort Gibson National Cemetery in Oklahoma.

* * * *

Who is considered a citizen of the Cherokee Nation today? Anyone who can prove they are descended from a person listed on the Dawes Rolls. These rolls are lists of people accepted by the Dawes Commission between 1898 and 1914 as members of the Cherokee (and four other nations). The Dawes Commission was formed to divide tribal land into plots, which were then divided among tribal members.

* * * *

British History

❑ ❑ ❑ ❑

What was Gandhi's role during the Boer War?
What event brought the full Privy Council together during Queen Victoria's reign?
What did soldiers do during the Christmas Truce of 1914?
Read on to find out.

King Henry VIII's Wives

In his quest for a male heir to succeed him, English King Henry VIII (1491–1547) married six times. His fourth marriage, to the German **Anne of Cleves** (1515–57) in 1540, was primarily for political reasons. Henry was urged to marry Anne to strengthen England's ties with Germany and increase the king's power over Holy Roman Emperor Charles V.

Anne was never actually crowned queen of England, and the marriage was annulled after six months because Henry greatly disliked Anne. She was granted land and continued to live in England as "the King's sister"; she even socialized with the king and his next wife, Catherine Howard. Anne died in 1557, the last survivor of Henry's six wives. She outlived him by ten years.

The following were Henry VIII's other wives:

- Catherine of Aragon (1485–1536), married 1509–33; divorced by Henry
- Anne Boleyn (ca. 1500–36), married 1533–36; executed by Henry
- Jane Seymour (ca. 1509–37), married 1536–37; died after childbirth
- Catherine Howard (1521–42), married 1540–42; executed by Henry
- Catherine Parr (1512–48), married 1543–47; widowed by Henry

King Henry VIII's Children

Although he is reputed to have had at least one illegitimate child, Henry VIII had only three legitimate ones: Mary, with first wife Catherine of Aragon; **Elizabeth,** with second wife Anne Boleyn; and Edward, with third wife Jane Seymour. Mary and Elizabeth both had their legitimacy called into question after Henry issued legal proclamations annulling his marriages to their mothers (with the marriages declared invalid, the girls were illegitimate according to law). Elizabeth was legally declared a bastard three separate times, once by the pope himself!

Edward became King Edward VI upon Henry's death and ruled for six years (1547–53), until his own death from tuberculosis. Mary became queen in 1553 and ruled until her death five years later. Elizabeth succeeded Mary, remained queen for more than 44 years, and was the last living legitimate child of Henry VIII. It is ironic that the most well known event of Henry's life, his divorce of Catherine and marriage to Anne Boleyn, was partly due to his belief that a woman could not rule England. His two daughters did just that, and the latter was one of the most powerful monarchs in history.

Henry VIII's Chief Ministers

Thomas Cranmer, Archbishop of Canterbury and the last chief minister to Henry VIII, was fortunate enough to be the only one of Henry's chief ministers the king didn't eventually have arrested (and usually executed) for treason. He was also one of the primary supporters of major religious reforms and the rise of Protestantism in England. Although he survived Henry and was still successful promoting reform during the reign of Edward VI, Cranmer's luck with English monarchs ran out when Mary I took the throne. Catholic Mary had no tolerance for religious reforms of any kind, and in 1555 she had Cranmer burned at the stake as a heretic.

The Royal House of Plantagenet

The royal Plantagenet family ruled England for more than 300 years, from King Henry II in 1154 to the overthrow of King Richard III by Henry Tudor (Henry VII) in 1485. The last member of the direct male line was Edward, Earl of Warwick, who was executed by Henry VII in 1499.

Margaret Pole, Countess of Salisbury, is widely acknowledged by historians as being the last of the Plantagenet dynasty. A prominent Catholic, the countess was a great supporter of Queen Catherine of Aragon when Henry VIII worked so hard to divorce her to marry Anne Boleyn. Lady Salisbury was executed for treason by Henry VIII in 1541 at age 67. During her execution, she refused to lay her head on the block, saying she was no traitor. Some accounts report that the executioner had to chase her around the scaffold, striking her repeatedly with the ax until she finally died.

Catholic Monarchs of England

The following were the last four Catholic monarchs of England:

- Henry VIII (1491–1547) reigned 1509–47; was Catholic until he broke with Rome and declared himself head of the Church of England.
- Mary I (1516–58), Henry's elder daughter, reigned 1553–58.
- Charles II (1630–85) reigned 1660–85; he became a Catholic on his deathbed.
- **James II** (1633–1701), reigned 1685–88; the last Catholic to be crowned King of England, he fled to France after Parliament called on his Protestant daughter Mary and her husband, William of Orange, to take the throne.

The Jacobite Pretenders

In 1689, the English Parliament invited Queen Mary II and her husband, William, to invade in order to depose her father, James II, and put a Protestant back on the throne. Even after Mary and William were crowned, many Catholics still considered James to be king and his young son (also named James) the rightful heir. The Jacobite line of succession continued to James II's grandsons, then passed to the descendants of James's younger sister, Henrietta Anne. The heirs of the Jacobite line are known as "pretenders" for their claim to a throne held by someone else, though none have actively claimed the crown since Prince Charles Edward Stuart led a failed rebellion in 1745.

The current Jacobite pretender is **Francis II,** Duke of Bavaria. Born on July 14, 1933, in Munich, Germany, Francis inherited the Jacobite claim from his father in 1996, and upon his death, the claim and all English rights will go to his younger brother, Max.

The Duke of Marlborough's Soldiers

On May 23, 1706, the forces of John Churchill, Duke of Marlborough (1650–1722), defeated the French at the Battle of Ramillies. This battle was part of the War of Spanish Succession, which broke out when European powers came together to prevent a member of the French Royal House of Bourbon from ascending the Spanish throne. The other European powers agreed that if this were allowed to happen, the French king would wield too much power.

The Battle of Ramillies drew nearly all of the Spanish Netherlands over to the side of the coalition. It was an acquisition that allowed a direct attack on France. When confronted with this sobering reality, Louis XIV was forced to seek peace over further turmoil, a circumstance that is thought to have helped shorten the war. When the dust finally settled, the French had lost some 8,000 soldiers and the coalition roughly 4,500.

One of Marlborough's men, 27-year-old **William Billinge,** was shot in the thigh while helping to save the Duke's life. He fought for the Hanoverians in the Scottish Rebellions of 1715 and 1745, the latter at 65 years of age. The last surviving man to have fought with the Duke of Marlborough, Billinge died in 1791 at the age of 112 at Fawfieldhead, Staffordshire. Curiously, he expired within 500 feet of his place of birth. Billinge was a soldier to the bitter end, which is why his epitaph includes the passage: "Billited by Death I quartered here remain. When the trumpet sounds I'll rise and march again."

Mistresses of Charles II

King Charles II of England was known for his many mistresses. The last survivor of Charles's primary mistresses, **Louise de Kéroualle,** Duchess of Portsmouth, died in her native France in November 1734. Diana, Princess of Wales, and Camilla, Duchess of Cornwall, are both descended from Louise through her illegitimate son by Charles. If Prince William ascends the throne, he will be the first British monarch to be descended from Charles II.

King Charles II of England

Children of King George III

King George III (1738–1820) is best known as the reigning British monarch during the American Revolutionary War. He is also the subject of the 1994 movie *The Madness of King George*. Around 1810—when King George began a speech with the address, "My Lords and Peacocks"—it was clear to all present that something was seriously wrong with the king. In the 1970s, his medical records were reviewed, and scientists determined that the king likely suffered from porphyria, a rare blood disorder. In more recent years, strands of the king's hair were found in the files of a London museum. Upon analysis, scientists discovered that the hairs contained massive amounts of arsenic—more than 300 times the toxic level. It is now believed that arsenic poisoning triggered the king's porphyria and caused him to exhibit symptoms of madness.

The last surviving child of King George III was **Princess Mary,** duchess of Gloucester and Edinburgh. She was the 11th child and fourth daughter of King George and Queen Charlotte and was married to Prince William Frederick, Duke of Gloucester. Mary died in 1857 at age 81.

The *Bounty*

On April 28, 1789, officer Fletcher Christian and eight crew members took control of the ship HMS *Bounty* from Captain William Bligh (1754–1817). Although most of the film versions of *Mutiny on the Bounty* depicted Bligh as a cruel captain, it is now surmised that the uprising wasn't necessarily a result of his mistreatment of the crew.

For many months preceding the mutiny, the *Bounty*'s sailors had been docked in Tahiti to collect breadfruit plants. While holding over in this paradise, many formed relationships with native women and understandably held little interest in returning to the hardships of the sea. Even acting lieutenant Fletcher Christian, the protagonist in the mutiny, had become interested in a Tahitian woman and was pondering desertion just before setting sail.

After the *Bounty*'s crew regrouped and set out to sea, Captain Bligh lambasted them for the alleged theft of coconuts. This episode, above all others, is believed to have been the spark that triggered the actual mutiny.

Factually speaking, things get clearer from this point. Christian and his mutineers ordered Captain Bligh and his loyalists into the *Bounty*'s launch, then set them adrift. They were equipped with minimal provisions, a sextant (a measuring device that uses the altitude of celestial bodies to determine latitude and longitude), and a pocket watch. Miraculously, Captain Bligh navigated the craft to Indonesia—a 3,600-mile journey that lasted seven weeks.

The mutineers went to Tahiti and eventually settled on remote Pitcairn Island. Some were killed by natives and others were captured and tried for mutiny. Three from this group were declared guilty and hanged. Modern-day Pitcairn Island is populated predominantly by descendants of the mutineers. When the rebel's settlement was finally discovered by the outside world in 1808, **John Adams** was the only mutineer still alive. He died on March 5, 1829.

The *Bounty* on Film

The *Bounty* incident spawned three Hollywood movies—two named *Mutiny on the Bounty* (1935 and 1962) and one named *The Bounty* (1984). Charles Laughton, Trevor Howard, and Anthony Hopkins took turns portraying Captain Bligh, and Clark Gable, Marlon Brando, and Mel Gibson performed yeoman's duty as the inimitable Fletcher Christian.

The 1935 and 1962 offerings (based on the novel of the same name) paint Captain Bligh as unduly brutal and sadistic, a fact that flies in the face of historical accounts. Likewise, Fletcher Christian is seen as a selfless saint, a condition that has more to do with artistic license than reality. The 1984 movie comes closest to the truth. It depicts both as simply men of their era and the mutiny itself as less noble than was previously implied.

Officers of the HMS *Bounty*

The *Bounty*'s carpenter, **William Purcell,** was constantly at odds with Captain Bligh. Nevertheless, he accompanied Bligh on his forced leave of the ship and 3,600-mile voyage to land. As a veteran sailor in the Royal Navy, Purcell knew well the grisly fate that awaited mutineers and likely decided that remaining with Bligh was the lesser of two evils.

Captain Bligh

The two men had been at odds since 1787, when Purcell signed on as the *Bounty*'s carpenter. Conscious of his special skills and rank, Purcell maintained that he should be exempted from such punishments as flogging. As a unionist, he added that he should be excused from ordinary sea duties as well.

Such demands did not sit well with Bligh. Within days, Bligh's logbook recorded incidents where Purcell refused "in a most insolent and reprehensible manner" to take part in general sea duties. Having just been reprimanded by Bligh for bad conduct, Purcell was likely returning the favor.

In their next run-in, Purcell successfully appealed to the *Bounty*'s senior warrant officer, stating that his rank should preclude him from unfair duties Bligh had ordered. This infuriated Bligh to the point that he refused Purcell further provisions until his work was done. The ship's log shows that Purcell ultimately cooperated.

Purcell was the only one of the *Bounty*'s loyalists that Bligh preferred charges against. This stemmed from their rocky dealings but may also have resulted from the captain's apparent distaste for union sympathizers. After being court-martialed, Purcell sailed on 14 more ships, then retired from the navy. He was the last surviving officer of the *Bounty* when he died on March 10, 1834, on the Gosport side of Portsmouth Harbor in England.

The Battle of Trafalgar

On October 21, 1805, a British naval fleet under the command of Admiral Horatio Nelson fought a combined French and Spanish fleet overseen by French Admiral Pierre Charles de Villeneuve. Known as the Battle of Trafalgar, the conflict consisted of 27 British ships squared off against 33 vessels in what can best be described as a classic mismatch. After the smoke of confrontation had lifted, 18 enemy vessels had slipped beneath the waves while British forces sailed away without the loss of a single ship.

The decisive victory destroyed any chance France had of invading Britain and forced French leader Napoleon Bonaparte to fight future battles on land only. More impressively, it raised the British Navy's status to world preeminence. Some 14,000 French and Spanish sailors were killed—approximately ten times the losses suffered by Great Britain.

British seaman **James Sharman** was approximately 19 at the time of the battle. He is believed to be one of the sailors who carried the fatally wounded Admiral Nelson (downed by a sniper's bullet) to the cockpit of his ship during the Battle of Trafalgar. In later years, Sharman became a personal friend of novelist Charles Dickens. The character Ham Peggoty in *David Copperfield* is based on Sharman. When he passed away in 1867 at the age of 82, Sharman was the last living person to have served on Nelson's ship at the Battle of Trafalgar.

Officers of Nelson's Trafalgar Fleet

The last surviving officer of Admiral Nelson's Trafalgar fleet was **Captain Robert Newman,** who is buried in a graveyard in Hounslow, a borough of London. He died on April 1, 1833, at age 90.

Rorke's Drift

The Anglo-Zulu War was fought in 1879 in Zululand (now eastern South Africa) between the Zulu people and British colonial forces. The Zulu king, Cetshwayo, had assembled a sizable army; the British forces in the area felt threatened and demanded he disband his force. When he refused, war broke out. Rorke's Drift was a remarkable battle because 145 British soldiers were able to fend off thousands of Zulu warriors, who eventually retreated. The last British survivor of Rorke's Drift was **Frank Bourne,** who was awarded the Distinguished Conduct Medal after the battle. Bourne died on Victory in Europe Day (May 8, 1945) at age 90.

* * * *

Napoleon III's son, Prince Louis, died fighting with British forces in the Anglo-Zulu War.

* * * *

The Boer War

The Boer War (1899–1902) was fought between Great Britain and the Boers (people of Dutch ancestry in South Africa) and ended with the surrender of the Boer forces to the British. The war was initiated by Alfred Milner, the British high commissioner of Cape

Colony, South Africa. By claiming the Dutch Boer republics of the Transvaal and Orange Free State, Milner hoped to annex the region's gold mines and create a Cape-to-Cairo confederation of British colonies.

Greatly underestimating their foes, British forces predicted that the war would end in a matter of months. Through pride, tenacity, and the use of guerrilla warfare, the Boers forced Britain to fight for more than two years. Only after Great Britain switched its strategy to include guerrilla tactics—including the burning of villages and the confiscation of foodstuffs—did that nation prevail.

The last Boer War veteran was British soldier **George Frederick Ives.** After the war, Ives moved to Canada, where he worked as a farmer and shipbuilder. When a *Daily Telegraph* piece featuring his story came to light, the ex-soldier was brought to the United Kingdom for the 1992 Remembrance Day ceremonies. Ives died in Canada in 1993 at age 111.

* * * *

Foretelling his future role as a man of peace, Mohandas Gandhi organized an ambulance corps and fronted a Red Cross unit during the Boer War.

* * * *

Queen Victoria's Privy Council

The Privy Council is the British king or queen's private council. The last surviving privy councilor of Queen Victoria (who reigned from 1837 to 1901) was **Sir James Lowther,** first Viscount Ullswater, who was appointed in 1898 and died in 1949 at age 93.

The following are the last surviving privy councilors of other British monarchs:

- Politician and diplomat Malcolm John Macdonald was the last surviving privy councilor of King George V (1910–36). Macdonald was appointed in 1935 and passed away in 1981 at age 80.

- World War II leader Sir Winston Churchill was the last surviving privy councilor of King Edward VII (1901–10). Churchill was appointed in 1907 and died in 1965 at age 90.
- Henry George Grey, Viscount Howick, was the last surviving privy councilor of King William IV (1830–37). Appointed in 1835, Grey died in 1894 at age 91.
- British diplomat Stratford Canning, later Baron Stratford de Redclyffe, represented his country for many years at the Ottoman court. He was the last surviving privy councilor of King George IV (1820–30). He was appointed in 1820 and died in 1880 at age 94.
- Robert Jocelyn, Viscount Jocelyn, later Earl of Roden, was the last surviving privy councilor of King George III (1760–1820). He was appointed in 1812 and died in 1870 at age 81.

* * * *

The full Privy Council now comes together on only two occasions: when a monarch dies and the council proclaims the accession of an heir, and when a monarch intends to marry. Queen Victoria was the last monarch to marry while on the throne.

* * * *

Queen Victoria's Children

Queen Victoria of Great Britain and her husband, Prince Albert, had nine children. The last surviving was the youngest, **Princess Beatrice.** Beatrice was just four years old when her father died; after his death, she was almost always by her mother's side. Beatrice met Prince Henry of Battenberg at a family wedding, and the two quickly fell in love. Queen Victoria was opposed to the engagement—it took the couple eight months to win her approval, and even then the queen only relented after the couple agreed to settle in Britain. They had been married just seven years when Henry succumbed to malaria while on an expedition in Africa in 1896. Beatrice died in 1944 at age 87.

* * * *

Princess Beatrice's daughter Victoria Eugénie ("Ena") married King Alfonso XIII of Spain in 1909. Ena passed the hemophilia gene on to her sons.

* * * *

Queen Victoria's Great-Granddaughters

Queen Victoria reigned for 63 years—up until her death in 1901. Her last surviving great-granddaughter was **Lady Katherine Brandram.** Lady Katherine was originally Princess Katherine of Greece (a daughter of King Constantine I and Queen Sophie; Queen Sophie was the daughter of Germany's Friedrich III and Princess Victoria, daughter of Queen Victoria).

Princess Katherine was born in 1913 during a traumatic time in Greece. Her father was forced to abdicate in favor of her brother Alexander in 1917 because the Allied powers viewed Constantine as "pro-German." Katherine was exiled to Switzerland with her parents. When Alexander died of blood poisoning in 1920 after being bitten by his pet monkey, Constantine returned to the throne.

After World War II broke out, Katherine began working for the Red Cross, spending most of her time caring for the wounded. In 1941, when the Germans invaded Greece, the family was exiled to South Africa, and Princess Katherine again nursed those who had been wounded in the war. Her patients often called her "Sister Katherine." After the war ended, Katherine married Richard Brandram, a British army officer. The couple had one child, Paul, who was born in 1948. Lady Katherine died in 2007 at age 94.

* * * *

King Constantine I was Prince Philip's uncle (Prince Philip's father, Prince Andrew, was Constantine's brother).

* * * *

Great-Grandchildren of Queen Victoria

One of Queen Victoria's great-grandchildren, **Count Carl Johan Bernadotte,** was still alive in 2009 at age 92. His parents were Princess Margaret and King Gustav VI Adolf of Sweden. Carl Johan had been Prince of Sweden until 1946, when he lost his right to succession after he fell in love with Kerstin Wijkmark, a divorced journalist, and married her against the wishes of his grandfather, King Gustav. At the time of his marriage, Carl Johan was 23 and his bride was 29. The ceremony took place in New York, making Carl Johan the first royal to marry in the United States. Kerstin died in 1987, and Carl Johan married his current wife, Gunnila, in 1988.

* * * *

Queen Elizabeth II is Victoria's great-great-granddaughter.

* * * *

The British Cavalry

The Battle of Loos in Belgium in 1915 was the British part of a British–French World War I offensive. British forces attacked German positions in Loos, while French forces battled the Germans in France. The Allied goal was to give the Russians some relief by forcing the Germans to divert resources from the Eastern Front. When the battle was over, the death tolls were horrific: More than 8,000 of the 10,000 British forces involved had been killed. **Albert Marshall** fought on horseback in the battle. When he died at age 108 in May 2005, Marshall was the last living person who had fought on horseback with the British cavalry.

World War I British Commissioned Officers

Noted composer and pianist **Conrad Leonard,** a second lieutenant who served in the trenches in World War I, was the last British commissioned officer of the war to survive. In 1935, he played for King George V at the London Palladium, and he continued to perform publicly until age 103. Leonard died in 2003; he was 104 years old.

British POWs in World War I

Harold Lawton was conscripted in 1916. He wanted to apply for officer training, but he knew he would not be able to afford the uniform. By April 1918, he found himself on the front line at Armentières in France. When the Germans swept past, Lawton and several others were forced to surrender. As the captives were transported to a prison, they traveled through the town of Lille. As they passed, townspeople tried to give them bread; Lawton was deeply touched and never forgot the kindness shown to him by the French people during this traumatic time.

Lawton was released when the war ended in November, and he enrolled at the University of Wales to study the French language. He then moved to Paris to study for a doctorate in Latin and French literature at the University of Paris. After finishing his doctorate, he obtained a junior teaching post at the Sorbonne. In 1930, Lawton returned to England to teach at University College, Southampton.

When war again broke out in 1939, Lawton was asked to teach British soldiers about French culture to prepare them for deployment. This work earned him a spot on the Nazi "wanted" list. Lawton joined Sheffield University as French department chair in 1950, and he spent the rest of his career there. In old age, he kept his mind sharp by working crossword puzzles and reading (most notably the French translations of *Harry Potter*). He also relaxed by enjoying a glass of malt whiskey every day. When he died on December 24, 2005, 106-year-old Harold Lawton was the last of Great Britain's World War I prisoners of war.

The Christmas Truce

On Christmas Day in 1914, an impromptu truce interrupted World War I, and combatants from both sides briefly met as friends in No Man's Land. Scottish soldier **Alfred Anderson,** the last living of Scotland's World War I veterans, remembers shouting, "Merry Christmas!" to the soldiers in the German trenches. The British and German soldiers climbed out of their respective trenches, shook hands, sang a few carols, and even kicked a ball back and forth. By the afternoon, the merriness was over and machine-gun fire filled the air again, but the brief peace gave the soldiers a comforting reminder of better times.

After Anderson was wounded by shrapnel and discharged in 1916, he moved to Scotland and took over his father's business. He passed away on November 22, 2005, at age 109.

The Battle of Jutland

The 1916 Battle of Jutland was the only major World War I naval battle between the German and British fleets. Although the British lost more ships in the fight, a larger percentage of the German fleet was destroyed, leaving Great Britain still the stronger sea power. **Henry Allingham,** a mechanic assigned to the armed trawler HMT *Kingfisher*, was the last survivor of this battle. Allingham also fought at the Somme and Ypres. After the war, Allingham married and started working for Ford Motor Company. After retiring, he continued playing golf until his eyesight failed him at age 93.

Allingham did not talk much about his war experiences until 2001, when he met Dennis Goodwin, a man who organized trips for veterans. On these trips, veterans traveled to battle sites to pay their respects to their lost friends. After meeting Goodwin, Allingham began discussing his experiences with reporters and students. Goodwin helped Allingham write his autobiography, which includes an introduction written by Prince Charles. At 112 years old in 2009, Allingham is believed to be Great Britain's oldest living man. He brought tears to the eyes of onlookers in November 2008 when he attempted (and failed) to lift himself out of his wheelchair to lay the Royal Air Force wreath at the Cenotaph on Remembrance Day.

The 1921 Anglo-Irish Treaty

Ireland's War of Independence pitted the Irish Republican Army against British forces in 1919 and ended with the signing of the Anglo-Irish Treaty in 1921. The treaty split Ireland into two parts: the Irish Free State and Northern Ireland, which remained a part of Great Britain.

Robert Barton was the last surviving signer of the treaty. Barton was born in County Wicklow to a wealthy Protestant family. Barton had served as an officer in the British Army, but he joined the Irish Republican forces after the Easter Rising. Barton signed the Anglo-Irish Treaty after British Prime Minister Lloyd George threatened that any representative who did not sign would be held responsible for the all-out war that would ensue. War followed regardless, however, and Barton fought on the antitreaty side in the civil war that broke out in Ireland the next year. Barton died on August 10, 1975, at his Glendalough Estate in County Wicklow.

* * * *

The organizers of the Easter Rising had planned for it to be a nationwide event. However, a series of mishaps forced them to confine it to Dublin.

* * * *

The Chamberlain Government

Neville Chamberlain served as British prime minister from 1937 to 1940. He is most remembered for his failure to prevent the outbreak of World War II. The last person to have served in the government of British Prime Minister Neville Chamberlain was **Horace Trevor Cox.** Cox studied German at Hanover University, and one of his teachers was a sister of one of Hitler's future field marshals. After graduating from Hanover, Cox worked at a factory in Berlin. Cox returned to Britain, and in 1937, he was elected to the House of Commons. Cox was knowledgeable about Germany and advised the British government to take Hitler's threats seriously. After the war began, Cox volunteered for the Welsh Guards and served in France. Cox died at age 97 on October 30, 2005.

The Sinking of the HMS *Hood*

In May 1941, the German battleship *Bismarck* fought the battle cruiser HMS *Hood*, the largest ship in Great Britain's Royal Navy. The *Hood* exploded and sank with 1,416 aboard. Only three were rescued from the waters, and the last survivor was **Ted Briggs.**

Born in 1923, Briggs joined the crew of the *Hood* at age 16. He had first viewed the ship when he was 12 years old; he wanted to serve on the ship so badly that he tried to join the navy at that time but was turned away because he was too young. Briggs retired from the navy in 1973 after 35 years of service. He served as president of the HMS *Hood* Association for many years. Briggs died October 4, 2008.

* * * *

Three days after the sinking of the Hood, *British warships attacked and sank the* Bismarck.

* * * *

Children of Winston Churchill

Prime Minister Winston Churchill is credited with holding Great Britain together during the dark days of World War II. Of Churchill's four children, **Lady Mary Churchill Soames** is the last surviving, still living as of 2009 at age 86.

The Princess Diana Crash

On August 31, 1997, Diana, Princess of Wales and ex-wife of Prince Charles, heir to the British throne, died from internal bleeding after the limo she was riding in crashed in a tunnel in Paris, France. She was 36 years old. Her companion, Dodi Al Fayed, and the driver were also killed. The fourth passenger, bodyguard **Trevor Rees-Jones,** suffered severe injuries but was the sole survivor. Investigations into the accident determined that the crash was caused by negligent driving—by both the driver of the limousine (who was drunk and speeding) and by the pursuing photographers. The princess and Al Fayed were not wearing seat belts.

Before becoming a bodyguard in 1994, survivor Rees-Jones was a paratrooper. He turned 40 in 2008 and was back to work (at a security firm) and playing rugby again.

* * * *

After the accident that killed Princess Diana, the paparazzi were severely criticized, but no criminal charges were filed against them.

* * * *

Literature

❑ ❑ ❑ ❑

How many of Mark Twain's children outlived him?
What prompted Pearl Buck to start her own orphanage?
Who thought time travel would eventually be possible?
All the answers can be found in the pages of this chapter.

People for Whom a Shakespearean Play Is Named

Of the 13 real-life people upon whom a Shakespearean play is based, the last living was **King Henry VIII,** who died in 1547.

The following are Shakespearean plays named after historical figures:

- *Coriolanus* (6th century B.C.)
- *Julius Caesar* (100–44 B.C.)
- *Antony and Cleopatra* (ca. 82–30 B.C. and 69–30 B.C., respectively)
- *Cymbeline* (Cunobelinus; ?–A.D. 42)
- *Macbeth* (ca. A.D. 1005–57)
- *King John* (ca. A.D. 1167–1216)
- *Richard II* (A.D. 1367–99)
- *Henry IV, Part I* (A.D. 1367–1413)
- *Henry IV, Part II* (A.D. 1367–1413)
- *Henry V* (A.D. 1387–1422)
- *Henry VI, Part 1* (A.D. 1421–71)
- *Henry VI, Part 2* (A.D. 1421–71)
- *Henry VI, Part 3* (A.D. 1421–71)
- *Richard III* (A.D. 1452–85)
- *Henry VIII* (A.D. 1491–1547)

Henry VIII

* * * *

Although the plays Coriolanus, Cymbeline, *and* Macbeth *are named after historical figures, the plots of these plays are entirely fictional.*

* * * *

Shakespeare's Descendants

Of the direct descendants of William Shakespeare, the last living was his granddaughter, **Elizabeth Hall.** She was born in 1608 to Susanna Hall (Shakespeare's daughter) and John Hall (a Stratford doctor). Elizabeth Hall married lawyer Thomas Nash in 1626. Nash died in 1647, and Elizabeth married John Barnard in 1649. Neither marriage produced offspring, however, and Elizabeth died in 1670.

The Nine Worthies

In medieval times, the following men were esteemed for their chivalry and were called "The Nine Worthies": Hector, Alexander, Julius Caesar, Joshua, David, Judas Maccabeus, King Arthur, Charlemagne, and Godfrey of Bouillon. The best-known reference to these important figures of history is in the Shakespearean comedy *Love's Labour's Lost.* **Godfrey of Bouillon,** the last living of these men, was a leader of the First Crusade. He died in 1100 at approximately age 40.

English Romantic Poets

William Wordsworth published *Lyrical Ballads* with Samuel Taylor Coleridge in 1798. It included "Tintern Abbey," which was considered the first major work of the English Romantic poets. Appointed Poet Laureate in 1843, Wordsworth died in 1850, a few days after his 80th birthday. He was the last of the greatest English Romantic poets.

The following were also English Romantic poets:

- John Keats (1795–1821) wrote "Ode on a Grecian Urn" and "La Belle Dame Sans Merci."
- Percy Bysshe Shelley (1792–1822) wrote "Ozymandias" and "One Word Is Too Often Profaned."
- Lord Byron (1788–1824) wrote "When We Two Parted" and "So, We'll Go No More a Roving."
- William Blake (1757–1827) wrote "The Tyger" and "A Poison Tree."
- Samuel Taylor Coleridge (1772–1834) wrote "Kubla Kahn" and "The Rime of the Ancient Mariner."

The Brontë Sisters

During a childhood spent in the isolation of the Yorkshire Moors, the Brontë sisters were inspired by the Romantic poets and went on to create several masterpieces of English literature. Although she did not reach the age of 40, **Charlotte Brontë** was the last survivor of the three Brontë writers. The writer of the Gothic romance *Jane Eyre* married Arthur Nicholls in 1854. She was pregnant when she succumbed to illness in 1855. The other Brontë sisters were Emily (1818–48), who wrote *Wuthering Heights,* and Anne (1820–49), author of *Tenant of Wildfell Hall.*

The Communist Manifesto and *Das Kapital*

Karl Marx was born in 1818 in Trier, Germany; his father was a lawyer. **Friedrich Engels** was born in 1820 in Barmen, Germany, to wealthy Protestant parents. After becoming friends with Karl Marx and German Socialist Moses Hess in 1842, Engels began to espouse communist beliefs. He worked at a textile mill for the next two years, and this work led to his interest in workers' rights. In 1848, Engels and Marx published *The Communist Manifesto.* Marx released the first volume of *Das Kapital* in 1867, and after Marx died in 1883, Engels finished the last two volumes. Engels died at 74 in 1895.

The Greatest Authors of 19th-Century Concord, Massachusetts

The last of the great 19th-century authors who lived in Concord, Massachusetts, was **Louisa May Alcott** (1832–88), author of *Little Women* and *Little Men*. Alcott was educated by her father, Bronson Alcott, a transcendentalist philosopher. Louisa enjoyed writing from a young age. She kept a journal and would often write plays that she and her sisters would perform.

When Louisa was in her teens, her family was struggling financially. Louisa began working but was frustrated by the few job opportunities available to women at the time. She worked various jobs—servant, seamstress, teacher, and governess. During this time in her life, Louisa wrote *Work: A Story of Experience*.

In the years preceding the Civil War, Louisa was writing articles for the *Atlantic Monthly*. Once war broke out, however, she signed up to work as a volunteer nurse. This took her to Washington, D.C., where she worked at Union Hospital. Unfortunately, Louisa contracted typhoid fever there, and the treatment she received (which involved mercury) led to health problems later in her life.

After the war, Louisa's publisher asked her to write a book for girls. This prompted Louisa to begin working on her masterpiece, *Little Women*.

The following are other well-known authors from Concord, Massachusetts:

- Henry David Thoreau (1817–62) wrote *Walden*.
- Nathaniel Hawthorne (1804–64) wrote *The Scarlet Letter* and *The House of Seven Gables*.
- Ralph Waldo Emerson (1803–82) wrote such essays and poems as "Self-Reliance" and "The Rhodora."

* * * *

Orchard House, the Alcotts' home on Lexington Road in Concord, Massachusetts, is now a national historic landmark.

* * * *

Louisa May Alcott is buried in the Authors Ridge area of Sleepy Hollow Cemetery, near her friends Henry David Thoreau, Nathaniel Hawthorne, and Ralph Waldo Emerson.

* * * *

The Alcott Sisters

The Alcott sisters grew up in Concord, Massachusetts. In 1868, Louisa May Alcott wrote *Little Women*, a masterpiece of American literature. The characters in the book were based on Louisa's sisters. The oldest sister, **Anna Alcott,** was the last survivor.

The Alcott sisters were:

- Elizabeth Sewall Alcott (1835–58) inspired Beth in *Little Women.*
- May Alcott Nieriker (1840–79) inspired Amy in *Little Women.*
- Louisa May Alcott (1832–88) inspired Jo in *Little Women.*
- Anna Alcott Pratt (1831–93) inspired Meg in *Little Women.*

* * * *

Each of the sisters in Little Women *had a central character flaw: Meg's was vanity, Jo's was a bad temper, Beth's was timidity, and Amy's was selfishness.*

* * * *

Children of Charles Dickens

Henry "Harry" Dickens, eighth child of Charles Dickens, was born on January 16, 1849. He had a successful law career and founded the *Gad's Hill Gazette* with his brother Edward. The last surviving child of the writer who best described life in mid-19th century London slums, Harry lived to see the Great Depression of the 1930s. He died on December 21, 1933, after he was struck by a motorcycle.

* * * *

A Christmas Carol *has never been out of print since Dickens first published it in 1843.*

* * * *

The Pulitzers

Joseph Pulitzer was born near Budapest, Hungary, in 1847. His father died when he was still just a child, and the family fell on hard times. As a teenager, Pulitzer tried to enlist in the Austrian army but was denied because of his poor eyesight. Pulitzer then tried joining the armies of several other European countries, but he was rejected each time. Because civil war had broken out in the United States, Pulitzer decided to try to enlist there.

Pulitzer arrived penniless at Castle Garden in New York City in 1864. He spoke very little English and at times had to resort to sleeping on park benches. However, he was finally able to enlist. He joined the Union Army First Regiment, New York (Lincoln) Cavalry in September 1864 and was discharged the following year. Next, he traveled to the western United States with an Austrian who had been his friend in the army; they could afford to travel as far as St. Louis. Once there, Pulitzer took any job he could find. He worked on a ferry and then as an undertaker during a cholera epidemic. He studied law and was admitted to the bar in 1868. He did not enjoy law, however, and started searching elsewhere for a job that held more interest for him.

When he began working as a reporter for a German newspaper, he knew he had found his calling. He rose to city editor, then managing editor, and then became part owner of the paper. In 1878, the *St. Louis Evening Dispatch* was offered at auction; Pulitzer bought it and soon took over the *Evening Post* as well. In this way, the *St. Louis Post-Dispatch* came into being.

Joseph Pulitzer died on his yacht near Charleston, South Carolina, in 1911. His will had a provision for the establishment of prizes that would encourage and reward excellence in the field of journalism. The first prizes were awarded in 1917. **Herbert Bayard Swope,** who died in 1958, was the last surviving recipient of the first Pulitzers. Swope received the Reporting prize for the *New York World* series of articles entitled "Inside the German Empire."

The following individuals also received Pulitzers in 1917:

- French Ambassador J. J. Jusserand (1855–1932) won the History prize for his book *With Americans of Past and Present Days.*
- Laura E. Richards (1850–1943) and Maude Howe Elliott (1854–1948) shared the Biography/Autography prize for their book *Julia Ward Howe.*

Descendants of Mark Twain

Mark Twain's last living direct descendant was **Nina Clemens Gabrilowitsch** (1910–66). Nina was the daughter of Twain's daughter Clara (1874–1962) and Ossip Gabrilowitsch, Clara's first husband. Ossip was the conductor of the Detroit Symphony Orchestra from 1918 until his death from stomach cancer in 1936.

Nina lived with her parents in Detroit until she enrolled at Barnard College. Nina studied theater at Barnard. She stayed in New York after graduation but was unsuccessful in her attempts to find work as an actor. After Ossip's death in 1936, Clara moved to Hollywood; Nina eventually joined her mother and tried to find work on the West Coast. She was unsuccessful there as well, and in 1966, Nina died of an apparent drug overdose. She left the bulk of her estate to the American Cancer Society.

* * * *

After Clara's death in 1962, Nina fought with Clara's second husband, Jacques Samossoud, over Clara's estate. In the end, Nina wound up with 35 percent of the estate while Jacques received 65 percent. Jacques died soon after Nina in 1966. After his death, his estate passed to Dr. William E. Seiler. After Seiler's death in 1978, the estate became the Mark Twain Foundation.

* * * *

Mark Twain and his wife, Livy, had four children, but only Clara outlived her father. Son Langdon died of diphtheria while still a toddler, oldest daughter Susie died of meningitis in her 20s, and daughter Jean drowned in a bathtub after suffering an epileptic seizure around age 20. Neither Susie nor Jean had any children.

Children of Jack London

Jack London was born in San Francisco in 1876. His family was quite poor, and by age ten, London was selling newspapers to bring in money. He held various other jobs for the next decade—he worked at a cannery, then as a window washer, then as a security guard. He even worked on a whaling boat in the Pacific at one time.

At age 19, he took a year-long course that covered everything most students learn in four years of high school. He then enrolled at the University of California at Berkeley. He had studied there for a year before the Klondike gold rush began. London went to the Klondike, but he did not find any gold—and he contracted scurvy. After he retuned from the Klondike, he began writing essays, short stories, news articles, and novels. His pieces at times appeared in such publications as the *Overland Monthly* and the *Atlantic Monthly*. In 1900, London married Bess Maddern, and they had two daughters before divorcing in 1904. During these years, London continued to write, covering the Russo-Japanese War and the 1906 San Francisco earthquake. Jack London died of kidney disease in 1916. *The Call of the Wild* (1903), *The Sea Wolf* (1904), and *White Fang* (1906) are classic Jack London titles.

Becky London, Jack London's younger daughter, was born in 1902. She married World War I veteran Percy Fleming in 1927. They owned and operated a stationery store and had two children—a daughter, Jean, and a son, Guy. In her later years, Becky became friends with a couple who owned the Jack London Bookstore in Glen Ellen, California. Becky lived in an apartment next door to the bookstore and occasionally came over to visit with customers. Becky died on March 26, 1992, at age 89. She was the last person to have known the world-famous author personally.

* * * *

> *"My place in society was at the bottom. Here life offered nothing but sordidness and wretchedness, both of the flesh and the spirit; for here flesh and spirit were alike starved and tormented."*
>
> *—Jack London, "What Life Means to Me," from* Revolution and Other Essays *(1910)*

* * * *

Sir Arthur Conan Doyle's Children

Sir Arthur Conan Doyle created fictional detective Sherlock Holmes and his sidekick Dr. Watson in 1886. Conan Doyle had two children by his first marriage, daughter Mary (1889–1976) and son Kingsley (1892–1918); and three by his second marriage, sons Denis (1909–55) and Adrian (1919–70) and daughter Jean (1912–97). **Dame Jean Conan Doyle,** the last living child of Sir Arthur Conan Doyle, died on November 18, 1997, at age 84. A volunteer with the Women's Royal Air Force in World War II, she rose to become its director.

The Hardy Players

British novelist and poet Thomas Hardy's acting group, the Hardy Players, was dissolved after his death in 1928 at age 87. The last surviving member of the group, **Norrie Woodhall,** recited Hardy's words on stage in 2007 at age 101. Ms. Woodhall was given her first part by Hardy himself in his 1928 stage production of *Tess of the D'Urbervilles*. Woodhall was still alive in 2008 at age 102.

Pre–World War II Nobel Prize in Literature

The Nobel Prize in Literature was first awarded in 1901. Of the 38 individuals who received the award before 1940, **Pearl Buck** (who won the prize in 1938) was the last survivor. Born Pearl Sydenstricker in 1892 in Hillsboro, West Virginia, she grew up in China, where her parents worked as missionaries.

In 1910, she began studying at Randolph College in Lynchburg, Virginia. After graduation she returned to China because her mother was very sick. In 1917, she married agricultural economist John Buck, and their daughter Carol was born in 1921. During delivery it was discovered that Buck had a uterine tumor, and a hysterectomy was performed. The Bucks later discovered that Carol suffered from the genetic disorder PKU; she grew up mentally disabled, and it became necessary to place her in an institution in the United States.

From 1920 until 1933, Buck taught English literature at Nanking University. In 1925, the Bucks adopted their daughter Janice. Buck wrote many stories during the 1920s, some of which were printed in such publications as *The Nation* and *Atlantic Monthly.* In 1931, Buck's novel *The Good Earth* was published; it was the best-selling book of 1931 and 1932. Buck and her husband divorced in 1934, and Buck moved to an old farmhouse in Pennsylvania to be near her daughter Carol. In 1935, she married her publisher, Richard Walsh, and over the next several years the couple adopted six more children. Pearl Buck died on March 6, 1973, at age 80.

* * * *

In 1942, Pearl Buck and Richard Walsh founded the East and West Association in an effort to promote cultural exchange and understanding between Asia and the West. During her work for this organization, Buck found that most adoption agencies would not take on cases of mixed-race children; the agency heads seemed to think it would be too difficult to find couples willing to adopt such children. This outraged Buck and led her to open Welcome House, her own adoption agency.

* * * *

Individuals with PKU cannot process phenylalanine, which is present in many foods. Years ago, the substance would build up in sufferers' bloodstreams and eventually cause brain damage. Today, newborns with PKU can be diagnosed and treated early. With treatment, individuals grow up normally.

* * * *

In 1904 and 1917, two writers were each awarded a Nobel literature prize (Frédéric Mistral and José Echegaray in 1904, and Karl Gajellerup and Henrik Pontoppidan in 1917). In other years (1914, 1918, 1935, 1940, 1941, 1942, and 1943), the committee decided not to award a literature prize at all.

* * * *

The Inklings

The literary group the Inklings was composed of Charles Williams (1886–1945), C. S. Lewis (1898–1963), Warren Lewis (1895–April 9, 1973) J.R.R. Tolkien (1892–September 2, 1973), Dr. R. E. Havard (1901–85) and **Owen Barfield** (1898–1997). Meeting on Tuesdays at the Eagle and Child pub in Oxford, they would read their latest works and discuss current events. The last survivor of the group was Barfield, who wrote *A History in English Words* and *Poetic Diction*. Barfield died in 1997 at age 99.

The First Jewish Encyclopedia Editorial Board

In the 1920s, an encyclopedia on Jewish history and culture was started in Germany. After ten volumes, the project was stopped when Adolf Hitler rose to power. The last surviving member of the project's editorial board was **Nahum Goldmann** (1895–1982). Goldmann survived World War II by moving to the United States in 1940. In 1972, using funds from German reparations, he completed the *Encyclopaedia Judaica* in English. The coeditor of the 1972 encyclopedia, Fred Skolnik, became editor of the second edition of *Encyclopaedia Judaica* in 2006.

The Big Seven Poets of the Scottish Renaissance

The Big Seven poets of the 20th century's Scottish Literary Renaissance were Robert Garioch, Norman MacCaig, Hugh MacDiarmid, George Mackay Brown, Sorley Maclean, **Edwin Morgan,** and Iain Crichton Smith. As of 2009, only Morgan, born in 1920, was still living. Morgan was named the first national poet of Scotland in 2004. He recently published his latest book, released a CD of his poems set to music, and celebrated his 89th birthday.

The National Book Awards

The National Book Foundation sponsors the National Book Awards. In 1950, the first year of the awards, three people were honored. **Nelson Algren** won the Fiction Award for *The Man with the Golden Arm*.

Algren's manuscript examined the tumultuous life of a back-alley card dealer with a morphine monkey on his back. The book, later made into a film starring Frank Sinatra, masterfully depicted the disintegration of the lead character against a gritty urban backdrop. Algren was well within his element with this subtext. The budding writer grew up in a poor immigrant neighborhood on Chicago's South Side; he witnessed the seedy side of life every day. With the prize-winning *The Man with the Golden Arm*, he conveyed firsthand experiences of such a world to an audience stunned by its bleakness.

Stories of the downtrodden struck a particular chord with Algren, as did exposés on corruption. *A Walk on the Wild Side* (1956) and *Chicago, City on the Make* (1951) illustrate the author's longing for fair play in a largely unfair world. Cataloging the life of a Depression-era drifter, *A Walk on the Wild Side* was hailed as a masterpiece by critics. "The book asks why lost people sometimes develop into greater human beings than those who have never been lost in their whole lives," explained Algren.

Algren's personal life mirrored this philosophy. Hospitalized on several occasions for depression, the author attempted suicide after *A Walk on the Wild Side* was first released. He wrote numerous books, many to rave reviews, before his career ended. Nelson Algren was the last survivor of the first three National Book Award winners when he passed away on May 9, 1981.

The following were the other recipients of the 1950 National Book Awards:

- Ralph L. Rusk (1888–1962) received the Nonfiction Award for *Ralph Waldo Emerson.*
- William Carlos Williams (1883–1963) received the Poetry Award for *Paterson: Book III* and *Selected Poems.*

Science Fiction's "Big Three"

The three people often considered the Big Three of science fiction are writer Robert Heinlein, biochemist-turned-novelist Isaac Asimov, and **Sir Arthur C. Clarke.** The last living of these was Clarke, who passed away at age 90 in March 2008 at his home in Sri Lanka.

Clarke was born in Minehead, England, in 1917. He developed a love for science during his grade school years and would regularly devour books by such fantasy writers as H. G. Wells and Jules Verne. In 1945, Clarke authored a paper that explained how communication satellites could work.

In 1947, Clarke published his first science fiction novel, *Prelude to Space,* and would produce scores more throughout his career. Developing an interest in undersea exploration during the 1950s, Clarke moved to Sri Lanka and concentrated his writing efforts around the depths of the Indian Ocean.

A 1962 polio attack left Clarke's body paralyzed, but his fertile imagination remained unimpaired. Much of the author's best work was yet to come.

A 1964 novel about space travel led to the epic 1968 film *2001: A Space Odyssey,* directed by Stanley Kubrick. The 1980s saw Clarke fronting two television shows: *Arthur C. Clarke's Mysterious World* (1980) and *World of Strange Powers* (1985). These introduced the master of imagination to an entirely new generation and furthered his fame.

Clarke is noted for his predictions concerning technology. Satellite television and the ability to land space probes on asteroids are among his direct hits. The world will have to wait until 2023 to see if dinosaurs will indeed be cloned from computer-generated DNA, and 2050 to see if time travel will become possible through cryonic suspension.

An Advocate for Science

Sir Arthur C. Clarke didn't just write science fiction—he helped make the technologies he imagined become reality. He believed that, through his books, he could inspire people to get involved in science and was a vocal advocate for scientific advancement, especially in space exploration. He was recognized several times for his contributions: He received the UNESCO Kalinga Award for advancing interest in science in 1962, and was nominated for the Nobel Peace Prize in 1994 for his key role in conceptualizing and developing geostationary communications satellites.

U.S. History

❑ ❑ ❑ ❑

Is it still possible to see remnants of the actual Mason-Dixon Line?
What was the Know-Nothing Party?
Did Aaron Burr regret shooting Alexander Hamilton?
This chapter has all these answers and then some!

The Original *Mayflower* Passengers

The first Pilgrims came to North America in 1620 on the ship *Mayflower.* The last living passenger was **Mary Allerton Cushman.** Born in Holland in June 1616, she married Thomas Cushman around 1636 in Plymouth, Massachusetts Bay Colony. Mary Cushman died on November 28, 1699, at age 83.

Mayflower Compact Signers

The Mayflower Compact, an agreement signed by 41 male Pilgrims before they landed at Plymouth, served as the basis of the government of their colony in eastern Massachusetts. **John Alden** was the last living of these signers. He died in 1687 at about 89 years of age.

The Mason-Dixon Line Surveyors

A dispute arose in the 1700s between the colonies of Maryland and Pennsylvania over the boundary line between their lands. The proprietors of each colony, the Penns of Pennsylvania and the Calverts of Maryland, took their argument to the British courts for resolution. In 1750, England's chief justice declared that a line of demarcation should run between southern Pennsylvania and northern Maryland at a point 15 miles south of Philadelphia. At the shared expense of both controlling families, British experts were hired to create this line.

A decade after the ruling, astronomer **Charles Mason** and surveyor Jeremiah Dixon began creating the line of demarcation. Their undertaking was a formidable one, and it took them five years to survey the 230 miles of land. In addition to the technical difficulties of establishing a reliable tangent line, the duo faced the potential hostilities of Native Americans who inhabited the area. The team planted a limestone marker at each mile point. These stones had an M on one side and a P on the other, and each was about three and a half feet long and weighed about 300 pounds. More ornate stones, featuring the Penn and Calvert coats of arms, were positioned at every fifth mile.

Far more than a boundary separating Pennsylvania and Maryland, the Mason-Dixon Line served to divide the North from the South in the years to come. To this day, original stone markers can still be found along the route.

Mason outlived his colleague Dixon by nine years, and was the last survivor of the Mason-Dixon Line surveyors when he died in 1786.

The Attack on the HMS *Gaspee*

Eighteen months before the Boston Tea Party, the British revenue schooner HMS *Gaspee* was burned by American patriots near Providence, Rhode Island. The central motive behind the attack was resentment and distrust of British efforts to regulate trade—it came on the heels of a series of taxes put into effect by the British in 1764.

The *Gaspee,* moored in Narragansett Bay, was seen by the colonists as a symbol of British heavy-handedness. Sent to enforce customs collections and to inspect vessels operated by colonists, the ship provoked immediate resentment. On June 9, the *Gaspee* grounded as it chased a ship; the colonists knew the *Gaspee* would be stuck where it was until high tide, and they took full advantage of the situation. Under the canopy of a moonless night, a group of angry patriots boarded the ship.

In the ensuing scuffle, the ship's commander, William Dudingston, was wounded by musket fire and forced to surrender his vessel. Dudingston was placed on a rowboat, and he and his crew went ashore. The colonists then burned the *Gaspee* within full sight of cheering colonists gathered along the shoreline. No one was killed in the *Gaspee* incident, which is a testament to the colonists' good faith. Theirs was simply a symbolic act against a system they felt was unfair.

During the aftermath, a British commission of inquiry attempted to round up those suspected of involvement. Their intention was to bring the suspects to England for trial, but the colonists strongly objected because the suspects would have zero chance of getting a fair trial in England. When the Rhode Islanders displayed a lack of memory regarding the incident, the Crown realized that a sea change had indeed occurred. In a statement that proved telling, the British collector of customs for Rhode Island offered, "There's an end to collecting a revenue and enforcing the acts of trade."

The *Gaspee* Affair served as a precursor to the American Revolution. American **Colonel Ephraim Bowen** (1753–1841) was the last surviving participant in the attack. Bowen was born in 1753 in Providence, Rhode Island, to Lydia Mawrey and R. Ephraim Bowen, a doctor. During the *Gaspee* incident, Bowen helped John Mawney, a medical student, attend to the wounded William Dudingston. Bowen went on to serve as a deputy quartermaster general during the Revolutionary War, and after the war, he opened a rum distillery in Pawtuxet. In 1838, he wrote a statement about the *Gaspee* incident. Bowen died in 1841.

The Boston Tea Party

On December 16, 1773, colonial patriots disguised as Native Americans boarded cargo ships in Boston Harbor and threw shipments of tea overboard in an act of defiance over taxes. **George Robert Twelves Hewes** was the last of these men to survive. About 31 years old at the time of what would become known as the Boston Tea Party, he lived until 1840.

The British response to the Boston Tea Party was to pass four laws that the colonists would refer to as the Intolerable Acts. The first law stipulated that the port of Boston would be closed until the colonists paid for the tea they had destroyed. The second law revoked the charter of the colony of Massachusetts and forbade town meetings. The third law introduced the Quartering Act, which required the colonists to provide quarters for British soldiers. The fourth law removed British officials from the jurisdiction of Massachusetts courts, meaning that only in England could legal action be taken against them.

The Continental-Confederation Congress

The Continental-Confederation Congress was an assembly of delegates that acted for the people of the colonies from 1774 to 1789. The Continental-Confederation Congress was first convened in response to the Intolerable Acts, which were passed by the British Parliament in 1774.

John Armstrong Jr. was the last survivor of the delegates to the Continental-Confederation Congress. Born in 1758, Armstrong attended Princeton but left in 1775 to serve in the Revolutionary Army. He was a member of the Continental-Confederation Congress from 1787 to 1788 and had a remarkable military career in later years, serving as a commissioned brigadier general during the War of 1812 and secretary of war under President James Madison (1813–14). Unfortunately, the capture of Washington, D.C., by the British during the War of 1812 occurred on his watch, and he was blamed. He died in 1843.

* * * *

Armstrong was one of 51 Pennsylvania delegates to the Continental-Confederation Congress.

* * * *

The "Committee of Five"

John Adams

The Committee of Five was appointed by the Continental-Confederation Congress to draft a statement declaring the colonists' reasons for wanting independence. The committee subsequently asked Thomas Jefferson to write the Declaration of Independence. The last member of this committee to die was **John Adams** of Massachusetts. He died a few hours after Jefferson on the 50th anniversary of the Declaration of Independence, which both had signed.

The following were the other members of the Committee of Five:

- Benjamin Franklin of Pennsylvania (1706–90)
- Roger Sherman of Connecticut (1721–93)
- Robert R. Livingston of New York (1746–1813)
- Thomas Jefferson of Virginia (1743–July 4, 1826)

Adams vs. Jefferson

John Adams and Thomas Jefferson were friends and collaborators during the 1770s and 1780s, but they became foes in the 1790s. In 1796, they ran against each other for the presidency, and Adams, a Federalist, won. In 1800, they ran against each other again, and Jefferson, a Democratic-Republican, won. Adams was so bitter that he did not even attend Jefferson's inauguration. The two reconciled in later years and wrote each other often. Before he died on July 4, 1826, Adams's last words were "Thomas Jefferson survives." Adams was, however, incorrect—Jefferson had died a few hours earlier.

* * * *

"Bear in mind this sacred principle, that though the will of the majority is in all cases to prevail... the minority possess their equal rights, which equal law must protect, and to violate would be oppression."

—From Thomas Jefferson's 1801 Inaugural Address

* * * *

Signers of the Declaration of Independence

Sometimes called the "birth certificate of the United States," the Declaration of Independence expressed the ideals of the yet-to-be-established nation. **Charles Carroll,** the last surviving signer of the Declaration, was born in Annapolis, Maryland, in 1737. He studied law in Paris and London and was a member of a prominent Maryland family. Before the Revolution, however, he could not practice law or even vote because he was Roman Catholic. Carroll was the only Roman Catholic among the 56 signatories.

Carroll helped draft Maryland's constitution and served in the Maryland State Senate from 1777 to 1800. He eventually became a Federalist and served in the U.S. Senate from 1789 to 1792; he was one of Maryland's first two U.S. senators. He resigned from the U.S. Senate when the Maryland legislature disqualified any members from its body who were also serving in the U.S. Congress. After he retired from politics in 1801, Carroll served on the first board of directors of the Baltimore & Ohio Railroad Company. When construction began on July 4, 1828, Carroll laid the cornerstone; this was his last public act. He died on November 14, 1832, at age 95.

* * * *

One signer noted that anyone reading the Declaration of Independence might not be able to tell which Carroll had signed it, since there were a number of Carrolls in the colonies. Charles Carroll heard this remark and added "of Carrollton" to his signature to ensure that there would be no confusion about which Carroll had signed it.

* * * *

In 1776, Carroll traveled to modern-day Canada with Benjamin Franklin in an attempt to persuade the Canadians to join the colonists' war against Britain. The trip was unsuccessful.

* * * *

Carroll was also the last survivor of the 37 Maryland delegates to the Continental-Confederation Congress.

* * * *

Widows of the Declaration of Independence Signatories

Elbridge Gerry represented Massachusetts at the Continental-Confederation Congress and signed the Declaration of Independence. Ten years later, at age 41, he married Ann Thompson, who was then about 33 years of age. In 1812, Gerry was elected vice president of the United States and served until his death on November 23, 1814, at age 70. Because of the state of the family's finances, the U.S. Senate voted to provide his vice presidential salary to his widow for the rest of his term. However, the House of Representatives refused to approve the arrangement. When **Ann Gerry** died in 1849 at age 85, she was the last surviving widow of a signer of the Declaration of Independence. Emily, a daughter of Elbridge and Ann Gerry, was the last surviving child of the signatories when she died in 1894.

Signatories of the Articles of Confederation

Congress passed the Articles of Confederation, in effect the first constitution of the United States, on November 15, 1777. The articles were active from 1781 until the U.S. Constitution took over in 1789. Of the 48 signers, the last to survive was **William Ellery** of Rhode Island, who died in 1820 at age 92.

Writers of *The Federalist Papers*

The Federalist Papers were 85 articles written for New York newspapers under the pen name "Publius" by Alexander Hamilton (1757–1804), John Jay (1745–1829), and **James Madison** (1751–1836). Appearing in 1787 and 1788, the purpose of these articles was to gain support for the new Constitution of the United States. The first article was written by Hamilton and appeared in the *New York Independent Journal* on October 27, 1787. It was not until an 1818 edition of the *Papers* was published by printer Jacob Gideon that the real names of the writers were revealed. Hamilton wrote 51 of the essays, Madison wrote 15, and Jay wrote 5; another 3 were jointly written by Madison and Hamilton, and the authorship of the remaining 11 is undetermined. Jay contributed such a small number because he was recovering from an illness during this time. The last survivor of the three writers was James Madison, who died in 1836 at age 85.

Signatories of the Constitution

The Constitution of the United States provides the fundamental laws of the country. In 1787, it was signed by a convention of delegates from all 13 original states except Rhode Island. The last of the 39 signers was **James Madison,** who later became the fourth president of the United States. Madison died on June 28, 1836, at age 85. Not only was he the last to survive, but his contribution to the creation of the document was so great that history has given him the title of "Father of the Constitution."

The Burr-Hamilton Duel

On July 11, 1804, U.S. Vice President **Aaron Burr** mortally wounded former Secretary of the Treasury Alexander Hamilton during a duel at Weehawken, New Jersey. Bitter differences between the two men can be traced to their philosophical stances (Burr was a Democratic-Republican, Hamilton a Federalist) as well as pivotal events that had pushed both to the breaking point.

Tensions began when Burr snatched a U.S. Senate seat away from Hamilton's father-in-law, Philip Schuyler. Hamilton also held a grudge against Burr for obtaining and publishing one of his private papers. In the document, Hamilton was highly critical of President John Adams, also a Federalist. The ensuing publicity proved embarrassing to Hamilton and widened rifts in the Federalist Party.

Burr blamed Hamilton for his defeat in the race for governor of New York in 1804. Burr had switched parties and run as a Federalist, but Hamilton urged New York Federalists not to support him. When Burr learned that Hamilton had also defamed him at a society dinner, he challenged him to a duel.

When the two faced off, each managed to squeeze off a round. Burr emerged unscathed but Hamilton wasn't so lucky. A bullet ripped through his spine and proved fatal. Some witnesses claim that Hamilton intentionally aimed into the air, not at his nemesis. Some also stated that Burr's manner immediately following the shooting suggested regret. Burr was indicted for murder in New York and New Jersey but was never tried. After the duel, Burr's political career went down in ruins.

Several years after the incident, Burr was tried for treason for attempting to start a new republic in the Southwest, but he was acquitted. When Burr died on September 14, 1836, at age 80, he was the last surviving participant of the 1804 duel.

The participants of the Burr-Hamilton duel were:

- Alexander Hamilton (died in 1804, one day after the duel)
- Nathaniel Pendleton, Hamilton's second in the duel (died in 1821)
- William Peter Van Ness, Burr's second in the duel (died in 1826)
- Aaron Burr (died in 1836)

* * * *

"Had I read Sterne more and Voltaire less, I should have known the world was wide enough for Hamilton and me."

—*Aaron Burr*

* * * *

Alexander Hamilton was born in the West Indies in 1757. His father was James Hamilton. His mother, Rachel Fawcett Lavine, was married to John Michael Lavine at the time of Alexander's birth, and Lavine threw her out of the house for adultery. James Hamilton abandoned the family in 1765, and his mother died in 1768. Alexander was able to thrive, however, because of his intelligence and strong work ethic.

* * * *

Federalists in Congress

Samuel Thatcher, a Massachusetts Federalist who served in the U.S. House of Representatives from 1801 through 1805, was the last surviving former Federalist member of Congress when he died a few days after his 96th birthday in 1872.

The Federalist Party

The Federalists believed that the United States needed a strong, organized central government that would pass tax laws, take on national and state debts, have a central bank, and encourage commerce and industry. In the foreign policy concerns of the time, the Federalists usually sided with Britain against France. George Washington, Alexander Hamilton, John Adams, and John Jay were prominent Federalists. Manufacturers, merchants, and bankers all tended to favor the Federalist Party. The Federalists were influential from 1787 (when *The Federalist Papers* were published) until 1796. The party began to fracture during Adams's presidency, and any remaining power the party had died with Hamilton in 1804.

* * * *

Hamilton was a captain during the Revolutionary War. One reason he became passionate about a strong central government was because of the disheartening inefficiency he witnessed during the war.

* * * *

Congress During the War of 1812

Because of problems related to trade during the European conflicts between Great Britain and France, President James Madison signed a declaration of war against Great Britain on June 18, 1812. The War of 1812 lasted for more than two years. **Ezekiel Bacon** of Massachusetts was in the U.S. House of Representatives at that time and lived until 1870, ultimately becoming the last remaining member of Congress from the time of the War of 1812. He died in Utica, New York, at age 94.

Members of Congress from the Whig Party

Kentucky Congressman **Addison White** held the distinction of being the last Whig to have served in the U.S. Congress. Elected to the 32nd Congress (1851–52), White later fought for the Confederates in the Civil War. He died on February 4, 1909, at age 84.

Who Were the Whigs?

The Whig Party (1834–56) was a political faction that was formed to oppose the authoritarian policies of President Andrew Jackson and the Democratic Party. The Whigs believed that Congress should overrule the executive branch—not vice versa—and promoted economic protectionism and internal programs of modernization that would develop roads, canals, railroads, and other infrastructure. In 1852, when a number of Whig antislavery backers blocked the nomination of their own incumbent, President Millard Fillmore, the party came apart. In 1856, the Whigs held their last political convention and then faded into history.

Governors from the Whig Party

The last surviving member of the Whig Party to have been a state governor was **Thomas Hill Watts.** Born in 1819 in what was then Alabama Territory, he carried on a career in law and government. During the Civil War he was first attorney general of the secessionist state of Alabama, then its governor for the last two years of the war. After the South surrendered, Watts returned to his law practice. He died at age 73 in 1892.

Members of Congress from the Mexican War

New York Democrat **Ausburn Birdsall** was a member of the 30th Congress (March 4, 1847–March 3, 1849). When he died at age 88 in 1903, he was the last person who had served in Congress during the Mexican War.

The Mexican War

Multiple events and circumstances led to the Mexican War. Major catalysts included the U.S. annexation of Texas in 1845 and U.S. President James K. Polk hinting at ambitions to seize California. The first strained United States/Mexican relations strongly because Mexico continued to claim Texas as its own (even though Texas had declared itself an independent republic ten years earlier). The latter made Mexico uneasy for obvious reasons.

Another factor leading up to the conflict was an ongoing border dispute between the two countries. The United States argued that the southern border of Texas was the Rio Grande, while Mexico held that the boundary line was the Nueces River farther north. At war's end, the United States emerged victorious and claimed California and New Mexico as its spoils.

Members of Congress from the Know-Nothing Party

The Know-Nothing Party, also called the American Party, was strong in the 1850s. Anti-immigrant and anti-Catholic, the Know-Nothing Party sought to prevent or hinder foreign-born residents from voting, holding office, or becoming citizens. Of the 40 members of Congress who belonged to it, the last surviving member was **Mark Trafton** of Massachusetts. A longtime minister, he served two years in the U.S. Congress during the late 1850s before losing his reelection bid. He returned to the ministry and died on March 8, 1901, at age 90.

* * * *

The Know-Nothing Party earned its name because when members were questioned about nativist organizations, they always replied that they knew nothing.

* * * *

Know-Nothing Governors

The Know-Nothing Party was especially popular among people who were apathetic about the slavery issue. Massachusetts Governor **Henry Joseph Gardner** was a member of the Know-Nothing Party and a supporter of antialien legislation. He died in 1892 at age 74, the last surviving governor to have been a member of the Know-Nothing Party.

Members of Congress from the Civil War

The Civil War began in April 1861 with the attack on Fort Sumter in Charleston, South Carolina, and ended when the last Confederates surrendered in April 1865. After serving during the war as an officer in the Union Army, **George Latham** of West Virginia was elected to the 39th Congress (March 4, 1865–March 3, 1867). When Latham died at age 85 in 1917, he was the last surviving member who had served in Congress during the Civil War.

Governors Who Fought in the Civil War

Of the 83 governors who served in the Civil War, the last surviving was Governor **Joseph Wilson Fifer** of Illinois. Fifer was born in Staunton, Virginia, in 1840, and his family moved to Illinois in 1857. When he was just a child, he heard a lawyer deliver an argument before a jury; from that moment on, he knew he wanted to be a lawyer.

When the Civil War broke out, Fifer and his brother enlisted. As a member of the 33rd Illinois Infantry, he was seriously wounded in 1863 when a musket ball passed through his body. Only the efforts of a surgeon and a compatriot who rode 50 miles for ice saved his life. After several months of recuperation, Fifer insisted on finishing his three-year tour of duty. After the war, he studied law and opened his own practice in Bloomington, Illinois, before he embarked upon a career in politics. He served as state's attorney, a state senator, and governor. President McKinley appointed Fifer to the Interstate Commerce Commission in 1899, and Fifer was reappointed by Theodore Roosevelt. After a long political career, Fifer died at age 97 in 1938.

* * * *

In 1924, Fifer's daughter, Florence Fifer Bohrer, was elected Illinois's first female state senator.

* * * *

Congressional Delegates from the Dakota Territory

Eleven men were congressional delegates from the Dakota Territory between 1861 and 1889. Republican **George Arthur Mathews,** who passed away at age 88 in 1941, was the last surviving delegate. Mathews served in the 51st Congress from March 4, 1889, until the territory was admitted into the Union (November 2, 1889) as the two states of North and South Dakota.

Members of Congress from the U.S. Entry into the Spanish-American War

The Spanish-American War began with an April 1898 Congressional Resolution for War with Spain and lasted until December 1898. The United States entered the war on the side of Cuba against Spain after the USS *Maine* exploded in Havana Harbor.

Of those who served in Congress during the Spanish-American War, Massachusetts representative **John Francis Fitzgerald** was the last to die. He campaigned with his grandson John F. Kennedy when the latter was running for Congress in 1946. Kennedy won the seat that Fitzgerald had held 50 years before. Fitzgerald passed away in 1950 at age 87, and ten years later his grandson was elected president.

* * * *

John Francis Fitzgerald often sang the song "Sweet Adeline" in an attempt to charm voters; this earned him the nickname "Honey Fitz."

* * * *

The Colorado Coal Field War

During the early 1900s, Colorado Fuel & Iron (CF&I), owned by John D. Rockefeller Jr. dominated mining in Colorado's Southern Coal Field. Miners were paid per ton of coal mined, so they received no payment for mine repair or maintenance work. Since the company owned all rental housing and shops, the system simply recycled wage dollars through the company's coffers.

In August 1913, Southern Coal Field miners went on strike to demand union recognition, eight-hour days, hourly pay, and the right to trade and live anywhere they wished. Company police evicted all strikers from company property, so the families moved to tent cities organized to defend against strikebreakers. The strikebreakers marauded with searchlights, random beatings, and occasional machine-gun hosings from the "Death Special"—a primitive armored car.

Soon CF&I execs asked themselves: "Why spend money on thugs? That's what the Colorado National Guard is for!" The governor obliged; the Guard arrived in October. Neutral at first, the Guard soon continued the terror. On April 20, 1914—just after Easter celebrations—the Guard assaulted, machine-gunned, sacked, and burned a camp at Ludlow. There were 21 fatalities, more than half of whom were women and children. The miners shot back at the Guard and began wrecking mines. Only the arrival of federal troops ended the "Ten-Day War." The strike finally ended in December 1914.

The miners lost the shooting war but won the PR war. Upton Sinclair led demonstrations against Rockefeller in New York and excoriated the media for covering up the ugly truth. Within a few years, the companies met most union demands.

The Coal Field War's last known survivor was **Mary Benich McCleary,** an 18-month-old tot on April 20. In the midst of the attack on that day, a teenage boy scooped up baby Mary in his jacket and ran, saving her life. Ms. McCleary passed away on June 28, 2007, at age 94.

Members of Congress During the Pearl Harbor Attack

New York Republican representative **Edwin Arthur Hall** was the last survivor of all the members in the U.S. Congress in 1941. He also served during the time Germany was invading Norway, Denmark, and France. He died at age 95 in the same month George W. Bush and John Kerry were holding the 2004 presidential debates.

Members of Congress from the Socialist Party

Only two members of the U.S. Congress have been elected under the banner of the Socialist Party. One was Meyer London from New York, who served from 1915 to 1919 and from 1921 to 1923. He died in 1926. The other was Wisconsin representative **Victor Berger,** who died in 1929 at age 69 and was thus the last surviving Socialist member of Congress.

Berger was born in Austria-Hungary in 1860 and moved to New England with his family in 1878. He moved to Milwaukee in 1880 to teach school, embarked upon a journalism career in 1892, and entered politics in 1911. He served in Congress from 1911 to 1913 and from 1923 to 1929.

✱ ✱ ✱ ✱

Berger was reelected to Congress in 1918, but the House refused to seat him because of his pacifist leanings.

✱ ✱ ✱ ✱

Berger was tried for espionage in 1919 and was found guilty. Judge Kenesaw Mountain Landis sentenced him to 20 years' imprisonment. The verdict was then overturned, however, and Berger did not serve any time.

✱ ✱ ✱ ✱

Foreign-Born U.S. Supreme Court Justices

Felix Frankfurter was born in 1882 in Vienna, Austria. After emigrating to America, he graduated from Harvard Law School and became Harvard's first Jewish professor of law. He was an associate justice of the U.S. Supreme Court from 1939 to 1962. When he died in 1965, he was the last living of the six foreign-born men who had served on the highest court in the land.

The following were the five other foreign-born justices:

- James Wilson (1742–98), born in Scotland, served on the Court from 1789 to 1798.
- James Iredell (1751–99), born in England, served on the Court from 1790 to 1799.
- William Paterson (1745–1806), born in Ireland, served on the Court from 1793 to 1806.
- David J. Brewer (1837–1910), born in Smyrna (in present-day Turkey), served on the Court from 1889 to 1910.
- George Sutherland (1862–1942), born in England, served on the Court from 1922 to 1938.

The First Social Security Beneficiaries

Of the approximately 28,000 charter beneficiaries of the U.S. Social Security System, **William Howard Weamer** was the last survivor. He had paid about $30 into the system before he received his first monthly check of $17.44 in January 1940. He had been a dairy worker, a mail carrier, and a member of the Pennsylvania House of Representatives. He was featured in a publication of the Social Security Administration in 1980, when he was 106 years old and receiving a $227 monthly check. He died in July of the following year.

The Kennedys

Joseph P. Kennedy Sr. and Rose Fitzgerald Kennedy had five daughters and four sons. Of the daughters, two are still living: Eunice Kennedy Shriver (founder of the Special Olympics and mother of Maria Shriver) and Jean Kennedy Smith (founder of Very Special Arts and former ambassador to Ireland). Kathleen Kennedy Hartington died in a plane crash in 1948, Rosemary Kennedy died in 2005, and Patricia Kennedy Lawford died in 2006.

The last surviving son is **Edward "Ted" Kennedy.** Joseph Jr. died in a military accident in World War II, and President John F. Kennedy and Senator Robert Kennedy were both assassinated. Ted, who has served as a U.S. senator since 1962, turned 77 years old in 2009.

Honorary Citizens of the United States

Six people have been named honorary citizens of the United States by the U.S. Congress. Of these six, the last to die was Catholic nun and religious organization founder **Mother Teresa** of Calcutta (1910–97), who received the honor in 1996. Born Agnes Gonxha Bojaxhiu in Albania, Mother Teresa helped abandoned children, the poor, the sick, and the dying through the Missionaries of Charity, a religious order she founded in 1950. She won the Nobel Peace Prize in 1979 and the Presidential Medal of Freedom in 1985. In the late 20th century, Mother Teresa's name became synonymous with care for the poor.

The following were the other five honorary U.S. citizens:

- William Penn (1644–1718) and Hannah Callowhill Penn (1671–1727), 18th-century founders of Pennsylvania (posthumously awarded in 1984)
- Marquis de Lafayette (1757–1834), French leader in the Revolutionary War (posthumously awarded in 2002)
- Raoul Wallenberg (1912–47?), Swedish diplomat and Holocaust hero (posthumously awarded in 1981)
- Winston Churchill (1874–1965), British prime minister during World War II (awarded in 1963)

* * * *

Raoul Wallenberg worked for the War Refugee Board in Hungary during World War II. He helped designate 30 safe houses and saved tens of thousands of Hungarian Jews. Soviet forces liberated Budapest in February 1945, and Wallenberg was last seen with Soviet officials in January 1945. He is believed to have died in a Soviet prison in 1947, but the exact details of his death are unknown.

* * * *

In 2007, a new book about Mother Teresa, Come Be My Light, *was published. It detailed Mother Teresa's intense doubts. Some took this to mean she did not really believe in her work. Others saw it differently—that the constant prayer of her life was a common one: "Lord, I believe; help my unbelief."*

* * * *

Inventions

❑ ❑ ❑ ❑

Who invented the lightbulb?
Who came to regret his contributions to the invention of television?
What made portable electronics possible?
We won't hold you in suspense—the answers can be found in the following pages.

The 19th Century's Best-Known Inventors

Thomas Alva Edison (1847–1931) was self-taught. When he was seven years old, his mother had a disagreement with one of his teachers. She pulled him out of school and homeschooled him from then on. He went on to become one of the greatest inventors of all time.

During his career, he invented the phonograph, the incandescent lightbulb, and the motion picture camera. Last survivor Edison also outlived the other major inventors of his era.

The following were other prolific 19th-century inventors:

- Humphrey Davy (1778–1829) invented the lightbulb.
- Louis-Jacques-Mandé Daguerre (1789–1851) produced the first permanent photographic image.
- Barthelemy Thimonnier (1793–1857) invented the first functional sewing machine.
- Walter Hunt (1796–1859) invented the safety pin and the first eye-pointed needle sewing machine.
- Elias Howe (1819–67) invented the first sewing machine with a lockstitch mechanism.
- Isaac Singer (1811–75) invented the first sewing machine with an up-and-down motion mechanism.

- Gottlieb Daimler (1834–1900) invented the prototype of the modern gas engine.
- Sir Joseph Wilson Swan (1828–1914) invented an electric lightbulb that could burn for more than 13 hours.
- Alexander Graham Bell (1847–1922) invented the telephone.
- Karl Benz (1844–1929) invented the internal-combustion engine.

* * * *

Thomas Edison allowed only positive discussion in his laboratory. When an experiment failed, Edison always stressed that the failure helped steer their work in the appropriate direction.

* * * *

Edison was hearing impaired, but he felt that this helped him in his work because it made it easier for him to concentrate.

* * * *

"Sleep is like a drug. Take too much at a time and it makes you dopey. You lose time and opportunities."

—Thomas Edison

* * * *

Children of Thomas Edison

The last living of inventor Thomas Edison's six children was his youngest son, **Theodore Edison,** who passed away in 1992 at age 94. When Theodore was a child, his father stated, "Theodore is a good boy, but his forte is mathematics. He may go flying off into the clouds with that fellow Einstein. And if he does . . . I'm afraid he won't work with me." However, after graduating from MIT with a degree in physics, Theodore started his career as a laboratory assistant for his father. He eventually accumulated more than 80 U.S. patents.

Major 19th-Century Photographic Inventors

English physicist **William Talbot** (1800–77) invented a method of creating photographic prints in 1838 and pioneered the use of flash photography. After a career in astronomy, mathematics, and archaeology, which included helping to decipher the cuneiform inscriptions at Nineveh, he died at age 77 in 1877. Talbot was the last surviving major 19th-century inventor in the field of photography.

The following were other great 19th-century photographic inventors:

- Joseph Nicéphore Niépce (1765–1833) produced the first photographic image.
- Louis-Jacques-Mandé Daguerre (1789–1851) produced the first permanent photographic image.

Last Living Person Who Knew Alexander Graham Bell

Pediatrician **Mabel Grosvenor,** granddaughter of telephone inventor Alexander Graham Bell, was the last survivor of those who personally knew Bell.

Dr. Grosvenor was the daughter of Elsie Bell Grosvenor (Alexander Graham Bell's eldest child) and Gilbert Grosvenor, the first president of *National Geographic* magazine. Some of Dr. Grosvenor's memories included performing scientific experiments with her grandfather, working as his secretary during her teen years, and participating in a women's suffrage march with her mother and grandmother in Washington, D.C., in 1913. Dr. Grosvenor was one of seven women who earned medical degrees from Johns Hopkins University in 1931. She died in 2006 at age 101.

Television Inventors

Working for RCA, Russian immigrant **Vladimir K. Zworykin** developed the first practical television camera in the late 1930s. Zworykin was born in Russia in 1889 and escaped during the Russian Revolution. He settled in Pittsburgh and earned his Ph.D. in physics in 1926. Zworykin began working for RCA in 1929. He died in 1982—the last surviving inventor in the field of television.

The following were other television inventors:

- Charles F. Jenkins (1867–1934) transmitted the first moving silhouette images.
- Paul Nipkow (1860–1940) came up with the idea of dissecting an image and transmitting it sequentially.
- John Logie Baird (1888–1946) invented a mechanical television system that used reflected light.
- Allen B. DuMont (1901–65) perfected the first commercially practical cathode-ray tube.
- Philo T. Farnsworth (1906–71) transmitted the first all-electronic television image.
- David Sarnoff (1891–1971) oversaw the manufacture of the first television sets.

* * * *

"Today we have . . . the transmission of sight for the first time. . . . Human genius has now destroyed the impediment of distance . . . in a manner hitherto unknown."

—Herbert Hoover during the first long-distance transmission of a live picture and voice (April 9, 1927)

* * * *

Philo T. Farnsworth grew to regret his contributions to television. He viewed TVs as machines through which people wasted unfathomable amounts of time.

* * * *

The First Synthetic Fiber

Nylon, the first synthetic fiber, was invented by DuPont chemists in the 1930s. Initially used for stockings and toothbrush bristles, it was diverted for military uses during World War II and was used for everything from parachutes to bomber tires. Once the war ended, women were eager to buy nylons again.

Joe Labovsky was the last survivor of the team that invented nylon. Labovsky was born in Kiev, Ukraine, in 1912. His family emigrated to the United States in 1923. Labovsy's father worked as a tailor for the DuPont family, and he was able to find his son a job as a chemist helper to Wallace Carothers at DuPont in 1930.

Labovsky went on to study chemical engineering at the Pratt Institute in Brooklyn. He had trouble finding work after he graduated in 1934, but he did eventually find a job digging ditches—again at DuPont. One day Wallace Carothers walked by as Joe was working, and Carothers stopped to chat. He soon recruited Joe for the nylon project, and—because most of the others working on the project were research chemists—Labovsky's chemical engineering background was an asset to the team. Labovsky was still alive in 2009 at age 96.

The Transistor

Walter Brattain (1902–87), William Shockley (1910–89), and **John Bardeen** (1908–91) invented the transistor in 1947. The transistor is a component of silicon chips; it replaced cumbersome vacuum tubes and made portable electronics possible. The three men were awarded the Nobel Prize in Physics in 1956.

John Bardeen was the last survivor of the team. Born in Madison, Wisconsin, on May 23, 1908, Bardeen loved math from an early age. He exhibited such brilliance that his parents and teachers moved him from third grade directly to junior high. Enrolling at the University of Wisconsin in 1923 at age 15, he went on to complete a master's degree in electrical engineering because he felt he would have the best job prospects in that field. He also earned a Ph.D. in mathematical physics from Princeton. Bardeen was awarded another Nobel Prize in Physics in 1972 for his contributions to the development of the theory of superconductivity. This made him the first person to receive two Nobel Prizes in the same field. Bardeen died on January 30, 1991.

The First General-Purpose Computer

In 1946, John Mauchly and **J. Presper Eckert** of the University of Pennsylvania completed development of the first general-purpose digital computer, the ENIAC. Funded during World War II by the U.S. Army to calculate ordnance trajectories, the ENIAC offered a thousandfold speed increase over electromechanical computers because it worked by sending electrons through semiconductors. One might liken it to the difference between e-mail and a typed, mailed letter.

The ENIAC could perform complicated equations some 50,000 times faster than a human being and had numerous practical applications going beyond military science. It weighed 27 tons, occupied 680 square feet, and gulped 150 kilowatts of juice. (It is a myth, however, that its power draw dimmed the lights in Philly.)

Mauchly died in 1980 at age 72, but his coinventor Eckert lived until age 76 in 1995, just as the Internet age was gathering steam (or rather, voltage).

Remote Control

In the 1950s, Zenith engineers Robert Adler (1913–2007) and **Eugene Polley** (1916–) developed the first practical wireless television remote controls, each using a different technology. Polley's Flashmatic used light beams, while Adler's Space Command device used high-frequency sound. In 1998 the two men accepted an engineering Emmy Award for their work in developing the television remote.

Polley, the last survivor of the two, received only $1,000 for his invention because Zenith selected Adler's technology as the most practical. Today's remotes, however, use light beams, just as Polley's device did. Holder of 18 patents, Polley was alive in 2009 at age 91.

Entertainment

❑ ❑ ❑ ❑

What was Mary Pickford's given name?
Who wrote some of the funniest scenes in The Wizard of Oz?
Who was writer Roald Dahl's first wife?
As luck would have it, the answers can be found in this very chapter.

The Ringling Brothers

The five Ringling brothers who started the family's circus business were Otto (1858–1911), Albert (1852–1916), Alfred (1861–1919), Charles (1863–1926), and John (1866–1936). The youngest brother, Henry (1868–1918), joined later, and a seventh brother, August (1854–1907), was not involved. In 1907, the brothers purchased the Barnum & Bailey Circus.

John Ringling was the last survivor of the seven brothers. Each of the brothers played a specific role in running the circus, and John's role was handling transportation. He masterminded the shift from traveling by wagon to traveling by rail, which greatly increased the reach of the show. John died of pneumonia in 1936.

* * * *

John Ringling and his wife, Mabel, acquired a vast art collection. Visitors can view their treasures at John and Mabel's Sarasota, Florida, mansion, which is now known as the John and Mabel Ringling Museum of Art.

* * * *

The Keystone Kops

No silent film comedy group was more famous than the Keystone Kops, a hilariously incompetent, undisciplined police force. **Hank Mann** was the last remaining of the original seven Keystone Kops. He died at age 84 in 1971. The following were the other original Keystone Kops:

- Charles Avery (1873–1926)
- Bobby Dunn (1890–1937)
- Edgar Kennedy (1890–1948)
- Slim Summerville (1892–1949)
- George Jesky (1891–1951)
- Mack Riley (1886–1963)

The Ziegfeld Girls

The chorus girls in Broadway producer Florenz Ziegfeld's (1867–1932) shows were universally known as "Ziegfeld Girls." The last living of these dancers was **Doris Eaton Travis.** Celebrating her 105th birthday in 2009, Travis was a "Ziegfeld Girl" in 1918, 1919, and 1920.

United Artists

The United Artists distribution company was founded in 1919 by Douglas Fairbanks Sr. (1883–1939), D. W. Griffith (1875–1948), Charlie Chaplin (1889–1977), and **Mary Pickford** (1892–1979). Pickford, who was nicknamed "America's Sweetheart," lived the longest. She was born in Toronto in 1892. Her father passed away when she was just five years old, and Mary began pursuing acting roles to help earn money for the family. She started in local productions, then joined a touring company, landed a role on Broadway in 1907, and began starring in movies in 1909. She went on to have her own production company (the first star to do so) and also became Hollywood's first millionaire. Pickford passed away in 1979.

* * * *

Mary Pickford's real name was Gladys Smith. She changed it in 1907 because her producer convinced her that the new name sounded more glamorous.

* * * *

Silent Film Superstars

Born Anita Pomares in 1910 in Queens, New York, **Anita Page** began her film career in 1925 as an extra in *A Kiss for Cinderella.* She was offered a contract with MGM as a result of that performance. As a leading lady and screen beauty in the late 1920s and early 1930s, she often received more than 10,000 fan letters per week, some of which were reportedly marriage proposals from Benito Mussolini. Most critics point to her performance in *Our Dancing Daughters* as her finest.

After Page married naval officer Herschel House in 1936, she retired from movies. She died in 2008 at age 98, the last surviving top star of the silent film era.

* * * *

Anita Page was also the last survivor of those who attended the 1929 Academy Awards ceremony. Page costarred in Broadway Melody, *which won best picture at the ceremony that year.*

* * * *

The Academy of Motion Picture Arts and Sciences Founders

Academy of Motion Picture Arts and Sciences is an honorary organization designed to promote the motion picture profession. It is best known for its efforts to recognize achievements of filmmakers through its annual Academy Awards. It was founded in 1927 by 33 men and 3 women, a group that included actors Mary Pickford and Douglas Fairbanks Sr., director Cecil B. DeMille, and producers Louis B. Mayer and Jack Warner.

The last surviving founding member was director **Henry King,** a stage actor who started directing silent films in 1915. King himself won the Best Director Academy Award for 1943's *The Song of Bernadette* and was the director of three of actor Gregory Peck's best films: *Twelve O'Clock High* (1949), *The Gunfighter* (1950), and *The Snows of Kilimanjaro* (1952). King passed away in 1982 at age 96.

Wives of Charlie Chaplin

Charlie Chaplin (1889–1977), considered by many to be the greatest star of silent films, was married four times: to Mildred Harris in 1918, **Lita Grey** in 1924, Paulette Goddard in 1933, and Oona O'Neill in 1943. The marriage to second wife Lita lasted from 1924, when she was 16 and he was 35, until 1928. Grey and Chaplin had two sons, Sydney and Charles Jr. In 1965, Grey wrote *My Life with Chaplin*. She died in 1995 at age 87—the last survivor of Chaplin's wives.

The Academy Awards

The first Academy Awards were given out in 1928. Of the four people who received major awards that year, **Janet Gaynor** was the last to survive. She retired from filmmaking in 1938 and passed away in 1984.

The following were the first Academy Award winners:

- Best Actor: Emil Jannings (1884–1950), for *The Way of All Flesh* and *The Last Command*
- Best Actress: Janet Gaynor (1906–84), for *Seventh Heaven, Street Angel,* and *Sunrise*
- Best Drama Direction: Frank Borzage (1893–1962), for *Seventh Heaven*
- Best Comedy Direction: Lewis Milestone (1895–1980), for *Two Arabian Knights*

Child Movie Stars of the 1920s

Child movie star **Jackie Cooper** (1922–) started appearing in movies in 1929. At age nine in 1931, Cooper was nominated for the Best Actor Academy Award for his performance in *Skippy*. The other nominees were adults: Lionel Barrymore, Richard Dix, Fredric March, and Adolphe Menjou. Although Cooper didn't win, he remains the only person in history younger than age 18 to have been nominated for the Best Actor Oscar. His career skyrocketed in the

1930s with such classics as *The Champ* and *Treasure Island*, both with Wallace Beery. In his later years Cooper turned to directing. In the 1970s and 1980s, he appeared as Perry White in all four *Superman* movies. Still living in 2009, Jackie Cooper is the last survivor of the major child movie stars of the 1920s.

* * * *

Cooper served as a captain in the U.S. Navy during World War II.

* * * *

Walt Disney Studios

In 1923, **Virginia Davis** starred in Walt Disney Studios' "Alice Comedies" series. In the movies, four-year-old Virginia interacted with animated characters. She appeared in 13 of the "Alice Comedies" and went on to perform in theater, in movies, and on TV. She later earned a degree from the New York School of Interior Design and worked as a decorating editor and a realtor. Miss Davis was alive in 2009 at age 90—the last survivor of Disney Studio's first employees.

* * * *

Diane Disney Miller was the last surviving child of Walt Disney. She was alive as of 2009 at age 75. Walt Disney used to take Diane and her sister, Sharon, to the park. He would patiently wait for them to have their fill of playing. While waiting for them, it occurred to him that there should be more options for things for parents to do with their children. This is how he came up with the idea for his theme parks.

* * * *

Romantic Teams of the 1930s

Loretta Young (1913–2000) and **Douglas Fairbanks Jr.** (1909–2000) starred in seven films together between 1929 and 1933. They died within months of each other in 2000, the last of the romantic pairs from the 1930s film era. Loretta Young and Douglas Fairbanks Jr. made the following films together:

- *The Careless Age* (1929)
- *Fast Life* (1929)
- *The Forward Pass* (1929)
- *Loose Ankles* (1930)
- *I Like Your Nerve* (1931)
- *The Slippery Pearls* (1931)
- *The Life of Jimmy Dolan* (1933)

Douglas Fairbanks Jr.

Metro Goldwyn Mayer (MGM)

Samuel Goldwyn (1879–1974) outlived Louis B. Mayer (1882–1957) by 17 years. Actually, Goldwyn was ousted from his own company before the merger, so he never had any part in the new company, though his name was retained. Goldwyn was born in Russia and emigrated to England in 1895. He then made his way to Canada and finally the United States. Upon his arrival in the United States in 1898, he became a leather glove salesperson. Goldwyn married Blanche Lasky in 1910 and convinced her brother Jesse L. Lasky and Cecil B. DeMille to go into film production with him. He went on to become one of Hollywood's most prolific producers. Goldwyn died in 1974.

The Marx Brothers

The five Marx brothers went from humble beginnings in New York City to become arguably the greatest comedy act in show business history. First performing on stage, they later achieved their greatest success in such films as *Duck Soup, A Night at the Opera, A Day at the Races,* and *Animal Crackers.* **Zeppo Marx,** the youngest of the brothers, died in 1979 at age 78. Zeppo played a straight man character in several of the Marx Brothers classics. The Marx brothers were

- Leonard "Chico" (1887–1961)
- Arthur "Harpo" (1888–1964)

- Milton "Gummo" (1893–April 21, 1977)
- Julius "Groucho" (1890–August 19, 1977)
- Herbert "Zeppo" (1901–79)

Marx Brothers' Writers

Irving Brecher, the last survivor of those who wrote for the Marx Brothers, died in 2008 at age 94. Brecher was born in the Bronx in 1914. While he was working at a local movie theater in 1933, he began to send one-liners to journalists; once in a while, the one-liners wound up in print. Some friends advised Brecher to try to find paying work this way, and he put an ad in *Variety* that pitched "Berle-proof gags—so bad not even Milton would steal them." Milton Berle himself saw the ad and offered Brecher $50 for a page of one-liners. Berle liked what Brecher submitted and offered Brecher a job on his radio show.

When Berle's show moved to Hollywood in 1937, Brecher went with him. Soon after moving there, Brecher was asked to help write some of the comedy scenes for *The Wizard of Oz.* Brecher then wrote the scripts for the Marx Brothers' films *Go West* and *At the Circus.* He was nominated for a Best Screenplay Oscar for the 1944 Judy Garland musical *Meet Me in St. Louis,* and he also wrote the screenplay for *Bye Bye Birdie.*

The Seven Little Foys

Irving Foy was the last surviving member of the Seven Little Foys, one of vaudeville's most popular teams of the early 1900s. The Foy family traveled across the country performing their act. Irving was quite young when he started performing, but he was a big hit. His father began their act by coming onstage with a carpetbag. After he set the bag down, Irving would climb out of it, to the delight of the audience. Irving and his father would then interact, with Irving singing and often mimicking his father. The show would usually end with Irving trying to pull his dad offstage. Irving performed into the 1930s and then moved to New Mexico, where he held several jobs, from managing movie theaters and ice cream parlors to working as a waiter or bartender. Irving died in 2003 at age 94.

* * * *

The Foy family's story was told in the movie The Seven Little Foys, *which starred Bob Hope and James Cagney.*

* * * *

Directors Guild of America

In 1936, a group of 13 directors banded together to form the Directors Guild of America. Their chief grievances against the studios of the time were that they were left out of significant script, casting, and editing decisions that often negatively impacted the films that would bear their names. These directors decided to band together to stand up for the integrity of their films because individual directors who tried to defend themselves were often fired.

The last living Directors Guild of America founder was Russian-born director **Rouben Mamoulian,** who passed away in 1987. Famous for such stage productions as *Porgy and Bess* and such movies as *Love Me Tonight,* Mamoulian was 90 years of age when he died.

* * * *

The day the founders announced the formation of the Directors Guild of America, the group received 100 applications. As of 2008, the guild had more than 13,000 members.

* * * *

Portrayers of Thomas Edison

Several years after the death of prolific inventor Thomas Edison, two film biographies were produced. Spencer Tracy (1900–67) portrayed Edison in *Edison, the Man* (1940), and **Mickey Rooney** (1920–) portrayed Edison in *Young Tom Edison* (1940). Mickey Rooney, the last surviving of the portrayers of Edison, was still doing live performances in 2009.

Ava Gardner's Husbands

Ava Gardner (1922–90) was married to three show business legends: Frank Sinatra, Artie Shaw, and **Mickey Rooney.** The only one of these still living as of 2009 was Rooney.

The Three Stooges

For decades the Three Stooges' act was synonymous with slapstick comedy. In the late 1950s, **Joe DeRita** joined Moe Howard and Larry Fine as the sixth man to be a Stooge. Because of his resemblance to the original Curly, he took the name "Curly Joe." DeRita became the last living stooge when Joe Besser died in 1988.

The following were the six "Three Stooges":

- Moe (Moses) Howard (1897–1975)
- Shemp (Samuel) Howard (1895–1955)
- Curly (Jerome) Howard (1903–52)
- Larry Fine (1902–75)
- Joe "Curly Joe" DeRita (1909–93)
- Joe Besser (1907–88)

Famous Dance Pairs

Of the following famous dance pairs, the only person alive as of 2009 was **Marge Champion.** Arthur and Kathryn Murray were the last surviving team in which both members survived. Among the most famous American dance partners of the 20th century were:

- Vernon (1887–1918) and Irene Castle (1893–1969)
- Fred Astaire (1899–1987) and Ginger Rogers (1911–95)
- Arthur (1895–1991) and Kathryn Murray (1906–99)
- Gower (1921–80) and Marge Champion (1919–)

Warner Brothers

Four Warner brothers founded Warner Bros. Pictures Inc. in 1923: Sam (1887–1927), Harry (1881–1958), Albert (1882–1967), and Jack

(1892–1978). They released *The Jazz Singer* in 1927. Warner Bros. became home to such stars as Errol Flynn, Humphrey Bogart, and James Cagney.

The most well known Warner brother, **Jack L. Warner,** was born in Canada in 1892 and outlived his brothers. He lost interest in the studio after the deaths of the other three brothers, and he sold it in 1967.

Al Jolson's Wives

Of entertainer Al Jolson's four wives, the last living was **Erle Jolson Krasna.** An X-ray technician at an army hospital in Hot Springs, Arkansas, she caught Jolson's eye while he was there entertaining wounded soldiers in June 1944. Their five-year marriage ended with Jolson's 1950 death. The couple had one child, Albert Jolson Jr.

In 1951, Erle Jolson married Oscar-winning screenwriter Norman Krasna. She had her son David during this marriage. Played by Barbara Hale in the 1949 movie *Jolson Sings Again*, Erle died on January 11, 2004, at age 81.

Classic Movie Monsters

Ben Chapman (1928–2008), who played the monster in the *Creature from the Black Lagoon* (1954) in the out-of-the-water scenes, passed away in 2008 at age 79. In his later years, he enjoyed attending autograph conventions and was kind and generous to his fans. The following were the other classic movie monster actors and their best-known characters:

- Lon Chaney Sr. (1883–1930), the Phantom of the Opera
- Bela Lugosi (1882–1956), Dracula
- Claude Rains (1889–1967), Invisible Man
- Boris Karloff (1887–1969), the Frankenstein monster, the Mummy
- Lon Chaney Jr. (1906–73), the Wolf Man

Female Stars of the Classic Monster Films

Gloria Stuart, who played the female lead in *The Invisible Man* (1933) with Claude Rains, was alive as of 2009. She also appeared in *Old Dark House* (1932) with Boris Karloff and was nominated for an Academy Award for her performance in 1997's *Titanic.* The following were other female stars of classic monster movies:

- Helen Chandler (1906–65) of *Dracula* (1930)
- Evelyn Ankers (1918–85) of *The Wolf Man* (1941)
- Elsa Lanchester (1902–86) of *Bride of Frankenstein* (1935)
- Mae Clarke (1910–92) of *Frankenstein* (1931)
- Zita Johann (1904–93) of *The Mummy* (1932)
- Josephine Hutchinson (1903–98) of *Son of Frankenstein* (1939)
- Valerie Hobson (1913–98) of *Bride of Frankenstein* (1935)

Classic Movie Monster Creators

Curt Siodmak was the writer who created the Wolf Man for the 1941 Lon Chaney Jr. classic of the same name. After he wrote that movie and *The Invisible Man Returns,* he specialized in writing science fiction. Siodmak died at age 98 in 2000.

The U.S. Postal Service's "Monster" Stamps

In 1997 the U.S. Postal Service released the popular "Classic Movie Monsters" stamps, featuring four of the most famous monster actors in their makeup. The last surviving of these actors was Wolf Man star Lon Chaney Jr. (1906–73). The following were the other actors (and monsters) on the "Classic Movie Monsters" stamps:

- Lon Chaney Sr. (1883–1930), the Phantom of the Opera
- Bela Lugosi (1882–1956), Dracula

- Boris Karloff (1887–1969), the Frankenstein Monster and the Mummy

Boris Karloff's Children

Film actor Boris Karloff's only living child as of 2009 was **Sara Karloff.** A frequent participant in autograph conventions, she celebrated her 70th birthday in 2008.

The "Singing Cowboys" of the 1930s and 1940s

Monte Hale died at age 89 in 2009. The following were other movie singing cowboys of the 1930s and 1940s:

- Tex Ritter (1905–74)
- Roy Rogers (1911–July 6, 1998)
- Gene Autry (1907–October 2, 1998)
- Eddie Dean (1907–March 4, 1999)
- Rex Allen (1920–December 17, 1999)

1930s Movie Gangsters

James Cagney (1899–1986), star of the classic films *The Public Enemy* and *Angels with Dirty Faces,* was the last survivor of the major old-time gangster movie actors. He started off as a song and dance man, and it's interesting to note that he preferred the Yankee Doodle Dandy role to the gangster parts. The following were other major gangster actors of the 1930s:

- Humphrey Bogart (1899–1957)
- Paul Muni (1895–1967)
- Edward G. Robinson (1893–1973)
- George Raft (1895–1980)

Female Costars of Golden Age Gangster Films

Of all the actresses who had female leads in the classic gangster films, **Karen Morley** (1909–2003), who appeared in *Scarface* (1932), lived the longest. The following were other gangster movie female costars:

- Jean Harlow (1911–37) of *The Public Enemy*
- Noel Francis (1906–59) of *I Am a Fugitive from a Chain Gang*
- Ann Sheridan (1915–67) of *Angels with Dirty Faces*
- Glenda Farrell (1904–71) of *I Am a Fugitive from a Chain Gang* and *Little Caesar*
- Ann Dvorak (1912–79) of *Scarface* and *G-Men*
- Margaret Lindsay (1910–81) of *G-Men*
- Priscilla Lane (1915–95) of *The Roaring Twenties*
- Helen Vinson (1907–99) of *I Am a Fugitive from a Chain Gang*

Humphrey Bogart's Wives

Of Humphrey Bogart's four wives, the last surviving is actress and costar **Lauren Bacall.** Married to Bogart from 1945 until his death in 1957, she celebrated her 84th birthday in 2008. Bacall was born Betty Joan Perske in New York City in 1924. After high school, she studied at the American Academy of Dramatic Arts and then went into modeling. A *Harper's Bazaar* cover led to a screen test, which in turn led to work in a wide range of movies. She acted with her husband in such films as *To Have and Have Not, The Big Sleep, Dark Passage,* and *Key Largo.* She performed on her own in such movies as *How to Marry a Millionaire, Murder on the Orient Express, The Fan,* and *My Fellow Americans.*

The Hope-Crosby "Road" Pictures

Bob Hope (1903–2003), Bing Crosby (1903–77), and Dorothy Lamour (1914–96) made seven "Road" movies together. The movies were so named because each was set in a different exotic location.

Hope, who also was famous for entertaining U.S. troops during wartime, was the last to die, on July 27, 2003, at age 100.

The "Road" pictures were:

- *Road to Singapore* (1940)
- *Road to Zanzibar* (1941)
- *Road to Morocco* (1942)
- *Road to Utopia* (1946)
- *Road to Rio* (1947)
- *Road to Bali* (1952)
- *Road to Hong Kong* (1962)

The Dead End Kids

The Dead End Kids got their start in the Broadway play *Dead End,* which was about New York tenement life in the 1930s. When Sam Goldwyn decided to produce a film based on the play in 1937, he recruited Humphrey Bogart and the young Broadway actors.

Bernard Punsly was the last surviving member of the Dead End Kids. He appeared in 19 of the movies before leaving the film industry in 1943 to join the army. After World War II, he entered medical school at the University of Georgia and eventually served as chief of medicine at a Los Angeles hospital. Punsly died at 80 in Torrance, California, on January 20, 2004.

Superman Creators

Superman brought adventures of "Good versus Evil" to young and old through popular comic books. Successful Superman movies and television shows followed. The character was created by artist Joe Shuster (1914–92) and writer **Jerry Siegel** (1914–96). Siegel, the last living cocreator, died on January 28, 1996, at age 81.

Batman Creators

The heroic characters of Batman and his sidekick, Robin, were created by artist **Bob Kane** (1916–98) and writer Bill Finger (1914–74). Kane, the last survivor, passed away on November 3, 1998.

Disney's "Nine Old Men"

The top Walt Disney Studios animators responsible for feature-length cartoons were known as Disney's "nine old men." The last living of the nine, **Ollie Johnston,** did key animation work on *Snow White, Pinocchio, Fantasia, Bambi, Cinderella, Alice in Wonderland, Peter Pan, Sleeping Beauty, 101 Dalmatians, The Jungle Book,* and more. He was proudest of his work on *Bambi.* Johnston died in 2008 at age 95.

Hanna-Barbera

Cartoon writer William Hanna (1910–2001) and artist **Joseph Barbera** (1911–2006) started their partnership at MGM Studios in the 1930s, but it wasn't until the 1960s that their names became household words.

Hanna-Barbera Productions' cartoon creations included *Tom and Jerry, The Flintstones, The Jetsons, Yogi Bear, Huckleberry Hound,* and *Scooby-Doo.* The last survivor was Barbera, who passed away on December 18, 2006, at age 95.

The Cannes Film Festival

Eleven films won the feature film Grand Prix award at the first Cannes Film Festival in 1946. The last surviving of the directors of these films was **Jean Delannoy,** who won for *La symphonie pastorale.* Starting his career as an actor in silent films, Delannoy turned to editing (he worked at Paramount's Paris office) and then to directing.

During the 1950s, Delannoy drew ire from both modernists and conservatives. French New Wave critics viewed his work as too mainstream and boring, while traditionalists found his films (particularly *L'éternel retour* and *Le garçon savage)* too provocative. Most critics, however, praise Delannoy for such films as *La Symphonie pastorale, L'éternel retour, Les Jeux sont faits,* and *Dieu a besoin des homes*. Still directing films in the 1990s, Delannoy passed away in 2008 at age 100.

* * * *

"Censorship believes it has protected youth's soul, whereas it has, at one and the same time, done it violence and dulled it."

—Jean Delannoy

* * * *

The Tonys

The Tony Awards, which recognize excellence in the theater, were first given in 1947. Of the six people who won major acting awards, **Patricia Neal** was the only one still alive in 2009.

Born Patsy Louise Neal in Knoxville, Tennessee, in 1926, Neal became interested in performing after appearing in functions at her local church. She attended Northwestern University for two years and then moved to New York. After settling in there, she began calling herself Patricia. She got her start performing on stage then began appearing in movies.

She married writer Roald Dahl in 1953 (they divorced in 1983). Patricia Neal is an esteemed actress, but she also became noted for her resilience after experiencing several personal tragedies. An accident forced her son, Theo, to undergo intense rehabilitation while he was still just an infant. Neal and Dahl lost their oldest daughter, Olivia, when she contracted measles encephalitis at just seven years old. At age 39 in 1965, Neal suffered three debilitating strokes. Her husband coached her through her rehabilitation, and she eventually returned to acting.

The following were the first Tony Award winners:

- Actor (dramatic): Fredric March (1897–1975), for *Years Ago*
- Actress (dramatic): Ingrid Bergman (1915–82), for *Joan of Lorraine*
- Actor (dramatic): Jose Ferrer (1909–92), for *Cyrano de Bergerac*
- Actress (dramatic): Helen Hayes (1900–93), for *Happy Birthday*
- Actor, supporting or featured (musical): David Wayne (1914–95), for *Finian's Rainbow*
- Actress, supporting or featured (dramatic): Patricia Neal (1926–), for *Another Part of the Forest*

* * * *

The February 22, 1965, Variety *headline mistakenly reported that Patricia Neal had died as a result of the strokes she had suffered.*

* * * *

Patricia Neal was pregnant when she suffered her strokes. Her daughter Lucy was born healthy six months later.

* * * *

Patricia Neal won the Best Actress Academy Award in 1963 for her performance in Hud.

* * * *

Winners of the Best Actor Oscar Before 1960

The last living male who won a Best Actor Academy Award prior to 1960 is **Ernest Borgnine.** He won his Oscar for the title role in 1955's *Marty.* Borgnine turned 92 in 2009.

Winners of the Best Actress in a Musical Tony Award Before 1960

The last living winner of a Best Actress in a Musical Tony Award prior to 1960 is **Nanette Fabray.** The winner of the 1949 award for *Love Life,* she turned 88 in 2008.

Winners of the Best Director Oscar Before 1970

The last surviving person to win a Best Director Academy Award prior to 1970 is **Mike Nichols.** He won his Oscar in 1968 for *The Graduate,* starring Dustin Hoffman, Anne Bancroft, and Katharine Ross. In 2008, at age 77, Nichols directed the popular film *Charlie Wilson's War.*

Winners of the Best Actor Tony Award Before 1970

The last living person who won the Best Actor Tony Award prior to 1970 is **Robert Morse** for *How to Succeed in Business Without Really Trying*. He turned 78 in 2009.

The Barrymore Siblings

Siblings John (1882–1942), Lionel (1878–1954), and **Ethel Barrymore** (1879–1959) made up one of the most famous Golden Age of Hollywood acting families. Lionel and Ethel are the only brother and sister to win Academy Awards for acting. Ethel, who passed away in 1959, was the last to die.

* * * *

Contemporary actress Drew Barrymore is John Barrymore's granddaughter.

* * * *

Hopalong Cassidy Sidekicks

Hopalong Cassidy, who was portrayed by former silent film leading man William Boyd, was one of the most popular western characters of the 1930s, 1940s, and 1950s. Throughout many movies and television series episodes, Boyd had many different sidekicks, including the legendary old codger "Gabby" Hayes and George Reeves, the future TV Superman. **Rand Brooks,** who played sidekick Lucky Jenkins in a dozen films, was the last surviving sidekick when he passed away in 2003. Before the Hopalong years, he played Charles Hamilton, Scarlett O'Hara's first husband in *Gone With the Wind.* In later years he owned the largest private ambulance company in Los Angeles.

Hopalong Cassidy's sidekicks were:

- George Reeves (1914–59)
- Jay Kirby (1920–64)

- Britt Wood (1885–1965)
- Andy Clyde (1892–1967)
- George "Gabby" Hayes (1885–1969)
- Edgar Buchanan (1903–79)
- Russell Hayden (1912–81)
- Brad King (1917–91)
- Jimmy Ellison (1910–93)
- Jimmy Rogers (1915–2000)
- Rand Brooks (1918–2003)

Judy Garland's Husbands

Of singer and actress Judy Garland's (1922–69) five marriages, the one between 1952 and 1965 to producer **Sidney Luft** was the longest and produced two children. Luft, who also produced Garland's 1954 movie *A Star Is Born,* died on September 15, 2005, at age 89.

The First Top Actors Who Were Knighted

Sir Alec Guinness died on August 5, 2000, outliving his mentor, Sir John Gielgud, by a little more than two months—the last surviving British actor to have been knighted before 1960.

Guinness was born in London in 1914 to Agnes Cuffe, a single mother. The identity of his father is a matter of dispute. Guinness believed that his father was Andrew Geddes, a banker. Others speculated that he may have been the son of Walter Guinness, of the Guinness brewing family.

Alec Guinness grew up quite poor but was able to begin attending boarding school at age six (most surmise this schooling was paid for by Andrew Geddes). Guinness was drawn to drama in school but could not afford to continue taking classes. At age 18 he began working as a copywriter at an advertising agency and then obtained a two-year scholarship to the Fay Compton Studio of Dramatic Art. After those two years, he started performing at a small theater, then—at age 24—he won the lead role in London's Old Vic Theatre production of *Hamlet*.

Guinness joined the Royal Navy in 1941. After the war, he went back to the stage, and then he began acting in films. Many fans revere Guinness for his role as Obi-Wan Kenobi in the *Star Wars* films.

The following were the first top actors who were knighted:

- Sir Ralph Richardson (1902–83) was knighted in 1947.
- Sir Michael Redgrave (1908–85) was knighted in 1959.
- Sir Laurence Olivier (1907–89) was knighted in 1947.
- Sir John Gielgud (1904–May 21, 2000) was knighted in 1953.
- Sir Alec Guinness (1914–August 5, 2000) was knighted in 1959.

The Rat Pack

Frank Sinatra's Rat Pack was comprised of five entertainers who performed together in Las Vegas in the 1960s and starred in the hit movie *Ocean's Eleven.* It consisted of: Peter Lawford (1923–84), Sammy Davis Jr. (1925–90), Dean Martin (1917–95), Frank Sinatra (1915–98), and **Joey Bishop** (1918–2007).

Bishop, who passed away on October 17, 2007, was the last surviving member of the Rat Pack. In the 1960s, Bishop starred in two television shows, a situation comedy and a talk show. *Who Wants to Be a Millionaire*'s Regis Philbin served in the latter as Bishop's sidekick.

Marilyn Monroe's Husbands

The last surviving husband of actress Marilyn Monroe was **James Dougherty,** who died in 2005 at age 84. He became a Los Angeles detective after their marriage. The following were Marilyn Monroe's husbands:

- James Dougherty (1921–August 15, 2005), married 1942–46
- Joe DiMaggio (1914–99), married 1954
- Arthur Miller (1915–February 10, 2005), married 1956–61

The Gabors

Long-time Hollywood celebrity **Zsa Zsa Gabor** is the last surviving Gabor sister. The Gabor sisters include

- Eva Gabor (1919–95), costar of the 1960s *Green Acres* television series
- Magda Gabor (1914–97)
- Zsa Zsa Gabor (1917–), star of *Moulin Rouge* (1952); more recently appeared in *Naked Gun 2½: The Smell of Fear* (1991)

Portrayers of Superman in Movies

Superman, who came from another planet to help the world fight crime, was portrayed by several actors over the years. The last living movie Superman is **Brandon Routh.**

The following actors have portrayed Superman in movies:

- George Reeves (1914–59) of *Superman and the Mole Men* (1951)
- Kirk Alyn (1910–99) of *Superman* (1948)
- Christopher Reeve (1952–2004) of *Superman* (1978), *Superman II* (1980), *Superman III* (1983), and *Superman IV: The Quest for Peace* (1987)
- Brandon Routh (1979–) of *Superman Returns* (2006)

Laurel & Hardy

Stan Laurel (1890–1965) and Oliver Hardy (1892–1957) made more than 100 comedy films together from the 1920s through the 1950s. Laurel played a naive, accommodating simpleton, while Hardy had big plans that always went awry. Laurel lived to age 74 and was the final living member of this memorable team.

George Burns and Gracie Allen

George Burns (1896–1996) and Gracie Allen (1895–1964) were married in 1926 and performed together for decades in vaudeville, radio, movies, and television. After Gracie's death in 1964, George continued to perform but never remarried. George Burns did reach his 100th birthday, though he was not able to hold the special performance in London that he had planned.

Abbott & Costello

One of the most popular comedy acts of vaudeville, radio, movies, and television, Abbott & Costello performed the world-famous "Who's on first?" routine. **Bud Abbott** (1895–1974) lived until age 78 and outlived Lou Costello (1906–59) by 15 years.

Martin & Lewis

After the comedy team's success in the early 1950s, Dean Martin (1917–95) and **Jerry Lewis** (1926–) broke up, with Martin beginning his highly successful television variety show and Lewis starring in movies. The last survivor, Jerry Lewis, was still active in charity work as of 2009 and received the Jean Hersholt Humanitarian Award at the 2009 Oscars.

Actors Nominated for Oscars for Portrayals of Henry VIII

A handful of actors have received Academy Award nominations for portrayals of English King Henry VIII. The last survivor was **Richard Burton,** who died in 1984 at age 58.

Actors nominated for Academy Award performances for Henry VIII were:

- Charles Laughton (1899–1962) won the Best Actor award for 1932/1933's *The Private Life of Henry VIII.*
- Robert Shaw (1927–78) was nominated for Best Actor in a Supporting Role in 1966's *A Man for All Seasons.*
- Richard Burton (1925–84) was nominated for Best Actor in 1969's *Anne of the Thousand Days.*

John Wayne "Killers"

Actor John Wayne's character was killed several times in movies, but only twice was he killed by identifiable actors: Bruce Dern's character in *The Cowboys* (1972) and the bartender played by Charles G. Martin in *The Shootist* (1976). Martin died in 1998, leaving Dern the last living identifiable actor to kill John Wayne in a movie. **Bruce Dern** was alive at age 72 in 2009.

* * * *

Bruce Dern's father, John, was Adlai Stevenson's law partner. His grandfather was governor of Utah and also served as secretary of war under Franklin Delano Roosevelt.

* * * *

Laura Dern, star of such movies as Blue Velvet, Wild at Heart, Rambling Rose, *and* Jurassic Park, *is Bruce Dern's daughter.*

* * * *

The TV Hall of Fame

The National Academy of Television Arts and Sciences conducted its first Hall of Fame inductions in 1984. Of the seven people selected that year, only **Norman Lear** was still living in 2009. The producer of such hit sitcoms as *All in the Family, Sanford and Son, The Jeffersons,* and *Good Times,* Lear turned 86 in 2008.

The following individuals were also inducted into the National Academy of Television Arts and Sciences Hall of Fame in 1984:

- Edward R. Murrow (1908–65)
- David Sarnoff (1891–1971)
- Paddy Chayefsky (1923–81)
- Lucille Ball (1911–89)
- William S. Paley (1901–90)
- Milton Berle (1908--2002)

Lucille Ball

Military History

❑ ❑ ❑ ❑

Did the Rough Riders actually ride *in Cuba?*
Why was the USS Panay *patrolling the Yangtze River in 1937?*
What was the goal of Operation Redwing?
This chapter answers these questions and more!

U.S. Veterans of the War of 1812

Why did America declare war on Great Britain in 1812? The Napoleonic Wars were still going on, with all British resources stretched to rupturing against France. When American ships defied the British embargo on French trade, British vessels seized U.S. ships and shanghaied their sailors into His Majesty's Navy. Many who remembered the Revolution felt George III needed a refresher course in "Respect for Our Former Colonists." On June 18, 1812, President James Madison signed a declaration of war against Great Britain.

Combat went on for three years in three main theatres: the Atlantic, the Deep South, and the Canadian border/Great Lakes. Most American incursions into Canada met with failure, but U.S. troops managed to burn the Parliament buildings at York (now Toronto). In reprisal, the British landed near Washington, D.C., and burned the White House and congressional buildings. The British also armed and encouraged restive Native Americans against the United States, leading to sporadic fighting. By 1815, with Napoleon defeated in Europe, both American and British sides realized that neither could win. They ended the war with a return to the prewar status quo.

About 286,000 soldiers served on the American side. According to the U.S. Department of Veterans Affairs, the last living U.S. veteran of the War of 1812 was **Hiram Cronk,** who died on May 13, 1905, at age 105. He was about 15 years old when the gunfire quieted down in 1815.

* * * *

The White House caught fire again on Christmas Eve 1929, while President Hoover was hosting a children's party. This time the culprit was a chimney flue. Given that the building has more than two dozen wood-burning fireplaces, it's a wonder more fires haven't started over the years. This one gutted the Oval Office and the West Wing.

* * * *

The Battle of Lake Erie

On September 10, 1813, an American flotilla under Commodore Oliver H. Perry faced a British flotilla off modern Sandusky, Ohio, for control of the Great Lakes. The fleets were tiny, but neither side had anything larger available in Lake Erie.

The Americans' shorter-range but heavier cannon dictated the need to fight the British at close quarters. Perry's flagship, USS *Lawrence,* ran a gauntlet of British cannon fire to close with HMS *Detroit,* while her comrade USS *Niagara* at first failed to close with her own designated target, HMS *Queen Charlotte.* When *Lawrence* was beaten to a pulp, Perry transferred his flag to *Niagara.* Crashing the British line in *Niagara,* Perry cut loose with both broadsides. *Queen Charlotte* and *Detroit* collided in the confusion, hampering their ability to return effective fire. After three hours of battle, the British struck their colors and were captured.

The Battle of Lake Erie was a major victory on the northern front in the War of 1812. It led to the recapture of Detroit (which had been taken by the British in August 1812) and forced the combined British and Native American forces (led by British General Procter and the Shawnee Chief Tecumseh) to flee to Canada.

The battle's last survivor was **Stephen Champlin,** Perry's cousin and the skipper of the schooner USS *Scorpion*. Crippled for life by a grapeshot volley while blockading Mackinac, Michigan, in 1814, Champlin served in the Navy until 1855. He became commodore on the retired list in 1862 and died in 1870 at age 80.

* * * *

"We have met the enemy, and they are ours. Two ships, two brigs, one schooner, and one sloop."

—Commodore Oliver H. Perry (to General William Henry Harrison after the Battle of Lake Erie)

* * * *

The Battle of Lake Champlain

Commodore Thomas McDonough led the American forces that defeated the British on Lake Champlain. **Hiram Paulding** was an acting lieutenant aboard the *Ticonderoga.* After an active career as a naval officer, he was given command of the Navy Yard in New York City at the start of the Civil War and was promoted to rear admiral in 1862. Paulding died on October 20, 1878, at age 81.

* * * *

Francis Scott Key wrote "The Star-Spangled Banner" after the Americans won the Battle of Baltimore in the War of 1812.

* * * *

Widows of U.S. War of 1812 Veterans

The U.S. Department of Veterans Affairs recognizes **Carolina King,** who died on June 28, 1936, as the last widow of an American veteran of the War of 1812.

Dependents of U.S. Veterans of the War of 1812

Esther A. H. Morgan died on March 12, 1946, at age 89. She is recognized by the U.S. Department of Veterans Affairs as the last dependent of an American War of 1812 veteran.

U.S. Officers of the War of 1812

The War of 1812 officially ended with the signing of the Treaty of Ghent in 1815. Captain **Walter Bicker** was the last surviving officer of the regular army who took part in the war. Born in New York City in 1796, Bicker joined the army as a lieutenant when he was 17 years old. He fought in the Battle of Plattsburgh. Bicker stayed in the army after the war and resigned in 1840. He passed away in 1886 in Far Rockaway, Long Island, at age 90.

The Battle of the Alamo

The siege of Alamo Mission, San Antonio de Valero, Republic of Texas, from February 23 to March 6, 1836, was part of Mexico's effort to subdue an insurgency. The Alamo Mission itself wasn't much of a fort, but General Antonio López de Santa Anna had to capture it if he wished to put down the Texan rebellion. Some 180 or so defenders, plus noncombatant women and children, holed up in the mission under Colonel William Travis, who hoped for reinforcements but got none.

On March 6, Santa Anna's numerically superior forces stormed the Alamo Mission, capturing it within three hours and ultimately killing (in some cases, executing) all its defenders, including Davy Crockett and Jim Bowie. The exact number of Mexican casualties is unknown but is estimated to have been about triple the Texan losses. The battle became one of history's great rallying cries, especially for the Texans, who avenged the Alamo six weeks later in the surprise attack at San Jacinto.

Not all the occupants of the Alamo perished; some noncombatants lived to describe the experience firsthand. One-year-old **Alejo Pérez Jr.** brought into the Alamo Mission by his mother, was too young to remember the battle. He survived it, later becoming a San Antonio police officer and then a city official. He almost lived to see World War I end, dying October 19, 1918, at age 83.

The Battle of San Jacinto

On April 21, 1836, less than two months after the fall of the Alamo and the death of its Texan defenders, General Sam Houston, with 900 soldiers, fought the 1,200-strong Mexican army under General Antonio López de Santa Anna. It was here that cries of "Remember the Alamo!" inspired soldiers.

The Battle of San Jacinto lasted only 18 minutes and resulted in the defeat of the Mexican forces, the capture of Santa Anna, and the effective end of the Texan rebellion. Only nine of Houston's soldiers were killed.

The last Texan survivor of the battle was **John Pickering,** who died on February 4, 1917, at age 99—more than 80 years after the battle.

U.S. Veterans of the Mexican War

According to the U.S. Department of Veterans Affairs, the last American veteran of the more than 78,000 who served in the Mexican War (1846–48) was Philadelphian **Owen Thomas Edgar,** who died on September 3, 1929, at age 98. Edgar served as a private aboard the *Potomac* and was about 17 years old at the end of hostilities.

Widows of U.S. Veterans of the Mexican War

Lena James Theobald, who died on June 20, 1963, at age 89, was the last widow of an American veteran of the Mexican War.

Dependents of U.S. Veterans of the Mexican War

The U.S. Department of Veterans Affairs has identified **Jesse G. Bivens** as the last living dependent of a U.S. Mexican War veteran. Bivens died on November 1, 1962, at age 94.

Veterans of the Indian Wars

Officially, the Indian Wars took place between 1817 and 1898. They included the Sioux wars, the Southern Plains conflicts, the Nez Percé War, and the Apache campaign.

The U.S. Department of Veterans Affairs recognizes the last veteran of those wars to be **Frederick Fraske,** who was born in Posen, Germany, in 1872. Fraske moved to Chicago with his parents and four brothers in 1877. He joined the army in 1894 to help his widowed mother. Fraske was assigned to Fort D. A. Russell in Cheyenne, Wyoming, and during his time there he was a letter carrier and helped with first aid.

Fraske was discharged after three years and three months of service. In later years he said he was glad he never had to battle any Native Americans during his time in service because he bore them no ill will and understood their plight. After his discharge, Fraske returned to Chicago and worked as a painter. He went into forced retirement at age 65 because climbing scaffolds was considered too dangerous for someone his age. After his retirement, Fraske worked as a security guard. He died in 1973 at age 101 and is buried in Niles, Illinois.

The Rough Riders

No Spanish-American War regiment is better known than the 1st U.S. Volunteer Cavalry (USVC): the "Rough Riders." Commanded primarily by Theodore Roosevelt, they distinguished themselves by their charge in the Battle of San Juan Hill in Cuba. Remembering his Dakota days, Roosevelt recruited mostly frontiersmen, athletes, and good marksmen for the 1st USVC.

What they did not do, however, was ride. There wasn't enough transport space for their horses, so the 1st USVC ran on foot up Kettle and San Juan hills.

To Roosevelt, the war was "bully": a grand, masculine adventure that also met a national need for a unifying conflict. Though the Rough Riders and their leader undoubtedly fought well in Cuba against some very determined Spanish defenders (who rarely get fair credit), they garnered outsize media attention. Unique, sexy, led by a flamboyant volunteer colonel—the Rough Riders were proved brave by their deeds, but the newspapers made them famous.

Jesse Langdon, the last living Rough Rider, died in 1975.

Buffalo Soldiers

Several African American regiments fought in the Spanish-American War. The 9th and 10th U.S. Cavalry, best known as the "Buffalo Soldiers," endured enormous bigotry in the service despite their proud reputation for valor and skill. They wrote one of their story's finest chapters in Cuba.

At San Juan Hill, war's confusion achieved in minutes what took Congress nearly a century: integration. Rough Riders, Buffalo Soldiers, and regular white troopers got mixed together in the jungle fighting. When you're thirsty, all canteens are the same color, and the Buffalo Soldiers shared fair credit for a key victory at San Juan Hill.

Australian Victoria Cross Recipients for Boer War Service

Six Australian men received the Victoria Cross for service during the Boer War. The last surviving was Lieutenant **Guy George Egerton Wylly.** On September 1, 1900, while wounded, he risked his own life to save one of his men. Lieutenant Wylly died in 1962 at age 81.

The USS *Panay*

Beginning in 1914, the U.S. Navy maintained a gunboat patrol to protect U.S. commerce and nationals on the Yangtze River. When Imperial Japan invaded the Chinese Republic in 1937, Western garrison troops and watercraft found themselves neutrals in a war zone.

As relations between the United States and Japan deteriorated, their presence grew more awkward. Even so, the Japanese tried hard to avoid incidents with Western garrisons—with one noteworthy exception.

On December 12, 1937, Japanese aircraft bombed and sank the Yangtze Patrol gunboat USS *Panay* off Nanjing, China. One officer, one enlisted soldier, and an Italian journalist died. Aircraft returned to sink two of the three tankers *Panay* had been escorting, and that day Japanese artillery shelled two British Yangtze River patrol boats.

American public opinion and the Franklin Roosevelt administration exploded in outrage. The Japanese fell all over themselves to apologize for the "mistake," but no one believed them. Even had U.S. cryptographers not decoded some Japanese messages proving the attack's deliberateness, Japan could not explain away a sudden attack against multiple ships (with which they were surely well acquainted). Why, then, did they do it? To test Western resolve? As a stern warning to stay out of Japan's way? More than 70 years later, speculation still thrives, but no one really knows.

Panay's last survivor, **Fon Huffman,** died at age 95 on September 4, 2008. After giving his lifebelt to a fellow survivor, Huffman paddled ashore on a mattress.

The Nanjing Massacre

The day after the *Panay* incident, Japanese forces followed the capture of Nanjing with an orgy of rape, robbery, torture, arson, and murder that shocked the world. However, it made less impact on U.S. public opinion than it deserved, partly due to China's extreme distance from America, and partly due to basic racism. Most European Americans of the day hardly saw Asians as equals.

The massacre itself lasted approximately two months. The photographs and contemporary eyewitness accounts that survive are graphic and detail a pattern of wanton sadism and murder, with women in particular singled out. The Japanese version was that they were rooting out enemy combatants, but since there's no record of China organizing military units composed of pregnant women or toddlers, that explanation doesn't hold water. We'll never know the final death toll, but it certainly reached into the hundreds of thousands.

• •

Australian Victoria Cross Recipients for Vietnam War Service

Keith Payne's battalion was attacked by a much larger North Vietnamese force on May 24, 1969. Although wounded in several places by shrapnel, Keith Payne led about 40 soldiers back to safety. He had those who were not wounded carry those who were on their backs as they crawled out to safety. He and World War II Private **Edward Kenna** were the only Australian recipients of the Victoria Cross still living as of 2009.

Operation Redwing

In June 2005, four U.S. Navy SEALs were sent on Operation Redwing, a mission to locate and capture or kill Taliban leader Ahmad Shah, who was believed to be in eastern Afghanistan. The four SEALs were Lieutenant Michael Murphy and Petty Officers Matthew Axelson, Danny Dietz, and **Marcus Luttrell.**

Once they reached Afghanistan, the SEALs were in the mountains, surveying the village below for signs of Shah. While there, they encountered three goat herders. Shortly after this encounter, the SEALs found themselves surrounded by dozens of Taliban fighters. Murphy, Axelson, and Dietz were killed in the firefight that followed. A helicopter coming to the SEALs' rescue was shot down with 16 Americans aboard, and all 16 died.

Luttrell was badly wounded but survived. Three villagers found him, carried him to their hut, nursed him, and hid him from the Taliban. Days later, the villagers contacted a U.S. military outpost nearby and helped U.S. forces rescue Luttrell. Awarded the Navy Cross in 2006, Luttrell turned 33 in 2008.

U.S. Presidents

❑ ❑ ❑ ❑

How did the Smithsonian Institution come into existence?
Which president defended the Amistad *rebels?*
Why was Lincoln's body exhumed in 1901?
You need look no further than this chapter to find out.

Artists Who Painted George Washington from Life

George Washington was painted from life numerous times. **Rembrandt Peale** (1778–1860), the last surviving major artist to paint Washington from life, was the son of another noted painter, Charles Willson Peale (1741–1827). Charles had already painted Washington six times by 1795, when he arranged for his son to paint the president while he painted next to him. (Rembrandt was nervous about painting the president, and having his father next to him helped calm him.) The younger Peale was just 17 years old. Washington was 63, and he died four years later.

The following were other major artists who painted George Washington from life:

- Robert Edge Pine (1730–88)
- Joseph Wright (1756–93)
- Charles Peale Polk (1767–1822)
- Gilbert Stuart (1755–1828)
- James Peale (1749–1831)
- John Trumbull (1756–1843)

* * * *

Gilbert Stuart's portrait of Washington is considered the "standard likeness," but Rembrandt Peale's painting in the Senate is also highly regarded.

* * * *

* * * *

"The likeness in features is striking, and the Character of the whole face is preserved & exhibited with wonderful Accuracy. It is more Washington himself than any Portrait of him I have ever seen."

—Chief Justice John Marshall,
on Rembrandt Peale's portrait of Washington

* * * *

Washington's Electors

In the first and second presidential elections, George Washington was elected by the unanimous vote of the Electoral College. The last surviving elector from the first, in 1789, was **Robert Smith** of Maryland. A veteran of the Battle of Brandywine in 1777, he went on to become Thomas Jefferson's secretary of the Navy and James Madison's secretary of state. Smith died in 1842 at age 85.

Washington's Cabinets

In 1795, Alexander Hamilton resigned his position as secretary of the Treasury because he wanted to devote more time and energy to his law practice. To continue Hamilton's financial programs, President George Washington chose **Oliver Wolcott Jr.** to replace Hamilton. At the end of Washington's administration, Wolcott was retained by John Adams and served until 1800. In later years, Wolcott went on to several terms as governor of Connecticut. The last living member of Washington's cabinet, Wolcott was 73 when he died in 1833.

Washington's Children

Although he had no natural children, George Washington had two stepchildren, **John Parke Custis** and Patsy Custis, from Martha Washington's first marriage. Martha had married Colonel Daniel Parke Custis in 1750, but he died in 1757, when Martha was 26. Martha then married George Washington in 1759.

The last survivor of the two children was John Parke Custis. Custis married Eleanor Calvert in 1774, and they had five children. After serving on Washington's staff at the Battle of Yorktown, Custis contracted typhoid fever and died on November 5, 1781.

* * * *

Patsy Custis died after suffering an epileptic seizure at age 17 in 1773.

* * * *

One of Martha Washington's descendants, Martha Custis Lee, was the wife of famed Confederate general Robert E. Lee. Part of Lee's inheritance from the Custises included an estate called Arlington, which was seized by the U.S. government during the Civil War and turned into Arlington National Cemetery.

* * * *

The Democratic-Republican Party

The name of the Democratic-Republican Party, which held the presidency from 1801 to 1829, now sounds like a contradiction in terms. It was the party of Thomas Jefferson and James Madison, founded in the early 1790s to oppose Alexander Hamilton's Federalist Party. Members of the party first called themselves "Republicans" to stress their antimonarchical stance. Federalists began to call their opponents "Democratic-Republicans" to stress their sympathies with the French Revolution, and the Republicans eventually came to refer to themselves the same way.

Neither modern major party really encompasses the core issues of the Democratic-Republican Party. Its members believed in literal constitutional interpretation and states' rights (as opposed to a strong federal government). The party favored the interests of workers and farmers, was unfriendly to banking and mercantile interests, and abhorred national debt. Its foreign policy generally took the side of the French in the ongoing Franco-British squabbles.

During the John Quincy Adams administration (1825–29), the Democratic-Republican Party gradually split into National Republican and Democratic factions. John Quincy Adams, the last Democratic-Republican president, ran on the National Republican ticket when he lost his 1828 reelection bid.

• •

John Adams's Cabinet

During the Revolutionary War, **John Marshall** served under General George Washington at Brandywine, Germantown, Valley Forge, and Monmouth. Marshall, a Federalist, was elected to represent Virginia in the U.S. Congress in 1799, and he served 15 months. In 1800, President John Adams appointed him secretary of state, and he served nine months there before Adams appointed him Chief Justice of the United States Supreme Court in 1801. He served in that position for 34 years.

Marshall presided over seven presidential inaugurations, from Thomas Jefferson to Andrew Jackson. Because of his influence in shaping the nature of the U.S. judicial system, he is considered by many to be history's most influential U.S. Supreme Court justice. When Marshall died in 1835 at age 79, all of Adams's other cabinet members had already passed away.

Children of John Adams

Of John and Abigail Adams's four children, the last living was **John Quincy Adams,** who served as the sixth president of the United States and then as a member of the House of Representatives. On February 21, 1848, he suffered a stroke while rising from his desk in the House of Representatives. He died two days later in the chambers of the Speaker of the House at age 80.

Election of 1804

In 1804, with the nation enjoying prosperity, president **Thomas Jefferson** easily won reelection over Federalist Charles Cotesworth Pinckney (1746–1825), a former minister to France. Jefferson was the last survivor of the 1804 electoral candidates, but only by 11 months.

Jefferson's Cabinet

Albert Gallatin was born in Geneva, Switzerland, in 1761. He immigrated to the United States in 1780 and served in the Revolutionary army. He was a member of the House of Representatives from 1795 to 1801 and constantly fought with Alexander Hamilton, the secretary of the Treasury.

Gallatin went on to serve as secretary of the Treasury under President Thomas Jefferson from 1801 to 1809, and under President James Madison from 1809 to 1814. During his tenure, he initiated the practice of providing Congress with detailed reports of the country's financial status. He also helped create the House Ways and Means Committee to ensure that the Treasury was held accountable by Congress.

After his cabinet service, Gallatin served as United States envoy extraordinary and minister plenipotentiary to France (1815–23), minister plenipotentiary to Great Britain (1826–27), and president of the National Bank of New York. In 1814, Albert Gallatin was one of the commissioners who negotiated the Treaty of Ghent that ended the War of 1812. In 1843, President John Tyler offered Gallatin his old position as secretary of the Treasury; however, the 82-year-old declined. When Gallatin passed away on August 12, 1849, at age 88, he was the last of Jefferson's cabinet secretaries.

Children of Thomas Jefferson

Thomas Jefferson's wife was Martha Wayles Skelton. Her first husband was Bathurst Skelton, but he died in 1768, after they had been married just two years. Martha Wayles Skelton and Thomas Jefferson were married in 1772. She had six children in the next ten years, but only two, **Martha Jefferson** and Mary Jefferson, lived past childhood. Martha Wayles Skelton Jefferson passed away in 1782, and Thomas Jefferson became president 19 years later.

The last living of Jefferson's six children was daughter Martha (1772–1836). Martha married Thomas Mann Randolph in 1790, and they had 11 children.

* * * *

Martha Jefferson Randolph's eighth child, James Madison Randolph, was born in the White House in 1806. He was the first child to be born there.

* * * *

Election of 1808

With the support of Thomas Jefferson, Democratic-Republican **James Madison** (1751–1836) beat Federalist Charles Cotesworth Pinckney (1746–1825). James Madison was the last survivor of the two candidates of the 1808 election.

Election of 1812

Although earlier in the year Democratic-Republican **James Madison** (1751–1836) had recommended war against Great Britain, he still won reelection. He also outlived Federalist/Peace candidate DeWitt Clinton (1769–1828).

* * * *

DeWitt Clinton is often called the Father of the Erie Canal because he was a strong proponent of the canal, which linked the East Coast to the Midwest.

* * * *

Madison's Cabinet

The last surviving member of James Madison's cabinet was Attorney General **Richard Rush.** In later years, he was secretary of the Treasury in President John Quincy Adams's administration, vice presidential running mate to Adams in his unsuccessful reelection campaign, a commissioner to England for President Andrew Jackson, and minister to France for President James K. Polk. Rush passed away on July 30, 1859, at age 78—41 years after his service in Madison's cabinet.

At President Jackson's request, Rush represented British scientist James Smithson's estate in the British Chancery Court. Smithson's will stipulated that his estate was to go to the United States to found "an establishment for the increase and diffusion of knowledge among men." On his return to the United States in 1838, Rush carried with him 11 boxes filled with $508,318 worth of British gold coins. This money was used to establish the Smithsonian Institution.

James Smithson

Scientist James Smithson (1765–1829) distinguished himself by bequeathing $508,318 to the U.S. government. As a research chemist, geologist, and mineralogist, the French-born blueblood certainly didn't need the money. His fortune had come from an inheritance left to him by his mother, Elizabeth Keate Hungerford Macie, a member of England's royal society. It was Smithson's wish that upon his death the bulk of his estate would pass to his nephew Henry James Hungerford. However, Smithson's will also stipulated that if no further heirs were born, the estate would pass to "the United States of America, to found at Washington, under the name of the Smithsonian Institution, an establishment for the increase and diffusion of knowledge." In 1835, upon Hungerford's passing, Smithson's wish became reality. Though Smithson's philanthropic motives remain unknown, the Smithsonian Institution, aka "our nation's attic," endures as a grand symbol of his generosity.

* * * *

Richard Rush was 33 years old when he began his term as attorney general, qualifying him as the youngest individual ever to serve in that position.

* * * *

Rush was the son of Dr. Benjamin Rush, who signed the Declaration of Independence for Pennsylvania.

* * * *

Presidents Born Under the Julian Calendar

The Julian calendar was used in most of Europe from the time of the Roman Empire until 1582, when Pope Gregory XIII advocated the Gregorian calendar, which is what we use today. The Gregorian version was adopted by most Catholic countries first and Protestant countries years later. When Great Britain and its colonies went to the Gregorian calendar in 1752, the conversion was achieved by omitting the days September 3 through September 13 that year.

James Madison was born in the British colony of Virginia in 1751, the year before the Gregorian calendar was adopted by Great Britain. The last surviving U.S. president to be born under the Julian calendar, Madison died in 1836.

The following presidents were also born under the Julian calendar:

- George Washington (1732–99)
- Thomas Jefferson (1743–1826)
- John Adams (1735–1826)

Why the Switch?

By 46 B.C., the civil calendar year varied considerably from the solar year. Julius Caesar came up with a calendar "patch" to fix it, and it worked... for the most part. By the 1200s, astronomers realized Caesar had been a bit imprecise. The solar year actually consisted of 365.242 days—not the 365.250 days Caesar's calendar allotted. In any given year the discrepancy does not make much difference; by the 1500s, however, the drift had pushed the Christian celebration of Easter (which is observed on the first Sunday after the first full moon after the spring equinox) quite far into the spring. In 1563, the Council of Trent proposed a fix.

The Council decided to drop ten days to correct the drift and to make new rules governing leap years. The new Gregorian calendar would diverge from the Julian at about three days per four centuries.

In 1582, only France, Luxembourg, Spain, Italy, Portugal, and Poland went Gregorian. Other European countries gradually followed suit. Japan did so in 1873, and China switched in 1912. Russia changed in 1918 after the Bolshevik takeover, and Greece changed in 1924.

Election of 1816

During the War of 1812, Democratic-Republican **James Monroe** (1758–1831) served his country as both secretary of war and secretary of state. He won the presidential election of 1816 over Federalist Rufus King (1755–1827) and was the last survivor of the two candidates.

* * * *

By the election of 1820, the Federalist Party was no longer a force in the United States, and Democratic-Republican James Monroe (1758–1831) ran unopposed. With the exception of Washington's two elections, this is the only U.S. presidential election that has been unopposed.

* * * *

Presidents Who Were Veterans of the Revolutionary War

George Washington, who died in 1799, and **James Monroe** were the only presidents who served in a military capacity in the Revolutionary War. Monroe, when a teenager, was a soldier under Washington at the historic crossing of the Delaware River and the subsequent victorious attack on the Hessian encampment at Trenton, New Jersey. Monroe died 31 years after Washington and 48 years after the Treaty of Paris officially ended the war. Like Adams and Jefferson before him, Monroe died on July 4, the anniversary of the signing of the Declaration of Independence. James Monroe was the last surviving person who had been both U.S. president and a veteran of the Revolutionary War.

James Monroe and John Quincy Adams's Cabinets

John McLean holds the distinction of being the last living cabinet member in the administrations of both Monroe and John Quincy Adams, serving as postmaster general under both presidents (1823–29). However, he is best known for his dissent in the Dred Scott case when he was a U.S. Supreme Court justice. He and Benjamin Curtis were the only justices who opposed the pro-slavery decision. After 31 years on the Supreme Court, McLean died on April 4, 1861—eight days before Confederate forces fired on the Union garrison in Fort Sumter and started the Civil War.

Children of James Monroe

Of Monroe's three children, **Maria Hester Monroe** (1803–50) was the last living. She was born in Paris, France, while her father was minister to that country. She married Samuel Lawrence Gouveneur in 1820, and hers was the first wedding to take place in the White House. She and Samuel moved to New York in 1825, after John Quincy Adams appointed Samuel postmaster of New York City. The couple eventually had three children, and Maria's father came and lived with them during his last years.

* * * *

"Monroe was so honest that if you turned his soul inside out there would not be a spot on it."

—Thomas Jefferson

* * * *

Children of John Quincy Adams

Charles Francis Adams, the last surviving son of John Quincy Adams, was born in Boston in 1807. Charles married Abigail Brown Brooks when he was 22 years old, and they had six children. He served in Congress from 1859 until 1861, when Abraham Lincoln appointed him minister to Britain. He later edited the *Life and Works of John Adams* and the *Memoirs of John Quincy Adams*. Charles Frances Adams died in 1886 at age 79.

Saint-Gaudens's Masterpiece

Charles Francis Adams's son Henry married Marian Hooper in 1862. In 1885, Marian became extremely depressed after her father's death, and she committed suicide. Henry Adams was devastated and commissioned sculptor Augustus Saint-Gaudens to create a memorial for her gravesite in Rock Creek Cemetery. Most consider the sculpture to be the artist's masterpiece. It is officially nameless but is commonly called *Grief.*

Presidents Born Under the Flag of Great Britain

John Quincy Adams (1767–1848), who died while serving as a member of Congress in 1848, was the last surviving U.S. president to be born under the British flag. Adams was born in Massachusetts in 1767, nine years before the signing of the Declaration of Independence.

The following were the other U.S. presidents who were born in British colonies:

- George Washington (1732–99)
- Thomas Jefferson (1743–1826)
- John Adams (1735–1826)
- James Monroe (1758–1831)
- James Madison (1751–1836)
- William H. Harrison (1773–1841)
- Andrew Jackson (1767–1845)

Presidents Whose Fathers Signed the Declaration of Independence

Two U.S. presidents' fathers signed the Declaration of Independence: Benjamin Harrison (1726–91), father of William Henry Harrison (1773–1841); and John Adams (1735–1826), father of **John Quincy Adams** (1767–1848). John Quincy Adams, who was nine years old when his father signed the famous document, was the last survivor.

Presidents Who Were Veterans of the War of 1812

Only two presidents served in the War of 1812: William Henry Harrison, who died shortly after election in 1841; and **Andrew Jackson,** who died 30 years after the war ended. Jackson, nationally famous for his role as commander at the Battle of New Orleans (1815), was the last surviving U.S. president who was a veteran of the War of 1812.

Election of 1824

Although Andrew Jackson received a majority of the popular vote and more electoral votes than the other candidates, he did not obtain a *majority* of the electoral votes. The House of Representatives settled the election in favor of John Quincy Adams after candidate **Henry Clay** threw his support to Adams. Clay was the last survivor of the four candidates. A major statesman of his day, he was known as the "Great Compromiser" because of his work in settling disagreements about slavery between the Northern and Southern states.

The following were the 1824 election candidates:

- Democratic-Republican William Crawford (1772–1834)
- Democratic-Republican Andrew Jackson (1767–1845)
- Democratic-Republican John Quincy Adams (1767–1848)
- Democratic-Republican Henry Clay (1777–1852)

Election of 1828

A national hero as the result of the War of 1812, Democratic-Republican Andrew Jackson (1767–1845) won the 1828 presidential election. Democratic-Republican **John Quincy Adams** (1767–1848), however, was the last survivor. Adams, the son of the second U.S. president and an influential antislavery leader, spent his entire life serving his country as diplomat and elected official. One of John Quincy Adams's finest hours was his 1841 Supreme Court defense of the *Amistad* slave ship rebels.

Amistad

In 1839, hundreds of Africans were captured near Sierra Leone and sold as slaves. They were boarded onto a slave ship and brought to Cuba. Once there, they were falsely classified as native Cuban-born slaves; the slave trade was technically illegal in Cuba at the time, but individuals who had been slaves for a long time could still be traded.

A Portuguese trader bought 36 of the slaves, and he had them boarded onto the schooner *La Amistad* to transport them to another port. Three days into the journey, the slaves broke free of their chains and attacked the crew. They spared two Cuban slavers aboard the ship because the Cubans agreed to steer the ship back to Africa. The Cubans initially headed toward Africa, but once it became dark, they gradually turned and headed for the United States.

More than a month later, the ship was found off Long Island by the U.S. Coastal Survey. The Cubans immediately claimed that the Africans were slaves and their property. The Spanish ambassador became involved and demanded the ship be returned to Spain. Abolitionists became involved as well and arranged for a translator to give the Africans' side of the story. The Africans told the translator that they had recently been kidnapped in Africa. The judge decided that the Africans should be freed. The case was appealed, and John Quincy Adams argued the Africans' case before the Supreme Court. He used the principle of habeas corpus in their defense. He argued that if the United States were to turn the Africans over to Spain, it would set a precedent that would threaten the freedom of all. His argument convinced the court, and it ruled in the Africans' favor.

"No Show" Presidents

Only two presidents, John Adams and his son, **John Quincy Adams,** did not attend the inauguration ceremonies of their successors. The last survivor of the two was John Quincy Adams, who refused to attend Andrew Jackson's first inauguration on March 4, 1829.

Fighting Words

The 1828 campaign was a nasty one, mostly because of resentments that remained after the last election, which was between the same individuals. Each opponent hurled incendiary insults at the other. Jackson's supporters claimed that Adams—during his years as a diplomat stationed in Russia—procured an American girl to service the needs of the Russian czar (this charge was completely false). Adams's supporters accused Jackson of adultery and accused Jackson's wife, Rachel, of bigamy because there was some confusion over the timing of her divorce from her first husband. When Rachel suffered a heart attack and died before she could attend his inauguration, a bitter, heartbroken Jackson blamed Adams and his supporters.

Election of 1832

This was the first presidential election where national political conventions chose the candidates. Democratic-Republican Andrew Jackson (1767–1845) won a landslide victory with 219 out of 268 electoral votes. However, Democratic-Republican **Henry Clay** (1777–1852) outlived Jackson by several years.

Jackson and Van Buren's Cabinets

Amos Kendall served as postmaster general for two U.S. presidents: Andrew Jackson (from 1835 to 1837) and Martin Van Buren (from 1837 to 1840). Belonging to the group of President Jackson's closest advisers known as the "Kitchen Cabinet," Kendall was extremely influential in the Jackson administration.

In 1857, Kendall established the Columbia Institution for the Instruction of the Deaf and Dumb and the Blind (today named the Kendall School) in Washington, D.C. The first students at the school were Kendall's five adopted deaf children. When Kendall died in 1869 at age 80, he was the last of Jackson and Van Buren's cabinet secretaries.

Children of Andrew Jackson

Andrew Jackson and his wife, Rachel, never had any children of their own. However, children of friends and relatives lived with the Jacksons at the Hermitage at times.

In 1808, the couple took in Rachel's infant nephew, one of a set of twins. It is unclear exactly why it became necessary for the Jacksons to take him in, but they adopted him and named him **Andrew Jackson Jr.** Although the boy grew up at the Hermitage, he remained close with his twin, who lived nearby. The Jacksons also took in Lyncoya, an orphaned Native American boy, and raised him as their own. Last survivor Andrew Jackson Jr. died as a result of a hunting accident in 1865.

Election of 1836

In this election, the Whig party chose to run three different candidates in different regions of the country. They estimated that their combined electoral votes would give them a majority in the electoral college. However, New Yorker **Martin Van Buren,** the Democratic candidate, won an absolute majority of electoral votes. He also outlived the other three candidates.

The following were the 1836 election candidates:

- Whig Hugh Lawson White (1773–1840)
- Whig William Henry Harrison (1773–1841)
- Whig Daniel Webster (1782–1852)
- Democrat Martin Van Buren (1782–1862)

Children of Martin Van Buren

Of the five Van Buren children, **Smith Thompson Van Buren** (1817–76) was the last to die. Smith Thompson married twice, first to Ellen James in 1842. She died in 1849, and he married Henrietta Eckford in 1855. Smith Thompson had four children from his first marriage and three from his second. He served as an aide to his father and helped write his speeches.

Election of 1840

Whig William Henry Harrison (1773–1841) campaigned as a candidate of the common man and easily won this election. His 8,445-word inaugural address on March 4, 1841, was the longest in history. Unfortunately, Harrison died only one month after his inauguration. Democrat **Martin Van Buren** (1782–1862) outlived him by more than 20 years.

William Henry Harrison and John Tyler's Cabinets

Known for his support of the Whig Party and opposition to slavery, **Thomas Ewing** served six years as a U.S. senator from Ohio. In

1841, he was appointed secretary of the Treasury by President William Henry Harrison. One month into his presidency, Harrison died and was succeeded by Vice President John Tyler. Tyler kept Ewing on until the latter resigned six months later because of Tyler's opposition to his plans for a central bank.

In 1849, Ewing was again selected to serve on a presidential cabinet; this time, President Zachary Taylor appointed him as the country's first secretary of the interior. In later years, Ewing again served as U.S. senator and frequently advised President Lincoln during the Civil War. When Thomas Ewing died in 1889 at age 81, he was the last living member of the cabinets of presidents William Henry Harrison and John Tyler.

* * * *

Civil War general William Tecumseh Sherman's father died when he was just nine years old, and the boy was sent to live with family friend Thomas Ewing because Sherman's mother had trouble providing for all eight of her children after her husband died. Sherman married Ewing's daughter, Eleanor, 21 years later.

* * * *

First Ladies Who Were Born in the 18th Century

Born in 1775, **Anna Harrison,** President William Henry Harrison's wife, was too ill to accompany her husband to his inauguration in 1841. Since he died after only one month in office, Anna never lived in the White House. She passed away in 1864 at age 88. All other first ladies born before 1800 had died years before her.

Children of William Henry Harrison

The last living child of William Henry Harrison was **John Scott Harrison,** who died in 1878 at age 73. A member of the U.S.

House of Representatives from Ohio, John was also the father of U.S. President Benjamin Harrison.

* * * *

William Henry Harrison's grandfather, Benjamin Harrison of Virginia, signed the Declaration of Independence.

* * * *

Wives of John Tyler

Widower John Tyler became the first president to marry while in office when, on June 26, 1844, he and **Julia Gardiner** were wed. Julia died 45 years later at age 69.

Children of John Tyler

John Tyler, who served as president from 1841 through 1845, was born in 1790, when George Washington was still in his 50s. Tyler had two wives, by whom he had 15 children—more than any other U.S. president. The last survivor of Tyler's children was **Pearl Tyler,** his youngest daughter, who died in 1947. She married Major William Mumford Ellis and had eight children.

Election of 1844

Democrat James K. Polk (1795–1849) advocated the immediate annexation of Texas, while Democratic-Republican **Henry Clay** (1777–1852) tried to shift the campaign to other issues. Polk won, but Clay lived the longest.

Polk's Cabinet

Often referred to as the "Father of American History," **George Bancroft** wrote a ten-volume history of the United States over the course of 50 years. The first volume was published in 1834, the last in 1874, and a revised edition in 1885.

An antislavery Democrat, Bancroft rose to political prominence in his native Massachusetts, then a bastion of the Whig Party. His support of James Polk's candidacy resulted in an appointment as secretary of the Navy and his founding of the Naval Academy at Annapolis, Maryland.

After a year and a half as secretary, Bancroft served in various diplomatic positions, including minister to Great Britain and minister to Germany. In 1845, he was the official eulogist of Andrew Jackson, and in 1865, he delivered Lincoln's official memorial address in the U.S. Congress. Bancroft died on January 17, 1891, at age 90.

Election of 1848

Military hero Zachary Taylor won this election, but the last survivor of the candidates was Senator **Lewis Cass.** Cass came to this election with a great résumé: brigadier general in the War of 1812, 18 years as governor of the Michigan Territory, secretary of war under President Jackson, and minister to France. After Cass lost this election, he won the new election to fill the Senate seat made vacant by his own resignation. Later, he served as secretary of state under President James Buchanan.

The following were the candidates of the 1848 election:

- Whig Zachary Taylor (1784–1850)
- Free Soiler Martin Van Buren (1782–1862)
- Democrat Lewis Cass (1782–1866)

Taylor's Cabinet

The last surviving member of President Zachary Taylor's cabinet was **Reverdy Johnson.** In 1849, he resigned his U.S. Senate seat to take the attorney general position. Johnson was an attorney involved in the Dred Scott case (1857). He personally opposed slavery and was instrumental in keeping Maryland from joining the Confederate states. During the Civil War, he again represented Maryland in the Senate (1863–68). In later years, Johnson practiced law and served for a short time as minister to England. He passed away at age 79 on February 10, 1876.

Children of Zachary Taylor

Of Taylor's six children, the last survivor was his daughter **Mary Taylor,** who was born in 1824 in Jefferson County, Kentucky. She married Major William Bliss in 1848 in Baton Rouge, Louisiana. Her mother, Margaret Mackall Smith Taylor, had not wanted her father to accept the presidential nomination; when he did so, she told him she would live in the White House but would not act as hostess at White House events. These duties fell to Mary, who performed them gracefully. Mary's first husband, William Bliss, died in 1853; several years later, Mary married Philip Dandridge of Winchester, Virginia. Neither marriage produced any children, however. Mary died in 1909.

* * * *

Zachary Taylor was 64 years old when he became president. He had spent the preceding years on the frontier, and those years and the stresses of the presidency wore Taylor down. After a hot July 4 listening to speeches at the foot of the Washington Monument, Taylor collapsed of acute indigestion. He died on July 9, 1850, and Vice President Millard Fillmore assumed the presidency.

* * * *

Whig Presidents

Starting as a group opposed to Andrew Jackson, the Whig Party advocated such issues as high tariffs, new canals, and better highways. **Millard Fillmore,** the last surviving person who had been a Whig Party president, died 21 years after leaving office (March 8, 1874).

The Whig Party presidents were:

- William Henry Harrison (1773–1841; president 1841)
- Zachary Taylor (1784–1850; president 1849–50)
- John Tyler (1790–1862; president 1841–45)
- Millard Fillmore (1800–74; president 1850–53)

* * * *

In 1853, President Millard Fillmore sent Commodore Matthew Perry to Japan with a letter to the emperor requesting a trading relationship between the two nations. The two countries signed a formal treaty the following year.

* * * *

Fillmore's Cabinet

Virginia lawyer **Alexander Hugh Holmes Stuart** served as secretary of the interior in President Millard Fillmore's cabinet from 1850 to 1853. In addition to occupying many state government positions, he served one term in the U.S. Congress. In 1861, Stuart was a delegate to the Virginia Secession Convention. Stuart voted against secession, but he was on the losing side of the 88–55 tally. Stuart died in 1891 at age 83—the last survivor of Millard Fillmore's cabinet.

Wives of Millard Fillmore

Fillmore's first wife, Abigail Powers, died of pneumonia in 1853. **Caroline Carmichael McIntosh,** the widow of a wealthy businessman, married former president Fillmore in 1858. She died in 1881 at age 68.

* * * *

Of President Fillmore's two children, son Millard Powers Fillmore was the last living. He died in 1889.

* * * *

Election of 1852

In this election, Winfield Scott lost Southern votes because of his opposition to slavery. Winner Franklin Pierce, on the other hand, had supported enforcement of the Fugitive Slave Law. After the election, last survivor **John Parker Hale** returned to the U.S. Senate, capping his career with the position of minister to Spain in the late 1860s.

The following were the candidates of the 1852 election:

- Whig Winfield Scott (1786–1866)
- Democrat Franklin Pierce (1804–69)
- Free Soiler John Parker Hale (1806–73)

Pierce's Cabinet

Franklin Pierce was the only president in history to have no turnover of his cabinet members. When **James Campbell** passed away on January 27, 1893, at age 80, he was the last living member of Pierce's cabinet. He had served as postmaster general from 1853 through 1857. A man devoted to the welfare of others, Campbell was vice president of Saint Joseph's Orphan Asylum for 45 years and served as president of Jefferson Medical College's board of trustees for 25 years.

Children of Franklin Pierce

Of Franklin Pierce's three sons, the last survivor was **Benjamin Pierce,** who was killed in a train accident in 1853. He was just 11 years old. The Pierce family had been returning from a vacation in Boston when the axle of the train they were riding in broke, and the train jumped the track. Benjamin was the only passenger killed in the accident.

Election of 1856

Without taking a strong position on slavery, James Buchanan appealed to as many voters as possible and won the election. Unlike the other two candidates, **John C. Fremont** would never reach the presidency, but he would be the last survivor, dying in 1890 at age 77. His career as an explorer and military officer was legendary.

The candidates of the 1856 election were:

- Democrat James Buchanan (1791–1868)
- American Party/Whig Millard Fillmore (1800–74)
- Republican John Charles Fremont (1813–90)

Presidents Who Were Born in the 18th Century

James Buchanan was born on April 23, 1791, and passed away on June 1, 1868—the last of the 18th-century chief executives.

The U.S. presidents who were born in the 1700s were:

- George Washington (1732–99)
- John Adams (1735–1826)
- Thomas Jefferson (1743–1826)
- James Madison (1751–1836)
- James Monroe (1758–1831)
- John Quincy Adams (1767–1848)
- Andrew Jackson (1767–1845)
- Martin Van Buren (1782–1862)
- William H. Harrison (1773–1841)
- John Tyler (1790–1862)
- James K. Polk (1795–1849)
- Zachary Taylor (1784–1850)
- James Buchanan (1791–1868)

James Buchanan

Election of 1860

Division among the Democrats and Republican candidate Abraham Lincoln's "everyman" image led to Lincoln's victory at the polls. After his presidential loss, **John Cabell Breckinridge** returned to the U.S. Senate in 1861. Several months later he was expelled for supporting the South's rebellion, and he joined the Confederate army as a general. The last few months of the war saw him as the Confederacy's secretary of war. After the fall of the Confederacy, Breckinridge spent a few years in Europe, later returning to the United States to his career as a lawyer and businessman. Even though he lived to be only 54, he outlived the other three candidates of the 1860 presidential election.

The following were the candidates of the 1860 election:

- Northern Democrat Stephen Arnold Douglas (1813–61)
- Republican Abraham Lincoln (1809–65)
- Constitutional Union John Bell (1797–1869)
- Southern Democrat John Cabell Breckinridge (1821–75)

Election of 1864

Recent Union victories in the Civil War enabled Republican Lincoln (1809–65) to defeat his former subordinate, Major General **George B. McClellan** (1826–85), a Democrat. McClellan later served as governor of New Jersey (1878–81).

Buchanan and Lincoln's Cabinets

Of the men who served in James Buchanan and Abraham Lincoln's cabinets, **Horatio King** was the last to die. Appointed postmaster general by President James Buchanan, King was in Lincoln's cabinet for only three days before Lincoln's new postmaster general, Montgomery Blair, replaced him. King was born in 1811 and died in 1897.

Children of Abraham Lincoln

Of Lincoln's four sons, only one, **Robert Todd Lincoln,** reached adulthood. Robert Lincoln was born in Springfield, Illinois, in 1843. He graduated from Harvard and then served on Grant's staff during the Civil War and was present at Lee's surrender at Appomattox. After the war, he studied law in Chicago and was admitted to the bar in 1867. His specialty was corporate law, and he often represented railroad companies. He served as secretary of war under President Garfield and minister to Great Britain during

Benjamin Harrison's administration. He was president of the Pullman Company from 1897 to 1911. He lived at his Vermont estate, Hildene, during his later years, and his last major public appearance was at the Lincoln Memorial dedication on May 30, 1922. Robert Lincoln died in 1926.

* * * *

Robert Todd Lincoln once nearly fell from a platform into the path of a moving train but was saved by Edwin Booth, brother of John Wilkes Booth, who would later kill Lincoln's father.

* * * *

Secret Service Agents—the President's Guards *and* Counterfeiter Fighters?

Two roles that fall under the umbrella of the United States Secret Service are protecting the president and fighting counterfeiters. What's the connection? It goes back to 1876, when the newly formed Secret Service was investigating a group of counterfeiters in Chicago, Illinois. A Secret Service informant began frequenting the Hub, a saloon that was the counterfeiters' regular hangout. Four counterfeiters hatched a plan to spring their talented buddy, Benjamin Boyd (an engraver), out of the Joliet penitentiary. They planned to steal Lincoln's body from Oak Ridge Cemetery in Springfield and demand Boyd's freedom as ransom. When one counterfeiter dropped out, the other three felt they still needed another participant. Unfortunately for them, they approached the informant, Lewis C. Swegles, who promptly told his boss—Patrick D. Tyrrell, the chief of the regional office of the Secret Service.

The night the counterfeiters went to the cemetery to carry out their plan, Secret Service agents were waiting for them. The counterfeiters bungled their mission in an amazing fashion, and Lincoln's body was never touched. The counterfeiters fled the scene but went right back to the Hub, where they were promptly arrested. After this event, the Secret Service gradually began protecting presidents, in addition to their original role of fighting counterfeiters.

The 1901 Exhumation of Lincoln's Body

After the 1876 plot to steal Lincoln's body, Lincoln's son Robert was worried that there might be another attempt in the future. In 1901, Robert arranged for his father to be reburied. This time he was encased in lead, a cage of steel, and tons of cement. Before the reburial took place, 22 people witnessed the opening of Lincoln's coffin. The last survivor of these witnesses was **Fleetwood Lindley,** son of one of the unofficial guardians of Lincoln's tomb. Lindley died in 1963, several days after he was interviewed by *LIFE* magazine. Lindley claimed that Lincoln was remarkably preserved—his skin was bronze in color, and some of the makeup the undertaker had used was still visible. Lindley remembered instantly recognizing Lincoln's blemish and hair.

Johnson's Cabinet

A professor at West Point and Washington University (St. Louis) before the Civil War, **John Schofield** became a major of the 1st Missouri Volunteer Infantry at the start of the war. By war's end, he had been promoted to brigadier general in the regular army. In 1868–69 he served as secretary of war in President Andrew Johnson's cabinet. After another 25 years of top military positions, he attained the highest military position, Commanding General of the Army (1888–95). On March 4, 1906, Schofield died in Florida at age 74.

* * * *

Andrew Johnson's impeachment revolved around the Tenure of Office Act. This act, which had been passed in 1867, stated that the president could not remove a cabinet official without the consent of Congress. After Andrew Johnson dismissed Edwin Stanton, John Schofield's predecessor as secretary of war, the House voted to impeach. He was tried in the Senate and was acquitted. In 1926, the Supreme Court ruled that the Tenure of Office Act was unconstitutional.

* * * *

Children of Andrew Johnson

Of Andrew Johnson's five children, **Martha Johnson** lived the longest. She married David Trotter Patterson in 1855, and they had two children. Martha served as White House hostess for her father because her mother was weak from tuberculosis. The White House had been neglected during the Civil War, and Martha worked hard to restore it. She had rugs replaced and took numerous presidential portraits out of storage and displayed them on the first floor. Martha died in 1901.

* * * *

Martha's husband, David Trotter Patterson, was a senator from Tennessee during his father-in-law's impeachment trial.

* * * *

Presidents Who Were Veterans of the Civil War

When Lincoln was assassinated in 1865, Vice President Andrew Johnson rose to the presidency. Every president for the rest of the century, with the sole exception of Grover Cleveland, was a veteran of the Civil War. The last surviving veteran president was **William McKinley,** who distinguished himself during the Civil War by rising from private to a brevet major. After serving almost five years as president, he was shot by anarchist Leon Czolgosz at the Pan-American Exposition in Buffalo, New York, on September 6, 1901. McKinley died eight days later.

The following were the Civil War veterans who became president of the United States:

- Ulysses S. Grant (1822–85), president 1869–77
- Rutherford B. Hayes (1822–93), president 1877–81
- James A. Garfield (1831–81), president 1881
- Chester Alan Arthur (1829–86), president 1881–85

- Benjamin Harrison (1833–March 13, 1901), president 1889–93
- William McKinley (1843–September 14, 1901), president 1897–1901

Lincoln's Bodyguard Unit

George Coates Ashmun, the last surviving bodyguard for Abraham Lincoln, aided security during Lincoln's second inauguration. In later years, Ashmun served as a surgeon with the 5th Ohio Infantry during the Spanish-American War and with the Students Army Training Corps during World War I. He was born in 1841 and died in 1929 at age 88.

Election of 1868

Republican Ulysses S. Grant (1822–85) was the military leader who brought the Civil War to a successful conclusion for the Union. His opponent, Democrat **Horatio Seymour** (1810–86), was a former New York governor and opponent of many of President Lincoln's policies during the war. Grant won the election, but Seymour was the last survivor. He died in 1886, a year after Grant.

Election of 1872

Republican **Ulysses S. Grant** (1822–85) won reelection over his opponent, Democrat/Liberal Republican Horace Greeley (1811–72). Perhaps best known today for popularizing the phrase, "Go West, young man," Greeley was one of the most important newspaper publishers of his day. Just before the election, Greeley's wife died, and he lost his newspaper company. He went insane and died before the electoral votes were even cast. Grant outlived him by 12 years.

Grant's Cabinet

James D. Cameron served as President Ulysses S. Grant's secretary of war from 1876 to 1877. Later he served 20 years as a U.S. senator from Pennsylvania (1877–97). When he died on August 30, 1918, at age 85, he was the last surviving of Grant's cabinet secretaries.

* * * *

James D. Cameron's father, Simon Cameron, also a U.S. senator, was President Abraham Lincoln's secretary of war at the beginning of the Civil War (1861–62).

* * * *

Children of Ulysses S. Grant

Jesse Root Grant, the last surviving child of Ulysses S. Grant, was born in St. Louis in 1858. He studied at the Cornell College of Engineering and went on to work as a mining engineer. He married Elizabeth Chapman in 1880, and they had two children. Jesse divorced Elizabeth in 1914 and soon married Lillian Burns Wilkins. Jesse died in 1934.

* * * *

Jesse accompanied his parents when they visited Queen Victoria in 1877. She described him as "a very ill-mannered young Yankee."

* * * *

Individuals Featured on U.S. Paper Currency

Ulysses S. Grant, who appears on the U.S. $50 dollar bill, was the last of the men pictured on current U.S. paper currency to die. In 1913, his image was placed on the bill, which was then called a $50 gold certificate because it was redeemable for gold.

U.S. paper currency available in 2008 (and the individual pictured on each):

- $1—George Washington, president 1789–97, died in 1799
- $2—Thomas Jefferson, president 1801–09, died in 1826
- $5—Abraham Lincoln, president 1861–65, died in 1865
- $10—Alexander Hamilton, first secretary of the treasury 1789–95, died in 1804
- $20—Andrew Jackson, president 1829–37, died in 1845
- $50—Ulysses S. Grant, Civil War general; president 1869–77, died in 1885
- $100—Benjamin Franklin, American Revolution leader and inventor, died in 1790

* * * *

Since 1969, denominations of more than $100 are no longer produced. Older, larger currencies featured Grover Cleveland, William McKinley, and Woodrow Wilson—all of whom died later than Grant.

* * * *

Election of 1876

The 1876 election was one of the messiest presidential elections in U.S. history. Democrat Samuel Jones Tilden (1814–86) won a majority of the popular vote and 184 electoral votes (185 was the magic number). Republican **Rutherford B. Hayes** (1822–93) won 165 undisputed electoral votes (19 from Florida, Louisiana, and South Carolina were disputed). In Oregon, the Democratic governor replaced a disqualified Republican elector with a Democrat, a shenanigan that was soon overridden.

Of those Southern African Americans who dared vote, most cast Republican ballots, which explains the rampant intimidation of Republican voters in Dixie. Ballot chicanery was also an issue because the parties printed their own ballots. To help illiterate voters "decide," the Democrats put pictures of Lincoln (a Republican icon) on some ballots. The states' electoral commissions,

generally Republican-friendly, disallowed enough such ballots to hand Hayes the electoral votes—and the proverbial mess hit the fan.

With inauguration fast approaching, the Republicans struck a deal to appease the Southern Democrats by withdrawing federal troops from Southern states. Thus Rutherford B. Hayes won, but African American residents of the South lost. Mocked as "Rutherfraud," Hayes served only one term but outlived Tilden.

Hayes's Cabinet

West Virginia lawyer and Civil War veteran **Nathan Goff** was appointed secretary of the Navy by President Rutherford Hayes in 1881; he served for the last few weeks of the Hayes administration. In later years, he served as a member of the U.S. House of Representatives and the U.S. Senate, and as a circuit court judge. When Goff passed away at age 77 on April 24, 1920, he was the last surviving member of Hayes's cabinet.

Children of Rutherford B. Hayes

Fanny Hayes was the last living child of President Hayes. She married Harry Eaton Smith, and they had one child, Dalton, who was born in 1898. Fanny passed away in 1950 at age 82.

Election of 1880

This election pitted two Civil War generals against each other. During the war, Republican James A. Garfield (1831–81) had been promoted to brigadier general at the age of 31. His opponent, Democratic former army general **Winfield Scott Hancock** (1824–86), had fought at Antietam, Fredericksburg, Chancellorsville, Gettysburg, and the Wilderness. An assassin's bullet during Garfield's first year as president left Hancock the last survivor.

Log Cabin Presidents

When President **James A. Garfield** (1831–81) was assassinated in 1881, he was the last surviving U.S. president who had been born in a log cabin. The following were the other U.S. presidents who were born in log cabins:

- Andrew Jackson (1767–1845)
- Zachary Taylor (1784–1850)
- Millard Fillmore (1800–74)
- Franklin Pierce (1804–69)
- James Buchanan (1791–1868)
- Abraham Lincoln (1809–65)

James A. Garfield

* * * *

Garfield was assassinated by Charles J. Guiteau, an attorney who had been turned down for a diplomatic post. Garfield lived for 11 weeks after the shooting, but he finally succumbed to infection and internal hemorrhaging.

* * * *

"The people are responsible for the character of their Congress. If that body be ignorant, reckless, and corrupt, it is because the people tolerate ignorance, recklessness, and corruption."

—James A. Garfield

* * * *

Garfield would sometimes entertain friends by writing in Greek and Latin simultaneously—one language with his right hand, and the other with his left.

* * * *

Children of James A. Garfield

James A. Garfield's last surviving child was his son **Abram Garfield,** who was just eight years old when his father was assassinated. Abram graduated from Williams College and became an architect. He married Sarah Granger Williams in 1897, and they had two children. After Sarah's death, Abram married Helen Grannis Mathews. Abram died in 1958 at age 85.

Presidents Who Never Had a Vice President

After President James A. Garfield was assassinated in Washington, D.C., in 1881, his vice president, **Chester Alan Arthur,** was sworn in as president. Arthur surprised everyone by rising above partisanship. In the process, however, he alienated many members of his own party, and the Republicans chose not to nominate him in the next election. Arthur died of kidney disease two years later, at age 56. He was the last living U.S. president to have never had a vice president.

The following four U.S. presidents never had vice presidents:

- John Tyler (1790–1862) took over when William Henry Harrison died in 1841. He served until 1845.
- Millard Fillmore (1800–74) became president when Zachary Taylor died in 1849. He served until 1853.
- Andrew Johnson (1808–75) took over when Abraham Lincoln was assassinated in 1865. He served until 1869.
- Chester Alan Arthur (1830–86) succeeded to the presidency when James A. Garfield was assassinated in 1881. He served until 1885.

* * * *

Theodore Roosevelt, Calvin Coolidge, Harry Truman, and Lyndon Johnson served without vice presidents after stepping up to the presidency, but they were all later elected to full terms with vice presidents.

* * * *

* * * *

The last living of Arthur's two children was son Chester, who passed away in 1937.

* * * *

Election of 1884

The Republicans lost support when their candidate James Blaine was accused of accepting bribes from railroad companies. Democratic candidate **Grover Cleveland** was embroiled in scandal as well, over allegations that he had fathered an illegitimate child ten years earlier. Cleveland countered that the story about him was not a secret. Maria Halpin had named him as the father of her child, and Cleveland had acknowledged the possibility. He had attended to her financial needs and the needs of the child (Oscar Folsom Cleveland) initially, but Maria Halpin continued to struggle with alcoholism, and the boy was given up for adoption (he went on to become a doctor). Cleveland won the election and was the last living candidate. The other two candidates died within 17 days of each other in 1893, and Cleveland died on June 24, 1908.

The candidates of the 1884 election were:

- Greenback/Anti-Monopolist Benjamin Franklin Butler (1818–January 11, 1893)
- Republican James Gillespie Blaine (1830–January 27, 1893)
- Democrat Grover Cleveland (1837–1908)

Election of 1888

Democrat **Grover Cleveland** (1837–1908) called for a reduction in tariffs, and this was one of the main issues in 1888. He beat Republican Benjamin Harrison (1833–1901) in popular votes; however, he lost in the Electoral College, and Harrison became president. Cleveland outlived Harrison by seven years.

Election of 1892

Sound currency was a major issue in this election, a rematch of the previous race. This time, Democrat **Grover Cleveland** (1837–1908) won a clear victory over Republican Benjamin Harrison (1833–1901). With this election, Grover Cleveland became the only person in history to be elected U.S. president for two nonconsecutive terms.

Grover Cleveland's Cabinets

Grover Cleveland appointed lawyer and newspaper editor **Hoke Smith** secretary of the interior in 1893. In later years, Smith became one of the most powerful figures in the Southern wing of the Democratic Party, serving as Georgia governor and U.S. senator. Known for his longtime support of education and opposition to railroad monopolies, Smith was also infamous for his efforts to deny African Americans civil rights. When Smith died on November 27, 1931, at age 76, he was the last living Cleveland cabinet member.

Children of Grover Cleveland

Of the six children born to Grover Cleveland and his wife, Frances Folsom, **Esther Cleveland** was the last living. Born in 1893, she married British Captain William Sydney Bence Bosanquet, and they had two children. Esther passed away in 1980.

* * * *

Esther's older sister Ruth was allegedly the inspiration for the Baby Ruth candy bar.

* * * *

Benjamin Harrison's Cabinet

John Wanamaker was the founder of one of the first department stores in the United States. Having started his first store in 1861, he is often credited with inventing the fixed price tag and the money-back guarantee. Always an innovator, he installed electric lights, elevators, and a restaurant in his huge Philadelphia store in the late 19th century. Concerned with business ethics long before that term was used, he was also the president of the Philadelphia YMCA for many years, active in his Presbyterian church, and a generous contributor to numerous charities. In 1889, he was appointed postmaster general of the United States by President Benjamin Harrison and championed free delivery of mail to rural areas. When he died at age 84 in 1922, he was the last living member of the Harrison cabinet.

Benjamin Harrison

Wives of Benjamin Harrison

Benjamin Harrison's first wife, Caroline Lavinia Scott, died in 1892. Four years later, Benjamin married her niece, **Mary Scott Lord Dimmick,** who died in 1948 at age 89.

Children of Benjamin Harrison

Benjamin Harrison had two children by his first wife and one by his second. **Elizabeth Harrison,** the child of his second wife and the last survivor of Harrison's three children, died in 1955. She was just four years old when her father died in 1901. She remembered bringing an apple pie to his bedside the night he passed away. He was unable to speak, but he looked at her and smiled. Elizabeth earned a law degree from New York University and was admitted to the Indiana and New York bars at the age of 22. She also founded *Cues to the News,* a newsletter for female investors. She married James Blaine Walker in 1921.

* * * *

Benjamin Harrison was nicknamed "Iceberg" because he hated small talk.

* * * *

Elections of 1896 and 1900

Republican William McKinley (1843–1901), supporting the gold standard and higher tariffs, beat Democrat/Populist **William Jennings Bryan** (1860–1925), the renowned Nebraska orator, in the presidential elections of 1896 and 1900. However, McKinley's assassination in 1901, shortly after his second inaugural, left Bryan the last survivor.

McKinley's Cabinet

Elihu Root, recipient of the 1912 Nobel Peace Prize, served as secretary of war (1899–1904) under President William McKinley and secretary of state (1905–09) under President Theodore Roosevelt. In the latter post, he was responsible for placing the consular service under civil service.

A U.S. senator from 1909 to 1915, Root undertook many important diplomatic missions for the United States in his later years. He also served as the first president for the Carnegie Endowment for International Peace (1910–25). When he died on February 7, 1937, a week shy of his 92nd birthday, he was the last living member of McKinley's cabinet.

Children of William McKinley

Neither of McKinley's daughters reached adulthood. The last survivor was **Katherine McKinley,** who died of typhoid fever in 1875 at age four.

Election of 1904

A hero in the Spanish-American War and the man who had successfully filled the boots of William McKinley after the latter's assassination, Theodore Roosevelt won this election. **Eugene Victor Debs,** who ran four times as the Socialist party candidate for president, died a few months after Alton Brooks Parker on October 20, 1926.

The following were the candidates of the 1904 election:

- Republican Theodore Roosevelt (1858–1919)
- Democrat Alton Brooks Parker (1852–May 10, 1926)
- Socialist Eugene Victor Debs (1855–October 20, 1926)

Eugene Debs

Born to French immigrants, Debs grew up a middle-class Midwesterner. In 1875, at age 20, he founded a railway workers' union, and his strong communication skills quickly made him a prominent labor leader. Jailed in 1894 for defying a federal injunction, he read the works of Karl Marx and became a committed socialist. He would get from three to six percent of the popular presidential vote four times as a socialist, the last in 1920 while a federal political prisoner.

Debs was in prison because of a speech he made encouraging World War I draft resistance. President Harding commuted Debs's sentence in 1921, but the labor advocate's health and strength were broken. He died in 1926, with the Communists mad at him for not blindly supporting Lenin. Debs always made up his own mind.

Theodore Roosevelt's Cabinet

At 16 years old, Ohio native **James Rudolph Garfield** was with his father, James A. Garfield, when the elder was assassinated in 1881. James Rudolph graduated from Columbia Law School in 1888. He married Helen Newell, and the couple had four children. He also went on to serve in various political and administrative capacities with the state and national governments. He was Roosevelt's secretary of the interior from 1907 to 1909. Like his president, James Rudolph was devoted to the conservation of the country's natural resources. Born in 1865, he died in 1950 at age 84.

Wives of Theodore Roosevelt

Roosevelt's first wife, Alice Hathaway Lee Roosevelt, died in 1884, two days after she had given birth to the couple's only child, Alice

Lee Roosevelt. Her death was a result of Bright's disease, and she actually died on the same day as Roosevelt's mother (who died of pneumonia). After the deaths of these two beloved women, Roosevelt ventured west to distract himself from his grief. Three years later, he married **Edith Kermit Carow.** Edith passed away in 1948 at age 87.

Children of Theodore Roosevelt

Of his six children, the last living was **Alice Lee Roosevelt,** his daughter with his first wife. After her mother died and her father headed west, little Alice was taken care of by her father's sister Anna. When Theodore Roosevelt returned from his trip, Alice was three years old. The little girl had a wild streak from an early age and during her teenage years she took up smoking (which was quite unusual for women at the time). She was also known for her quick wit and sharp tongue. Alice married Nicholas Longworth (who would eventually rise to Speaker of the House) in the East Room of the White House in 1906. The marriage was amicable but distant, and both had affairs. When Alice did have a daughter, Paulina, 18 years after the marriage, it was obvious to most that the child's father was Senator William Borah of Idaho rather than Longworth. Both men adored the little girl, however. Alice Roosevelt Longworth died in 1980 at age 96.

* * * *

"If you can't say something good about someone, sit right here by me" was one of Alice Roosevelt Longworth's favorite maxims. She had it embroidered on a pillow that she kept in her study.

* * * *

"I can either run the country or control Alice—not both."

—Theodore Roosevelt,
when questioned about his daughter's antics

* * * *

* * * *

After her daughter, Paulina, died suddenly in 1957, Alice Roosevelt Longworth raised her granddaughter, Joanna Sturm, who was ten years old at the time. Joanna's father had passed away in 1951.

* * * *

Bearded Presidents

Benjamin Harrison was the last surviving bearded president, dying in 1901, just after the turn of the 20th century. Presidents who sported beards during their presidency were:

- Abraham Lincoln (1809–65), president 1861–65
- Ulysses S. Grant (1822–85), president 1869–77
- Rutherford B. Hayes (1822–93), president 1877–81
- James A. Garfield (1831–81), president 1881
- Benjamin Harrison (1833–1901), president 1889–93

* * * *

William Howard Taft, who lived until 1930, was the last president to sport a mustache in office and the last mustached president to die.

* * * *

Election of 1908

Theodore Roosevelt chose not to seek another term and threw his support to **William Howard Taft,** who had served as Roosevelt's secretary of war. Taft won the 1908 election, served four years as president, and later became chief justice of the U.S. Supreme Court. He died in 1930 at age 72.

The candidates of the 1908 election were:

- Democrat William Jennings Bryan (1860–1925)
- Socialist Eugene Victor Debs (1855–1926)
- Republican William Howard Taft (1857–1930)

Taft's Cabinet

United States Secretary of War during the entire Second World War, **Henry L. Stimson** served in the same post three decades earlier, under President William Howard Taft. In 1940, Franklin Roosevelt chose Stimson, a Republican, to obtain more support for his military policies. In total, Stimson served on the cabinets of four U.S. presidents: secretary of war for Taft (1911–13), Roosevelt (1940–45), and Harry Truman (1945), and as secretary of state for Herbert Hoover (1929–32). Stimson was a key player in the controversial decision to drop the atomic bombs on the Japanese cities of Hiroshima and Nagasaki in August 1945. When Stimson died on October 20, 1950, at age 83, he was the last living Taft cabinet member.

Hiroshima and Nagasaki

Strategic opportunity and symbolic impact were chiefly in mind when Hiroshima and Nagasaki were chosen as nuclear targets during World War II. Both cities were picked for their comparatively light war damage, with Hiroshima singled out as the initial target due to its favorable "bowl-like" geography between mountains. As a backup to the principal target city of Kokura, Nagasaki ran out of luck when smoke cover forced the B-29 bomber *Bockscar* to ditch Kokura in favor of an alternate target. Kyoto had once been on the nuclear hit list but was removed by Secretary Stimson when he argued that its cultural significance as the ancient capital of Japan precluded its destruction.

Children of William Howard Taft

Taft had three children, and his daughter **Helen Taft** was the last survivor. She graduated magna cum laude from Bryn Mawr in 1915 with degrees in history, economics, and politics. After her sophomore year at Bryn Mawr, her mother had a stroke, and Helen took a leave from school to serve in her mother's place at White House events. Helen became dean of Bryn Mawr in 1917 (at age

25). She left to pursue her doctorate at Yale then returned as dean in 1925. She married Frederick J. Manning, a professor of history at Swarthmore, and the couple had two daughters. Helen passed away in 1987 at age 95.

Election of 1912

The Republican Party was divided. President **William Howard Taft** became its nominee, but Theodore Roosevelt ran as the candidate of the new Progressive Party. With the Republican vote split between the two, Democrat Woodrow Wilson won the election. The last survivor of the 1912 election was William Howard Taft, who died in 1930 at age 72. He ended his career as chief justice of the U.S. Supreme Court—the only president in history who has held that position.

The following were the candidates of the election of 1912:

- Progressive Theodore Roosevelt (1858–1919)
- Democrat Woodrow Wilson (1856–1924)
- Socialist Eugene Victor Debs (1855–1926)
- Republican William Howard Taft (1857–1930)

Presidents Born in Virginia

More U.S. presidents have been born in Virginia than in any other state. **Woodrow Wilson** was the last surviving Virginian president, passing away on February 3, 1924.

The following presidents were born in Virginia:

- George Washington (1732–99), Westmoreland County
- Thomas Jefferson (1743–1826), Albemarle County
- James Madison (1751–1836), Port Conway
- James Monroe (1758–1831), Westmoreland County
- William H. Harrison (1773–1841), Berkeley
- John Tyler (1790–1862), Greenway

- Zachary Taylor (1784–1850), Orange County
- Woodrow Wilson (1856–1924), Staunton

* * * *

Eleven vice presidents were born in New York, more than in any other state. The last surviving New York vice president was Nelson Rockefeller, who served with president Gerald Ford from 1974 until 1977. He died in 1979 at age 70.

* * * *

Election of 1916

Democrat Woodrow Wilson (1856–1924) was reelected in a close race, primarily because many people were grateful to him for keeping the United States out of World War I. Although he lost, Republican **Charles Evans Hughes** (1862–1948) lived to see World War II, dying in 1948. Before the election of 1916, he had been governor of New York and an associate justice of the U.S. Supreme Court. After the election, he was U.S. secretary of state (1921–25) and chief justice of the U.S. Supreme Court (1930–41).

* * * *

President Wilson never had an inaugural ball; he felt it was unnecessary and too expensive.

* * * *

Woodrow Wilson's Cabinet

A Republican turned Progressive Party leader, New Yorker **Bainbridge Colby** was appointed secretary of state by Democratic President Woodrow Wilson. Taking office shortly after the end of World War I, he served during the last year of the Wilson administration. Joining Wilson's law firm in 1921, he practiced law until his retirement. When Colby died in 1950 at age 80, he was the last former member of Woodrow Wilson's cabinet.

Wives of Woodrow Wilson

Woodrow Wilson's first wife was Ellen Louise Axson, who died of Bright's disease in 1914. Wilson married his second wife, **Edith Bolling Galt,** in 1915. During his 1919 tour of the country to promote the Versailles Treaty, Wilson suffered a stroke that partially paralyzed him. While he was recuperating, Edith helped keep all official matters running smoothly. Before she died in 1961 at age 89, she participated in President Kennedy's inaugural parade.

Children of Woodrow Wilson

Of the three Wilson children, **Eleanor Wilson** was the last survivor. She married Secretary of the Treasury William Gibbs McAdoo at the White House in 1914, and the couple had two daughters. Eleanor passed away in 1967 at age 77.

Election of 1920

Warren G. Harding, U.S. senator from Ohio and a compromise candidate at the Republican convention, easily won the 1920 election. Third party candidate Eugene Debs had conducted his presidential campaign from his federal prison cell in Atlanta, Georgia, where he was serving time for violating the wartime espionage law. He received almost a million votes. However, neither Debs nor Harding lived long afterward. The third candidate, **James Middleton Cox,** a newspaper publisher, congressman, and Ohio governor, outlived both opponents by more than 30 years.

The following were the candidates of the election of 1920:

- Republican Warren G. Harding (1865–1923)
- Socialist Eugene Victor Debs (1855–1926)
- Democrat James Middleton Cox (1870–1957)

Warren G. Harding and Calvin Coolidge's Cabinets

The last survivor of the cabinets of Warren G. Harding and Calvin Coolidge was **Herbert Hoover.** A mining engineer by profession,

Hoover was praised throughout his life for his humanitarian work. During World War I, as head of the Food Administration, he helped assure sufficient food supplies for Allied nations. After the war he headed the American Relief Administration, which provided food for 350 million people. He then served as chairman of the Boys' Clubs of America. After serving as secretary of commerce under both Harding and Coolidge, Hoover was elected the 31st president of the United States in 1928.

Hoover was blamed for the stock market crash of 1929 and the subsequent Great Depression, and he lost his 1932 reelection bid to Franklin Roosevelt by a large margin. After World War II, Hoover helped get food to starving people in war-torn countries. When he died on October 20, 1964, at age 90, he was the second oldest former president in history behind John Adams, who had lived about six months longer than Hoover. (Gerald Ford and Ronald Reagan would also reach age 90.)

* * * *

Because he was independently wealthy before he entered the White House, Hoover donated his presidential salary to charity.

* * * *

Election of 1924

Although Democrats pointed to the scandals of the Harding administration, most people were enjoying economic prosperity and voted for Calvin Coolidge. Democratic candidate and constitutional lawyer **John William Davis** lived decades beyond his 1924 opponents. Shortly before his death, he unsuccessfully defended the doctrine of "separate but equal" public education before the U.S. Supreme Court in the *Brown v. Board of Education* case.

The following were the candidates in the election of 1924:

- Progressive/Socialist Robert Marion La Follette (1855–1925)
- Republican Calvin Coolidge Jr. (1872–1933)
- Democrat John William Davis (1873–1955)

Presidents Who Served as Mayors

As of 2009, only three United States presidents have served as mayors of cities or towns. Lincoln's successor, Andrew Johnson, was once mayor of Greeneville, Tennessee; Grover Cleveland served as mayor of Buffalo, New York; and **Calvin Coolidge** was mayor of Northampton, Massachusetts. The last living of these three presidents was Coolidge. He worked his way up the political ladder. First he served as mayor of Northampton from 1910 to 1911, then he became, in succession, a member of the Massachusetts legislature, Massachusetts lieutenant-governor, Massachusetts governor, U.S. vice president, and president. He died in 1933.

Children of Calvin Coolidge

Of Coolidge's two sons, the last survivor was **John Coolidge,** who was born in Northampton, Massachusetts, in 1906. He graduated from Amherst College in 1928 and began working for the New York, New Haven and Hartford Railroad. John married Florence Trumbull, daughter of the governor of Connecticut, in 1929. The couple had two daughters. Gifts from John made Vermont's President Calvin Coolidge State Historic Site possible. John often visited the site and would discuss the Coolidge family with visitors. He would not always let on that he himself was a Coolidge, however. John died in 2000 at age 93.

* * * *

In June 1924, Calvin Coolidge's other son, Calvin Jr., died at age 16 of an infected blister. His death plunged his father into severe depression. Coolidge did not seek reelection in 1928.

* * * *

Election of 1928

Republican **Herbert Hoover** (1874–1964) defeated Democrat Alfred Emanuel Smith (1873–1944) in the 1928 election and was its last living candidate. Hoover died on October 20, 1964, at age 90.

* * * *

Hoover was almost two years old when General George Armstrong Custer and his troops were killed at the Battle of the Little Bighorn; at age 87, Hoover heard that astronaut John Glenn had become the first American to orbit Earth.

* * * *

Children of Herbert Hoover

The last survivor of Herbert Hoover's two sons was **Allan Hoover.** Allan was a mining executive and investment banker, and he and his wife, Margaret, had three children. Allan passed away in 1993 at age 86.

Election of 1932

With the nation in the grip of the Great Depression, Franklin Delano Roosevelt's message of economic reform appealed to the average voter. He won his first of four consecutive elections. The last survivor of this election was Socialist **Norman Mattoon Thomas,** who lived to see the election of Richard Nixon in 1968.

The following were the candidates of the election of 1932:

- Democrat Franklin D. Roosevelt (1882–1945)
- Republican Herbert Hoover (1874–1964)
- Socialist Norman Mattoon Thomas (1884–1968)

* * * *

Franklin Roosevelt was distantly related to Theodore Roosevelt (they were fifth cousins). Eleanor Roosevelt was Theodore Roosevelt's niece, making her Franklin Roosevelt's fifth cousin, once removed.

* * * *

Election of 1936

Voters approved of Democrat Franklin D. Roosevelt's (1882–1945) economic measures and he won by a landslide, garnering all but eight electoral votes. Republican **Alfred "Alf" M. Landon** (1887–1987) not only was the last survivor of this election, he also lived to be older than any other major party presidential candidate in history. Landon died in 1987 at age 100.

* * * *

Strom Thurmond, a candidate in the 1948 election, lived about five months longer than Landon, but Thurmond was a minor party candidate.

* * * *

Election of 1940

Democratic candidate **Franklin D. Roosevelt** (1882–1945) was running for his third term, and Republican Wendell Wilkie (1892–1944) ran on a pro-business platform and criticized Roosevelt for breaking with the tradition of Washington's self-imposed limit of two presidential terms. Roosevelt won by another landslide (449 to 82 electoral votes). After this election, Wilkie worked against isolationist tendencies in the United States, supporting unlimited aid to Britain early in 1941. He died in 1944, a year before Roosevelt.

Election of 1944

Republicans argued against a 16-year presidency, while Democrats insisted that it was in the country's best interest not to change administrations in the middle of World War II. Republican **Thomas E. Dewey** (1902–71) lost the election, but he survived Democrat Franklin Roosevelt (1882–1945) by more than 25 years.

Franklin D. Roosevelt's Cabinet

James A. Farley managed Franklin D. Roosevelt's first two presidential campaigns and was Roosevelt's postmaster general from 1933 through 1940. Farley opposed Roosevelt's run for a third term of office and quit his cabinet post in 1940. He died on June 9, 1976, at age 88 and was the last survivor of Roosevelt's cabinet.

Children of Franklin D. Roosevelt

Of the six children of Franklin and Eleanor Roosevelt, the last survivor was eldest son **James Roosevelt,** who was born in 1907. James graduated from Harvard in 1930 and commanded a Marine battalion during World War II. In 1954, James was elected to Congress and served for 11 years. He resigned to serve as United States representative to the United Nations Economic and Social Council. He married four times and had seven children. James died at age 83 in 1991.

* * * *

Franklin Roosevelt barely served 12 years as president. He died on April 12, 1945—just five months after his fourth election.

* * * *

Election of 1948

Civil rights issues split the Democratic Party three ways for this election, but the fighting spirit of Harry S. Truman and his pledge to carry out the Roosevelt legacy enabled him to achieve a victory.

Strom Thurmond was the undisputed last survivor of this election, going on to serve nearly a half century in the U.S. Senate.

The following were the candidates of the election of 1948:

- Progressive Henry Wallace (1888–1965)
- Republican Thomas E. Dewey (1902–71)
- Democrat Harry S. Truman (1884–1972)
- States' Rights Democrat James Strom Thurmond (1902–2003)

* * * *

Strom Thurmond's last term in office ended just after his 100th birthday.

* * * *

Truman's Cabinet

Denver attorney **Charles F. Brannan** was President Harry Truman's secretary of agriculture from 1948 to 1953. When Brannan died on July 2, 1992, at age 88, he was the last of the more than 30 people who served in Truman's cabinet.

Presidents Who Were Veterans of World War I

Only two U.S. presidents served in the military during World War I. Dwight D. Eisenhower, a graduate of West Point, held various staff appointments, including service under General John J. Pershing. Eisenhower, who was president from 1953 to 1961, died in 1969.

Harry S. Truman (1884–1972) saw combat in France as a field artillery officer during World War I and died 54 years after the end of the war. Truman, who served as president from 1945 to 1953, was the last surviving U.S. president who was a veteran of the First World War.

* * * *

Harry S. Truman was also the last survivor of the presidents born before 1900. His wife, Elizabeth Virginia Wallace Truman, was the last of the first ladies born before 1900.

* * * *

Elections of 1952 and 1956

The leader of the Allied armies in Europe in World War II, Republican **Dwight D. Eisenhower** (1891–1969) opposed Democrat Adlai Stevenson (1900–65) in the presidential elections of 1952 and 1956, with Eisenhower winning crushing victories each time. Eisenhower outlived Stevenson by several years.

Eisenhower's Cabinet

The last survivor of President Eisenhower's cabinet was **William P. Rogers,** who served as Eisenhower's attorney general from 1957 to 1961. When not engaged in government assignments, Rogers ran a flourishing law practice. Also, for almost five years (1969–73), he was President Richard Nixon's secretary of state. When Rogers died on January 2, 2001, he was 87 years old.

* * * *

Rogers served as a lieutenant commander in the United States Navy during World War II and was chairman of the presidential commission on the 1986 space shuttle Challenger *accident.*

* * * *

Election of 1960

The first televised presidential debates may have been the deciding factor in this election. Democrat John F. Kennedy (1917–63) excelled in the debates and won a very close race. Kennedy was assassinated on November 22, 1963, and Republican **Richard M. Nixon** (1913–94) was the last of the 1960 candidates to survive. He eventually won the presidency (in 1968).

The Cuban Missile Crisis

In October 1962, President John F. Kennedy was shown reconnaissance photographs of the construction of Soviet missile installations in Cuba. On October 22, he initiated a naval quarantine of Cuba to prevent the arrival of additional weapons. On October 28, Soviet leader Nikita Khrushchev announced that his country would dismantle the installations. It was assumed the United States also agreed not to invade Cuba in the future.

Robert S. McNamara was secretary of defense during these negotiations. He served in that post for Kennedy from 1961 to 1963 and continued until 1968 under the Johnson administration. He was heavily involved in the conduct of the Vietnam War during that time. Born in 1916 and still alive as of 2009, he is the last survivor of President Kennedy's group of major Cuban Missile Crisis advisers.

Election of 1964

Democrat Lyndon Baines Johnson (1908–73) entered this election less than one year after he succeeded assassinated President John F. Kennedy. After a campaign that depicted Republican **Barry M. Goldwater** (1909–98) as a dangerous extremist, Johnson won in a landslide. Goldwater lived 25 years longer than Johnson.

Election of 1968

The Democratic Party lost votes to third-party candidate **George C. Wallace** because Lyndon Baines Johnson had expanded civil rights. The party lost even more votes because of its apparent inability to bring the Vietnam War to a conclusion. The end result was Republican Richard Nixon's victory. Wallace outlived the other two candidates, however. While competing in the next presidential election's Democratic primaries in 1972, Wallace was paralyzed in both legs after an attention-seeking assassination attempt by Arthur Bremer.

The following were the candidates in the election of 1968:

- Democrat Hubert Horatio Humphrey (1911–78)
- Republican Richard Milhous Nixon (1913–94)
- American Independent George Corley Wallace (1919–98)

* * * *

The character Travis Binkle in the movie Taxi Driver *was partially based on Arthur Bremer.*

* * * *

Arthur Bremer was released from prison in 2007.

* * * *

Election of 1972

In one of the greatest landslides in U.S. presidential election history, Republican Richard Nixon (1913–94) won reelection, gathering 520 electoral votes to 17 for Democrat **George McGovern** (1922–). McGovern carried only Massachusetts (14 votes) and Washington, D.C. (3 votes). Nixon won the popular vote by approximately 18 million votes, only to resign the presidency 21 months later. In 2008, McGovern celebrated his 86th birthday.

Children of Pre-1960 Presidents

When Harry Truman's only child, novelist Margaret Truman, died in 2008 at age 83, **John S. D. Eisenhower,** son of President Dwight Eisenhower, became the only living child of a pre-1960 U.S. president. The year 1960 is significant because all presidents serving before 1960 were born in the 18th and 19th centuries; all after have been born in the 20th century.

In addition to being a retired brigadier general, John Eisenhower is one of America's most respected military historians. He turned 86 in 2008.

Presidents Who Reached 90 Years of Age

With the resignation of Richard Nixon in 1974, **Gerald Ford** became president. Ford was formerly head of the Republican minority in the House of Representatives. He was also a member of the Warren Commission that investigated the Kennedy assassination, and he secretly kept the FBI informed about the Warren Commission investigation.

When Ford died at 93 years and 5½ months old, he was the oldest former U.S. president in history. He was also the last living of the four chief executives to reach 90 years of age.

The following were the other presidents who lived to their 90th birthdays:

- John Adams, 90 (1732–1826), president 1797–1801
- Herbert Hoover, 90 (1874–1964), president 1929–33
- Ronald Reagan, 93 (1911–2004), president 1981–89

Presidents Who Didn't Go to College

Harry S. Truman (1884–1972), who died in 1972, was the last living president who did not attend a college or university.

The following were the other U.S. presidents who did not attend college:

- George Washington (1732–99)
- Andrew Jackson (1767–1845)
- Martin Van Buren (1782–1862)
- Zachary Taylor (1784–1850)
- Millard Fillmore (1800–74)
- Abraham Lincoln (1809–65)
- Andrew Johnson (1808–75)
- Grover Cleveland (1837–1908)

Presidents Who Served as College Presidents

Three U.S. presidents served as college or university presidents before ascending to the presidency of the country. Of the three, **Dwight D. Eisenhower** was the last. He passed away on March 28, 1969.

The following were the U.S. presidents who served as college presidents:

- James A. Garfield (1831–81), Hiram College
- Woodrow Wilson (1856–1924), Princeton University
- Dwight D. Eisenhower (1891–1969), Columbia University

Children of President John F. Kennedy

John F. Kennedy, one of the most popular U.S. presidents of the 20th century, was assassinated in Dallas, Texas, on November 22, 1963. He and his wife, Jacqueline, had three children: **Caroline Bouvier Kennedy,** who turned six years old four days after her father died, John Fitzgerald Kennedy Jr., who turned three years old two days after his father's death, and a newborn son, Patrick Bouvier Kennedy, who had died earlier in 1963. Caroline was the last survivor of the children. Turning 51 years old in 2008, she is a lawyer and an author. She is also a founder of the Profiles in Courage Award. Her brother John died in an airplane crash in 1999.

Ronald Reagan's "Kitchen Cabinet"

Earle M. Jorgensen, founder of a steel distribution company and one of Ronald Reagan's closest advisers, died in 1999 at age 101. He was part of a group of advisers that was referred to as Reagan's Kitchen Cabinet because they met informally. The following were other members of Reagan's Kitchen Cabinet:

- Alfred Bloomingdale (1916–82) was a grandson of the department store founder.
- Justin Dart (1907–84) was the son-in-law of Charles Walgreen, founder of Walgreens drugstores.
- Holmes Tuttle (1906–89) was a California auto dealer.
- William French Smith (1917–90) was Reagan's personal attorney.
- Jaquelin Hume (1905–91) was a dried foods producer.
- Leonard Firestone (1907–97) was the son of the founder of Firestone Tire & Rubber Co.
- Henry Salvatori (1901–97) founded an oil company.

Presidents Who Were Not Born in Hospitals

The last U.S. president who was not born in a hospital was **George H. W. Bush.** He was born in 1924 in a private home in Milton, Massachusetts. As of 2009, Bush was alive and well at age 84. The only U.S. presidents born in hospitals (as of 2009) were Jimmy Carter (1924–), Bill Clinton (1946–), George W. Bush (1946–), and Barack Obama (1961–).

Presidents Named James

More U.S. presidents have carried the first name of James than any other name. The last surviving was **James "Jimmy" Carter** (1924–), who was still alive in 2009. The other U.S. presidents named James were:

- James Monroe (1758–1831)
- James Madison (1751–1836)
- James Polk (1795–1849)
- James Buchanan (1791–1868)
- James A. Garfield (1831–81)

Vice Presidents Named John

The most common first name for U.S. vice presidents is John. Of the five men with this name, the last was Franklin Roosevelt's first vice president, **John Nance Garner.** Garner died in 1967.

Election of 1976

When President Gerald Ford (1913–2006) ran for election in 1976, he was defeated by Democratic former Georgia governor **Jimmy Carter** (1924–).

Although Carter lost to Ronald Reagan in the next election, he was lauded during his later years for his humanitarian efforts. He even won the 2002 Nobel Peace Prize. The last survivor of this election, Carter celebrated his 84th birthday in 2008.

Election of 1984

This election resulted in a reelection landslide for Republican Ronald Reagan (1911–2004). Democrat **Walter Mondale** (1928–) lost the popular vote in 49 states, carrying only Washington, D.C., and his home state of Minnesota (by fewer than 4,000 votes). Mondale, the last survivor of the 1984 election, celebrated his 81st birthday in 2009.

* * * *

For all elections after 1984, all participants were still alive as of 2009.

* * * *

Wives of Ronald Reagan

Of the six presidents to be married more than once, Ronald Reagan was the only one who was divorced, and both wives survived him. The last survivor of the two wives was his second wife, First Lady **Nancy Davis Reagan,** who celebrated her 87th birthday in 2008. Reagan's first wife, Academy Award–winning actress Jane Wyman, died in September 2007 at age 90.

Asian History

❑ ❑ ❑ ❑

Who was the last World War II Japanese soldier to surrender?
What was Deng Xiaoping's role in the Tiananmen Square massacre?
Why did Le Duc Tho decline the Nobel Prize?
All the answers are in this chapter.

The Original Siamese Twins

When Chang and **Eng** were born in Siam (modern-day Thailand) in 1811, they were joined at the chest. The two traveled the world on exhibition tours and eventually settled in North Carolina. There they took the last name Bunker, married sisters, and had 10 and 11 children, respectively. At one point, they consulted with medical professionals about the option of surgical separation, but most experts at the time deemed the procedure too risky. On January 17, 1874, Eng awoke to find that Chang had died in his sleep. Eng expired several hours later, reportedly of shock and sorrow.

* * * *

Understandably, Chang and Eng struggled with their coexistence. At one point, Chang took to drinking heavily, which led Eng to join a temperance society. Eng lectured on behalf of the society at times, and during his lectures Chang stood next to him and drank from a flask the whole time.

* * * *

The Legendary Flying Tigers

Long Qiming is the last man in China to have been a member of the American Volunteer Group known as the Flying Tigers. During World War II, the Tigers flew supplies from India to China and were credited with downing more than 2,500 Japanese aircraft.

World War II Japanese Soldiers Discovered on U.S. Territory

Japanese World War II veteran sergeant **Shoichi Yokoi** was discovered on the island of Guam in April 1972 after spending 27 years hiding in its jungles. Yokoi knew the war was over but feared he would be killed if captured. In order to survive undetected, Yokoi lived in a cave and emerged only to obtain food and necessary articles. His diet consisted of coconuts, bananas, mangoes, papaya, breadfruit, eels, snails, and rats, and his clothing was painstakingly assembled from the fibers of wild hibiscus plants and tree bark.

After being discovered by local hunters Jesus Duenas and Manuel DeGracia, Yokoi was returned to Japan. There he received a hero's welcome for his enduring loyalty but waved off the attention. "It is with much embarrassment that I have returned alive," explained Yokoi.

Life in Japan was far from the spartan affair Yokoi had experienced in Guam. After marrying and becoming accustomed to modern life, Yokoi became a television personality. With 27 years of self-survival tactics under his belt, Yokoi advocated the benefits of an austere lifestyle. The plucky survivor died of a heart attack in 1997 at age 82.

The Last World War II Japanese Soldier to Surrender

Lieutenant **Hiroo Onoda** did not stop fighting for Imperial Japan in the Philippines until March 1974. Two fellow soldiers had been killed in gun battles with local authorities over the years, but Onoda remained at large, believing that the war was still ongoing. He brushed off any contrary talk as a trick.

Onoda finally gave up when his commanding officer was flown to the Philippines to order his surrender. He returned to Japan in 1974 and immigrated to Brazil the following year.

In 2004, the 82-year-old Onoda was honored by the Brazilian air force for his remarkable military record. He was still alive as of 2009.

Major World War II Figures

Madame Chiang Kai-shek, wife of Nationalist Chinese leader Chiang Kai-shek, was the last surviving major figure of World War II. In 1943, in an attempt to obtain support for China in its war with Japan, she became the second woman ever to address a joint session of Congress. Madame Chiang Kai-shek died on October 23, 2003, at age 105.

1940s Monarchs Who Reigned Through the End of the 20th Century

King Bhumibol Adulyadej of Thailand (born 1927) ascended to the throne in 1946, just seven years after the country's name changed from Siam. Well-liked by his people, he was still reigning as of 2009.

The Batang Kali Massacre

In December 1948, Britain's Scots Guards killed 24 unarmed Malaysian men. The incident has been compared to the My Lai massacre in Vietnam. The Batang Kali Massacre has never been fully investigated by either British or Malaysian authorities. The only survivor, **Chong Hong,** was 82 years old in 2008. He was 22 years old at the time of the massacre, and he survived by pretending to be dead.

The "Gang of Four"

After the 1976 death of People's Republic of China founder Mao Zedong, four key Communist party leaders, known as the Gang of Four, were arrested and accused of committing crimes during the Cultural Revolution.

The Cultural Revolution, a political campaign launched by Communist party chairman Mao Zedong and executed by the Gang of Four, was designed to eradicate political rivals and revolutionize Chinese society. Student groups called Red Guards were indoctrinated with marching orders to "smash the four olds" (ideas, culture, customs, and habits). Their work included the destruction of temples, artwork, books—anything considered connected to traditional or foreign cultures. But the abuses didn't end there. Writers, artists, and other free thinkers were subjected to public criticism, humiliation, and physical abuse. Millions of people were sent from the cities to the country to perform manual labor. Thousands were killed outright by the Red Guard or committed suicide as a last-ditch effort to end their torment.

When Mao Zedong died in 1976, Hua Guofeng assumed power. The members of the Gang of Four were arrested and imprisoned after attempting a coup d'état. They were publicly tried in 1980 and found guilty of treason. The last survivor of the Gang of Four, **Yao Wenyuan,** died December 23, 2005.

The following were the other members of the Gang of Four:

- Jiang Qing (1914–91)
- Wang Hongwen (1935–92)
- Zhang Chunqiao (1917–April 21, 2005)

* * * *

Jiang Qing was Mao Zedong's widow.

* * * *

Founders of the People's Republic of China

Lifelong Communist **Deng Xiaoping** followed Mao Zedong on the harrowing 1934–35 "Long March"—a 6,000-mile trek the Communist army undertook to flee south China and the Nationalist army. The Communists headed north to reestablish a base in Yan'an. For his loyalty, Xiaoping would rise to the top of the Chinese Communist Party. After attaining de facto power in 1978, Xiaoping would implement "Socialism with Chinese Characteristics," a new model for Chinese economic reform. The system featured state ownership of a large portion of the economy while allowing individual entities the ability to participate in markets.

Trumpeting the values of the new arrangement, Xiaoping proclaimed: "Poverty is not socialism; to be rich is glorious." The quote directly countered the "Better to be poor under socialism than rich under capitalism" proclamation endorsed by the Gang of Four and their followers. With this mind-set leading the way, Xiaoping implemented major changes toward a market-based economy.

Xiaoping's push toward economic prosperity over Mao Zedong–era nationalism continues to this day. In an additional move, Xiaoping helped open trade between China and the West. By 1985, this new influx of capital accounted for 20 percent of China's gross national product. The last of the People's Republic of China's major founders, Deng Xiaoping was 92 years old when he died in 1997.

Tiananmen Square

When protestors took to Peking's Tiananmen Square demanding an end to political corruption in April 1989, not many people noticed. The group, comprised heavily of students, assembled peaceably to push for democratic reform from a government it viewed as corrupt. Over time, however, the crowd grew in volume. By May, there were approximately one million people in the square, with countless more staging protests on the city's streets. People from all walks of life were standing beside the students in solidarity against the government. Fearing a civil war, Deng Xiaoping sent in the military to break up the demonstration. His efforts failed. An uneasy standoff persisted for the rest of the month.

On June 4, the situation turned deadly. The army opened fire on unarmed protestors in the streets. No one knows for certain what triggered the violence, but an estimated 3,000 people were killed during the massacre, with an additional 10,000 sustaining injuries. Opinion is divided on Xiaoping's role in the incident. Some claim that the leader issued a "no shoot" order to his soldiers, while others—including former premier Li Peng (who himself has been blamed for the slaughter)—maintained that Xiaoping thought the actions were necessary to maintain control. Due to global media coverage, China's heavy-handed actions were condemned by nations across the world.

Individuals Who Have Declined a Nobel Prize

Only two people in the 106-year history of the Nobel Prize have declined the award. Jean-Paul Sartre, who was awarded the 1964 Nobel Prize in Literature, was the first to decline, and **Le Duc Tho,** who was awarded the 1973 Nobel Peace Prize, was the other. The last survivor of the two, Tho, died on Oct. 13, 1990, one day before his 79th birthday. He fought the French and the Americans in Vietnam and was instrumental in arranging the cease-fire of 1973 that resulted in the American withdrawal. He declined the prize because he did not believe that peace had truly been established.

The "Eight Immortals"

Besides the Eight Immortals of Chinese mythology, the term has been applied to eight of the People's Republic of China's Communist Party leaders. These men all participated in the Long March, and after the death of Mao Zedong in 1976, they introduced the economic reforms that brought about China's prosperity after 1980. The last living of these eight was **Bo Yibo,** who died in 2007 at age 98.

The following were the other Eight Immortals:

- Song Renqiong (1909–2005) was a general in the People's Liberation Army.
- Yang Shangkun (1907–98) served as president of China from 1988 to 1993.
- Peng Zhen (1902–April 26, 1997) was chairman of the National People's Congress from 1983 to 1988.
- Deng Xiaoping (1904–February 19, 1997) was China's chief policy maker from 1980 to 1989.
- Chen Yun (1905–95) was a member of the Chinese Communist Party Politburo for 53 years (1934–87).
- Wang Zhen (1907–93) served as vice president of China from 1988 to 1993.
- Li Xiannian (1909–92) served as president of China from 1983 to 1988.

Who was the last witness to the crash that killed Knute Rockne?
Why is there an oak from Germany's Black Forest
on the grounds of a Connellsville, Pennsylvania, high school?
Why was Byron Nelson excused from World War II service?
You are about to find out.

The First Modern Olympic Games

The first Olympic Games of modern times were held in Athens in April 1896. Of the 14 participating nations, Greece, Germany, France, and Great Britain sent the largest delegations. **Sir George Roberts,** a British discus thrower, was the last surviving Olympic athlete to have competed that year. He died in London in 1967 at age 94.

19th-Century Major-League Baseball Players

Right-handed pitcher **Ralph Miller** played in 29 games for the Brooklyn Bridegrooms and Baltimore Orioles during the 1898 and 1899 seasons. He had a record of 5 wins, 17 losses. When he died in 1973 at age 100, Miller was the last surviving 19th-century major-league player.

* * * *

As of 2006, 12 former major-league baseball players had reached the age of 100. The oldest of all time was Chet Hoff, who pitched for the New York Yankees when they were still known as the Highlanders. Nicknamed "Red," he died in 1998 at age 107.

* * * *

Pittsburgh Players of the First World Series

In 1903, the Boston Americans played the Pittsburgh Pirates in Major League Baseball's first World Series. Boston beat Pittsburgh in five games out of eight. **Tommy Leach** was the last surviving Pittsburgh Pirates player. Just 25 years old at the time, five feet six inches tall, and very thin, he hit four triples in the series. As of 2008, no other player has hit more than three triples in a World Series. Leach's major-league career lasted for 20 years, 14 of which were with Pittsburgh. Leach died in 1969 at age 91.

Boston Players of the First World Series

Freddy Parent was Boston's shortstop in the first World Series in 1903. His batting average for the series was .281, and his major-league career lasted from 1899 to 1911 (1899, St. Louis; 1901–07, Boston; 1908–11, Chicago White Sox). He died at age 96 on November 2, 1972, in the era of Carlton Fisk, Carl Yastrzemski, and Reggie Smith.

Britain's Great Triumvirate

Three legendary golfers, Harry Vardon, James Braid, and **John Henry "J. H." Taylor,** were known as the "Great Triumvirate" in the late 19th and early 20th centuries. These golfers won 16 of the 21 British Opens between 1894 and 1914. Taylor, who won the Opens of 1894, 1895, 1900, 1909, and 1913, was the last survivor. A founder and first president of the British PGA, he passed away at age 91 in 1963.

The "Great Triumvirate" were:

- Harry Vardon (1870–1937), six-time British Open champion
- James Braid (1870–1950), five-time British Open champion
- J. H. Taylor (1871–1963), five-time British Open champion

Pre–World War I Heavyweight Boxing Champions

Boxing champion **Jess Willard** was born on December 29, 1881. Six feet six inches tall, he reigned as heavyweight champ from April 5, 1915, through July 4, 1919. He passed away on December 15, 1968—just before his 87th birthday and five days after Joe Frazier's bout with Oscar Bonavena. Willard was the last survivor of the heavyweight boxing champions before the United States entered World War I.

Pre-World War I heavyweight champions were:

- 1882–92 John Lawrence Sullivan (1858–1918)
- 1892–97 James John Corbett (1866–1933)
- 1897–99 Robert James Fitzsimmons (1862–1917)
- 1899–1905 James Jackson Jeffries (1875–1953)
- 1905–06 Marvin Hart (1876–1931)
- 1906–08 Tommy Burns (1881–1955)
- 1908–15 John "Jack" Johnson (1878–1946)
- 1915–19 Jess Willard (1881–1968)

The 1918 Boston Red Sox

This was the last Red Sox team to win the World Series until 2004. Third baseman **Fred Thomas** died in 1986 at age 93. He started with Boston on April 22, 1918, and played off and on throughout the year. However, he started every game of the World Series. Boston won the Series in six games, and Thomas got two hits in 17 at-bats. He remained in the majors for the 1919 and 1920 seasons.

Notre Dame's Four Horsemen

The most famous players of 1920s college football were the "Four Horsemen" on Knute Rockne's Notre Dame team. Sportswriter Grantland Rice helped make this Notre Dame backfield famous by comparing them to the Four Horsemen of the Apocalypse: "Outlined against a blue-gray October sky, the Four Horsemen rode again. In dramatic lore, they are known as famine, pestilence, destruction and death. These are only aliases. Their real names are Stuhldreher, Miller, Crowley, and Layden." The Four Horsemen led Notre Dame to a 1923 national championship, a 1925 Rose Bowl win over Stanford, and a 26–1–2 record from 1922 to 1924. Halfback **Jim Crowley,** who went on to coach at Fordham, was the last surviving horseman, dying in 1986 at age 83.

The following were the Four Horsemen of Notre Dame:

- Harry Stuhldreher, quarterback; College Football Hall of Fame induction 1958; died 1965
- Elmer Layden, fullback; College Football Hall of Fame induction 1951; died 1973
- Don Miller, halfback; College Football Hall of Fame induction 1970; died 1979
- Jim Crowley, halfback; College Football Hall of Fame induction 1966; died 1986

* * * *

Crowley's high school coach was Curly Lambeau, founder of the Green Bay Packers. At Fordham, Crowley coached Vince Lombardi, who would become a Packers legend.

* * * *

The U.S. Postal Service issued an honorary Four Horsemen stamp in 1998.

* * * *

The 1927 Yankees

The 1927 New York Yankees was arguably the best professional baseball team of all time. Players included Babe Ruth (1895–1948), Lou Gehrig (1903–41), Earle Combs (1899–1976), and Tony Lazzeri (1903–46). Shortstop **Mark Koenig,** the last survivor of the team, played major-league ball from 1925 through 1936, including five

World Series: 1926, 1927, and 1928 for the Yankees; 1932 for the Cubs; and 1936 for the Giants. He passed away on April 22, 1993, at age 88.

Inventors of Major Sports

Basketball is the only major team sport that is native to the United States. Also the most popular indoor team sport in the world, it was invented in Springfield, Massachusetts, by **James Naismith** (1861–1939), who arranged the first game in December 1891. Naismith played the game only twice because he felt he committed too many fouls (he believed this was because his extensive experience in wrestling and football made physical contact come naturally to him). In 1936, basketball was added as an Olympic sport. After many years as a professor of physical education at the University of Kansas, Naismith died in 1939.

The following were founders of other major American team sports:

- Baseball: Alexander Joy Cartwright (1820–92)
- American football: Walter Camp (1859–1925)

The "Four Musketeers"

Between 1927 and 1932, four French tennis players won six consecutive Davis Cups. They also won numerous Wimbledon and French championships in the 1920s and 1930s. **René Lacoste** (1904–96) was the last member of the team, outliving Jean Borotra by two years. Lacoste retired from the team in 1928 because of health problems. The other three played until 1933 or 1934.

The following were the other Four Musketeers of French tennis:

- Jacques Brugnon (1895–1978)
- Henri Cochet (1901–87)
- Jean Borotra (1898–1994)

French Players of the First World Cup

The World Cup began when 13 teams met in Uruguay in 1930. Eight South American nations, four European nations, and the United States were represented. France achieved the first goal of the games in its 4–1 win over Mexico. The goal was scored by **Lucien Laurent,** who died in 2005 at age 97. He was the last living player of the 1930 French World Cup team.

Witnesses to the Rockne Crash

The greatest Notre Dame University football coach in history, Knute Rockne compiled an impressive record during his time as head coach (1918 to 1930): 105 wins, 12 losses, and 5 ties. At age 43, he finished the 1930 season with a 10–0 record and the national championship.

On March 31, 1931, Rockne took off on a flight to Los Angeles; he was planning to serve as an adviser on a Hollywood movie about Notre Dame. One of his plane's wings broke en route, and the small craft dropped into a Kansas wheat field. He and the other four people aboard were killed. **James Easter Heathman,** a farmer's son who was 14 at the time of the crash, heard the plane coming down and immediately drove to the site with his father. In his last years, Heathman took visitors to the crash site; he did this without charge out of respect for Rockne's memory. He was the last living witness to the crash when he died in 2008 at age 90.

The Original Pittsburgh Steelers

In 1933, its first year of existence, the Pittsburgh Steelers football team was called the Pittsburgh Pirates. **Ray Kemp** was the only African American on the team at the time and one of only two in the NFL (Joe Lillard of the Chicago Cardinals was the other). When Kemp died in March 2002 at age 94, he was the last survivor of Pittsburgh's original team.

The First Masters

Golf legend Bobby Jones and investment banker Clifford Roberts founded the Masters Tournament in 1934. Initially named the Augusta National Invitation Tournament, it was renamed the Masters in 1939. Of the 70 men who played in the first tournament, **Errie Ball** is the last living. He was 15 years old when he began his career in 1926 at the British Open. In 1930, Bobby Jones encouraged him to come to the United States to play. He did, and he stayed into the 21st century. Ball was still playing golf in 2008 at age 97.

The 1936 U.S. Olympic Track Team

The U.S. Olympic Track Team of 1936 is most noted for the historic performance of Jesse Owens at the games in Nazi Germany. The last survivor of the team was **John Woodruff,** a grandson of former Virginia slaves who was born in Connellsville, Pennsylvania, in 1915. He grew to be six feet three and one quarter inches tall and earned national recognition in high school by running 880 yards in 1:55.1 twice in one week. This feat led to a scholarship offer from the University of Pittsburgh. Woodruff had not planned to attend college, but when he went to apply for jobs after high school, he found only racist rebuffs. Woodruff headed for Pittsburgh—the first in his family to attend college.

After arriving in Pittsburgh, Woodruff competed with the track team, but when other schools refused to compete against blacks, he stayed behind in Pittsburgh. Woodruff earned money by working on the campus grounds and cleaning the football stadium after games. He completed his freshman year before heading to the Berlin Olympics.

Woodruff's 800-meter race at Berlin started off badly. He became boxed in by other runners, and he came to an almost dead stop in the confusion. These circumstances, however, allowed him room to get to the outside of the pack. Once there, Woodruff blew past the other runners. The result was a thrilling come-from-behind victory—and a gold medal.

After college, Woodruff joined the army, where he fought in World War II and Korea and rose to the rank of lieutenant colonel. After his retirement from the military, he settled in New York and went into coaching and officiating. Woodruff moved to an assisted-living facility in Arizona with Rose, his wife of nearly 40 years, and passed away in 2007 at age 92.

* * * *

Woodruff once ran the 800 meters in 1:49.9, which was only a tenth of a second off the world record.

* * * *

Each Berlin winner was awarded a Black Forest oak sapling from the German government. Woodruff's oak is on the grounds of his old high school in Connellsville, Pennsylvania.

* * * *

The Baseball Hall of Fame

When the Baseball Hall of Fame opened in 1936, it inducted five players. **Ty Cobb** (1886–1961) was the last surviving inductee. Cobb received the most votes that year and is a strong contender for the title of baseball's greatest player of all time. He is also a competitor for the title of baseball's surliest player ever.

Cobb was born in Narrows, Georgia. His father wanted him to work in business; baseball was always Cobb's chief interest, however, and his father finally decided to stop trying to dissuade his son. Some explain Cobb's brutishness by pointing to the fact that his father never got to see him play in the majors. Cobb seemed to never stop trying to prove himself.

He was rumored to file his spikes before games to make his slides more intimidating (during his playing years he never addressed this topic, but he did deny it after retirement). Cobb once went after a heckler in the New York stands and gave him a severe beating, even though the fan was disabled from a workplace accident. Cobb went after a groundskeeper in Augusta, Georgia, in another bizarre display, and he even went after the groundskeeper's wife when she tried to break up the fight.

No one could take issue with Cobb's performance on the field, however. When he retired after the 1928 season, he held 90 records. When he died in 1961, he was worth $12 million, mostly a result of his investments in Coca-Cola and United Motors (now GM). Only three former teammates and one Baseball Hall of Fame representative attended his funeral.

The following were the other four players who were inducted into the first Hall of Fame class:

- Christy Mathewson (1880–1925)
- Walter Johnson (1887–1946)
- Babe Ruth (1895–1948)
- Honus Wagner (1874–1955)

A Domestic Incident

Cobb's mother shot his father in a horrible accident on August 8, 1905. Cobb's father suspected his wife of infidelity, and told her he had to go out of town. That night he came back to spy on her. When Amanda Cobb saw a figure creeping around on the porch outside her bedroom, she grabbed a shotgun and fired it twice. Amanda was arrested for voluntary manslaughter, but was later acquitted after she said she had mistaken her husband for an intruder.

* * * *

Once, when Cobb was walking with his wife on the streets of Detroit, they were victims of an attempted mugging. When the gun Cobb was carrying failed to fire, Cobb chased the mugger down and beat him with the pistol.

* * * *

* * * *

Babe Ruth and Ty Cobb were intense rivals. Ruth hit for the fences, but Cobb strongly believed in the strategy of hits, steals, and RBI. Cobb hit for the fences during one game, just to prove he could. He pounded three homers in that game.

* * * *

Negro Leagues All-Star Team

The Baseball Hall of Fame Committee on Negro Baseball Leagues selected players it felt were the finest in the leagues to make up an all-star team. Only one of those players was still alive in 2008—right fielder **Monte Irvin.** He was born on February 25, 1919, and spent many years in the Negro Leagues. After the color line was broken, Irvin joined the New York Giants in 1949, batting .458 (11 hits in 24 at-bats) in the 1951 World Series. He played in the major leagues until 1956.

The Negro Leagues All-Star team included:

- Josh Gibson, catcher; born December 21, 1911, in Buena Vista, Georgia; died January 20, 1947
- Oscar Charleston, center fielder; born October 14, 1896, in Indianapolis, Indiana; died October 5, 1954
- Pop Lloyd, shortstop; born April 25, 1884, in Gainesville, Florida; died March 19, 1965
- Martin Dihigo, second baseman; born May 24, 1905, in Matanzas, Cuba; died May 20, 1971
- Satchel Paige, pitcher; born July 7, 1906, in Mobile, Alabama; died June 8, 1982
- Judy Johnson, third baseman; born October 26, 1899, in Snow Hill, Maryland; died June 15, 1989
- Cool Papa Bell, left fielder; born May 17, 1903, in Starkville, Mississippi; died March 7, 1991

- Buck Leonard, first baseman; born September 8, 1907, in Rocky Mountain, North Carolina; died November 27, 1997
- Monte Irvin (Monford Merrill Irvin), right fielder; born February 25, 1919, in Columbia, Alabama

The Gashouse Gang

The 1934 St. Louis Cardinals major-league baseball team fought an uphill battle to the World Series, where they beat the Detroit Tigers. Their star pitcher, Dizzy Dean, became a legend that season.

The last surviving player on the team was second baseman **Burgess Whitehead.** Whitehead played with the Cardinals from 1933 through 1935, before moving on to five years with the New York Giants. After World War II, he played one season with the Pittsburgh Pirates. Whitehead passed away at age 83 in 1993.

* * * *

The 1934 Cardinals were nicknamed the Gashouse Gang because many agreed they bore a strong resemblance to the tough characters who hung out in Manhattan's Gashouse District.

* * * *

A Three-Soda Salute

In the sixth inning of the seventh game of the 1934 World Series, the St. Louis Cardinals were winning handily. St. Louis baserunner Ducky Medwick slid into third with his spikes up and proceeded to kick Tigers third baseman Marvin Owen. The Detroit crowd let the outfielder have it in the next half of the inning, pelting him with hot dogs and soda bottles. He left the field three times, but each time he came back, the fans began pelting him again. The baseball commissioner ended the situation himself by throwing Medwick out of the game.

Negro League Umpires

Bob Motley is the last living man to have umpired in baseball's Negro Leagues. In 2007, he and his son released the memoir *Ruling Over Monarchs, Giants & Stars: Umpiring in the Negro Leagues & Beyond.* As of 2008, Motley was 84 years old.

Baseball's DiMaggio Brothers

Hall of Famer Joe DiMaggio (1914–99) played 13 years for the New York Yankees. One of the greatest players in history, his 56-game hitting streak in 1941 has never been broken. His older brother, Vince DiMaggio, who played with five National League teams for a total of ten years, passed away in 1986. The third (and youngest) brother, **Dom DiMaggio,** was a center fielder with the Boston Red Sox for 11 seasons (1940–42, 1946–53). Nicknamed the "Little Professor," he still holds the record for the longest consecutive game hitting streak in Red Sox history. Dom died in 2009 at age 92.

Professional Golf Greats of the 1940s

Byron Nelson, the last of the professional golf greats of the 1940s, was born on February 4, 1912, in Waxahachie, Texas. His first experience with golf came in 1922 as a caddie. He defeated Ben Hogan in a caddie championship a year later, then went on to a career in business while continuing to play golf in his spare time. With the coming of the Great Depression, jobs became more difficult to come by, and Nelson turned pro in 1932. He won five major golf championships and 11 straight tournaments in 1945. By 1946, Nelson was able to afford a ranch in Texas, and he retired. Nelson died in 2006 at age 94.

The following were the greatest golfers of the 1940s:

- Ben Hogan (1912–97), Masters (2), U.S. Open (4), British Open (1), PGA (2)
- Sam Snead (1912–2002), Masters (3), U.S. Open (0), British Open (1), PGA (3)
- Byron Nelson (1912–2006), Masters (2), U.S. Open (1), British Open (0), PGA (2)

* * * *

Byron Nelson was nicknamed "Lord Byron" as a tribute to his kind, gracious manner.

* * * *

Byron Nelson was excused from service during World War II because he was a hemophiliac.

* * * *

Pro Football Hall of Fame

The Pro Football Hall of Fame inducted its first group of players in 1963. Of those 17 men, **Sammy Baugh,** a veteran of 16 seasons (1937–62) with the Washington Redskins, was the last survivor.

Quarterback Baugh was primarily responsible for the development of the forward pass into a major offensive weapon; he threw with stunning accuracy. In one 1947 game, Baugh passed for 355 yards and 6 touchdowns.

"Slingin' Sammy" is also widely recognized as the best punter in professional football history, holding the records for highest career punting average (45.1 yards per kick) and highest season punting average (51.4 yards in 1940). Baugh passed away in 2008 at age 94.

Major-League Pitchers Who Won More than 30 Games in a Single Season

In the history of major-league baseball, only 11 pitchers have won more than 30 games in one season, and since 1917, only one has: Detroit's **Denny McLain** in 1968. He won 31 games that year and was still alive at age 64 in early 2009.

McLain grew up on the South Side of Chicago and was a mighty force on the Detroit Tigers' mound until age 26. His won/lost records from 1965 to 69 were 16–6, 20–14, 17–16, 31–6, 24–9. By age 28, he was washed up and released by the Atlanta Braves. What in the name of Cy Young happened?

For one thing, his pitching shoulder had been junked, perhaps by overwork. His off-field troubles began with gambling, then bookmaking, then underworld contacts. In 1970, McLain was suspended from baseball for gambling. He declared bankruptcy that year and again in 1977. A jury sent him up the river for racketeering in 1984, and in 1997 another jury convicted McLain and an associate of taking more than $2 million from a workers' pension fund.

At this writing McLain, a free man, trades commodities for a living. Sentimental baseball fans dare hope that doesn't change.

Major-League Pitchers with ERAs of Less than 1.15

In 1968, St. Louis right-hander **Bob Gibson** finished the season with a 1.12 Earned Run Average (ERA). He was the last living major-league pitcher to have an ERA of less than 1.15. Four other men have achieved the feat, all before 1915: Mordecai Brown (1.04 in 1906), Christy Mathewson (1.14 in 1909), Walter Johnson (1.14 in 1913), and Dutch Leonard (1.01 in 1914).

The Baseball Hall of Fame's Pioneer or Executive Category

Of the 26 men and one woman elected to the Baseball Hall of Fame's Pioneer or Executive Category, only general manager **Lee MacPhail** was still living as of 2009. After holding the position of Baltimore Orioles general manager, he became director of player personnel for the New York Yankees, then served as president of the American League in the 1970s and 1980s. Born on October 25, 1917, MacPhail was inducted by the Hall of Fame Veterans Committee in 1998.

The American West

❑ ❑ ❑ ❑

Who was the first Mormon to run for President?
Did the Donner party follow the normal western route?
Who was the last survivor of the Battle of the Little Bighorn?
If you're intrigued, you're also in luck—
the answers can be found in this very chapter.

The Joseph Smith Murder

After founding the Mormon Church in 1830, Joseph Smith searched for a peaceful place to settle down with his followers. But wherever they went, trouble followed.

First they settled in Kirtland, Ohio. By 1838, the other residents of that city were resentful of the Mormons and their increasing numbers, and Smith and his followers moved to Far West, Missouri. They were there less than a year before opposition rose up. They fled to Commerce, Illinois, and renamed the town Nauvoo (Hebrew for "beautiful place"). This settlement was peaceful for several years, and the town became powerful; it was the second largest city in the state after Chicago. It was during this time that the Mormons began to practice polygamy, and this—together with their growing numbers and power—again aroused resentment from neighboring communities.

Smith served as mayor and chief judge in Nauvoo, and when a community newspaper published an article critical of the Mormons, Smith ordered the newspaper's offices shut down. This action sparked outrage and riots. Authorities from nearby Carthage arrested Smith and his brother Hyrum and charged them with inciting a riot. On June 27, 1844, a large mob attacked the Smith brothers and supporters **John Taylor** (1808–87) and Dr. Willard Richards (1804–54) at the Carthage jail. Hyrum was shot in the face and died instantly; Joseph was shot multiple times and died as he tried to escape through a second-story window. The last of the four men was Taylor, who was shot four times but survived. In 1880, after the death of Brigham Young, Taylor became the third president of the Mormon Church. He died in 1887 at age 78.

Joseph Smith Founds a New Church

When Joseph Smith was 14 years old, he struggled over which church to join. His mother attended a local church, but his father did not. Not sure what to do, he began to pray about it. According to Smith, one day as he was praying, God and Jesus appeared and told him that all existing churches had deviated too much from Jesus's original teachings. A few years later, an angel named Moroni appeared to Smith and told him about a set of gold plates that contained a record of ancient Americans who were visited by Christ after his resurrection. Smith found the plates buried near his family farm, and four years later the angel helped him translate them. Smith published the Book of Mormon in 1830. Today the sacred text steers Mormon followers who believe that their church is the authentic restoration of the church established by Jesus Christ during New Testament times.

* * * *

Joseph Smith justified the practice of polygamy by pointing to the figure of Abraham in the Old Testament. Smith is believed to have had nearly 30 wives, though he claimed to have only one.

* * * *

In April 1844, Joseph Smith announced his candidacy for the office of president of the United States. He was killed two months later.

* * * *

The Donner Party

In 1846, farmers George and Jacob Donner and businessman James Reed succumbed to the land fever that was sweeping the country. Their families had plenty of land and money in Springfield, Illinois, but they were anxious to attain more wealth out west.

On April 16, 1846, the Donner party headed to Independence, Missouri. The party consisted of nine wagons (including the Reed family's luxurious, cumbersome wagon) carrying 87 people. The group left Independence on May 12, after the spring rains had subsided. The journey they were undertaking would take them 2,500 miles, across plains, deserts, the Great Basin, and three mountain ranges. It was necessary to arrive at Sutter's Fort in California ahead of the snows that blanketed the Sierra Nevada Mountains in the winter.

The group came upon the Little Sandy River (in present-day Wyoming) on July 20. Up to that point the journey had been smooth, but here they made the fatal mistake of attempting a shortcut George Donner knew about from reading Lansford Hastings's *The Emigrant's Guide to Oregon and California.* Although Hastings described this shortcut in his publication, no one had ever tested it.

The first obstacle they encountered was dense brush, and it was a battle to get the wagons through. Next they faced a maze of canyons that took them a month to navigate. Finally they came across the Great Salt Lake Desert. The group struggled through five blistering days and freezing nights to make the 80-mile trek that *The Emigrant's Guide* had led them to believe would be only 40 miles.

By the time the group made it out of the desert, it was early September. They soon began noticing snow flurries—the first sign of the coming winter. They were discouraged but trudged on, as there would be no point in turning back now. In early November they became trapped in the snowy Sierra Nevada Mountains, 150 miles from their destination. All they could do was build rough cabins and settle in until the worst of the winter was over. They had little, if anything, left to eat. The group was trapped for four months. Before they were rescued, 40 had died, with some of the forlorn survivors having resorted to cannibalism. The last living member of the Donner party was **Margaret Breen,** who died in 1935. She was only one year old at the time of the tragedy and remembered nothing of it.

* * * *

With the exception of the Donner party, all the groups that left Independence, Missouri, in 1846 arrived in California safely.

* * * *

✱ ✱ ✱ ✱

The "shortcut" the Donner party used was actually 125 miles longer than the regular route.

✱ ✱ ✱ ✱

George Donner was chosen as the captain of the Donner party because James Reed's superior attitude annoyed the rest of the group.

✱ ✱ ✱ ✱

At the End of Their Ropes

On October 5, James Reed and John Snyder (the driver of one of the wagons) got into an altercation, which was mostly the result of frayed nerves over their plight. James Reed stabbed Snyder after Snyder struck him with his whip, and Snyder died from the stab wound. Most of the group considered Reed a murderer after the incident, and he was banished from the party. Reed made it to Sutter's Fort in late October and tried to recruit people to go back into the mountains to search for the rest of the group. He was unsuccessful for weeks, however, because most men from the area were off fighting the Mexicans for control of California.

The Brigham Young Party

In 1846, Brigham Young led Mormon settlers on a 1,500-mile westward migration. After halting for the winter of 1846–47, Young continued west with an advance party of 148 people. On July 24, 1847, he arrived at the mouth of Emigration Canyon. Here, he declared, "This is the right place," and continued down the valley to establish the permanent settlement of Salt Lake City. The last survivor of the people who were with Young when he made this statement was his six-year-old nephew, **Lorenzo Sobieski Young.** Son of Brigham's brother Lorenzo Dow Young and Persis Goodall, he died in 1924 at age 83.

Murieta's Gangs

One of the most famous outlaws of the Old West, Joaquín Murieta turned to crime after his mining claim was unjustly taken, his wife raped, and his brother murdered. After years on the run, he was killed by a Texas Ranger in 1853. His head was taken for identification purposes and put on display in a museum in Sacramento, California. The last living member of Murieta's gangs was **Avelino Martinez,** who tended and sold horses acquired by the gangs. Martinez was a *vaquero* and a cook in later years. When he died on August 8, 1936, he was 112 years old.

The Battle of the Little Bighorn

Between 1874 and 1875, miners and crews mapping the route for the Northern Pacific Railroad were venturing onto Native American lands in western South Dakota, even though this area had been given to the Sioux under the 1868 Fort Laramie Treaty. The Native Americans began attacking intruders, and in the spring of 1876, the U.S. government started a military campaign against the Sioux and Cheyenne. Lieutenant Colonel George Armstrong Custer and soldiers of the 7th Cavalry fought an encampment of approximately 2,000 people on June 25, 1876, in Montana. All 263 soldiers and scouts in Custer's direct command were killed. It is believed that the last survivor of the battle was Lakota Sioux **Dewey Beard,** who died in 1955.

* * * *

Had Dewey Beard lived another four years, he would have outlived the best-known movie actor to have played Custer, Errol Flynn, who died in 1959.

* * * *

U.S. 7th Cavalry

Before the Battle of the Little Bighorn, the U.S. 7th Cavalry divided into four battalions, with Lieutenant Colonel George Armstrong Custer in command of two (236 men in all) and Major Marcus A.

Reno and Captain Frederick W. Benteen each commanding one of the others. Reno had approximately 140 men in his command, and Benteen had 100.

Benteen was ordered to move left to scout the area, and he was also instructed to attack any Native Americans he might encounter. Custer ordered Reno to march parallel to and a short distance from Custer's column. Approximately four miles from the Little Bighorn River, Custer ordered Reno to move up and attack; Reno was told that Custer would soon follow and lend his support. Reno's men soon came upon several hundred Indians and commenced the fight. After losing many men, Reno realized the futility of the situation and his group retreated to some bluffs in the distance. They tried to dig in, but had few tools or supplies. Benteen came upon Reno with his men, and the two conferred over how to proceed. They had no idea, but Custer and his men were being slaughtered right about this time.

Reno and Benteen finally decided to descend from the bluffs. A ways into the descent, a battle scene came into view, but they could not discern exactly what was happening. Soon the Native Americans were coming toward them, however, and they again retreated to the bluffs. They exchanged gunfire with the Native Americans for some time, but the Native Americans left once it became dark. They did return the next day, but reinforcements also arrived, and the Native Americans fled.

Once the reinforcements arrived, the troops began to scour the area and realized what had become of Custer and his men. All the soldiers in Custer's battalions died at the Little Bighorn, but there were survivors in the other battalions. **Lieutenant Charles Varnum** was the head of Custer's scouts on the fatal day of June 25, 1876. Riding with Major Reno's battalion, he survived, and his testimony at a later inquiry helped exonerate Reno after charges of cowardice were leveled against him for his actions at the Little Bighorn. When Varnum passed away in 1936, he was the last member of the U.S. 7th Cavalry to die.

* * * *

Two of Custer's brothers also died in the Battle of the Little Bighorn.

* * * *

Children of U.S. 7th Cavalry Survivors

Blacksmith Henry Mechling was under Benteen's command and died in 1926. His daughter, **Minnie Grace Mechling Carey,** the last living child of a 7th Cavalry survivor, passed away in 2006 at age 99.

The Nez Percé War of 1877

For three months in 1877, Chief Joseph's 700 Nez Percé battled the U.S. Army as they retreated to Idaho. They were outnumbered by the 2,000-strong U.S. Army contingent, but they fought with great dignity and courage. Chief Joseph surrendered on October 5, 1877, in the Bear Paw Mountains in Montana.

Josiah Red Wolf, born about 1872, was the last survivor of the Nez Percé War of 1877. He went on to become a farmer, a cobbler, and a country musician. He died in Idaho in 1971.

* * * *

> *"I am tired of fighting. . . . It is cold, and we have no blankets. The little children are freezing to death. My people, some of them, have run away to the hills, and have no blankets, no food. No one knows where they are—perhaps freezing to death. I want to have time to look for my children, and see how many of them I can find. Maybe I shall find them among the dead. Hear me, my chiefs! I am tired. My heart is sick and sad. From where the sun now stands I will fight no more forever."*
>
> *—From Chief Joseph's surrender speech*

* * * *

Gunfight at the O.K. Corral

On October 26, 1881, the most famous gunfight in the history of the American West occurred in the silver mining town of Tombstone, Arizona. Lasting about 30 seconds, the shoot-out left three members of the Clanton-McLaury gang dead and three members of the

Earp/Holliday faction wounded. Only one man was left unscathed—**Wyatt Earp,** who also was the last survivor of the fight when he died in Los Angeles, California, in 1929. Western movie stars Tom Mix and William S. Hart were pallbearers at his funeral.

The following men took part in the O.K. Corral gunfight:

Ike Clanton (1847–87), left before the shooting started

Frank McLaury (1848–81), shot to death

Tom McLaury (1853–81), shot to death

Billy Clanton (1862–81), shot to death

John H. "Doc" Holliday (1851–87), wounded on the hip

Virgil Earp (1843–1905), shot in the leg

Morgan Earp (1851–82), shot in the shoulders

Wyatt Earp (1848–1929), not wounded

* * * *

"You're looking for a fight and now you can have it."

—Wyatt Earp, to the Clantons and McLaurys

* * * *

Good Guys?

Popular sentiment casts Holliday and the Earps as "the good guys," but others see Clanton and the McLaurys as victims of an outrageous abuse of power. Though Clanton and the McLaurys were accused of being illegally armed, Wyatt Earp and Doc Holliday were not officers of the law at the time either, so they were illegally armed as well.

* * * *

Sheriff Behan witnessed the shoot-out and arrested Holliday and the Earps. A month later a Tombstone judge ruled that the homicides were justified.

* * * *

Buffalo Bill Cody's Wild West Show

Born Phoebe Ann Moses, **Annie Oakley** (1860–1926) was so good with a gun as a youngster that she was able to pay off the mortgage on her mother's house with proceeds from the game she shot. She took the name "Annie Oakley" when she formed a sharpshooting act with her husband, Frank Butler. They joined Buffalo Bill and his show in 1885 and toured with it for 17 years. She retired in 1922 and died on November 23, 1926, the last major star of the show to die. The other major stars of Cody's Wild West Show were Lakota Sioux Chief Sitting Bull (1831–90) and Buffalo Bill Cody (1846–1917).

The Jesse James Death House

Robert Ford was Jesse James's friend and partner in crime. He even lived with James, but at the same time he was plotting to kill the outlaw to claim the $10,000 reward offered by Missouri Governor Tom Crittenden. As James stood on a chair to dust a picture, Bob Ford saw his chance, and he took it.

Outlaw Jesse James's son, **Jesse Edward,** was the last survivor of the six people in the house when his father was shot in the back of the head on April 3, 1882. In 1921, he played his father in the movie *Jesse James Under the Black Flag*. He passed away in Los Angeles, California, in 1951 at age 75.

The people at the James home at the moment of Jesse James's death were:

Jesse Woodson James (1847–82)

Zerelda (Zee) Mimms (1845–1900), Jesse's wife

Jesse Edward James (1875–1951), Jesse's son

Mary Susan James (1879–1935), Jesse's daughter

Charles Ford (died 1884), Bob Ford's brother

Bob Ford (died 1892), Jesse's killer

The Younger Brothers

The James-Younger gang included Jim (1848–1902), John (1851–74), Bob (1853–89), and **Cole Younger** (1844–1916), Jesse and Frank James, and an assortment of other outlaws. John Younger was killed by Pinkerton agents in 1874. Two years later, Cole, Jim, and Bob, along with the James boys, attempted to rob a bank in Northfield, Minnesota. After the fatal shooting of several gang members, the Youngers were forced to go on the run. Finally surrendering to authorities, each of the Youngers was sentenced to 25 years in prison. Bob died in jail and Cole and Jim were released in 1901, having served their full sentences. The last living Younger brother was Cole, who in his final years lectured and wrote his autobiography, *The Story of Cole Younger by Himself.* He died on March 21, 1916.

Old West Outlaws

On October 5, 1892, the Dalton Gang attempted to rob two banks in Coffeyville, Kansas. The town marshal, three citizens, and four of the five gang members, including Grat and Bob Dalton, were killed. **Emmett Dalton,** the youngest Dalton brother at 19 years of age, was the only survivor. Hit by 23 shotgun pellets and almost lynched, he was sent to prison for life. Pardoned after 14 years, he devoted much of his later life to working for prison reform. He died on July 13, 1937.

Old West Lawmen

Born in 1865 in New Mexico, **Elfego Baca** became a deputy sheriff in Socorro County. In 1884, Baca attempted to stop a band of cowboys from firing their guns while riding through the town of Frisco. Baca shot one of their horses, which fell on its rider and crushed him to death. Baca was chased to the shelter of a small shack, where he was attacked by as many as 80 Texas cowboys who fired an estimated 4,000 rounds of ammunition at the building. After 36 hours, he walked out, unharmed. Even if the real numbers are only one-tenth of those in the story, they are still astounding. After a lifetime of public service as a deputy U.S. marshal, sheriff, district attorney, and mayor, Baca died on August 27, 1945.

* * * *

In 1958 the Walt Disney Company produced a television series that included several episodes devoted to Elfago Baca's life and legend. Robert Loggia starred in the title role.

* * * *

Old West Lawmen Who Died in the Line of Duty

Western legend Bat Masterson called **Bill Tilghman,** an Old West lawman, buffalo hunter, and scout "the greatest of us all." His career began in 1889 and included stints as deputy sheriff of Dodge City, Kansas; sheriff of Lincoln County, Oklahoma; and deputy U.S. marshal. He was shot and killed while attempting to arrest a corrupt prohibition officer in Cromwell, Oklahoma, in 1924. Tilghman was 70 years old.

The Wild Bunch

The Wild Bunch outlaw gang, which included Butch Cassidy and the Sundance Kid, was active during the late 1800s and early 1900s. **Laura Bullion,** who died in 1961 in her 80s, was the last surviving member of the Wild Bunch. The hit movie *Butch Cassidy and the Sundance Kid,* starring Paul Newman and Robert Redford, was released eight years after her death.

The Lincoln County War

The Lincoln County War started on February 18, 1878, after Lawrence Murphy and Jim Dolan killed John Tunstall, Billy the Kid's boss. After Tunstall's death, the others battled for control of the county. The war basically ended in a draw after federal troops came in.

George Coe was the last living participant of New Mexico's Lincoln County War. After fighting alongside Billy the Kid, he was granted amnesty by New Mexico Governor Lew Wallace in 1884. Coe died in 1941 at about 85 years of age.

Transportation

❑ ❑ ❑ ❑

Who invented the automobile?
Which Wright brother lived the longest?
Who was the last survivor of Howard
Hughes's around-the-world flight?
All the answers are in this chapter.

Steamboat Inventors

Robert Livingston Stevens (1787–1856), the last survivor of the steamboat inventors, helped design and build the *Phoenix*. He then sailed the ship from New York to Philadelphia, and the journey marked the first time a steamboat successfully navigated the ocean.

The following were also steamboat inventors:

- James Rumsey (1743–92) was the first American to launch a boat propelled by steam.
- John Fitch (1743–98) launched a steamboat that utilized paddles.
- Robert Fulton (1765–1815) built the first commercially practical steamboat.
- Patrick Miller (1731–1815) built a boat with paddle wheels.
- William Symington (1763–1831) outfitted Miller's boat with a steam engine.
- Claude-François-Dorothée, marquis de Jouffroy d'Abbans (1751–1832) navigated a steamboat on the River Seine in 1783.

Locomotive Inventors

American inventor and manufacturer **Peter Cooper** (1791–1883) designed and built the *Tom Thumb* locomotive, which proved that a train could run along steep, curvy terrain. Cooper reached 92 years of age in 1883, the last surviving locomotive inventor.

The other 19th-century locomotive inventors were:

- Richard Trevithick (1771–1833) invented the high-pressure steam engine and also built a self-propelled engine.
- William Hedley (1779–1843) built the first commercially practical steam locomotive.
- George Stephenson (1781–1848) invented the first steam locomotive engine.

* * * *

In 1854, Cooper endowed the Cooper Union for the Advancement of Science and Art, which today is one of the most prestigious colleges devoted to architecture, art, and engineering.

* * * *

Peter Cooper is also credited with inventing Jell-O.

* * * *

Automobile Inventors

The invention of the automobile cannot be credited to only one or two people the way the cotton gin is to Eli Whitney or the airplane is to the Wright brothers. Of the major inventors of the automobile, **James Frank Duryea** (1869–1967) was the last to survive. With brother Charles Edgar, he built a working gasoline-powered automobile in 1893. Three years later the brothers sold the first commercially produced American automobile.

The following were other major automobile inventors:

- Siegfried Marcus (1831–98) built a one-cylinder engine with a carburetor.

- Gottlieb Daimler (1834–1900) invented the first practical internal-combustion engine.
- Karl Benz (1844–1929) earned the first patent on a gas-fueled car.
- Charles Edgar Duryea (1861–1938) founded Duryea Motor Wagon Company, the first company to build and sell gasoline-powered cars.
- Robert Bosch (1861–1942) developed the magneto, which produced the current that ignited internal-combustion engines.

* * * *

In 1895, James Duryea won the first auto race ever held in the United States. The race covered 54 miles—from Chicago's Jackson Park to Evanston, Illinois.

* * * *

Individuals with Automobiles Named After Them

Ferdinand "Ferry" Porsche, who died in 1998 at age 88, built the first sportscar with the name Porsche in 1948. Porsche was the last living of those who had major automobiles named for them.

Automobiles and the people they are named for include:

- French explorer Antoine de la Mothe Cadillac (1658–1730)
- U.S. President Abraham Lincoln (1809–65)
- Armand Peugeot (1849–1915)
- David Dunbar Buick (1854–1929)
- Karl Benz (1844–1929) and Mercedes Daimler (1834–1900) (daughter of cofounder Gottlieb Daimler)

- Sakichi Toyoda (1867–1930), founder of Toyota (the spelling was changed so it would be easier to pronounce)
- Walter Chrysler (1875–1940)
- Race car driver Louis Chevrolet (1878–1941)
- Henry Ford (1863–1947)
- Ransom Eli Olds (1864–1950), namesake of the Oldsmobile
- August Horch (1868–1951)
- Enzo Ferrari (1898–1988)
- Soichiro Honda (1906–91)
- Ferrucio Lamborghini (1916–93)
- Ferdinand Porsche (1875–1951) and Professor Ferdinand "Ferry" Porsche (1909–98)

The Wright Brothers

On December 17, 1903, Wilbur and **Orville Wright** flew the first motor-powered airplane at Kitty Hawk, North Carolina. Today that plane hangs in the National Air and Space Museum in Washington, D.C. Wilbur died of typhoid fever in 1912, nine years after the historic flight. Orville died on January 30, 1948.

* * * *

The Wrights' niece, Ivonette Miller (1896–1995), daughter of the inventors' brother Lorin, was the last living person to have flown in an airplane piloted by a Wright brother (Orville).

* * * *

Hughes's Flight

On July 10, 1938, Howard Hughes and four crew members took off from New York City. Their goal was to break the record for the fastest around-the-world flight. They returned not even four days later with a new record that was less than half the previous time. The last survivor of the crew was copilot **Edward Lund,** who had first met Hughes when he welded model planes for the 1930 Hughes movie *Hell's Angels.* Lund died in 1988 at age 82.

* * * *

Howard Hughes's father invented a drill bit that earned him a fortune. Both his parents passed away when Hughes was 17, leaving him a millionaire.

* * * *

Pre–World War II British Motor Racing

Tony Rolt, the last of the British motor racers from before World War II, died in February 2008 at age 89. During World War II, Rolt was captured at the defense of Calais and sent to a German prisoner of war camp. After trying to escape several times, he ended up at Colditz Castle, a facility designed for prisoners who had made multiple escape attempts. There he was a key member of the team that devised an escape by glider. The castle was liberated by the U.S. Army before the glider could be tried. After the war, Rolt returned to automobile racing and later started a motor manufacturing company.

Pre–World War II Indianapolis 500 Drivers

The last surviving driver who raced in auto racing's Indianapolis 500 before it was closed down due to World War II was **George Connor.** Passing away on March 29, 2001, at age 94, he raced in seven of the annual races prior to 1942.

U.S. Civil War

❑ ❑ ❑ ❑

What was the Great Locomotive Chase?
Why did Pickett's Charge fail?
Who was held responsible for the horrors of Andersonville?
Read on to find out.

Union Soldiers

Of the 2.2 million Union Army veterans of the Civil War, **Albert Woolson** was the last to survive.

Woolson was born in 1847 in Antwerp, New York. He was a drummer during the war and was about 18 years old when the conflict ended in 1865. After the war, he worked as a carpenter, married, and had eight children.

Woolson died on August 2, 1956, at the age of 109. Vice President Richard Nixon attended Woolson's funeral, and that same year he was posthumously awarded a Congressional Gold Medal.

Like Father, Like Son

Woolson's father, Willard, also served during the Civil War. He enlisted in 1861. When more than a year passed and Albert and his mother had not heard any news of Willard, they contacted the army. They discovered that Willard was at a hospital in Minnesota, being treated for wounds suffered during the Battle of Shiloh. Albert and his mother journeyed across the Great Lakes to see Willard, who died soon after they arrived in Minnesota. Albert enlisted in 1864.

Confederate Soldiers

Most historians believe that the last Confederate veteran of the Civil War was **Pleasant Crump** of Alabama, who died in 1951 at age 104. Others who died later claimed to be the last Confederate; their service could not be proven, however, and most were believed to have been too young to have actually served in the war.

Civil War Generals

Adelbert Ames of Maine was the last of the Civil War's 1,008 generals (583 Union and 425 Confederate) to survive.

Born in 1835, Ames graduated from West Point at the start of the war in 1861. For his heroism at the Battle of Bull Run, Ames received the Congressional Medal of Honor. After the Civil War, he served as a provisional governor, Republican senator, and governor (all for the state of Mississippi) before becoming a businessman in Lowell, Massachusetts. During the Spanish–American War, Ames was appointed brigadier general of volunteers. He died in 1933 in his winter home in Florida at age 97.

Confederate Generals

At the outbreak of the Civil War, **Felix Robertson** resigned from West Point to join the Confederacy. He enlisted as a second lieutenant of artillery and fought at Shiloh, Murfreesboro, and Chickamauga, as well as in the 1864 Atlanta campaign. Robertson was the last surviving Confederate general when he died April 20, 1928, in Waco, Texas, at age 89.

* * * *

Last survivor Felix Robertson was also the only Texas-born Confederate general.

* * * *

Widows of Civil War Generals

General James Longstreet, General Robert E. Lee's second in command, was a corps commander at the Second Battle of Bull Run and the Battle of Gettysburg. At Antietam and Chickamauga, he led the wings of the Confederate armies. He became a member of the Republican Party after the Civil War and was appointed surveyor of customs in New Orleans and minister to Turkey by President Ulysses S. Grant. He incurred the hatred of many of his fellow Confederates because of his work with Northern leaders.

In 1889, Longstreet's wife of 41 years, Maria, died; eight years later, at age 76, he married 34-year-old **Helen Dortch,** who outlived him by 58 years. After her husband died, she devoted her life to political activism and the defense of her husband's military record. She passed away in May 1962.

Defending Longstreet

During the war, General James Longstreet was considered one of the Confederacy's finest soldiers. After the war, however, former Confederate generals John Gordon (later Longstreet's political rival) and Jubal Early leveled vicious attacks against him, falsely accusing him of deliberately disobeying General Lee's orders, causing the crushing defeat at Gettysburg, and, ultimately, the loss of the war.

Longstreet's military record wasn't the real issue, it was just the most convenient way to smear his character and assign a scapegoat for the South's defeat. The real problem was his politics. Longstreet became a Republican in a Democrat-dominated South after the war, and he actively supported Reconstruction. He also befriended many of his former Union enemies, such as General Dan Sickles and Ulysses S. Grant. His worst sin, however, was that he openly criticized General Lee's actions at Gettysburg, and proud Southerners would not tolerate negative words about their beloved general.

Battle Between the *Monitor* and the *Merrimac*

In history's first battle of ironclad gunboats, the U.S. Navy's USS *Monitor* faced the Confederacy's CSS *Virginia* (also known as the *Merrimac*) in 1862. The engagement ended in a stalemate. The last survivor of the two crews was **Thomas Taylor,** an African American who served aboard the *Monitor.* Taylor, who died on March 7, 1932, at age 84, is buried in Putnam, Connecticut.

Great Locomotive Chase

On April 12, 1862, civilian James Andrews and 19 Union Army volunteers commandeered an empty locomotive on the Atlanta-to-Chattanooga route of the Western & Atlantic Railroad. They headed north, stopping from time to time to cut telegraph lines and burn bridges in an attempt to disrupt Confederate lines of communication. Called the Great Locomotive Chase, or Andrews's Raid, the stolen train, the *General*, was chased by three other locomotives over a stretch of 87 miles before the raiders were captured near the Tennessee state line. Andrews and seven of the soldiers were executed as spies.

On March 25, 1863, six of the raiders received the first Congressional Medals of Honor ever awarded. Two of the raiders, Martin Hawkins and **John Reed Porter,** missed the train's departure. They were arrested as spies and were eventually reunited with their cohorts once the others were captured. Porter was the last living of those involved in the raid when he died on October 15, 1923, at age 84.

* * * *

Andrews's Raid was the subject of the 1956 Walt Disney movie The Great Locomotive Chase. *Fess Parker played the role of James Andrews.*

* * * *

Pickett's Charge at the Battle of Gettysburg

In what would go down in history as Pickett's Charge, the forces of Confederate General George Pickett led the march up Cemetery Ridge on the last day of the Battle of Gettysburg, Pennsylvania, in 1863. Nearly 12,000 soldiers marched more than a mile under heavy fire, and some managed to break through the Union line. However, lacking support behind and facing intense Union bombardment, they could not hold their ground; they retreated, having suffered horrific losses.

Virginia Infantry **Captain Frank Nelson,** born December 25, 1843, was the last survivor of the men who took part in the famous charge. Nelson died in 1936.

* * * *

"I was ordered to take a height, which I did, under the most withering fire I have ever known . . . "

—General George Pickett, in a letter to his wife after his ill-fated charge

* * * *

Battle of Monocacy

On July 9, 1864, near Frederick, Maryland, General Jubal Early's 15,000 Confederate troops defeated General Lew Wallace's 6,000 Union soldiers during the Battle of Monocacy. However, the battle served its purpose for the North because it delayed the Confederates and enabled Union troops to reinforce Washington, D.C.—thus preventing the Confederates from capturing the city.

Private Judson Spofford, who fought for the Union, was the last survivor of the Battle of Monocacy. He died in 1937 at age 91 in an Idaho veterans' hospital that he had personally financed and donated to the federal government years before.

Famous Civil War Commanders

Of the dozens of Civil War commanders, only about nine lived into the 20th century. The last remaining survivor was **Nelson Miles,** who passed away in 1925 at 85 years old. After the Civil War, he became one of the most successful commanders in the Indian Wars (defeating Sitting Bull, Chief Joseph, and Geronimo) and served as Commanding General of the U.S. Army during the Spanish–American War.

Dates of the passing of other major Union (U) and Confederate (C) Civil War commanders include:

- 1860s: Lewis A. Armistead (C), John Buford (U), A. P. Hill (C), Stonewall Jackson (C), Albert S. Johnston (C), Philip Kearney (U), John H. Morgan (C), Leonidas Polk (C), Jeb Stuart (C)
- 1870s: Braxton Bragg (C), John C. Breckinridge (C), Richard S. Ewell (C), David G. Farragut (U), Nathan B. Forrest (C), Henry W. Halleck (U), John B. Hood (C), Joseph Hooker (U), Robert E. Lee (C), George G. Meade (U), George E. Pickett (C), Raphael Semmes (C), George H. Thomas (U)
- 1880s: Ambrose E. Burnside (U), Ulysses S. Grant (U), Winfield S. Hancock (U), John A. Logan (U), George B. McClellan (U), John Pemberton (C), Philip H. Sheriden (U)
- 1890s: Pierre G. T. Beauregard (C), Don Carlos Buell (U), Benjamin F. Butler (U), Abner Doubleday (U), Jubal A. Early (C), Joseph E. Johnston (C), John Pope (U), Fitz John Porter (U), William S. Rosecrans (U), William T. Sherman (U)
- 20th century: Simon Bolivar Buckner (C; 1914), Joshua Lawrence Chamberlain (U; 1914), Wade Hampton (C; 1902), Oliver O. Howard (U; 1909), James Longstreet (C; 1904), Nelson A. Miles (U; 1925), John S. Mosby (C; 1916), John Schofield (U; 1906), Joseph Wheeler (C; 1906)

Widows of Union Veterans

Gertrude Janeway was the last widow of a Union veteran to survive. Her husband, John Janeway, joined the 14th Illinois Cavalry at age 19 and served the last year of the conflict, spending several months as a prisoner of war. They were married in 1927 when she was 18 and he was 81. John died at age 91 in 1937, and Gertrude died at age 93 in 2003.

* * * *

One of the last Confederate widows, Maudie Cecilia Hopkins, died in 2008 at age 94. The Daughters of the Confederacy says there are several Confederate widows still alive, but they do not want any publicity.

* * * *

Jewish Civil War Veterans

At the time of the American Civil War, about 85 percent of the country's 150,000 Jews lived in the North. Of the more than 7,000 Jewish war veterans on both sides, Union soldier **Daniel Harris** was the last to survive. Born in 1846, he died in New York City in 1945, several weeks before World War II ended in Europe.

Civil War Veterans Who Became U.S. Senators

John Hollis Bankhead was a captain in the Confederate Army before serving in both houses of the Alabama legislature after the war. Bankhead was also a U.S. congressman for 20 years and a U.S. senator for another dozen years. When he died in 1920 at age 77, he was the last U.S. senator who had served in the Civil War.

Andersonville Prison Military Commission Members

Andersonville Prison, or Camp Sumter, was built in Georgia by the Confederacy during the Civil War to hold Union prisoners. The first POWs arrived at the camp in February 1864. Within six months, there were 32,000 men being held in a space designed for little more than 10,000.

Conditions at the camp were beyond atrocious. Andersonville foreshadowed Nazi concentration camps, with malnourished inmates suffering from dysentery, scurvy, and malaria. Prisoners drank from the same stagnant water stream that they bathed in and used as a toilet. Some prisoners lived completely outdoors, and many died from exposure. The camp's death rate was more than 100 men per day during the summer.

After the war, a military commission convicted Andersonville's commandant, Captain Henry Wirz, of war crimes. He was hanged in 1865 at the current site of the U.S. Supreme Court building in Washington, D.C. Subsequent studies of Andersonville assert that Wirz, a Swiss immigrant, was unfairly singled out as the kingpin of prisoner abuses. Mismanagement and severe shortages of food, medicine, and materials are now regarded as the chief sources of Andersonville's horrors.

The last survivor of the Andersonville military commission was **John Howard Stibbs.** A colonel with the Iowa Infantry during the war, Stibbs rose to brevetted brigadier general, U.S. Volunteers. In 1910, at the age of 70, he wrote a detailed description of the Wirz trial to highlight the horrors for which Wirz was deemed responsible. Stibbs died in 1916 at age 76.

Commissioned Officers of the Confederacy

Samuel A'Court Ashe of North Carolina was the last surviving commissioned officer of the Confederate States Army. He died in 1938 at age 98.

Women's History

❑ ❑ ❑ ❑

Why did Lucretia Mott refuse to use cotton cloth and sugar cane?
Why did Lucy Stone refuse to pay taxes on her house?
How many women have been pictured on U.S. currency?
We won't hold you in suspense—the answers can be found on the following pages.

Prominent Women at the Birth of the United States

Of the most celebrated women who participated in the birth of the United States, **Dolley Madison** (1768–1849) lived the longest. She married James Madison in 1794, and while her husband served as Jefferson's secretary of state, Dolley served as cohost at White House events with the widowed Jefferson. She was a gracious, welcoming hostess and continued these duties from 1809 to 1817, while her husband was president.

The following were other notable women involved in the establishment of the nation:

- Mercy Otis Warren (died 1814) was a playwright, historian, and political activist.
- Abigail Smith Adams (died 1818) was the wife of President John Adams and mother of John Quincy Adams.
- Mary Hays McCauly, aka Molly Pitcher (died 1832), was the wife of an artilleryman, and she suffered alongside him at Valley Forge. When her husband was wounded during the Battle of Monmouth on June 28, 1778, she took over his position and operated his gun under heavy fire.
- Betsy Ross (died 1836) was a flag maker.

* * * *

Dolley married her first husband, lawyer John Todd Jr. in 1790. He died of yellow fever three years later, leaving Dolley with a young son, Payne.

* * * *

Famous Women of the Old West

Phoebe Moses, more commonly known as **Annie Oakley,** was the last surviving member of a select group of notable women of the Old West. The most famous marks-woman in U.S. history, Oakley toured with vaudeville troupes, circuses, and Buffalo Bill's Wild West Show. She died in 1926.

The following were other well-known women of the Old West:

- Jenny Lind (died 1887), singer
- Myra Belle Shirley, aka Belle Starr (died 1889), outlaw
- Martha Jane Canary, aka Calamity Jane (died 1903), mountain woman
- Nellie Cashman (died 1925), humanitarian, miner, businesswoman

Women's Suffrage Leaders

Alice Paul was an American women's suffragist whose efforts helped lead to the U.S. Constitution being amended in 1920 to grant women the right to vote. She died at the age of 92 on July 9, 1977—two years before suffrage leader Susan B. Anthony was honored with her image on the $1 coin.

The following were other women's suffragists:

- Lucretia Mott (died 1880) was an abolitionist and women's rights activist. She helped organize the Seneca Falls Woman's Rights Convention. She refused to use cotton cloth, cane sugar, and other goods produced through slave labor, and she often sheltered runaway slaves in her home.

- Sojourner Truth (died 1883) was a former slave and prominent abolitionist and women's rights activist. She was famed for her simple yet powerful oratory, especially her 1851 "Ain't I a Woman?" speech.
- Lucy Stone (died 1893) recruited many (Susan B. Anthony and Julia Ward Howe, for instance) to the cause of women's suffrage. After her marriage, she and her husband put their house in her name. She refused to pay property taxes on it at one point, claiming she should not have to pay taxes because she did not have the right to vote.
- Amelia Bloomer (died 1894) was a suffragist, editor, temperance leader, and tireless volunteer. She also became known for wearing "bloomers" (trousers underneath a skirt).

- Frances E. Willard (died 1898) served as president of the Woman's Christian Temperance Union from 1879 to 1898 and lectured across the country on prison, education, and labor reform.
- Elizabeth Cady Stanton (died 1902) helped organize the Seneca Falls convention and worked to liberalize divorce laws and other laws that made it difficult for women to leave abusive relationships.
- Susan B. Anthony (died 1906) helped found the Equal Rights Association. In 1872, she voted in a presidential election in an attempt to show that under the Constitution, women should already have the right to vote. She was arrested, tried, convicted, and ordered to pay a fine. She never paid the fine, and the authorities did not pursue the case.
- Emmeline Pankhurst (died 1928) was a British suffragist who founded the Women's Franchise League and the Women's Social and Political Union. She went to jail 12 times in 1912.
- Carrie Chapman Catt (died 1947) founded the League of Women Voters.

* * * *

When Lucy Stone was a child, her father would at times quote the Bible as a way of confirming the righteousness of a woman's place in society. Lucy vowed to learn to read Hebrew and Greek so she could prove that certain passages had been translated incorrectly. Stone studied Greek and Hebrew at Oberlin College.

* * * *

"Rosies"

"Rosie the Riveter" was a nickname given to American women who took on essential jobs at manufacturing plants while U.S. men were away serving in the military during the two world wars. Seattle's Museum of Flight honored 102-year-old **Florence Abrahamson** in 2005 for her work at De Havilland Aircraft Company during World War I and for her work at Boeing during World War II. She is the last living woman to have worked at aircraft plants during both wars.

The WAVES Program

In August 1942 women were accepted into the general Navy service for the first time since World War I in what was termed "Women Accepted for Volunteer Emergency Service," better known as WAVES. Women had served in the Navy during World War I, but most did only clerical work. In their service under the WAVES program, they were able to become officers and they also repaired aircraft and worked on code breaking. They still did not see combat, however. In 1995, the last surviving officer of this program, **Laura Rapaport Borsten,** authored *Once a WAVE: My Life in the Navy, 1942–1946*. She died August 11, 2003, at age 91.

Women Pictured on U.S. Currency

Suffragist and abolitionist **Susan B. Anthony,** who died in 1906 at 86 years old, was the last living of the three women who have been pictured on circulating U.S. money. Anthony is featured on dollar coins issued in 1979, 1980, 1981, and 1999. Martha Washington (1732–1802) is on the $1 silver certificates from 1886, 1891, and 1896, and Sacagawea (ca. 1788–1812) is pictured on a dollar coin issued starting in 2000.

Women Pictured on Commemorative Coins

Eunice Kennedy Shriver is the last living woman to have been featured on a U.S. commemorative coin. Founder of the Special Olympics and a lifelong humanitarian, Shriver is featured on the 1995 Special Olympics World Games silver dollar. She was 87 years old as of this writing.

The following women have also been pictured on U.S. commemorative coins:

- Queen Isabella of Spain (died 1504), Christopher Columbus's patron; featured on the 1893 Columbian Exposition quarter dollar
- Virginia Dare (date of death unknown), first English colonist born in America; pictured with her mother, Eleonor Dare, on the 1937 Roanoke Island half dollar

Female Recipients of the Nobel Prize in Physics

The last surviving woman to receive the Nobel Prize in Physics was **Maria Goeppert-Mayer.** She shared the 1963 prize with American Eugene Paul Wigner and German J. Hans D. Jensen for her contributions to the explanation of magic numbers. Goeppert-Mayer died in 1972.

Female Winners of the Nobel Prize in Chemistry

The last surviving woman to receive the Nobel Prize in Chemistry was Britain's **Dorothy Crowfoot Hodgkin.** She won the chemistry prize in 1964 for her contributions to the understanding of the structures of biochemical substances. Hodgkin passed away in 1994.

Television

❑ ❑ ❑ ❑

Which TV star patented the first artificial heart?
Which actor in a TV western was six feet six inches tall?
Earth Day is on which actor's birthday?
This chapter answers these questions and more!

The Lone Ranger

Clayton Moore (1914–99) played the title role in *The Lone Ranger* for seven years out of the series' eight-year run. However, for reasons known only to the show's producers, **John Hart** was hired to replace Moore during the 1952–53 season. Jay Silverheels (1919–80) played Tonto throughout the entire series.

Hart turned 91 on December 13, 2008, and has appeared at recent autograph conventions.

* * * *

John Hart is also the last survivor of another 1950s western, Hawkeye and the Last of the Mohicans. *Hart played Hawkeye, and horror film star Lon Chaney Jr. (1906–73) played Chingachgook.*

* * * *

Jay Silverheels grew up in Canada and was the son of a Mohawk chief. He got his start in Hollywood as a stuntman and appeared in Key Largo *in 1948.*

* * * *

Tonto usually called the Lone Ranger "kemo sabe," which means "trusty scout."

* * * *

The Jack Benny Show

During the course of *The Jack Benny Show*'s 15-year run, there were many actors who played recurring but infrequent roles. However, the regular cast consisted of Jack; his wife, Mary Livingstone; Eddie Anderson; Don Wilson; and **Dennis Day.** The last living of these was Day, who was known for his impressions of Adolf Hitler and W. C. Fields. Day was also an Irish tenor and ran a television production company and a restaurant chain. Day died of Lou Gehrig's disease in 1988 at age 70.

Pre-1960 Best Comedic Actor Emmy Award Recipients

The last living male honored as Best Actor in a Comedy prior to 1960 was **Sid Caesar.** Celebrating his 86th birthday in 2008, he won the Emmy in 1951 for his work on *Your Show of Shows.*

What's My Line?

What's My Line? was a popular New York City–based television show in the 1950s and '60s, during which panelists attempted to guess the occupations of the show's guests. The last surviving regular cast member of the series, **Arlene Francis,** passed away on May 31, 2001, at age 92.

The following were other regular cast members of *What's My Line?*:

- Dorothy Kilgallen (died 1965), played a regular panelist
- Bennett Cerf (died 1971), played a regular panelist
- John Charles Daly (died 1991), played a moderator

I Love Lucy

TV Guide bestowed its "Greatest TV Star of All Time" designation to **Lucille Ball,** who was the last living of the four stars of her 1950s show when she passed away on April 26, 1989. After starting her career as a Goldwyn Girl, Ball rose to become the first woman to head a major television studio.

The following were other *I Love Lucy* cast members:

- William Frawley (died 1966), played Fred Mertz
- Vivian Vance (died 1979), played Ethel Mertz
- Desi Arnaz (died 1986), played Ricky Ricardo

The Roy Rogers Show

Roy Rogers and his wife, **Dale Evans,** starred in *The Roy Rogers Show*, one of early television's most popular kids' westerns. Evans was the last to survive, passing away in 2001 at 88 years old. Roy Rogers had passed away two and a half years earlier.

I Married Joan

This 1950s television comedy series featured radio star Joan Davis and comedian Jim Backus (also famous for his roles as Thurston Howell on *Gilligan's Island* and the voice of cartoon character Mr. Magoo). The last surviving cast member was supporting actor **Sheila Bromley,** who passed away at age 95 in 2003.

My Little Margie

This popular 1950s television comedy series featured **Gale Storm** as Margie Albright. She followed up *My Little Margie* with another successful series, *The Gale Storm Show.* Storm, born in 1921, is the last surviving regular cast member of both shows. In recent years she has been in contact with fans through her Web site, www.galestorm.tv.

Our Miss Brooks

This high school television series starred Eve Arden in the title role. Of the major cast members, **Gene Barry,** who played Gene Talbot, is the last survivor. Prior to *Our Miss Brooks*, Barry starred in the 1953 science fiction classic film *The War of the Worlds,* as well as three other successful television series: *Bat Masterson, Burke's Law,* and *The Name of the Game.* Most recently, he made a cameo appearance in Steven Spielberg's 2005 production of *War of the Worlds.*

1950s Dummy/Puppet Shows

Children's television shows featuring marionettes, puppets, and ventriloquist dummies were popular in the 1950s. Of the stars on the top shows, **Paul Winchell** of *The Paul Winchell and Jerry Mahoney Show* was the last to survive, passing away at age 82 in 2005.

The following were other stars from 1950s dummy/puppet television shows:

- Burr Tillstrom (died 1985) of *Kukla, Fran and Ollie*
- Fran Allison (died 1989) of *Kukla, Fran and Ollie*
- Shari Lewis (died 1998) of *The Shari Lewis Show*
- Buffalo Bob Smith (died 1998) of *Howdy Doody*

* * * *

Winchell was also an accomplished inventor. He held the patent for the first artificial heart.

* * * *

Walt Disney's *Davy Crockett*

Fess Parker, who played Davy Crockett for Walt Disney on television, was the last survivor. Later, Parker became identified with another frontier character, Daniel Boone. He celebrated his 84th birthday on August 16, 2008. Since his Davy Crockett and Daniel Boone days, Parker has opened a luxury inn and a vineyard in California.

Pre-1960 Best Comedic Actress Emmy Award Winners

The last living female to win the Best Actress in a Comedy prior to 1960 was **Nanette Fabray.** Reaching her 88th birthday in 2008, she won the 1956 award for her performance in Sid Caesar's *Caesar's Hour.*

* * * *

Actress Shelley Fabares is Nanette Fabray's niece.

* * * *

Captain Kangaroo

The *Captain Kangaroo* children's television series ran from the 1950s through the 1980s. The last survivor was **Robert Keeshan** (1927–2004), who played the captain. Hugh Brannum (1910–87) played his friend Mr. Green Jeans.

Gunsmoke

In 1955 *Gunsmoke* started its 20-year prime-time run to become the longest lasting TV western of all time. The last surviving member of the original cast is **James Arness,** who portrayed Marshal Matt Dillon. Arness celebrated his 85th birthday in 2008.

The following were other original cast members of *Gunsmoke*:

- Milburn Stone (died 1980) played Doc Adams
- Amanda Blake (died 1989) played Kitty Russell
- Dennis Weaver (died 2006) played Chester Goode

* * * *

James Arness is six feet six inches tall. To get scenes to look right on camera, actors he worked with often had to stand on crates.

* * * *

James Arness was wounded in Anzio, Italy, during World War II and was awarded a purple heart.

* * * *

Contemporary actor Matt Dillon was named after the Gunsmoke *marshal.*

* * * *

The Honeymooners

Showcasing Jackie Gleason as bus driver Ralph Kramden and Art Carney as sewer worker Ed Norton, this early situation comedy became a television classic. Weekly fights with Kramden's wife, Alice, played by Audrey Meadows, and get-rich-quick schemes with Norton were trademarks of the series. **Joyce Randolph,** who played Norton's wife, Trixie, was the last living of the four major cast members of *The Honeymooners.* She turned 83 in 2008.

Perry Mason

In this classic television crime series (and in 1980s made-for-TV movies), Raymond Burr played brilliant attorney Perry Mason. **Barbara Hale,** in the role of his secretary, helped him solve many of his cases. Hale was still alive as of 2009.

The following were other *Perry Mason* cast members:

- Ray Collins (died 1965) played Lieutenant Arthur Tragg
- William Talman (died 1968) played Hamilton Burger
- William Hopper (died 1970) played Paul Drake
- Raymond Burr (died 1993) played Perry Mason

* * * *

Raymond Burr's official biography listed two marriages and one child, with one former wife and the child being deceased. Burr did have one brief marriage that ended in divorce, but the other marriage and the child were made up in an attempt to hide Burr's homosexuality. When Burr died in 1993, he left his estate to Robert Benevides, his longtime companion.

* * * *

Raymond Burr enjoyed cultivating orchids, and he named one after Barbara Hale.

* * * *

The Real McCoys

This popular series featured the comic adventures of the McCoy hillbilly family, headed by Walter Brennan as Grandpa Amos, Richard Crenna as Luke, and **Kathleen Nolan** as Kate. The last survivor of the adult stars of *The Real McCoys* is Nolan, who turned 75 in 2008.

Disney's *Zorro*

Disney's *Zorro* television series aired in the late 1950s with Guy Williams in the title role. The last living regular cast member was **Don Diamond,** who played Corporal Reyes. Years after *Zorro,* Diamond costarred as Crazy Cat in the *F-Troop* comedy series and did voice work for Zorro cartoons. He reached his 87th birthday in 2008.

The Lawman

This John Russell western featured **Peter Brown** as Deputy Johnny McKay. In the mid-1960s he also starred as Texas Ranger Chad Cooper in *Laredo.* The last living star of *The Lawman,* he turned 73 in 2008.

The Rifleman

Johnny Crawford played Mark McCain, the son of Chuck Connors's Lucas McCain, for the entire five-year run of this television series. Celebrating his 63rd birthday in 2009, Crawford is the last surviving regular cast member of the show.

Bonanza's Cartwright Family

Pernell Roberts played Adam Cartwright for the first six seasons of this series' 15-year run. He voluntarily left the successful show to pursue other interests. In 2008, he turned 80 years old.

The following were *Bonanza*'s other original Cartwrights:

- Dan Blocker (died 1972) played Hoss
- Lorne Greene (died 1987) played Ben
- Michael Landon (died 1991) played Joe

* * * *

Bonanza regular David Canary is not included because he was not one of the original cast members; he was added to the cast after Roberts quit.

* * * *

Dennis the Menace

Based upon Hank Ketcham's comic strip, this classic television series told of the adventures of Dennis, a child who is always getting into mischief and annoying his neighbor Mr. Wilson. Jay North (1951–) is still living, and the last surviving adult star of this series is **Gloria Henry,** who played Dennis's mom. She turned 86 in 2009.

Rawhide

The popular television western *Rawhide* featured Eric Fleming as trail boss Gil Favor, **Clint Eastwood** as drover Rowdy Yates, Paul Brinegar as Wishbone the cook, and a host of other cowboys. The last survivor is Eastwood, who has since become known for his spaghetti westerns; Dirty Harry movies; stint as mayor of Carmel, California; and skill at movie directing. He celebrated his 78th birthday in 2008.

Rocky and His Friends

Rocky and His Friends, later renamed *The Bullwinkle Show,* was one of the top TV cartoon series of the 1950s and '60s. The last living voice actor for the series is **June Foray,** who turned 90 years old in 2008. Foray not only was the voice of Rocky the Flying Squirrel, but she also provided the voices for almost all of the female characters on the show. In recent years she has been busy writing her autobiography.

The Flintstones

The popular television cartoon series *The Flintstones* appeared for the first time in 1960. Of the performers who provided the voices for major characters, **Jean Vander Pyl** (Wilma Flintstone) was the last to survive, passing away in 1999 at age 79. Vander Pyl also was the voice of Rosie the Robot in the cartoon series *The Jetsons.*

The following were other *Flintstone* voice actors:

- Bea Benaderet (died 1968) played Betty Rubble
- Alan Reed (died 1977) played Fred Flintstone
- Mel Blanc (died 1989) played Barney Rubble and Dino the Dinosaur

Car 54, Where Are You?

Joe E. Ross (1914–82), or Officer Toody, and **Fred Gwynne** (1926–93), who played Officer Muldoon, were partners in the early 1960s television comedy series *Car 54, Where Are You?* Last survivor Gwynne would follow this series by playing Herman Munster in *The Munsters,* his best-known role.

The Beverly Hillbillies

This 1960s series was about some hillbillies who struck oil and moved to Beverly Hills. As of 2009, 71-year-old **Max Baer Jr.** (Jethro) and 75-year-old **Donna Douglas** (Elly May) are still with us.

The following were other stars of *The Beverly Hillbillies:*

- Irene Ryan (died 1973) played Granny
- Raymond Bailey (died 1980) played Mr. Drysdale
- Harriet E. MacGibbon (died 1987) played Mrs. Drysdale
- Nancy Kulp (died July 10, 1991) played Miss Hathaway
- Buddy Ebsen (died 2003) played Jed Clampett

The Jetsons

One of the most popular 1960s television cartoon series was the space-age show *The Jetsons.* **Janet Waldo,** who provided daughter Judy's voice, turned 91 in 2009. She is the last living character voice actor for the show.

The Fugitive

In this 1960s television series, David Janssen portrayed innocent death row escapee Dr. Richard Kimble, who was pursued by Lieutenant Gerard, played by **Barry Morse.** The real perpetrator, a one-armed man, is being sought by Kimble. The last surviving cast member was Morse, who died in 2008 at age 89.

My Favorite Martian

With **Ray Walston** as the Martian and Bill Bixby as his earthling friend, Tim O'Hara, this science-fiction comedy flew through three seasons on CBS. The last survivor of the series' stars was Walston, who passed away on January 1, 2001, at age 86.

The Addams Family

Of the adult cast members of the television comedy show *The Addams Family,* only **John Astin,** who played Gomez Addams, is alive. Astin turned 79 in 2009.

The following were other adult actors on *The Addams Family:*

- Marie Blake (who was credited as "Blossom Rock" on the show), played Grandmama; she died in 1978.
- Ted Cassidy played Lurch; he died in 1979.
- Carolyn Jones played Morticia; she died in 1983.
- Jackie Coogan played Uncle Fester; he died in 1984.

Gilligan's Island

One of the most popular comedies of the 1960s, *Gilligan's Island* was the story of seven people on a boat tour who were stranded on a deserted island in the Pacific. The group consisted of the boat's captain, the first mate (Gilligan), a movie star, a professor, a millionaire and his wife, and a young woman named Mary Ann. As of 2009, three of the stars were still alive: 84-year-old "professor" **Russell Johnson,** 75-year-old "movie star" **Tina Louise,** and 70-year-old "Mary Ann" **Dawn Wells.**

The Munsters

This series featured the strangest family on 1960s television aside from the Addams family. The last survivors of *The Munsters* are **Butch Patrick** ("Eddie Munster") and **Pat Priest,** ("Marilyn"). As of 2009, Patrick is 55 years old and Priest is 72.

Get Smart

The 1960s spy spoof *Get Smart* starred Don Adams as agent Maxwell Smart; **Barbara Feldon** as his sidekick, Agent 99; and Edward Platt as the chief. Adams passed away in 2005, and Platt died in 1974, making Feldon the last survivor. She turned 77 years old in 2009.

Green Acres

Of the two major stars of this television series about a New York couple that moved to the sticks, **Eddie Albert,** who played Oliver Wendell Douglas, was the last survivor. Albert passed away at age 99 in 2005. Eva Gabor, who played Lisa Douglas, passed away in 1995.

* * * *

Two members of the supporting cast of Green Acres *are alive as of 2009: Tom Lester (Eb Dawson), who is 70, and 92-year-old Frank Cady, who played Sam Drucker on the show.*

* * * *

Eddie Albert was awarded a Bronze Star for rescuing 142 wounded marines during the World War II Battle of Tarawa.

* * * *

Eddie Albert was a dedicated environmentalist. He helped promote the first Earth Day, which took place on his birthday—April 22, 1970.

* * * *

Dragnet 67

The realistic TV detective series *Dragnet 67* was based in Los Angeles with Jack Webb (1920–82) starring as Sergeant Joe Friday, and **Harry Morgan** as his partner, Bill Gannon. Morgan, born April 10, 1915, is the last survivor of the two.

Top Television News Anchors of the 1960s

Walter Cronkite, often called "The most trusted man in America," was the *CBS Evening News* anchor from 1962 to 1964 and from 1967 to 1981. The last survivor of the major television news anchors of that era, he turned 92 in 2008.

The following were other top TV news anchors of the 1960s:

- Chet Huntley (died 1974), NBC
- Frank Reynolds (died 1983), ABC
- Howard K. Smith (died 2002), ABC
- David Brinkley (died 2003), NBC

Best Actor Emmy Award Winners for a Pre-1970 Drama Series

The last living male to win the Emmy for Best Actor in a Drama Series prior to 1970 was **Bill Cosby** for his work in *I Spy.* He won the award three consecutive years.

The Odd Couple

Between 1970 and 1975, two of the most watched guys on television were actors Tony Randall and **Jack Klugman.** Starring in *The Odd Couple,* Randall was Felix Unger, the neat freak, and Klugman played slob Oscar Madison. Shortly after the series ended, Klugman went on to star

as a medical examiner on another popular TV series, *Quincy M.E.* Randall passed away in 2004 at age 84, making Klugman the last survivor. He was 87 years old as of 2009.

* * * *

> The Odd Couple *series was based on the Neil Simon (1927–) play and movie of the same name. In the 1968 movie, Jack Lemmon (1925–2001) played Felix Unger and Walter Matthau (1920–2000) was Oscar Madison.*

* * * *

Sanford and Son

Producer Norman Lear's *Sanford and Son* starred Redd Foxx as junk dealer Fred Sanford and **Demond Wilson** as his son, Lamont. One of the top situation comedies of the decade, it ended when Foxx decided to move on to other ventures. The last surviving major cast member of the series was Wilson, who turned 62 in 2008. After the show ended, he worked on the short-lived series *The New Odd Couple* from 1982 to 1983 before becoming a minister. In 1994 he founded Restoration House, a vocational training organization for former prison inmates.

Stars from TV's Golden Age Who Were "Juniors"

Probably the three best-known "juniors" of pre-1980 television were **Max Baer Jr.** of *The Beverly Hillbillies,* **Efrem Zimbalist Jr.** of *77 Sunset Strip* and *The F.B.I.*, and Alan Hale Jr. of *Gilligan's Island.* As of 2009, Zimbalist (age 90) and Baer (age 71) were still living.

* * * *

> *Actress Stephanie Zimbalist (of* Remington Steele *fame) is Efrem Zimbalist Jr.'s daughter.*

* * * *

World War I

❑ ❑ ❑ ❑

How many women served in the U.S. Navy during World War I?
Who was the last World War I veteran who fought for France?
How does a pilot come to be called an "ace of aces"?
Read on to find out.

U.S. World War I Veterans

West Virginian **Frank Buckles** joined the U.S. Army at age 15. He drove ambulances in France during World War I, and spent three and a half years as a prisoner of war in the Philippines during World War II. In 2008, still in good health at age 107, Buckles was honored at the White House by President George Bush as the last survivor of the four million Americans who served their country during the First World War.

* * * *

To get to Europe, Buckles traveled aboard the Carpathia, *the ship that had rescued* Titanic *survivors just five years before.*

* * * *

African American World War I Veterans

Before his death in December 2006 at age 113, **Moses Hardy** was the last living African American who served in the military during the First World War. The child of former slaves, Hardy served in France during the war. He was considered the second oldest man in the world by Guinness World Records at the time of his death.

U.S. Navy Veterans of World War I

Lloyd Brown was born and raised in Missouri's Ozark Mountains, where his father ran a trading post. After lying about his age, 16-year-old Brown joined the Navy during the First World War and was assigned to the battleship *New Hampshire*'s gun crew. In later years, he spent three decades as a firefighter in Washington, D.C. Brown died on March 29, 2007, at age 105.

Female U.S. Sailors of World War I

Charlotte L. Winters, age 109, died in a Maryland nursing home on March 22, 2007. She was the last living of the 11,000 women who served in the Navy during World War I. Designated yeoman, these women handled clerical, translation, drafting, and designing positions during the war. After World War I, Winters remained as a civilian worker at the Washington Navy Yard. She was a member of the American Legion for 88 years.

Ottoman Empire Veterans of World War I

The last surviving Ottoman Empire veteran of the First World War was Turkey's **Yakup Satar.** A soldier at the Second Battle of Kut (1916–17), he was captured by the British and held in captivity until the end of the war. When Satar died in 2008, he was 110.

Canadian Veterans of World War I

Clarence Laking saw duty during World War I as a signaler, setting up field telephones to the trenches. When he passed away on November 26, 2005, at age 106, several of Canada's First World War vets were still alive, but Laking was the last one who had seen action on the front lines.

Canadian Women Who Served During World War I

Enlisting in 1914 in her native England, **Alice Strike** served in a clerical position in the Royal Flying Corps during the First World War. She passed away in a veterans hospital in Halifax, Nova Scotia, in December 2004 at age 108. When she died, she was also the oldest Canadian veteran of the war.

Australian World War I Veterans

In early 1918 **John Campbell Ross** enlisted in the army. He never left Australia during his time of service, but he is considered the country's last surviving World War I veteran. Campbell was also Australia's oldest man when he died on June 3, 2009, at age 110.

* * * *

Campbell is also Australia's oldest man.

* * * *

Australian Recipients of the Victoria Cross for World War I Service

Lieutenant **William Joynt** personally led his men against heavy enemy fire, taking dozens of prisoners during World War I. At one point, as 20 enemy soldiers approached him with rifles aimed, he forced them to surrender by aiming a pistol at their officer. When Joynt died in 1986 at age 97, he was the last remaining of the Australian recipients of the Victoria Cross for action in World War I. Of the total 64 recipients, 18 had died in action during the war.

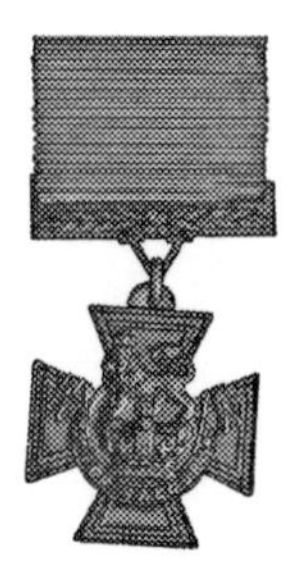

German World War I Veterans

Erich Kaestner served four months on the Western Front in 1918. He passed away in January 2008 at age 107. He was predeceased by his wife of 75 years, who died in 2003 at age 102.

World War I Veterans Who Fought for France

France's last surviving veteran of World War I was Italian **Lazare Ponticelli.** He died on March 12, 2008, at age 110, making him the last of the 8.5 million men who fought for France. Ponticelli was a member of the Foreign Legion when he served in the Argonne region of France. Later he fought for his home country against the Austrians. After World War I, Ponticelli and his brothers started a smokestack manufacturing business. During World War II, he worked for the French Resistance.

Native French World War I Veterans

In World War I, France lost 1.4 million of its 8.5 million soldiers. The last surviving veteran who was born in France was **Louis de Cazenave.** A veteran of 1916's Battle of the Somme, he died in 2008 at age 110. In an interview for *Le Monde* newspaper two years before his death, he said, "War is something absurd, useless, that nothing can justify."

British Veterans of the Battle of Passchendaele

The Third Battle of Ypres, also called the Battle of Passchendaele, was a major British offensive launched on July 31, 1917. British bombings and nearly constant rain had turned the battlefield into a swamp, which became so deep that thousands of British soldiers drowned in it. The British and the German sides suffered more than 250,000 casualties each during the three-month-long battle.

The last survivor of Passchendaele is **Harry Patch,** who was a plumber before he was drafted in 1916. He was wounded during the battle when a German shell exploded and killed most of the men in his machine-gun unit.

After the war Patch went back to plumbing. He married twice (he outlived both wives) and had two sons. He did not talk about his war experiences very much until after he met other survivors at a memorial service in Belgium in 2004. Patch celebrated his 110th birthday in 2008.

* * * *

Patch is also the last British soldier to have served in the trenches during World War I.

* * * *

U.S. Veterans Wounded in Combat During World War I

Al Pugh, who is believed to be the last surviving U.S. World War I veteran who was wounded in the war, died in January 2004. Although he was a victim of a wartime mustard gas attack, he lived to be 108 years old.

World War I Aces

James William Pearson was the last surviving WWI ace. As an American with the Royal Flying Corps in 1917 and 1918, he is credited with 12 air victories. He died in 1993 at the age of 97.

U.S. Aces of World War I

Of the pilots who fought with the American forces in the First World War, the last surviving man who shot down at least five planes, making him an ace, was **Arthur Raymond Brooks.** He flew 120 missions with the 139th Aero Squadron and shot down six enemy planes. After the war, he worked as an engineer at Bell Laboratories for more than 30 years. Brooks died in 1991 at age 95.

World War I Ace of Aces

If a soldier has five or more victories in World War I air combat he is designated an "ace." If he has more victories than anyone else from his country, he is his country's "ace of aces." Of the ace of aces from the participating countries of World War I, U.S. pilot **Eddie Rickenbacker** lived the longest, passing away on July 23, 1973. Rickenbacker was part of the first combat mission by an American squadron in April 1918 and eventually became commander of his squadron in September of that year. The 26 aerial victories he had during the war included a mission where he single-handedly took on seven German planes over enemy lines—and shot down two of them. Rickenbacker was awarded the Congressional Medal of Honor in 1930.

The ace of aces for each of the major World War I countries:

- Australia: Robert Little (died 1918)
- Canada: William Avery "Billy" Bishop (died 1956)
- France: René Paul Fonck (died 1953)
- Germany: Baron Manfred von Richthofen (died 1918)
- Great Britain: James Thomas Byford McCudden (died 1918)
- Ireland: George McElroy (died 1918)
- Italy: Francesco Baracca (died 1918)

European Monarchs at the Beginning of World War I

King Ferdinand I of Bulgaria entered World War I on the side of the Central Powers and abdicated after their defeat in 1918. He died on September 10, 1948, at age 87, making him the last living of the European monarchs who reigned at the start of World War I.

The following were other European monarchs reigning when World War I began:

- Carol I (died 1914), king of Romania from 1881 to 1914
- Franz Josef I (died 1916), Austrian emperor from 1848 to 1916
- Mehmed V (died 1918), sultan of the Ottoman Empire from 1909 to 1918
- Nicholas II (died 1918), Russian tsar from 1894 to 1917
- Peter I (died 1921), king of Serbia from 1903 to 1921
- Constantine I (died 1923), king of Greece from 1913 to 1917 and 1920 to 1922
- Ferdinand I (died 1927), king of Romania from 1914 to 1927
- Albert I (died 1934), king of Belgium from 1909 to 1934
- Alexander I (died 1934), Serbia's prince regent from 1914 to 1918 and later king
- George V (died 1936), king of England from 1910 to 1936
- Wilhelm II (died 1941), German emperor and king of Prussia from 1888 to 1918
- Vittorio Emanuele III (died 1947), king of Italy from 1900 to 1946

Versailles Treaty Signatories

William Morris Hughes was prime minister of Australia from 1915 through 1923. He holds the record for the longest service as a member of Australia's House of Representatives, entering with the first parliament in 1901 and leaving in 1952. When he died in 1952 at age 88, Hughes was the last person to have signed the Versailles Treaty, which ended World War I.

Members of Congress During World War I

The last living Congress member who served during the years of World War I was Georgia representative **Carl Vinson.** His first term began two years before World War I, and he continued to serve until the first part of the Vietnam War in 1965. Born in 1883, Vinson died in 1981.

Crime and Criminals

❑ ❑ ❑ ❑

Which criminal was personally captured by J. Edgar Hoover? Who was the last participant in the Bonnie and Clyde ambush? Which outlaw gang contemplated raiding the gun exhibits at FBI headquarters? If you are intrigued, you've stumbled upon the right chapter.

Famous Pirates

Jean Laffite, the leader of a band of 19th-century pirates in the Gulf of Mexico, fought on the side of the United States in the War of 1812 (notably at the Battle of New Orleans). There is no record of how he died, but it happened in about 1826.

Other famous pirates include:

- Sir Henry Morgan (died 1688)
- Captain William Kidd (died 1701)
- Edward Teach, aka Blackbeard (died 1718)

"The Untouchables"

"The Untouchables" were members of a squeaky-clean task force led by federal agent Elliot Ness. The group was known for being immune to the bribes and corruption prevalent during Prohibition. The supreme test of the group's image came when the agents set the screws to notorious alcohol bootlegger Al Capone. After an agent was offered a bribe by one of Capone's underlings, he declined and went straight to Ness. Considerable press coverage of the incident proved to the underworld that these "untouchable" lawmen were on a bootleg-busting mission and could not be bought.

Just after the St. Valentine's Day Massacre in 1929, agent **Albert H. Wolff** (who claimed he could bust through a speakeasy door "like nobody's business") transferred to Chicago from the hills of Kentucky. One of Ness's original 11 untouchables, Wolff retired from law enforcement in 1945 and became a restaurateur. He served as a technical consultant to Kevin Costner during the filming of *The Untouchables* (1987). Wolff died in 1998 at age 95, making him the last survivor of the group.

Notable Criminals from the 1930s

A member of the "Ma" Barker Gang, Public Enemy No. 1 **Alvin Karpis** (aka "Old Creepy") was personally captured by FBI Director J. Edgar Hoover in 1936. FBI agents tracked him down in spite of his recent face-lift. He had been wanted for months for robbery, kidnapping, and murder. After spending a record 26 years in Alcatraz Prison, Karpis overdosed on sleeping pills and died in Spain in 1979.

Other famous 1930s criminals:

- Clyde Barrow of Bonnie and Clyde (died May 23, 1934)
- Bonnie Parker of Bonnie and Clyde (died May 23, 1934)
- John Dillinger (died July 22, 1934)
- George "Baby Face" Nelson (died November 27, 1934)
- Kate "Ma" Barker (died 1935)
- Al Capone (died 1947)
- George "Machine Gun" Kelley (died 1954)

* * * *

Karpis had been involved in the kidnappings of brewer William Hamm and banker Edward George Bremer.

* * * *

The Bonnie and Clyde Ambush

Six law enforcement officers shot outlaws Bonnie Parker and Clyde Barrow to death in Louisiana on May 23, 1934. The two had been wanted for murder, robbery, and kidnapping.

The last officer to survive was **Ted Hinton,** who wrote the book *Ambush: The Real Story of Bonnie and Clyde*. Born in 1904, Hinton died of cancer in October 1977.

The Brady Gang

Alfred Brady, **James Dalhover,** and Clarence Lee Shaffer Jr. were responsible for three murders during the 1930s in addition to 150 holdups and robberies over a span of only six months. Obsessed with weapons, the gang stole and repaired machine guns from American Legion monuments and even contemplated raiding the gun exhibits at the FBI headquarters in Washington, D.C.

On October 12, 1937, Dalhover was captured in Bangor, Maine, and 27-year-old Brady and 21-year-old Shaffer were killed in gun battles with FBI agents. On November 18, 1938, last survivor Dalhover, then age 32, was electrocuted at the Indiana State Penitentiary for his part in the murder of Indiana state police officer Paul Minneman, the first Indiana state police officer killed in action.

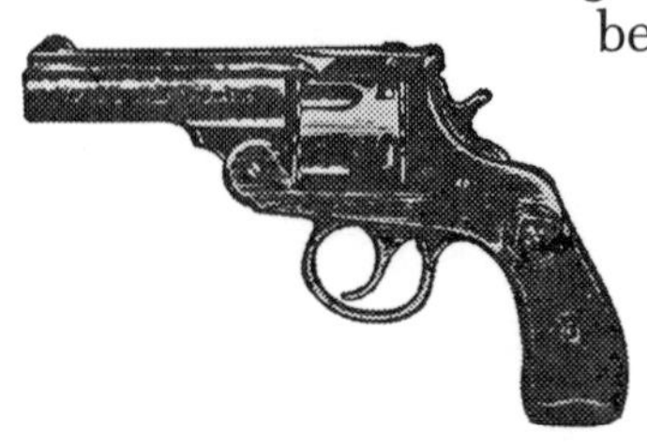

The Great Brink's Robbery

On January 17, 1950, seven armed men entered the Brink's Building in Boston's North End and stole $1.2 million in cash and $1.5 million in checks and securities. In 1956, eight men were sentenced to life in prison for their involvement in what was at the time the largest robbery in U.S. history. The last survivor of these criminals was **Adolph Maffie,** who died in 1988 at 77 years old. He had been released from prison in 1969 after the governor of Massachusetts commuted his sentence.

* * * *

Although eleven men were involved in planning the robbery, because two died before they could be brought to trial and one plead guilty, only eight men were actually tried.

* * * *

Less than $1 million of the money stolen during the Brink's robbery was ever recovered.

* * * *

Actor Paul Sorvino played Adolph Maffie in the 1978 motion picture The Brink's Job.

* * * *

Miranda v. Arizona

In the 1966 landmark case *Miranda v. Arizona,* the U.S. Supreme Court decided that police must thoroughly inform arrested individuals of their rights, including the right to remain silent, the right to

a lawyer, and an explanation that anything said to officials could be used against him or her at trial.

The case came about when Ernesto Miranda (1941–76) of Phoenix was arrested for armed robbery. While in police custody, Miranda signed a written confession admitting not only to the robbery but also to a recent kidnapping and rape. After being convicted for his role in the robbery, Miranda's attorneys appealed, arguing that their client hadn't understood his right against self-incrimination.

The case made it to the Supreme Court. The justices overturned Miranda's conviction, and he was released. He was later retried for the same crime and convicted, even though his confession was not introduced as evidence.

Miranda was paroled in 1972, after serving 11 years. In 1976, he was stabbed and killed during a bar fight. A suspect in the stabbing chose to exercise his Miranda rights and not speak with police. The suspect was later released.

The last surviving justice who ruled on the case was **Byron R. White,** who cast a dissenting vote. White argued that requiring officers to remind suspects of their right to remain silent would severely hinder an officer's efforts at extracting information from suspects. White died in 2002 at age 84.

The following were other Supreme Court justices involved in the *Miranda v. Arizona* decision:

- Hugo Black (died 1971) served 1937–71 (majority)
- John M. Harlan II (died 1971) served 1955–71 (dissent)
- Earl Warren (died 1974) served 1953–69 (majority)
- Tom Clark (died 1977) served 1949–67 (dissent)
- William O. Douglas (died 1980) served 1939–75 (majority)
- Abe Fortas (died 1982) served 1965–69 (majority)
- Potter Stewart (died 1985) served 1958–81 (dissent)
- William J. Brennan Jr. (died 1997) served 1956–90 (majority)

The Revolutionary War

❑ ❑ ❑ ❑

Who was nicknamed the "Gamecock General of the American Revolution"?
Why did Europeans fight in the Revolutionary War?
What is the Society of the Cincinnati?
All the answers are in this chapter.

U.S. Veterans of the Revolutionary War

The American Revolution was fought between Great Britain and its 13 colonies on the eastern shoreline of North America. It began in 1775, lasted through the Continental army's victory in 1781 at Yorktown, and officially ended with the Treaty of Paris in 1783. Most of the Colonial soldiers who fought in the war were poorly trained and ill equipped; their British counterparts, on the other hand, were professional soldiers, many with actual battle experience. Thus, the phrase "the world turned upside down" describes the thoughts of many in Europe when news spread of a Colonial victory.

The last American veteran of the Revolutionary War was Colonial soldier **Daniel F. Bakeman,** who died on April 5, 1869, at age 109. Bakeman was 21 years old at the end of hostilities in 1781. He was the last survivor of the approximately 217,000 men who fought for independence from Great Britain, and he lived to see three other major U.S. wars, including the American Civil War.

Widows of U.S. Veterans of the Revolutionary War

Due to the high mortality rate of women during the late 1700s and early 1800s, often caused by childbirth complications and disease, men were often married multiple times—and to women much younger than themselves. This would explain how **Catherine S. Damon,** born in 1814, is acknowledged by the U.S. Department of Veterans Affairs to have been the last widow of an American veteran of the Revolutionary War when she died on November 11, 1906, at age 92.

Dependents of U.S. Veterans of the Revolutionary War

Phoebe M. Palmeter, who died April 25, 1911, at age 90, was the last dependent of a Revolutionary War veteran.

U.S. Generals of the Revolutionary War

Brigadier General **Thomas Sumter,** nicknamed "The Gamecock General of the American Revolution" for his bravery in battle, represented South Carolina after the war as a U.S. congressman. He died June 1, 1832, at 97 years old. Fort Sumter in Charleston Harbor is named after Thomas Sumter.

Europeans Who Fought in the Revolutionary War

The Colonials might have lost the war but for some support from these knowledgeable Europeans:

- Baron von Steuben, an out-of-work Prussian officer, taught the Continental army helpful tactics, drills, organizational methods, and sanitation tips (all lamentable deficiencies in Washington's army). He later settled in New York, where Congress awarded him a well-deserved pension.
- Kazimierz Pulaski, a Polish rebel fleeing a Russian death sentence, organized his own cavalry regiment for the Colonial cause. He died

in October 1779 after a charge at Savannah—perhaps the only fitting end for an arrogant but dashing horse soldier.

- Tadeusz Kosciuszko was a Polish engineer who initially came to America seeking work. He read the Declaration of Independence and wept: Its values were the same as his own. As a colonel of Continental engineers, his military engineering wisdom aided the colonists. After the war, he went home to fight against the Russians.
- The Comte de Rochambeau, a French general, led 6,000 French regulars at the decisive Battle of Yorktown in 1781. He returned to France and joined the French Revolution, then narrowly escaped beheading during the Reign of Terror.
- The Marquis de Lafayette, a French soldier who paid his own way to America, was commissioned a major general of the Continental army in 1777. He fought with distinction and helped secure the key to victory: French intervention. In 1824, President Monroe invited Lafayette to tour the country and accept the tremendous public acclaim due a national hero. Lafayette died in 1834, the last surviving major Continental army general.

British Generals of the Revolutionary War

Lord **Charles Cornwallis** was the last to survive of the key generals who fought for Great Britain during the Revolutionary War. He was also the only one to live to see the 19th century, passing away in 1805. Modern American accounts often paint Cornwallis in bumbler's colors. That's quite unfair, considering the Yorktown Campaign was the only major failure in the long career of this capable administrator and general.

Cornwallis's first commission was as an ensign of the famous Grenadier Guards in 1756, and he rose in rank on his own merit. Before the war, he considered Colonial complaints legitimate;

during it, he beat Washington's forces as often as not.

How, then, did he lose? The Continental army could replace its losses, but Cornwallis largely could not. Penned up at Yorktown in 1781 by a larger Franco-American army and low on supplies, Cornwallis counted on the Royal Navy to come to his rescue with supplies and reinforcements. The French fleet thwarted that plan during the naval Battle of the Chesapeake. Cornwallis had to surrender to General George Washington, essentially ending the war.

After the war, he became Marquess Cornwallis in 1792, led successful campaigns against Indian and Irish rebels, and twice served as governor-general of India. Cornwallis passed away during his second governor-generalship, and his tomb overlooks the Ganges River at Ghazipur, India.

The following were other major British Revolutionary War generals:

- Thomas Gage (died 1787)
- John Burgoyne (died 1792)
- Sir Henry Clinton (died 1795)
- Sir William Howe (died 1799)

The Battle of Bunker Hill

The first real battle of the Revolutionary War occurred in June 1775. Although it has gone down in history as the Battle of Bunker Hill, the fighting actually took place on Boston's Breed's Hill. About half of the 2,000 British troops who fought in the battle were killed or wounded, while approximately 400 American colonists were injured or killed. Although the colonists were forced to retreat, they demonstrated that they were a match for the experienced British troops. The last American survivor of the battle, **Samuel Follett,** lived until 1854.

* * * *

When he was seven years old, John Quincy Adams and his mother witnessed the Battle of Bunker Hill from the top of a hill near their home south of Boston. Adams said it was a sight he would never forget.

* * * *

The Battle of Kings Mountain

Kings Mountain, another major battle of the Revolutionary War, took place on October 7, 1780, in northwest South Carolina. During the engagement, American colonists surrounded and defeated part of British General Cornwallis's army, causing the rest of his force to retreat. The British suffered three times as many casualties as the colonists during the battle. The last surviving soldier of Kings Mountain was colonial **Isaac Thrasher.** A letter he wrote in 1860 has been preserved, and this date qualifies him as the last survivor. However, the date of his death is not known.

General George Washington's Life Guards

After the start of the Revolutionary War, 180 mounted men were directed to accompany General George Washington (1732–99) at all times; this group was given the name "Life Guards." At times when Washington was near the British, this group would increase in number to 250 men, but when it was disbanded in 1783, the group had just 64 members. The last surviving member was **Nathaniel Berry** of Randolph, Maine. When he passed away on August 20, 1850, at 94, he was buried next to his wife, Lydia, in Randolph.

The Society of the Cincinnati

Continental army officers founded the Society of the Cincinnati in 1783. The mission of the society is to always remember the principles behind the Revolutionary War and the founding of the United States. More than 2,000 of the army's 5,500 officers joined the society. Its first president was George Washington, who served from the society's founding until his death, when he was succeeded by Alexander Hamilton. The last survivor of the original members was Congressman **Ebenezer Elmer,** who died on October 18, 1843, at age 91. Elmer served as a surgeon during the Revolutionary War.

* * * *

The Society of the Cincinnati was named after the Roman hero Cincinnatus, who twice led his country in battle. When each crisis was over he was offered powerful positions, but instead of accepting, he always quietly returned home to his normal work of plowing his fields.

* * * *

Signatories of the Paris Peace Treaty

Eight years after it began, the Revolutionary War officially ended with the signing of the Paris Peace Treaty of 1783. David Hartley signed for Britain's King George III, while John Adams, Benjamin Franklin, and **John Jay** signed for the newly created United States of America. Six years later, President George Washington appointed Jay the first chief justice of the U.S. Supreme Court. He died at age 83 on May 17, 1829, the last surviving signatory of the treaty.

Business

❑ ❑ ❑ ❑

What's the secret behind the success of Wal-Mart?
Who partnered with Henry R. Luce to found TIME?
Who is the last surviving grandchild of John D. Rockefeller Sr.?
We won't hold you in suspense—the answers
can be found on the following pages.

Merriam-Webster

In 1831, brothers George (1803–80) and Charles Merriam (1806–87) of Springfield, Massachusetts, started G. & C. Merriam Co., a printing and bookselling business. In 1843, they purchased the copyright to Noah Webster's *American Dictionary of the English Language.* Four years later they published the first Merriam-Webster dictionary with the help of Webster's son William and son-in-law Chauncey A. Goodrich. George and Charles's brother, **Homer Merriam,** joined the company in 1855; he served as company president from 1892 to 1904. Noah Webster died in 1843 at age 84. Homer was the last survivor, passing away in 1908 at 95.

Wells Fargo

In 1852, Henry Wells and **William Fargo** founded Wells, Fargo & Company. Their goal was to provide banking services and express delivery to the American West. The company's greatest accomplishment at the time was the establishment of a stagecoach line in the 1860s. Later, in addition to handling matters related to the business, Wells founded Wells College in Aurora, New York, while Fargo became mayor of Buffalo, New York. The last surviving founder was Fargo, who died at 64 years old in 1881.

Currier & Ives

The company Currier & Ives started in 1857 when lithographer Nathaniel Currier (1813–88) made bookkeeper **James Ives** a full partner in his business. Currier & Ives eventually became one of the most successful publishers of lithographs in history. The last survivor of the pair was Ives, who died in 1895 at 71.

Smith Brothers

In 1866, brothers **William Smith** and Andrew Smith took over their father's cough drop company in Poughkeepsie, New York. The Smith brothers placed their bearded faces on the front of each box of cough drops and obtained a trademark of the images. The word "trade" appeared under the picture of William on the left of the cough drop box, the word "mark" was under Andrew on the right—and these became their nicknames to millions of customers.

Andrew died in 1894, but William lived until 1913. Smith Brothers cough drops are still being sold with the two familiar pictures on the box, albeit a little smaller than what appeared on the original packaging.

Dow Jones

Dow Jones & Company was founded in 1882 by Charles Henry Dow (1851–1902), Edward Davis Jones (1856–1920), and **Charles Milford Bergstresser.** Two years later the company began publishing stock price averages, and in 1889 the company established *The Wall Street Journal.* Bergstresser was the last to survive of the three founders, passing away in 1923 at age 64.

* * * *

Bergstresser's name was not included in the company name simply because the three men agreed that Dow Jones & Company sounded better than Dow Jones & Bergstresser.

* * * *

There were eleven stocks in Dow's first average, and nine of those were railroad stocks.

* * * *

* * * *

The Wall Street Journal calls itself "the daily diary of the American dream." The first issue of the paper was only four pages long.

* * * *

Harvard Business School

In 1910, Harvard Business School graduated its first class, which consisted of 33 students. By 1983, all had died except **Harold T. Johnson,** former vice president of a Wall Street brokerage firm. He was 94 years old when he passed away on April 15, 1983.

National Department Stores

Among the founders of the best-known U.S. department stores still successful in the early 21st century, **Samuel M. "Sam" Walton** was the last to survive. He passed away in 1992 at age 74. Walton opened his first department store in 1962; it would become part of one of the world's largest chains of retail stores—Wal-Mart.

Walton grew up in Oklahoma and Missouri during the Great Depression. He began his retail career at JCPenney in Iowa, and in 1944, he opened a deep-discount Ben Franklin store in Newport, Arkansas. His strategy: Buy super cheap, sell cheap. The store was so successful that in 1950 the landlord wouldn't renew Walton's lease (he wanted to give the cash cow to his son). But Walton didn't go away empty handed: The discounting and land ownership lessons he learned would become the core of his future business model.

Next, Walton bought a five-and-dime in Bentonville, Arkansas. By 1962, with more than a dozen five-and-dimes operating profitably, he was ready for department stores. When the first Wal-Mart opened in Rogers, Arkansas, Walton stuck to several key principles: property ownership, no unions, low prices, low costs, and austerity. Manufacturers had to let Wal-Mart reps investigate their operations for ways to cut costs and give Wal-Mart a better price. His method worked—and continues to work—because his customer base cares about lower prices above all.

Other national department store founders include:

- Rowland Hussey Macy (died 1877) started Macy's in 1851.
- Marshall Field (died 1906) bought his first store in 1865.
- Richard W. Sears (died 1914) and Alvah C. Roebuck (died 1948) founded Sears, Roebuck and Co. in 1893.
- Sebastian S. Kresge (died 1966) opened S. S. Kresge in 1899; it became Kmart in 1977.
- James Cash Penney (died 1971) started JCPenney in 1907.

* * * *

Wal-Mart founder Sam Walton drove an old pickup truck, and there were no plush offices at his company's headquarters.

* * * *

Ernst & Young

In 1903, Cleveland native **Alwin C. "A. C." Ernst** and his brother, Theodore, started the accounting firm of Ernst & Ernst. Three years later, Scotland-born Arthur Young and his brother, Stanley, started the Arthur Young & Company accounting firm. A. C. died shortly after Arthur in the same year—1948. Although there is no record of the two men having ever met, their names became linked when their companies merged in 1989 to form Ernst & Young.

Black & Decker

Black & Decker Manufacturing Company began as a machine shop founded in 1910 by **Alonzo Galloway Decker** and Samuel Duncan Black in Baltimore. Its first plant of 12,000 square feet was built in 1917, and today Black & Decker is one of the world's largest and most successful manufacturers of power tools. Black was president from 1910 until his death in 1951; Decker took over the position and held it until his own death five years later at age 72.

TIME

Henry R. Luce spent his early years in China, where his parents worked as missionaries. Briton Hadden, the son of a stockbroker, grew up in Brooklyn. The two met at Connecticut's Hotchkiss School. Both went on to Yale, where they worked on the student newspaper, the *Yale Daily News,* and joined the secret society Skull and Bones. Though they had opposite personalities, they also had common literary interests. After struggling in journalism jobs after graduation, they agreed to collaborate on a news magazine. They approached fellow Bonesmen for funding and published the first issue of *TIME* in 1923. The erratic Hadden was the magazine's primary innovator, promoting the smug, reader-magnetic "we know everything" writing style that became known as "*TIME*style."

A mere two weeks after Hadden's untimely death in 1929, Luce took Hadden's name off *TIME*'s masthead. Hadden's will left his *TIME* stock to his family and stipulated that it was not to be sold for 49 years, but Luce had control of it within a year. His friends called him "Father *TIME*"; others called him "Il Luce," in reference to Italian dictator Benito Mussolini, who was called "Il Duce."

During and after World War II, Luce lost some of his journalistic balance and began yielding to propaganda. He was anticommunist and anti-isolationist, convinced that the United States must accept the mantle as the free world's bastion against the Red Menace. Though his prediction for the Cold War came true, the shift of focus in Luce's publications toward his political agenda was noted by readers and was not universally approved.

Luce also founded *Fortune* and *Sports Illustrated* and purchased and reinvented *Life* magazine. By the 1960s, he controlled the largest publishing empire in the United States. Luce's editorial reign at *TIME* lasted until his retirement in 1964, and he passed away in 1967.

U.S. Billionaires of the 1960s

By the early 21st century, there were approximately 400 billionaires in the United States. During the 1960s, only three could claim this status: H. L. Hunt (1889–1974), Howard Hughes (1905–76), and

J. Paul Getty. The last died June 6, 1976, just two months after Hughes.

Getty grew up the son of oil tycoon George Getty, one of America's first billionaires. His patrimony got him an easy start in life, but most of the modern Getty fortune grew through his savvy investments. In 1949, Getty picked a winner by purchasing the rights to a tract of Saudi desert that had never produced petroleum; it soon did. The tycoon moved to England, where he spent most of his remaining years.

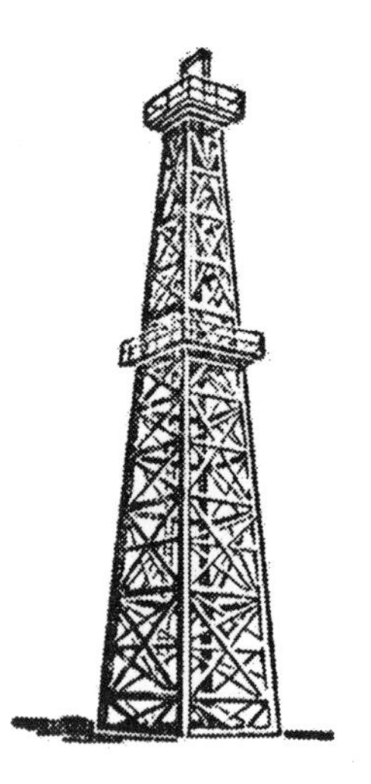

* * * *

J. Paul Getty was also the last survivor of the American oilmen who began their businesses before World War II. This group included Henry M. Flagler (1830–1913) and John D. Rockefeller (1839–1937).

* * * *

Getty left the bulk of his estate to the J. Paul Getty Museum in Malibu, California.

* * * *

Contemporary actor Balthazar Getty is J. Paul Getty's great-grandson.

* * * *

Gallo Wine

In 1932, brothers **Ernest Gallo** and Julio Gallo founded E and J Gallo Winery, one of the largest winemakers in the world. Julio died in a car accident in 1993 at age 83. Ernest passed away peacefully in 2007 at 97 years old.

Grandchildren of John D. Rockefeller Sr.

Through his Standard Oil Company, John D. Rockefeller Sr. (1839–1937) started the family fortune; it passed on to his three daughters and one son. His last surviving grandchild is **David Rockefeller,** who earned a Ph.D. in economics in 1940. One of the most powerful people in banking in the United States, he celebrated his 93rd birthday in 2008.

Hewlett-Packard

The technology company Hewlett-Packard (HP) was founded in 1939 by **William Hewlett** and David Packard (1912–96). Five years earlier, both had graduated from Stanford University as electrical engineers. Using a garage as their laboratory, the pair developed their first product, an instrument to test sound equipment. In their first year of business, their revenue was about $5,000. By the time Hewlett, the last surviving founder, died on January 12, 2001, the company had almost $50 billion in annual revenue and 85,000 employees.

H&R Block

Brothers **Henry Bloch** and Richard Bloch (1926–2004) founded the tax preparation company H&R Block in 1955. In 2004, the company had about 22 million clients and operated in 11 countries. The last to survive, Henry Bloch, turned 86 years old in 2008.

* * * *

When naming their company, the Bloch brothers altered the spelling of their last name so prospective customers would immediately know how to pronounce it.

* * * *

African American History

❑ ❑ ❑ ❑

How was Africatown, Alabama, established?
Who encouraged Dorothy West to finish The Wedding,
a work she had set aside for 30 years?
Who were the Scottsboro Boys?
You need look no further than this chapter to find out.

Underground Railroad Conductors

The Underground Railroad was a secret network of people who helped African Americans escape from slavery. Conductors on the Underground Railroad led fugitives from one station to the next. **Hiram Wertz** of Quincy, Pennsylvania, was reported to be the last conductor. Starting in 1845 (when Wertz was still in his teens), Wertz helped approximately 50 slaves escape to freedom. A 1911 newspaper article notes him as the last Underground Railroad conductor, but his date of death was not recorded.

Supreme Court Justices Who Ruled on *Dred Scott v. Sanford*

In the *Dred Scott v. Sanford* case of March 1857, the Supreme Court decided that neither free nor enslaved African Americans could become U.S. citizens. The ruling also made slavery legal in all U.S. territories. The last surviving justice to decide on the case was **John Archibald Campbell,** who was on the bench from 1853 to 1861. He died in 1889 at age 77.

The following were other Supreme Court justices who ruled on *Dred Scott v. Sanford*:

- Peter Daniel (died 1860) served 1842–60
- John McLean (died 1861) served 1830–61

- Roger Brooke Taney (died 1864) served 1836–64
- John Catron (died 1865) served 1837–65
- James Moore Wayne (died 1867) served 1835–67
- Robert Grier (died 1870) served 1846–70
- Samuel Nelson (died 1873) served 1845–72
- Benjamin Robbins Curtis (died 1874) served 1851–57

* * * *

The court's majority of seven included five justices from Southern or border states. The two dissenters, Justices Benjamin Robbins Curtis and John McLean, were from Massachusetts and Ohio, respectively.

* * * *

The Last Slave Ship

Beginning in 1808, it was technically illegal to bring slaves from Africa into the United States; this law was often violated, however. The last recorded case of a slave ship entering the United States was in 1859, when the *Clotilde* docked in Mobile Bay, Alabama, with more than 100 slaves from an area of western Africa near present-day Benin. More than 30 of the slaves escaped and established the settlement Africatown in southern Alabama, where they practiced the customs of their homeland. One of Africatown's leaders, **Cudjo Lewis,** was the last survivor of the *Clotilde* slaves. He died in 1935 at age 114, impoverished and embittered toward the Americans who had bought him and the Africans who had sold him.

* * * *

Africatown is now part of Pritchard, Alabama—a suburb of Mobile. More than 12,000 people live in Africatown today, and many of these residents can trace their roots back to the original Africatown settlers.

* * * *

Children of Frederick Douglass

Frederick Douglass was born in Maryland in 1818, the son of a female slave; all that's known about his father is that he was white. Douglass grew up surrounded by the brutality of slavery. He was sent to live in Baltimore when he was eight, and there he began to read and first heard about the abolitionist movement.

As a teenager, Douglass was sent to work on a farm. During these years he was given minuscule rations and was whipped every day. Douglass escaped to Massachusetts in 1838 and began his antislavery work and got married. He and his wife had five children. **Charles Remond Douglass** (1844–1920) was the last surviving child. He served in the Union army during the Civil War.

* * * *

"What, to the American slave, is your 4th of July? I answer: a day that reveals to him, more than all other days in the year, the gross injustice and cruelty to which he is the constant victim. To him, your celebration is a sham;... your sermons and thanksgivings, with all your religious parade and solemnity, are, to Him, mere bombast, fraud, deception, impiety, and hypocrisy—a thin veil to cover up crimes which would disgrace a nation of savages."

—Frederick Douglass,
"The Meaning of July Fourth for the Negro"

* * * *

African American Members of Congress from the Reconstruction Era

A slave until the Civil War, **John Roy Lynch** (1847–1939) represented Mississippi in the U.S. congress from 1873 to 1877 and from 1882 to 1883. He also served as a delegate to the Republican

National Conventions in 1872, 1884, 1888, 1892, and 1900. During the Spanish-American War, Lynch was appointed a major and a paymaster of volunteers by President William McKinley, and in 1901, he became a paymaster in the regular army. He retired from the army in 1911 and practiced law in Chicago until his death at age 92 in 1939—the last black member of congress from the Reconstruction era.

African American Widows of the Civil War

Daisy Anderson, the last African American widow of the Civil War, died in 1998 at 97 years old. In 1922, at age 21, she married 79-year-old Robert Anderson, a former slave and Union army veteran. A *New York Times* obituary stated that his owner's sadistic wife would have Anderson whipped and salt and pepper rubbed into the wounds. Daisy said that the scars on his back were as wide as her fingers. A self-made man, Anderson became the owner of a 2,000-acre ranch in Nebraska, where he employed 20 workers. He died in 1930.

Buffalo Soldiers

Late 19th-century Native Americans gave the nickname "Buffalo Soldiers" to the African American soldiers of the U.S. Army. At age 16 in 1910, **Mark Matthews** joined the all-black Tenth Cavalry. He later served under General John J. Pershing in the pursuit of Mexican revolutionary Pancho Villa. When Matthews died at age 111 in 2005, he was the last of the original Buffalo Soldiers.

The Harlem Renaissance

The Harlem Renaissance refers to the rich production of works in literature, art, and music by African Americans during the 1920s and '30s. Primarily based in Harlem, New York, the movement had a lasting influence on American culture in general.

The last of the prominent players in the Harlem Renaissance to survive was writer **Dorothy West.** West was born in Boston and published her first story at age 14. After her short story "The Typewriter" was awarded a prize by the Urban League in 1926, she moved to New York. West's work paved the way for countless African American women writers. She passed away in 1998 at age 91.

* * * *

Dorothy West started the book The Wedding *during the 1960s but then set it aside. Jacqueline Kennedy discovered West's work during the 1990s, and she persuaded West to finish the book.* The Wedding *was published in 1995, and Oprah Winfrey made it into a miniseries starring Halle Berry in 1998.*

* * * *

The Scottsboro Boys

In 1931, nine African Americans aged 13 to 21 were accused of raping two white women on a freight train passing through Alabama. A six-year legal fiasco ensued. Questionable standards of proof, all-white juries, inept defense counsel, and the intimidating mobs outside the courthouses made fair trials nearly impossible. In fact, three rounds of trials were necessary because the U.S. Supreme Court deemed the first two convictions unfair and threw them out.

Eight of the nine "Scottsboro Boys" were eventually sentenced to Alabama's electric chair, but their sentences were later commuted to prison time. Four of the men were released in 1937, shortly after the last round of verdicts. The other five were gradually paroled, the last in 1950—after spending 19 years in prison.

At the first trial, defendant **Clarence Norris** stunned everyone by claiming that he alone was innocent, and all the other defendants had raped the women; later, it was revealed that he had been coerced into making these statements. Paroled in 1946, Norris broke parole and moved to New York, where he remained a fugitive for years. During the 1960s, the NAACP helped him clear his name. In 1976, Alabama's parole board voided Norris's violation and declared him innocent of any crime, whereupon Governor George Wallace issued a pardon. Norris died in New York at age 76 in 1989—the last survivor of the Scottsboro Boys.

* * * *

The boys came to be called the Scottsboro Boys because they were held in a jail in Scottsboro, Alabama, after they were arrested.

* * * *

The ninth Scottsboro Boy was 12-year-old Roy Wright. A mistrial was declared when jurors demanded the death penalty even though the prosecution had recommended life in prison because of his young age.

* * * *

The Tuskegee Airmen

In 1941, an African American air pursuit squadron was established in Tuskegee, Alabama. Commonly known as the Tuskegee Airmen, the group was one of the finest fighter squadrons in World War II. Servicemen trained in the program included pilots, navigators, bombardiers, and support personnel.

The last general officer among the Tuskegee Airmen was **Lucius Theus.** A first sergeant with Tuskegee's basic training squadrons, he entered Officer Candidate School at war's end and eventually rose in rank to become director of accounting and finance in the U.S. Air Force's office of the comptroller. Major General Theus was born in 1922 and died on October 15, 2007. He is buried in Arlington National Cemetery.

Brown v. Board of Education Justices

The 1954 Supreme Court case *Brown v. Board of Education* unanimously overturned the *Plessy v. Ferguson* decision that established the "separate but equal" doctrine. The justices ruling on Brown decided that segregation laws violated the equal protection clause of the 14th Amendment. Justice **Stanley Reed,** the last living member of this court, died at 95 years old on April 2, 1980—less than three months after fellow *Brown v. Board of Education* Justice William O. Douglas.

After retiring from the court in 1957, Reed served on President Dwight D. Eisenhower's Civil Rights Commission.

The following were other Supreme Court justices who decided *Brown v. Board of Education:*

- Robert Jackson (died 1954) served 1941–54
- Harold Burton (died 1964) served 1945–58
- Felix Frankfurter (died February 22, 1965) served 1939–62
- Sherman Minton (died April 9, 1965) served 1949–56
- Hugo Black (died 1971) served 1937–71
- Earl Warren (died 1974) served 1953–69
- Tom Clark (died 1977) served 1949–67
- William O. Douglas (died 1980) served 1939–75

Brown v. Board of Education Attorneys

The Supreme Court's decision in the *Brown v. Board of Education* case ended school segregation in the United States. **William T. Coleman Jr.** was the last surviving attorney who worked on the case. He coauthored the brief that was presented to the court.

In 1975, Coleman became the second African American to hold a position in a U.S. president's cabinet when Gerald Ford appointed him secretary of transportation. Over the years, presidents Eisenhower, Kennedy, Johnson, and Nixon asked him to join various presidential commissions, such as the U.S. Arms Control and Disarmament Agency and the Committee on Government Employment Policy.

In 1995, Coleman received the Presidential Medal of Freedom, which is the highest honor a civilian can receive from the U.S. government. Coleman celebrated his 88th birthday in 2008.

The March on Washington for Jobs and Freedom

In August 1963, the most famous civil rights march in U.S. history was held in Washington, D.C. Best known as the event at which

Reverend Martin Luther King Jr. gave his "I Have a Dream" speech, it featured most of the major leaders of the civil rights movement. The last surviving speaker is **John Lewis,** who, at 23, was the head of the Student Non-Violent Coordinating Committee (SNCC) during the march. Today, Lewis is a U.S. congressman from Georgia.

The following were the other speakers at the March on Washington:

- Martin Luther King Jr. (died in 1968), founder of the Southern Christian Leadership Conference (SCLC)
- Walter Reuther (died in 1970), president of the United Auto Workers union
- Whitney Young (died in 1971), president of the National Urban League
- A. Philip Randolph (died in 1979), president of the Brotherhood of Sleeping Car Porters
- Roy Wilkins (died in 1981), president of the NAACP
- Dr. Eugene Carson Blake (died in 1985), vice chair of the National Council of Churches of Christ in America
- Rabbi Joachim Prinz (died in 1988), president of the American Jewish Congress
- James Farmer (died in 1999), president of the Congress of Racial Equality (CORE)
- Matthew Ahmann (died in 2002), founder of the National Catholic Conference for Interracial Justice

* * * *

Shortly before the March on Washington, James Farmer had been participating in demonstrations in Plaquemine, Louisiana. He was imprisoned for "disturbing the peace" and missed the march. CORE aide Floyd McKissick read Farmer's speech to the Washington crowd.

* * * *

Assassinations

❑ ❑ ❑ ❑

Who was the last survivor of Lincoln's pallbearers?
Why did Oscar Collazo and Griselio Torresola
attempt to assassinate President Truman?
Who was the last living member of the Warren Commission?
Read on to find out.

The Lincoln Assassination

On April 14, 1865, actor John Wilkes Booth murdered Abraham Lincoln in Ford's Theatre in Washington, D.C., while the president and his wife were viewing the comedy *Our American Cousin* from a balcony box. The last surviving occupant of the assassination box was **Major Henry R. Rathbone,** who died in a mental asylum in 1911. Of the five people in the box, three would be killed by another person; the other two would spend time in mental asylums.

The following were the occupants of Abraham Lincoln's balcony box when Lincoln was assassinated:

- Abraham Lincoln, U.S. president from 1861 to 1865, died on April 15, 1865 (the day after he was shot).
- John Wilkes Booth, Lincoln's assassin, was killed by federal troops two weeks after he shot Lincoln.
- Mary Todd Lincoln, Lincoln's wife, was committed to a mental asylum for a short time in 1875. She died in 1882.
- Clara Harris, Major Rathbone's fiancée, was murdered by Rathbone in 1883.
- Major Henry R. Rathbone died in 1911 in a German mental institution.

Convicted Conspirators in President Lincoln's Assassination

The last living convicted conspirator in the assassination of President Abraham Lincoln was **John Surratt,** who died of pneumonia on April 21, 1916.

Conspirators in Lincoln's assassination and their fates:

- John Wilkes Booth, mastermind of Lincoln's assassination, was shot to death while attempting to escape on April 26, 1865.
- Lewis Powell stabbed U.S. Secretary of State William H. Seward, but Seward recovered. (The assassinations of Seward and Vice President Johnson were part of the conspiracy, but these assassination attempts were unsuccessful.) Convicted of conspiracy to commit murder and treason, Powell was hanged July 7, 1865.
- George A. Atzerodt was assigned to kill Vice President Andrew Johnson, but he never got very close to the vice president; most historians believe he merely wimped out. Convicted of conspiracy to assassinate the president, Atzerodt was hanged July 7, 1865.

Vice President Andrew Johnson

- David E. Herold guided Lewis Powell to Seward's home. Convicted of conspiracy to commit murder and treason, Herold was hanged July 7, 1865.
- Mary E. Surratt owned the boardinghouse where the conspirators met. Convicted of conspiracy to assassinate the president, Surratt was hanged July 7, 1865.
- During early conspiracy plans, Michael O'Laughlen, a boyhood friend of Booth's and a former Confederate soldier, was assigned to help kidnap Lincoln. Convicted of conspiracy, O'Laughlin received a life sentence. He died of yellow fever in prison in 1867.
- Edman Spangler held Booth's horse during the assassination. Charged with conspiracy to assassinate the president, Spangler was sentenced to six years. Pardoned by President Andrew Johnson due to lack of evidence in March 1869, Spangler died in 1875.

- Dr. Samuel A. Mudd harbored Booth and Herold during their escape attempt. Mudd was charged with conspiracy and sentenced to life in prison, but he was pardoned by President Johnson in March 1869 for his lifesaving efforts at Fort Jefferson during a yellow fever outbreak. Mudd died of pneumonia in 1883.
- Samuel Arnold was involved in the early plans to kidnap President Lincoln. He was convicted of conspiracy and sentenced to life in prison. President Johnson pardoned Arnold in March 1869 because of his minimal role and early attempt to break from the conspirators. Arnold died of tuberculosis in 1906.
- John Surratt also participated in the early plans to kidnap President Lincoln. He remained a fugitive until November 27, 1866, when he was apprehended in Alexandria, Egypt. He was charged with conspiracy, but a deadlocked jury resulted in Surratt's release in 1868. Surratt died of pneumonia on April 21, 1916.

* * * *

Vice President Johnson and Secretary of State Seward were also targeted because the conspirators were aiming to overthrow the federal government and Johnson and Seward were first and second in line for the presidency, respectively.

* * * *

Lincoln Assassination Conspiracy Trial

Ohio native and lawyer **Henry L. Burnett** was a major in the Ohio Cavalry during the Civil War. In 1865, he was called to Washington, D.C., to head the investigation into the assassination of Abraham Lincoln. He served as one of the judge advocates in the trial. In later years, Burnett served as U.S. district attorney in New York. When he died on January 4, 1916, at age 77, he was the last survivor of the Lincoln conspirators' military tribunal.

* * * *

Democrat Alexander Hamilton Coffroth served in Congress during the last two years of the Civil War. When he died in 1906 at age 78, he was the last living person who had served as a pallbearer at President Abraham Lincoln's funeral.

* * * *

Witnesses to the Lincoln Assassination

Of everyone in Ford's Theatre the night Abraham Lincoln was shot, **Samuel James Seymour** was the last to survive. He was five years old when he heard the shot, saw Lincoln slump over, and watched Booth drop to the stage. Before Booth got up and fled, the boy cried out, "Hurry, hurry, let's go help the poor man who fell down!" Seymour died in 1956 at age 96, a few weeks after he appeared on the television game show *I've Got a Secret*.

The Assassination of Mohandas Gandhi

In 1948, a group of men conspired to assassinate Indian leader Mohandas Gandhi. They believed Gandhi had betrayed Hindus, and they also blamed him for the partition of India. **Gopal Godse,** whose brother was the actual assassin, was the last surviving conspirator. He served 16 years in prison and died on November 26, 2005, at age 85.

The Truman Assassination Attempt

On November 1, 1950, two Puerto Rican nationalists attempted to assassinate U.S. President Harry Truman. **Oscar Collazo** and Griselio Torresola tried to force their way into Blair House, where Truman was living while the White House was being renovated.

During the gunfight with Secret Service agents and White House police officers, Torresola mortally wounded Officer Leslie Coffelt. President Truman, who had been napping, was awakened by the gunfire. Truman went to the window to see what was going on; no one knows if Torresola saw Truman in the window, but—fortunately for the president—the dying Coffelt shot and killed Torresola before he could take aim at the president. Torresola's cohort, Collazo, was wounded, as were two other police officers.

Collazo was sentenced to death, but a week before the execution date, Truman commuted Collazo's sentence to life in prison. In 1979, President Carter commuted the sentence again, and Collazo was set free. He died in 1994 at age 80.

* * * *

A plaque on the gate in front of Blair House commemorates Officer Leslie Coffelt's heroism during the attempt on President Truman's life.

* * * *

Oscar Collazo and Griselio Torresola were followers of Pedro Albizu Campos, a Harvard graduate who had served in the U.S. army during World War I. He served in an African American unit, and the intense racism he witnessed during his service left Campos embittered toward the United States.

* * * *

The Kennedy Assassination

On November 22, 1963, President John F. Kennedy was fatally shot as he proceeded in a motorcade through the streets of Dallas, Texas. **Nellie Connally,** wife of Texas Governor John Connally, was the last survivor of those riding in the limousine with Kennedy. Connally passed away on September 1, 2006.

Passengers in the car in which President Kennedy was assassinated:

- President Kennedy, who sat in the right rear seat, died soon after being shot on November 22, 1963.
- Special Agent Roy Kellerman, who sat in the front passenger seat, died in 1984.
- Agent William Greer, the driver, died in 1985.
- Governor Connally, who sat in the right jump seat in front of President Kennedy, died in 1993.
- First Lady Jacqueline Kennedy, who sat in the left rear seat, died in 1994.
- Nellie Connally, who sat in the left jump seat in front of Jacqueline Kennedy, died in 2006.

The Warren Commission

The last living member of the Warren Commission, which investigated the John F. Kennedy assassination, was **Gerald Ford.** Ford later became the 38th U.S. president after the resignation of Richard Nixon. He died on December 26, 2006, at age 93.

The following were the members of the Warren Commission:

- Allen W. Dulles (1893–1969), a private attorney who had served as director of the Central Intelligence Agency under Republican Dwight D. Eisenhower
- Richard B. Russell (1897–1971), Democratic U.S. senator from Georgia and chairman of the Senate Armed Services Committee
- Thomas Hale Boggs (1914–72), Democratic U.S. representative from Louisiana and majority whip
- Earl Warren (1891–1974), chief justice of the U.S. Supreme Court
- John J. McCloy (1895–1989), a private attorney who had served as assistant secretary of war under Democrat Franklin D. Roosevelt
- John Sherman Cooper (1901–91), Republican U.S. senator from Kentucky

- Gerald R. Ford (1913–2006), Republican U.S. representative from Michigan and chairman of the House Republican Conference

The Martin Luther King Jr. Assassination

Reverend Martin Luther King Jr. called on Americans to work to truly make the United States the land of the free. He traveled to Memphis, Tennessee, in April 1968 to show solidarity with garbage workers who were striking over low wages and poor working conditions. On April 4, King was killed by an assassin while standing on the balcony outside his motel room; he had been scheduled to lead a protest march that evening.

The last hour of King's life was spent in his motel room with Reverend Ralph Abernathy and Reverend **Samuel "Billy" Kyles.** Abernathy died in 1990, leaving Kyles as the last survivor. Kyles, the longtime pastor of Monumental Baptist Church in Memphis who helped integrate the school system, restaurants, and buses of Memphis, was still alive as of 2009.

* * * *

Martin Luther King Jr. received hundreds of death threats in his lifetime. His Montgomery, Alabama, home was bombed (and his wife and children were inside it at the time), and he was once stabbed during a book signing appearance at a Harlem department store.

* * * *

The motel where Martin Luther King Jr. was killed is now the National Civil Rights Museum.

* * * *

Canadian History

❑ ❑ ❑ ❑

Which former Canadian prime minister is the only one buried outside of Canada?
Who was the last surviving member of the Canadian bicycle infantry?
Who was the last surviving crew member of the SS Caribou?
This chapter answers these questions and more.

Canada's Fathers of Confederation

The Fathers of Confederation were government leaders who helped form the nation of Canada from British colonies and territories during the 1860s. The last survivor was Sir **Charles Tupper,** who passed away in 1915 at age 94. A native of Nova Scotia, Tupper was a medical doctor, newspaper editor, federal judge, and legislative leader. In 1896, he became Canada's prime minister at age 74—the oldest person to ever hold the office.

Canadian Province Namesakes

Two of the 13 provinces of Canada were named after individual people. The last surviving was Queen Victoria's sixth child, Princess **Louise Caroline Alberta,** who lived in Canada from 1878 to 1883 while her husband, the Marquis of Lorne, served as governor general. She died in 1939 at age 91. Prince Edward Augustus (1767–1820), Duke of Kent and Queen Victoria's father, also had a province named after him: Prince Edward Island.

Foreign-born Prime Ministers of Canada

Of Canada's 22 prime ministers, only four were born outside the country. The last surviving of these was **John Turner** of the Liberal Party. Turner took office in June 1984 after Pierre Trudeau retired; Turner lost in the September general election, however, and served as prime minister for only a few months. Born in Richmond, England, Turner reached his 79th birthday in 2008.

The following were other foreign-born Canadian prime ministers:

Alexander Mackenzie

- Sir John A. Macdonald (died 1891) served 1867–73 and 1878–91; born in Glasgow, Scotland
- Alexander Mackenzie (died 1892) served 1873–78; born in Dunkeld, Scotland
- Sir Mackenzie Bowell (died 1917) served 1894–96; born in Rickinghall, England

* * * *

As of 2009, Richard B. Bennett is the only Canadian prime minister buried outside Canada. He was prime minister from 1930 to 1935, but in 1939, discouraged by lack of voter support, he moved to Britain. He purchased a mansion, became a viscount, and served in the House of Lords from 1941 to 1947. He died in 1947 at age 76 and is buried in Dorking, England.

* * * *

Knighted Canadian Prime Ministers

The last surviving Canadian prime minister to be knighted by the British monarchy was **Sir Robert Borden,** who passed away in 1937 at 82 years old. Borden served as Canada's leader throughout World War I and later focused his attention on making Canada diplomatically independent. He also served as a business leader and a university chancellor. Borden was knighted by King George V in 1914. Five years later, legislation was passed that prohibited the British sovereign from granting knighthood to Canadian citizens.

The following Canadian prime ministers were also knighted:

- Sir John A. Macdonald (died 1891) served 1867–73 and 1878–91
- Sir John Abbott (died 1893) served 1891–92
- Sir John Thompson (died 1894) served 1892–94
- Sir Charles Tupper (died 1915) served in 1896
- Sir Mackenzie Bowell (died 1917) served 1894–96
- Sir Wilfrid Laurier (died 1919) served 1896–1911

Canadian Bicycle Infantry Members

During World War I, all countries fighting in Europe used bicycle-mounted soldiers to one extent or another. Canada had five bicycle infantry battalions, and they were used primarily to spy behind enemy lines and to move with foot soldiers. The bicyclists often carried their own machine guns and suffered unusually high casualty rates. The last surviving member of the Canadian bicycle infantry was **W. D. Ellis,** who died in 1996 at 100 years old.

World War I Veterans from New Brunswick

Lazare Gionet, a farmer, fisherman, barber, and cook, was 20 when he volunteered for the Canadian Army during the First World War. When he passed away on April 1, 2005, at age 108, he was the last surviving World War I veteran from the province of New Brunswick.

Canadian Victoria Cross Recipients for World War II Action

Ernest "Smokey" Smith rode Canada's rails looking for work during the Depression. In 1940, Smokey enlisted in the Seaforth Highlanders of Canada, where he was promoted to corporal and then busted to private *nine* times. Future events showed that

Smokey's strengths lay more in combat than in military drill and discipline.

On October 22, 1944, near Italy's Savio River, the Seaforths faced a German tank and infantry assault. While protecting a wounded Seaforth comrade, Smokey disabled a German tank, then repelled two German infantry charges. His actions saved his buddy's life. For valor the size of British Columbia, King George VI personally gave Smokey the Victoria Cross (VC), Canada's highest military award, at Buckingham Palace.

Canada long made much more of Smokey's achievements than he did. His frequent comment was, "They could have wiped me out in no time if they'd known I was practically all by myself." After the war, Smokey married Esther Weston, who bore him a son and daughter. He reenlisted for the Korean War, but the army didn't want to risk losing a living icon. Assigned recruiting duties as a sergeant, this time Smokey kept his stripes.

After retirement in 1964, the Smiths started a successful travel agency in Vancouver. Smokey used his celebrity for the good of his country, often donating his time to speak in schools and talk with young people. He passed away on August 3, 2005, at age 91—the last living of the 16 Canadian World War II VC recipients.

* * * *

Ernest "Smokey" Smith doesn't recall the story behind his nickname, but a good guess might be his exceptional speed in track as a teenager.

* * * *

Crew of the SS *Caribou*

On October 14, 1942, the German submarine *U-69* sank the Canadian ferry SS *Caribou* on its run between North Sydney, Nova Scotia, and Port aux Basques, Newfoundland. Only 101 of its 237 passengers and crew survived. Of the 46 crew survivors, **John Matthews** was the last—he passed away on February 14, 2008, at 84. After the *Caribou* sank, Matthews was saved by a lifeboat. However, because the lifeboat was overcrowded, the occupants had to rotate between the boat and the freezing water.

Science

❑ ❑ ❑ ❑

How old was Franklin Delano Roosevelt when he contracted polio?
Why was Pluto reclassified as a dwarf planet?
Who was the last surviving key member of the Manhattan Project?
We won't hold you in suspense—the answers
can be found on the following pages.

National Academy of Sciences

Established by an act of Congress in 1863, the National Academy of Sciences provides advice to the U.S. government on scientific and technological issues. As of 2006, approximately 2,000 American scientists and 350 foreign associates were members of the academy. The last survivor of the original members was chemist **Oliver Wolcott Gibbs,** who was born in New York City in 1822. He studied in Germany and France, then became a professor of chemistry at the Free Academy (now called the College of the City of New York). Gibbs died in 1908 at age 86.

* * * *

Mt. Gibbs in Yosemite National Park is named after Oliver Wolcott Gibbs.

* * * *

Children of Louis Pasteur

French chemist Louis Pasteur (1822–95) is known for his germ theory, for originating the process of pasteurization, and for his work on the prevention of anthrax, rabies, and other diseases. Of his five children, daughter **Marie-Louise Pasteur** was the last survivor, passing away in 1934 at age 76.

The Reed Commission

In 1900, Walter Reed, a U.S. army medical officer, and three acting assistant surgeons—James Carroll, **Aristides Agramonte,** and Jesse Lazear—formed the Reed Commission. Also known as the Yellow Fever Commission, it studied the ways yellow fever might be transmitted among U.S. troops in Cuba. Tests on volunteers demonstrated that the bites of some mosquitoes transmitted yellow fever; before this time, many had believed the disease was transmitted from person to person.

The last surviving commission member was Agramonte, who was born in Puerto Principe, Cuba, in 1868. He had a mild case of yellow fever as a child in Cuba, and he was therefore immune to the disease later in life. Agramonte immigrated to the United States with his family when he was three years old. He earned his medical degree from the College of Physicians and Surgeons in New York in 1892, and he was soon appointed assistant bacteriologist with the New York Health Department. In May 1898, the U.S. surgeon general appointed Agramonte acting assistant surgeon in the U.S. Army, and he was then appointed to the Reed Commission. He died in 1931 at age 63.

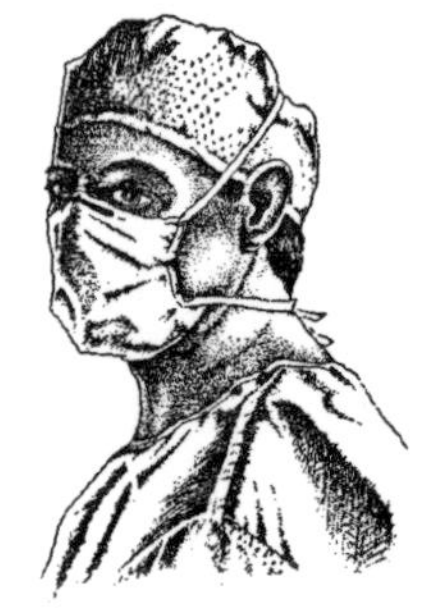

* * * *

Acting assistant surgeon Jesse Lazear died of yellow fever in 1900, during the commission's studies. No one is sure if he purposely infected himself as part of the experiment or if it happened accidentally.

* * * *

Yellow fever killed 9,000 people in New Orleans in 1853.

* * * *

American College of Surgeons

Founded in 1913, the American College of Surgeons had more than 70,000 members in 2008, making it the world's largest organization of surgeons. The last survivor of the association's founders was **Dr. Fayette Clay Ewing,** who died in 1956 at age 94.

Discoverers of Major Vitamins

During the 18th century, scientists realized that citrus fruit prevented scurvy, but no one understood how. Many scientists began working on the puzzle, including **Charles Glen King** of the University of Pittsburgh and Albert Szent-Györgyi of Szeged, Hungary. They both discovered the substance vitamin C around the same time in 1928. Szent-Györgyi was awarded the 1937 Nobel Prize, but most scientists believe King should have been recognized as well. Szent-Györgyi died in 1986, making King (who died in 1988) the last survivor.

The following were discoverers of other major vitamins:

- Elmer Verner McCollum (1879–1967) discovered vitamin A in 1913, vitamin B in 1916, and vitamin D in 1922.
- Henrik Carl Peter Dam (1895–1976) and Edward Adelbert Doisy (1893–1986) discovered vitamin K in 1935.

Developers of Major Vaccines

Jonas Salk (1914–95), who developed the killed-virus polio vaccine in 1954, lived until 1995 and is considered the last surviving discoverer of a major vaccine.

The following were developers of other major vaccines:

- Edward Jenner (1749–1823) developed the smallpox vaccine in 1796.
- Louis Pasteur (1822–95) developed the rabies vaccine in 1885.
- Charles Nicolle (1866–1936) developed the typhus vaccine in 1909.
- Albert B. Sabin (1906–93) pioneered the oral live-virus polio vaccine in the late 1950s.

* * * *

Jonas Salk refused to patent the polio vaccine because he wished to see it distributed as quickly as possible.

* * * *

Franklin Delano Roosevelt contracted polio in 1921, when he was 39 years old. In 2003, researchers at the University of Texas Medical Branch in Galveston reported that it is possible Roosevelt actually had Guillain-Barré syndrome (which exhibits symptoms similar to polio), but this remains a subject of debate.

* * * *

A Killer Reined In

Polio is a virus that is spread from person to person via unwashed hands, shared objects, and contaminated food or water. Symptoms include fever, headache, fatigue, vomiting, and limb pain. Some of those infected go on to develop the more serious form of the disease, which causes problems such as loss of reflexes and floppy limbs.

Of the thousands of Americans infected during the 1916 polio epidemic, 6,000 died and 27,000 survived but were paralyzed. During the 1950s, there was an average of 20,000 cases in the United States each year. Widespread vaccinations began in 1955, and by 1960 the number of U.S. cases was down to 3,000. In 1979, only 10 cases were reported in the United States.

Most children in the United States today receive four doses of the polio vaccine, the first at two months of age and the fourth at around age five. Polio has been eradicated from many areas of the world, but outbreaks still occur in Asia and Africa.

The Planets

English astronomer Sir William Herschel (1738–1822) discovered Uranus in 1781. In 1845, the existence of the planet Neptune was predicted independently by **John Couch Adams** (1819–92) of England and Urbain Jean Joseph Le Verrier (1811–77) of France. When he passed away at age 72 in 1892, Adams was the last living of the discoverers of the eight planets of the Earth's solar system.

* * * *

Humans have known about Mercury, Venus, Mars, Jupiter, and Saturn since prehistoric times because these planets are visible to the naked eye.

* * * *

Odd Planet Out?

Clyde Tombaugh (1906–97) discovered Pluto in 1930. In more recent years, researchers have found many problematic bodies in our solar system. Scientists were faced with either assigning planetary status to many more bodies or reclassifying Pluto. In 2006, the International Astronomical Union stipulated that planets have to fulfill the following criteria:

1) the body must orbit the Sun
2) the body must be big enough for gravity to quash it into a round ball
3) the body must have cleared all other debris (including asteroids and comets) out of its orbit

Pluto was reclassified as a dwarf planet because it did not fulfill the third criterion. Astronomers are aware of more than 40 dwarf planets and believe they will find hundreds more in the future.

The reclassification was controversial, however. Many scientists contend that Earth, Mars, Neptune, and Jupiter have not cleared their orbits either. Pluto actually ventures into Neptune's orbit at times, and there are 10,000 asteroids in Earth's orbit and 100,000 in Jupiter's. Most scientists believe that the definition of a planet still needs further revision. Stay tuned.

* * * *

When Ceres, the largest asteroid in the solar system, was discovered in 1801, many hailed it as the tenth planet. It was later reclassified as an asteroid.

* * * *

Penicillin

In 1928, Alexander Fleming discovered penicillin, an antibiotic mold that could kill bacteria. The last surviving member of the team that developed the means of mass producing the drug was **Norman Heatley** of Oxford University. Awarded Oxford's first honorary doctorate in medicine in 1990, Heatley died in 2004, several days short of his 93rd birthday.

* * * *

By the end of World War II, penicillin had saved millions of lives. Doctors used it to clean wounds and treat pneumonia, tuberculosis, diphtheria, and scarlet fever.

* * * *

Fermi's Scientists

Nuclear physicist **Franco Rasetti** was the last survivor of the group of scientists led by Enrico Fermi (1901–54) that first split the atom in the 1930s. Born in Castiglione del Lago, Italy, Rasetti studied and worked in Italy, Canada, Scotland, and the United States. In the 1940s, Rasetti broke with Fermi over the development of the atomic bomb and shifted his research efforts to the fields of geology and paleontology. He died on December 12, 2001, at age 100.

The Manhattan Project

Edward Teller was born in Budapest, Hungary, in 1908. After studying in Germany, he moved to the United States in 1935 to teach at George Washington University. During World War II, he worked on the Manhattan Project to develop the atomic bomb and was later one of the founders of what would become the Lawrence Livermore National Laboratory. Teller died on September 9, 2003, at age 95, the last surviving key member of the Manhattan Project.

J. Robert Oppenheimer

J. Robert Oppenheimer, the scientific director of the Manhattan Project, might be called the midwife of nuclear weapons. Born in 1904 and educated at Harvard and overseas, Oppenheimer's passions included Sanskrit, art, and literature. Under FBI surveillance since before World War II, Oppenheimer's left-wing politics brought him onto the radar of the McCarthyist movement of the early 1950s.

After World War II, Oppenheimer opposed plans to manufacture the more powerful hydrogen bomb. In 1954, Edward Teller, who also worked on the Manhattan Project, expressed doubts about Oppenheimer during hearings regarding Oppenheimer's security clearance. Oppenheimer's clearance was revoked, and Teller became a sellout in the eyes of the physics community. Oppenheimer withdrew from public life, and he died of throat cancer in 1967.

Einstein-Era Physicists

After emigrating from Germany in the 1930s, **Hans Bethe** taught at Cornell University and assisted in the development of the first atomic bombs. He was awarded the 1967 Nobel Prize in physics. Born on July 2, 1906, Bethe was the last major physicist of his era when he died on March 6, 2005.

* * * *

Alive as of 2008, 77-year-old physicist Bernhard Caesar Einstein is the last living grandchild of Albert Einstein.

* * * *

Individuals Who Have Won Two Nobels

Three men and one woman have received two Nobel Prizes. The last living of these was scientist and humanitarian **Linus Pauling.** Pauling won the 1954 Nobel Prize in Chemistry for his studies on the nature of the chemical bond and the structure of molecules and crystals. He also won the 1962 Nobel Peace Prize for his efforts to stop aboveground nuclear testing because of the risks of cancer and birth defects. Pauling died in 1994 at age 93.

The following people also received two Nobels:

- Marie Curie of France—Nobel Prize in Physics (1903) and Nobel Prize in Chemistry (1911)
- John Bardeen of the United States—Nobel Prize in Physics (1956 and 1972)
- Frederick Sanger of the United Kingdom—Nobel Prize in Chemistry (1958 and 1980)

Individuals Who Were Not Permitted to Accept the Nobel Prize

Four Nobel Prize recipients have been forced by their governments to either decline or return their prizes. Adolf Hitler kept Richard Kuhn, **Adolf Butenandt,** and Gerhard Domagk from accepting their prizes. The Soviet government forced the fourth, Russian writer Boris Pasternak, to return his prize. The last survivor of these four men was German biochemist Butenandt (1903–95), who was awarded the 1939 Nobel Prize in Chemistry for his work on sex hormones. Hitler refused to allow him to accept the prize, however, in retaliation for the Nobel committee bestowing a prize upon pacifist Carl von Ossietzky. A few years after the fall of Nazi Germany, Butenandt was finally able to accept the prize. He died in 1995 at age 91.

* * * *

Butenandt's work made the development of birth control pills possible.

* * * *

Married Couples Who Have Won the Nobel Prize

Four married couples have won Nobel Prizes. The last survivor was Swedish economist **Gunnar Myrdal,** who received the 1974 Nobel Prize in Economic Sciences for his work in the theory of money and economic fluctuations and for his analysis of the interdependence of economic, social, and institutional phenomena. He passed away in 1987 at age 88. His wife, Swedish diplomat Alva Myrdal, won the 1982 Nobel Peace Prize for her disarmament efforts.

The following were other married couples who have won the Nobel Prize:

- Marie Curie (1867–1934) and Pierre Curie (1859–1906) won the 1911 Nobel in Chemistry for their research into spontaneous radioactivity.
- Irène Joliot-Curie (1897–1956) and Frédéric Joliot (1900–58) won the 1935 Nobel in Chemistry for their synthesis of new radioactive elements.
- Gerty Cori (1896–1957) and Carl Cori (1896–1984) won the 1947 Nobel in Physiology or Medicine for their discovery of the course of the catalytic conversion of glycogen.

DNA

Maclyn McCarty, the last survivor of the team that proved DNA is responsible for transmitting genetic information, died in 2005 at age 93. In addition to decades of groundbreaking laboratory research, he was a vice president and physician-in-chief at Rockefeller Hospital, as well as chairman of the New York City Public Health Research Institute.

Movies

❑ ❑ ❑ ❑

Who is the last surviving star of Gone with the Wind?
What method of travel did Fay Wray's family use when they moved to Arizona?
What movie had John Dillinger seen just before he was gunned down outside the Biograph Theater?
If you're intrigued, you've stumbled upon the right chapter.

The Birth of a Nation

The Birth of a Nation, the 1915 D. W. Griffith epic of the Civil War period, is one of the most famous movies of the silent era. The last survivor of its major cast members was screen legend **Lillian Gish.** Gish was born in 1893; she moved to New York City with her family and began acting at age five. Gish knew Mary Pickford growing up, and it was Pickford who introduced her to D. W. Griffith. Gish spent most of her time working, mostly on the stage. She was also extremely devoted to her mother and sister. She never married and left no descendants when she passed away in 1993 at age 99.

The Sheik

The Sheik (1921), which starred Rudolph Valentino, was one of the great silent movies. Cast in small roles as Arab children were eight-year-old **Loretta Young** and her two sisters Sally Blane and Polly Ann Young. Last survivor Loretta was born in Salt Lake City in 1913. Her parents separated when she was two years old, and Loretta moved to Hollywood with her mother and siblings. She started acting at age four. Loretta eloped with a costar at age 17, but the marriage was annulled the following year. She married Tom Lewis in 1940, and the couple had two sons before divorcing in 1969. Loretta married her third husband, Jean Louis, in 1993, and they were together until his death in 1997. She passed away in 2000 at age 87.

* * * *

Loretta Young became pregnant while having an affair with Clark Gable. To avoid a scandal, Young feigned illness and had the child in secret. The next year she reappeared with an "adopted" daughter, Judy.

* * * *

The Phantom of the Opera

Noted for the superb performance by Lon Chaney, *The Phantom of the Opera* (1925) is one of the best known silent films. For the rest of her life, **Mary Philbin,** who played Christine, was best remembered for her performance in this movie. She died in 1993 at age 90.

* * * *

The love of Philbin's life was producer Paul Kohner, but the two never married because he was Jewish and she was Catholic.

* * * *

My Best Girl

"America's Sweetheart" Mary Pickford had one of her biggest hits with this 1927 movie. Her costar was future husband **Charles "Buddy" Rogers.** Married ten years after *My Best Girl* premiered, they remained wedded until her death in 1979. Rogers lived for another 20 years, passing away in 1999 at age 94.

The General

This classic 1927 Buster Keaton silent comedy was based upon an actual locomotive chase that occurred during the Civil War. The last surviving major cast member was female lead **Marion Mack,** who passed away in 1989.

The Jazz Singer

The Jazz Singer (1927), the first major sound movie, featured Broadway superstar Al Jolson in the title role. **Robert Gordon,** who passed away in 1990 at 77, was the last member of *The Jazz Singer* cast to survive. He played Jolson's character as a 13-year-old.

Wings

Wings (1927) was a story about two friends who fall in love with the same girl and later become fighter pilots in World War I. This was the first movie (and the only silent one) to win the Best Picture Academy Award. **Charles "Buddy" Rogers,** who in later years was married to actress Mary Pickford, was the last surviving major cast member of *Wings*. Born in 1904, Rogers died in 1999.

All Quiet on the Western Front

All Quiet on the Western Front won the 1930 Best Picture Academy Award. Last surviving cast member **Lew Ayres,** who several years later played Dr. Kildare in a series of hospital drama movies (not to be confused with the television series starring Richard Chamberlain), died in 1996.

* * * *

A conscientious objector during World War II, Lew Ayres refused to bear arms. He served as a medic and was awarded three Silver Stars.

* * * *

Frankenstein

This 1931 movie is the granddaddy of horror films; it is still haunting and effective. Boris Karloff is impressive as the mistreated monster who terrorizes the local community, and there are other fine performances by Colin Clive, **Mae Clarke,** and Edward Van Sloan. **Marilyn Harris,** who played the child Maria, was the last cast member when she died in 1999 at age 75. Clarke, who passed away in 1992 at age 81, was the last surviving adult member of the cast. She played Henry Frankenstein's fiancée, Elizabeth.

Little Caesar

This classic 1931 gangster movie is still fascinating. Edward G. Robinson is Enrico Bandello, the ruthless killer who takes over a gang of criminals. Robinson did such a convincing job with the role that others identified him with the character throughout his career. The last surviving star was **Douglas Fairbanks Jr.,** son of the legendary silent film star. Fairbanks became a superstar in his own right and died at the age of 90 in 2000.

King Kong

This thrill-packed 1933 monster movie has achieved screen-classic status, thanks to the imaginative and skillful use of special effects and on-target direction. A giant ape is brought from the jungle to New York, where it escapes and wreaks havoc in the city; the memorable climax on the Empire State Building is a masterpiece. The last major cast member of *King Kong*, **Fay Wray** starred as the beauty the beast found irresistible. Wray died on August 8, 2004, at age 96.

* * * *

Fay Wray was born in Alberta, Canada, in 1907. Her family moved to Arizona by stagecoach when she was three years old.

* * * *

Duck Soup

A wild offering of one-liners plus a famed mirror sequence put this 1933 comic romp in the Marx Brothers Hall of Fame. Groucho plays Rufus T. Firefly, the president of Freedonia, who ineptly wages war upon a scheming non-Marxist neighboring land. *Duck Soup*'s last surviving cast member was **Leonid Kinskey,** who played the agitator. Kinskey died in 1998 at age 95.

It Happened One Night

In this 1934 film, **Claudette Colbert** plays a spoiled girl who runs away from her daddy and sets off to marry her gigolo boyfriend. She is accompanied on this crazy odyssey by a story-hungry reporter (Clark Gable). This delightful romance was a forerunner to all the great screwball comedies of the '30s. Gable and Colbert make the ideal bickering couple.

Colbert, the last surviving cast member of the film, passed away at her home in Barbados on July 30, 1996, at age 92.

* * * *

It Happened One Night *took home all the major Academy Awards in 1935, including Best Picture, Best Director, Best Actor, and Best Actress.*

* * * *

The Thin Man

Starring William Powell and Myrna Loy as Dashiell Hammett characters Nick and Nora Charles, this 1934 murder mystery set the stage for many sequels. The last major cast member of *The Thin Man* was Irish-born **Maureen O'Sullivan,** star of the *Tarzan* movies. O'Sullivan died at age 87 in 1998.

* * * *

Maureen O'Sullivan was actress Mia Farrow's mother.

* * * *

Manhattan Melodrama

Of the large cast of *Manhattan Melodrama* (1934), only one person remained alive as of 2009—actor and comedian **Mickey Rooney.** Since his first movie role in 1926, Rooney has made at least one movie each year for the past 80-plus years for the longest film career on record.

* * * *

On July 22, 1934, outlaw John Dillinger was shot to death by federal agents as he left the Biograph Theater in Chicago after viewing Manhattan Melodrama.

* * * *

Mutiny on the Bounty

Mutiny on the Bounty (1935) is a classic movie adventure. Charles Laughton is unforgettable as the heartless Captain Bligh, whose treatment of the crew provokes mutiny. Clark Gable excels as first mate Fletcher Christian. The only player still alive as of 2008 is Mexican actress **Movita Castaneda,** who was born in 1917.

* * * *

Movita Castaneda was briefly married to Marlon Brando in the 1960s. The couple had one son, Miko, and a daughter, Rebecca.

* * * *

The Petrified Forest

This 1936 film marked Humphrey Bogart's first major screen part. Fleeing from the law, vicious gangster Duke Mantee and his gang hold a small group of people hostage at a desert café. Among those trapped are a dreamy-eyed intellectual, played by Leslie Howard, and the waitress he falls for, played by Bette Davis. Even today the film has plenty of tension, and the three luminous stars play off each other impressively. Last survivor **Genevieve Tobin** died in 1995 at age 95. She played Mrs. Chisholm, a wealthy tourist.

Gone with the Wind

This stirring 1939 romantic spectacle is among the best and most memorable of all Hollywood productions. Based on Margaret Mitchell's compelling novel of the South during the Civil War, the epic tells the story of an aristocratic plantation family and its involvement with that war. Vivien Leigh is magnificent as Scarlett O'Hara, the spoiled beauty, and Clark Gable is at his best as the dashing Rhett Butler. **Olivia de Havilland,** one of the superstars of the golden age of Hollywood, was alive as of 2009.

* * * *

> *After* Gone with the Wind *became a blockbuster, producer David O. Selznick realized he had underpaid author Margaret Mitchell for the rights (he had bought them for $50,000). He then paid her an additional $50,000.*

* * * *

The Wizard of Oz

This 1939 tale about a Kansas farm girl who's spirited off to the land of Oz still tingles with freshness. Garland is memorable as Dorothy, and such songs as "Over the Rainbow" are unforgettable. The charming cast also includes Frank Morgan, **Ray Bolger,** Jack Haley, Bert Lahr, Billie Burke, and Margaret Hamilton. For added measure, the superb songs of E. Y. Harburg and Harold Arlen blend beautifully with the photography of Harold Rosson.

The last surviving cast member of this classic fantasy film was Ray Bolger, who played the Scarecrow in need of a brain. He died five days after his 83rd birthday in 1987, outliving Dorothy, the Tin Man, the Cowardly Lion, the witches, and even the Wizard himself.

Mr. Smith Goes to Washington

This 1939 film is among the best of director Frank Capra's comedy-dramas. **Jimmy Stewart** gives a stirring performance as a forthright freshman senator who encounters corruption in the nation's capital. It's an inspiring portrait of how elected officials ought to behave. Last survivor Stewart died in 1997. The other cast members—Jean Arthur, Claude Rains, Edward Arnold, Guy Kibbee, and Thomas Mitchell—had died years earlier.

Ninotchka

This 1939 movie is one of the brightest screen comedies Hollywood has ever turned out. It represents the very best of two comedy veterans—director Ernst Lubitsch and screenwriter Billy Wilder. An austere Russian agent, played by Greta Garbo, is sent to Paris to sell a former duchess's jewels. There she meets debonair playboy Melvyn Douglas, who woos her desperately. The sparkling script superbly celebrates love and spontaneity. The last surviving cast member was **Gregory Gaye,** who played Count Alexis Rakonin. He died in 1993 at age 92.

The Story of Alexander Graham Bell

This 1939 movie is the only film to star Loretta Young and her three sisters, Polly Ann Young, **Georgiana Young,** and Sally Blane. The last survivor was Georgiana, who died in 2007 at age 84.

* * * *

Georgiana Young and Ricardo Montalbán were married for 63 years.

* * * *

The Roaring Twenties

In this 1939 film, World War I army pals James Cagney, Humphrey Bogart, and **Jeffrey Lynn** run into each other again. But now, Cagney is a gangster. He is fantastic as a New York bootlegger. Jeffrey Lynn, who died at age 86 in 1995, was the last living star.

Rebecca

Alfred Hitchcock adapted this award-winning 1940 story from Daphne du Maurier's novel about a naive woman (played by **Joan Fontaine**) who marries a brooding British nobleman and finds that she must live in the shadow of Rebecca—his beautiful first wife.

Hitchcock deftly combines romance, comedy, suspense, and mystery, with sets in Monte Carlo and Cornwall. Fontaine, Judith Anderson, and Laurence Olivier perform superbly and receive excellent support from George Sanders, Nigel Bruce, Gladys Cooper, Florence Bates, and Reginald Denny. Joan Fontaine was alive as of 2009.

* * * *

Fontaine is the younger sister of Gone with the Wind *star Olivia de Havilland. The two are legendary rivals.*

* * * *

The Sea Hawk

Avast, ye swabs! When Warner Brothers launches a big-budget pirate picture in 1940 with Errol Flynn, the all-time king of the swashbucklers, you can be sure it's a winner. Flynn stars as a privateer rooting out treacherous Spaniards on the high seas and in the court of Her Majesty Queen Elizabeth I. There's plenty of colorful action in this adaptation of the novel by Rafael Sabatini.

The last cast member of *Sea Hawk* to survive was **Gilbert Roland,** who played a pirate captain. Born Luis Antonio Damaso de Alonso in Juarez, Mexico, in 1905, Roland achieved popularity in both silent and sound films. Credited with more than 100 movies, he was also one of the most popular actors in television guest roles in the 1950s, 1960s, and 1970s. He died at age 88 in 1994.

* * * *

Gilbert Roland's father, grandfather, and great-grandfather were all matadors.

* * * *

The Fighting 69th

This 1940 movie follows the exploits of the most famous Irish regiment of World War I. Starring James Cagney and Pat O'Brien, it was popular with American fans concerned about the war in Europe.

The last surviving star of the film was **Jeffrey Lynn,** who played Sergeant Joyce Kilmer, a celebrated poet. Lynn passed away in 1995 at age 86.

* * * *

Joyce Kilmer's most famous poem was "Trees," which ends with these well-known lines: "Poems are made by fools like me,/But only God can make a tree."

* * * *

The Great Dictator

This 1940 film was an effective spoof of Adolf Hitler with Charlie Chaplin in a dual role; he plays a Jewish barber and Adenoid Hynkel, the dictator of Tomania. Jack Oakie is also outstanding as Benzino Napaloni, the ruler of the rival country of Bacteria. *The Great Dictator*'s last living cast member was **Paulette Goddard,** who passed away at age 79 in 1990.

* * * *

Paulette Goddard was Charlie Chaplin's companion from 1936 to 1942. Their relationship was scandalous for the time because it was never clear if they were actually married. Goddard lost the role of Scarlett O'Hara in Gone with the Wind *because she could not validate the relationship by showing producer David O. Selznick a marriage certificate.*

* * * *

Citizen Kane

Orson Welles's 1941 masterpiece is about a tyrannical newspaper publisher who built a vast empire. Every moment of the story, which parallels the career of William Randolph Hearst, is filled with intelligence, excitement, and pure entertainment. Welles cowrote, directed, and starred in this magnificent production, which broke new ground in cinematic craftsmanship. Seeing it today is still a remarkable experience, and it surely will remain a gem among Hollywood's offerings. **Ruth Warrick,** who played Kane's first wife, was the last living cast member, passing away on January 15, 2005.

How Green Was My Valley

This heartwarming 1941 drama about life in a Welsh coal-mining town won the Best Picture Academy Award. Much effort was lavished on exquisite production detail, giving eloquent class to the film, which was based on Richard Llewellyn's novel of the same name. **Maureen O'Hara,** born in 1920 in a suburb of Dublin, Ireland, was the last living star of this movie. She was alive and well in 2009.

The Maltese Falcon

This 1941 film is the king of the crime capers, smartly executed by director John Huston with zip, punch, and even a bit of sentiment. Humphrey Bogart is private-eye Sam Spade, hot on the trail of a mysterious statuette in this remake of a 1931 film (both films were based on the Dashiell Hammett novel). He's backed to the hilt with memorable supporting parts from his client (played by Mary Astor), Sydney Greenstreet as the Fat Man, and Peter Lorre as Joel Cairo. Character actor **Elisha Cook Jr.,** who played killer Wilmer Cook, was the last living major cast member, passing away in 1995 at the age of 91.

Casablanca

Intrigue, romance, and a superb moody atmosphere make this taut 1942 melodrama one of the best World War II films. Humphrey Bogart, in a memorable performance, is in top form as the owner of a Casablanca nightclub. He helps an old flame (played by Ingrid Bergman) and her husband (played by **Paul Henreid**) escape the Nazis. This classic, witty thriller earns more appreciation with each year that goes by. It also starred Conrad Veidt, S. Z. Sakall, Peter Lorre, and Sydney Greenstreet. The last surviving star was Henreid, who died in 1992 at age 84.

Woman of the Year

Spencer Tracy and **Katharine Hepburn** are charming in this 1942 story about a sportswriter and a famed political columnist who seems to know about everything except sports. The acting and dialogue are tops. Fay Bainter, William Bendix, Reginald Owen, Roscoe Karns, Minor Watson, and Dan Tobin are in supporting roles. The last surviving cast member, Hepburn, died in 2003 at age 96.

* * * *

Woman of the Year *was the first pairing of Tracy and Hepburn on the screen.*

* * * *

Going My Way

Bing Crosby is perfectly cast as a young priest in a New York slum parish in this sentimental 1944 comedy. Barry Fitzgerald also shines as the elderly pastor who is charmed by the personable newcomer. Crosby, perhaps at the top of his film career, sings "Swinging on a Star" and "Too-ra-Loo-ra-Loo-ra." Supporting work is provided by **Risë Stevens,** Frank McHugh, Gene Lockhart, James Brown, and Porter Hall.

Opera singer Risë Stevens, who played an old friend of Crosby's character, is the last survivor of *Going My Way,* passing her 95th birthday in 2008. Stevens was born in the Bronx in 1913 and studied at Juilliard.

Bing Crosby

* * * *

Risë *is the Norwegian word for laughter.*

* * * *

Song of Bernadette

Jennifer Jones won the Best Actress Academy Award for her portrayal of Bernadette in the 1943 religious film *Song of Bernadette*. She celebrated her 90th birthday in 2009. All major players of her supporting cast have passed away.

The Lost Weekend

This 1945 film is a stark, powerful drama about a struggling writer, played by Ray Milland, who becomes an alcoholic. Milland gives a striking performance, which effectively and sympathetically illuminates his desperate character. Billy Wilder's script and direction are relentless in providing the details of personal pain, dejection, and terror. Howard da Silva is exceptional in a supporting role as a bartender. There are other good performances from **Jane Wyman,** Philip Terry, Doris Dowling, and Frank Faylen. The last survivor of the cast was Jane Wyman, who four years later would go on to win a Best Actress Oscar for her performance in *Johnny Belinda.* Wyman passed away in 2007 at age 90.

* * * *

> The Lost Weekend *won Oscars for Best Picture, Best Director, and Best Actor.*

* * * *

It's a Wonderful Life

This 1946 movie is perhaps Frank Capra's best film; it shows his uniquely warm and charming blend of humor. **Jimmy Stewart** is superb as a small-town businessman who beats his brains out most of his life. When he decides to end it all because he thinks he's a failure, a guardian angel, played by Henry Travers, appears to show him his accomplishments. Donna Reed plays Stewart's wife. It is film sentimentality done to perfection and displayed with a silver lining—a Christmas favorite and a wonderful movie. Also with Lionel Barrymore, Thomas Mitchell, Ward Bond, and Gloria Grahame. The last surviving major star was Jimmy Stewart, who died on July 2, 1997.

Key Largo

This tense, electrifying 1948 gangster yarn set in the Florida Keys saw Humphrey Bogart and Edward G. Robinson make the sparks fly as adversaries. Robinson plays a sinister criminal who holds a group of people captive at a remote hotel during a violent storm; Claire Trevor plays his moll. Bogey is an ex-GI who stands up to Robinson. Bogey's real-life wife and costar in this movie, **Lauren Bacall,** is the last remaining cast member. Bacall, who turned 84 in 2008, published the latest volume of her autobiography in 2005.

The Treasure of the Sierra Madre

This 1948 film is one of those rare Hollywood movies that tells a vivid story and provides a message. The objective is reached because of the excellent direction and screenwriting of John Huston, the vitality of the original novel by the mysterious B. Traven, the intense and realistic mood created by the superb photography of Ted McCord, and the stunning acting. Humphrey Bogart, Walter Huston, and Tim Holt star as three prospectors who find gold and are then done in by greed. Barton MacLane, **Bruce Bennett,** and Alfonso Bedoya star in supporting roles. Bennett, who played Cody, was the last living major cast member of *The Treasure of the Sierra Madre*.

Herman Brix

Bruce Bennett's given name was Herman Brix, and he was a talented athlete. He played in the 1925 Rose Bowl for the University of Washington, and he won a silver medal as a shot-putter at the 1928 Olympics. Grantland Rice once called him "America's greatest athlete." In 1934, Tarzan creator Edgar Rice Burroughs—dissatisfied with the way Hollywood was portraying his character—decided to film his own Tarzan movie. He personally chose Brix to play the title character in *The New Adventures of Tarzan*. Later, Brix changed his name to Bruce Bennett and went on to make another 100 films. He passed away on February 24, 2007, at age 100.

Hamlet

Even if you find Shakespeare heavy going, you'll probably appreciate this absorbing 1948 screen version of his magnificent play. Laurence Olivier stars as the melancholy Dane, and it's one of the greatest film performances of all time. Direction, also by Olivier, is on target too; he presents the great drama with clarity and effective moody atmospherics. The last survivor is **Jean Simmons,** alive in 2009 at age 80. Simmons was nominated for Best Supporting Actress for her performance as Ophelia.

All the King's Men

This 1949 film is a gripping, high-powered drama about political corruption in Louisiana, based loosely on the career of Huey Long. Most notable is the electrifying portrayal by Broderick Crawford as Willie Stark, the honest small-town politician who is elected governor and is eventually overwhelmed by power. *All the King's Men* won the Best Picture Academy Award in 1949. Actress **Mercedes McCambridge,** who won an Academy Award for her portrayal of reporter Sadie Burke, was the last living cast member when she passed away in 2004, days before her 88th birthday.

* * * *

Mercedes McCambridge also performed the demonic voice of the possessed child in The Exorcist *(1973).*

* * * *

McCambridge appeared in Johnny Guitar *with Joan Crawford, and the two feuded bitterly. Crawford once even dumped McCambridge's wardrobe along an Arizona highway.*

* * * *

The Third Man

This 1949 film is one of the best thrillers in the history of cinema. Graham Greene's story about vile black market operations in Vienna after

World War II is still fresh because of Carol Reed's direction, excellent acting, and Anton Karas's haunting zither music. Joseph Cotton portrays an American who writes westerns. He's in search of Harry Lime, a mystery man of dubious morals played by Orson Welles—and therein lies the fascinating tale. Trevor Howard and Alida Valli are excellent in supporting roles. The last surviving major cast member of *The Third Man* was female lead **Alida Valli,** who died at age 84 in 2006.

She Wore a Yellow Ribbon

In this 1949 film, John Wayne is excellent as a cavalry officer about to retire. But before he can leave the range, he faces a last encounter with some Native Americans. The film has all of director John Ford's vintage ingredients: quality acting, beautiful photography, and a good story. Joanne Dru, John Agar, Ben Johnson, Harry Carey Jr., Mildred Natwick, Arthur Shields, Victor McLaglen, and George O'Brien also star. The last survivor—a man often cast in Ford-Wayne westerns—was **Harry Carey Jr.,** who turned 88 in 2009.

Harvey

Mary Chase's touching play about a middle-age tippler with an imaginary huge white rabbit as his companion came to the screen in 1950 with all the wonderful dialogue and memorable moments firmly in place. Jimmy Stewart is marvelous as the gentle Elwood P. Dowd, under pressure by his relatives to enter a mental hospital. Josephine Hull also stands out as the perplexed sister who is constantly apologizing for Dowd's nutty behavior. The engrossing story wisely questions the true definition of insanity. There are other good performances from Victoria Horne, **Peggy Dow,** Cecil Kellaway, and Jesse White. Dow is the last remaining star. After this movie and the following year's *Bright Victory,* Ms. Dow retired from show business. She was alive at age 81 in 2009.

Singin' in the Rain

Gene Kelly, Donald O'Connor, **Debbie Reynolds,** and Jean Hagen sparkle in this marvelous 1952 musical spoof about Hollywood during the period when talkies first replaced silent films. Rita

Moreno, Cyd Charisse, Douglas Fowley, and Millard Mitchell also star in what many critics consider the greatest Hollywood musical of all time. The last surviving major cast member is Debbie Reynolds, who was alive at age 77 as of 2009. Jean Hagen passed away in 1977, Gene Kelly in 1996, and Donald O'Connor in 2003.

* * * *

Debbie Reynolds is the mother of actress and writer Carrie Fisher.

* * * *

Rear Window

Director Alfred Hitchcock combines sophisticated comedy with superlative suspense scenes in this 1954 movie about a news photographer confined to his wheelchair who witnesses a murder. Jimmy Stewart plays the photographer, and Grace Kelly is charming as his girlfriend. The tension builds and becomes almost excruciating as Hitchcock works his magic. Raymond Burr, Judith Evelyn, Wendell Corey, and Thelma Ritter perform well in supporting roles. The last surviving cast member was **Frank Cady,** who played the upstairs neighbor of Raymond Burr's character. Cady reached his 92nd birthday on September 8, 2008.

* * * *

Cady is also known as the only actor to hold a role as a recurring character in three situation comedies simultaneously. He played the part of Sam Drucker in The Beverly Hillbillies, Green Acres, *and* Petticoat Junction.

* * * *

Seven Samurai

Beautifully directed by Akira Kurosawa, this epic 1954 action film is one of the most striking of them all—both violent and poetic. In 16th-century Japan, a lethal gang of 40 bandits threatens to wreak havoc on a farming village. The menaced citizens go out and hire seven professional soldiers—the samurai—who agree to ward off the invaders. The film has been duly celebrated by fans and critics around the world for its humor, heroism, and humanity. **Minoru Chiaki** was the last survivor of the seven samurai in the movie. He died of heart failure in 1999 at age 82.

12 Angry Men

A better title might have been *One Angry Man* because in this 1957 movie, Henry Fonda plays a conscientious and moral juror at the trial of a teenager accused of killing his father. The sensational cast also includes Ed Begley Sr., Martin Balsam, **Jack Klugman,** Lee J. Cobb, E. G. Marshall, Jack Warden, Edward Binns, Joseph Sweeney, Robert Webber, George Voskovec, and John Fiedler. As of 2009, only one of the actors that played the jurors was alive—Jack Klugman. Klugman later went on to star in two very successful television series. He played Oscar Madison in *The Odd Couple* and a medical examiner in *Quincy, M.E.* Klugman celebrated his 87th birthday in 2009.

Vertigo

This 1958 Alfred Hitchcock thriller about a detective who's drawn into a complex plot because he fears heights is arguably the director's best film. Each piece of the puzzle is fascinating in its own right, and the result is a haunting study with Jimmy Stewart as the unraveling detective and **Kim Novak** as the mystery woman. Barbara Bel Geddes, Henry Jones, and Tom Helmore help to make this a superb cinema experience. The last surviving major cast member is Kim Novak, who celebrated her 76th birthday in 2009.

Rio Bravo

Famed director Howard Hawks is in top form for this 1959 story about a sheriff trying to prevent the bad guys from helping a killer escape the town jail. Hawks has assembled a fine cast that includes John Wayne as the sheriff, Dean Martin as the town drunk, and Ricky Nelson as the young cowhand ready to prove his manhood. **Angie Dickinson** is the love interest. Also with Walter Brennan, Ward Bond, Claude Atkins, and Bob Steele. Dickinson, who turned 77 in 2008, is the last survivor of the movie's top cast members.

World War II

❑ ❑ ❑ ❑

Who was the last to survive of World War II's Allied leaders?
Who managed to escape being fingered for the assassination attempt on Hitler—and lived to tell about it for many years?
Who was the last living relative of Anne Frank?
Read on to learn about these and other last survivors of World War II.

The 1938 Munich Agreement Signatories

On September 29, 1938, leaders of Great Britain, France, and Italy signed the Munich Agreement, which allowed Adolf Hitler to take over the Sudetenland region of Czechoslovakia. British and French leaders felt this might satisfy the German leader's desire for expansion, but they were proved terribly wrong when Hitler invaded the rest of Czechoslovakia the following year. The Munich Agreement has gone down in history as a prime example of the futility of appeasing an aggressor. The last surviving signatory of the Munich Agreement was French statesman **Edouard Daladier,** who died in 1970 at age 86.

The Munich Agreement signatories were:

- Neville Chamberlain (1869–1940), Britain
- Benito Mussolini (1883–1945), Italy
- Adolf Hitler (1889–1945), Germany
- Edouard Daladier (1884–1970), France

Medal of Honor Recipients for Heroism at Pearl Harbor

Fourteen men were awarded the Congressional Medal of Honor for valor displayed on December 7, 1941, at Pearl Harbor, Hawaii. The last living survivor, **John Finn,** was wounded more than 20 times

* * * *

At the time of the Pearl Harbor attack, most photographers used black-and-white film. Although some color photos of the fighting exist, the image on the cover of this book is a still from the 2001 film Pearl Harbor, *which recreates the events that occurred on December 7, 1941.*

* * * *

Last Horse Cavalry Charge

While defending the Bataan Peninsula in January 1942, **Colonel Edwin P. Ramsey** made the last horse cavalry charge in U.S. military history. Escaping before the Bataan Death March, he helped organize guerrilla fighters against Japanese forces in the Philippines. Colonel Ramsey spoke at the dedication ceremony of the U.S. Cavalry Exhibition at the Ronald Reagan Presidential Library in June 2005, and was alive as of 2009.

Torpedo Squadron Eight at Midway

On June 4, 1942, during the Battle of Midway, 29 of the 30 men in the USS *Hornet*'s Torpedo Squadron Eight were killed during an attack on Japanese forces. Only one, Navy Ensign **George H. Gay Jr.,** survived. After his plane was shot down, he survived in the water for more than a day before being rescued. After the war, Gay worked as a commercial airline pilot. He died in 1994 at age 77.

Crew Members of Kennedy's *PT-109*

On August 2, 1943, John F. Kennedy's World War II torpedo boat, *PT-109*, was sunk by a Japanese destroyer in the Solomon Islands. Two crew members were killed, and the remaining 11 managed to swim to safety. **Gerard E. Zinser** was the last of these men to survive. In later years, Zinser worked for the U.S. Postal Service. When he passed away on August 21, 2001, he was 83 years old.

Leaders of the Warsaw Ghetto Uprising

Marek Edelman was the last living leader of the famous 1943 armed uprising of Jews against the Nazis in the Warsaw, Poland, ghetto. He also took part in the Warsaw Uprising of 1944 and was still living as of 2009. In the post–World War II years, he has spoken out in favor of freedom and justice, supporting the trade union movement Solidarity in Communist Poland, and condemning atrocities in former Yugoslavia.

Chaplains from Omaha Beach

On June 6, 1944, Allied Forces landed on Omaha Beach in Normandy, France. **Lieutenant Colonel George Russell Barber** was one of the chaplains who ministered to the wounded and dying there. He also served as chaplain at the Battle of the Bulge and during the Korean War. Lieutenant Colonel Barber passed away on December 17, 2004, at age 90, making him the last surviving Omaha Beach chaplain.

Conspirators in the Plot to Assassinate Hitler

On July 20, 1944, Colonel Claus von Stauffenberg (1907–44) planted a bomb in an attempt to assassinate Adolph Hitler. Hitler survived, and most of the conspirators were immediately executed. Carl Friedrich Goerdeler (born 1884) and Alfred Delp (born 1907) went into hiding; however, both were captured and, after months of torture, they were executed by the Nazis on February 2, 1945.

Of the approximately 100 people involved in the plot to assassinate Hitler, **Philipp von Boeselager** was the last to survive. Boeselager was frustrated over horrific military losses and had also heard that Jews and gypsies were being killed outright. When he was approached by conspirator Major General Henning von Tresckow in 1942, Boeselager did not hesitate; he even obtained the explosives. After the assassination attempt failed, suspects were rounded up. Some were tortured and killed, but none of them ever mentioned Boeselager's name. Lucky for him, after passing on the explosives, he made it back to his unit on the Eastern Front without arousing any suspicion. Boeselager passed away in May 2008 at age 90.

* * * *

The judge who presided over assassination conspirator Alfred Delp's case, Roland Freisler, died one day after Delp's execution when an American bomb landed on his courtroom.

* * * *

The French Jewish Resistance Group CRIF

Founded in 1944 at the height of World War II, CRIF *(Conseil Representatif des Institutions Juives de France)* was an organization committed to helping French Jews leave Nazi-occupied areas of their country. One of the founders was **Adam Rayski,** a journalist with the communist press. After the war, he left the communist party and took on the task of writing the definitive history of the French Jewish resistance. Rayski died in 2008 at age 95.

The Filthy Thirteen

In 1944 and 1945, paratroopers of the 101st Airborne Division led invasions into Nazi-held Europe. One group of the division, called the Filthy Thirteen, was famous for both their nonconformity and their fighting skills. In preparation for D-Day, they gave themselves mohawk haircuts and donned war paint.

The last survivor of the Filthy Thirteen is Oklahoma native **James "Jake" McNiece.** He made four combat jumps behind German lines in World War II, including in Normandy, Holland, and the siege of Bastogne. McNiece turned 90 years old in 2009.

Flag Raising at Iwo Jima

Two American flags were raised at Iwo Jima on February 23, 1945: an original flag and later a larger flag that was featured in the famous Joe Rosenthal photograph. **Charles Lindberg** (who had no relation to the famous aviator) was the last survivor of the six men who raised the first flag. He passed away in 2007 at age 86.

Of the men in the photograph, **John Bradley** was the last to die, passing away on January 11, 1994, at age 70. He was played by actor Ryan Phillippe in the 2006 Clint Eastwood movie *Flags of Our Fathers*.

Witnesses to Germany's Surrender

General Dwight D. Eisenhower and other top British, Russian, and U.S. military leaders were present in the War Room of the Supreme Headquarters of the Allied Expeditionary Force in Reims, France, on May 7, 1945—the day Germany surrendered. The last person alive of those present is **Captain Ted Bergmann,** who was working in Paris at the time as a radio public relations officer. His supervisor caught wind of the fact that something big was about to happen in Reims, and he sent Bergmann to cover it. In later years, Bergmann produced the hit television series *Three's Company*. He is still living as of 2009.

Viewers of Hitler's Dead Body

Rochus Misch, who turned 91 in 2008, was the last living person to have seen the dead bodies of Adolph Hitler and Eva Braun in their Berlin bunker in 1945. Misch served as a bodyguard and telephone operator for Hitler throughout the war.

Soldiers Who Captured Goering

On May 8, 1945, four American soldiers, including **Ed Frye** and Lieutenant Jerome Shapiro, an Orthodox Jew, captured Nazi leader Reich Marshal Hermann Goering in Austria. Frye covered Goering with a machine gun while Shapiro disarmed him. Frye passed away in February 2009 at age 85, making him the last of the four soldiers.

"Big Three" Leaders at Yalta Conference

Franklin Roosevelt

In 1945, the leaders of the "Big Three" Allied powers—the United States, Great Britain, and Russia—met at Yalta and held their most most important wartime meeting. U.S. President Franklin Roosevelt and British Prime Minister **Winston Churchill** agreed to some of Stalin's demands to allow Soviet military strength in post-war Eastern Europe. The last of these leaders to die was Winston Churchill, who passed away in 1965 at age 90.

Leaders who attended the Yalta Conference were:

- Franklin Roosevelt (1882–1945), United States
- Joseph Stalin (1879–1953), Soviet Union
- Winston Churchill (1874–1965), Great Britain

Potsdam Conference's "Big Three"

In this last meeting of World War II's "Big Three" Allied leaders, President **Harry Truman** replaced the deceased Franklin Roosevelt and Clement Atlee replaced Winston Churchill, whose party had lost the 1945 general election and with it his position as prime minister. The last survivor of the three was President Truman, who died December 25, 1972.

Leaders who attended the Potsdam Conference were:

- Joseph Stalin (1879–1953), Soviet Union
- Clement Atlee (1883–1967), Great Britain
- Harry Truman (1884–1972), United States

Nuremburg Trial Criminals

At the Nuremburg trials after World War II, **Rudolf Hess,** Adolph Hitler's private secretary and later deputy fuehrer, was sentenced to life in Spandau Prison in Berlin. He died in 1987 at age 93, the last surviving of the 21 major war criminals tried at Nuremburg.

* * * *

Hess flew to Scotland in 1941—allegedly to convince Great Britain to drop out of the war.

* * * *

U.S. Prosecutors at Nuremberg

Born to a Romanian Jewish family, **Benjamin B. Ferencz** was brought to the United States as an infant. After graduating from Harvard Law School and serving as an enlisted man in General George Patton's Third Army, he was chosen to be part of a team sent to Berlin to find evidence of Nazi genocide. At age 27, he became chief prosecutor for the United States in the Einsatzgruppen case, one of the 12 Nuremberg Trials. Einsatzgruppen were German military units charged with murdering civilian citizens of occupied countries and prisoners of war. All 24 defendants were convicted, and 14 were sentenced to death.

After the war, Ferencz taught international law at Pace University in New York and was a founder of the Pace Peace Center. Still alive as of 2009, Ferencz is the last living American prosecutor at the Nuremberg Trials.

U.S. Interrogators at Nuremberg

As a native of Luxembourg, U.S. Army intelligence officer **John Dolibois** spoke fluent German. He was one of five men assigned to interrogate the German war crime defendants at the Nuremberg Trials. Born in 1918, Dolibois was still alive as of 2008, making him the last surviving American interrogator at Nuremberg.

World War II Axis Leaders

After World War II, Adolph Hitler (1889–1945) of Germany committed suicide, Benito Mussolini (1883–1945) of Italy was murdered, and **General Hideki Tojo** of Japan was executed. The last of these Axis leaders to survive was Tojo, who was tried and found guilty of war crimes—including conducting biological experiments on prisoners of war. He was executed by the Allied forces in 1948.

Five-Star Generals and Admirals

During World War II, armies from various countries fought together, which at times presented the problem of a U.S. officer commanding an Allied officer of a seemingly higher rank. To address this problem, the United States implemented the five-star military rank on December 14, 1944, with the promotion of four Army generals and three Navy admirals. Another admiral was promoted a year later, followed by another general about six years later. No one has been promoted to this rank since. Of these nine men, the last to die was **General Omar N. Bradley** (1893–1981).

U.S. five-star generals and admirals and the date they received the rank:

Army

- General George C. Marshall, December 16, 1944
- General Douglas MacArthur, December 18, 1944
- General Dwight D. Eisenhower, December 20, 1944
- General Omar N. Bradley, September 20, 1950

Navy

- Admiral William D. Leahy, December 15, 1944
- Admiral Ernest J. King, December 17, 1944
- Admiral Chester Nimitz, December 19, 1944
- Admiral William F. "Bull" Halsey, December 11, 1945

Air Force

- General Henry H. Arnold, December 21, 1944 (promoted during his service with the U.S. Army Air Corps; became a five-star Air Force general when this branch of the service was created in 1947)

* * * *

The highest U.S. military rank of all time is General of the Armies of the United States. It has been awarded to only two men—World War I General John J. "Black Jack" Pershing in 1919 and General George Washington in 1976 (posthumously).

* * * *

The Liberation of Auschwitz

Approximately 1.6 million people, including as many as 1.5 million Jews, were killed at Auschwitz, the largest Nazi death camp. On January 27, 1945, four Soviet Army divisions liberated the camp. The last surviving commander of these divisions, **General Vasily Petrenko,** died on March 21, 2003, at age 92. In an interview with BBC Radio in 2001, the general said some of the first things he saw upon entering the camp were suitcases filled with children's boots and piles of children's eyeglasses.

Relatives of Anne Frank

Anne Frank (1929–45) was a Jewish girl who wrote a diary while she and her family hid from the Nazis in the Netherlands. When the family was discovered, she was sent to her death at the Bergen-Belsen concentration camp. Her diary is now recognized as one of the most important autobiographical works of the 20th century. **Buddy Elias,** a cousin of Anne Frank and her last surviving relative, turned 83 years old in 2008.

Yasukuni Swordsmiths

During the Second World War, Japanese swordsmiths made katanas, or samurai swords, for officers of the Japanese Imperial Army at Yasukuni Shrine in Tokyo. The last living of the swordsmiths was **Naoji Kariya,** who was 91 in 2008.

The Supreme Court of the United States

❑ ❑ ❑ ❑

Which Supreme Court ruling attempted to define obscenity?
Which ruling made it difficult
for public officials to defend themselves against libel?
Which ruling declared racial quotas unconstitutional?
Read on to find out.

McCulloch v. Maryland

In this 1819 case, the Supreme Court decided that the federal government had the power to create a bank, even though the U.S. Constitution did not specifically mention this power. The *McCulloch v. Maryland* decision led to a strengthening of the federal government vis-à-vis the states. The last surviving member of the Court who ruled on this case was **Joseph Story,** who died at age 65 in 1845.

Lochner v. New York

In *Lochner v. New York* (1905), a state law prohibiting bakers from working more than 60 hours per week was declared unconstitutional by the Supreme Court. A 5–4 majority opinion cited New York's violation of due process and the "right of contract between employers and employees" as running afoul of 14th Amendment protections. Critics believed the ruling would promote a laissez-faire form of capitalism, where treatment of individual workers was given short shrift against the unfettered pursuit of profits.

The ruling ushered in the "Lochner era," a period that saw a number of worker protection laws come to an end. But the ruling was short-lived. In 1937 the Supreme Court effectively overturned *Lochner* when *West Coast Hotel v. Parrish* made it legal to impose minimum-wage regulations on private employers.

The last survivor of the court members who presided over *Lochner* was **Oliver Wendell Holmes Jr.** One of the most respected justices in Supreme Court history, Holmes wrote a dissenting opinion in the case, arguing, "This case is decided upon an economic theory which a large part of the country does not entertain." He died in 1935, two days before his 94th birthday.

Schenck v. United States

In this 1919 case, the Supreme Court unanimously decided that the government can prevent freedom of speech if that speech presents a "clear and present danger." As secretary of the Socialist Party, Charles Schenck had printed and distributed thousands of leaflets promoting opposition to the draft during World War I. With antagonistic directives such as "Assert your rights" and "Do not submit to intimidation" prompting the populace to rebel, the Court ultimately felt that Schenck's actions fell well outside of First Amendment protections. Schenk spent six months in prison as a result of the ruling.

The last survivor of this Court was Tennessee's **James C. McReynolds.** A former attorney general in President Woodrow Wilson's administration, McReynolds was noted for his abrasiveness. A rumor circulated that Wilson appointed him to the Court to get him out of the Cabinet. McReynolds died in 1946 at age 84.

Korematsu v. United States

The court ruling over *Korematsu v. United States* (1944) decided that the federal government could lawfully remove people of Japanese ancestry from locations that were susceptible to Japanese attack during World War II. The case evolved as a result of a major American initiative that forcibly relocated Japanese Americans to internment camps during World War II. In addition to being displaced from their homes and communities, more than 100,000 relocated citizens faced substantial hardships. These included overcrowding, temperature extremes (many camps were located in the desert), insufficient heat, and inadequate food supplies.

Fred Korematsu refused the order and was subsequently prosecuted and convicted. His challenge of the order's constitutionality rose to the Supreme Court level. The Court reasoned that the measure might appear racist in nature, but it was not. Bolstering the argument,

Justice Hugo Black delivered the court opinion, explaining that the United States maintained such a right, given the fact that its shores were currently being threatened by hostile forces. In his dissent, Justice Frank Murphy called the court's ruling a "legalization of racism."

Stanley F. Reed was the last surviving justice who ruled on *Korematsu v. United States.* He passed away in 1980 at age 95.

* * * *

Beginning in 1990, $1.6 billion in reparations were paid to some 82,210 surviving Japanese Americans.

* * * *

Roth v. United States

In this 1957 case, New York publisher Samuel Roth was accused of distributing obscene materials through the mail. He had been sending advertisements for such publications as *Wanton by Night* and *American Aphrodite Number Thirteen* to random individuals. Roth was arrested after authorities received complaints from several recipients. Roth was charged with violating the Comstock Act, an 1872 act that prohibited sending obscene materials through the mail. Roth was found guilty in the U.S. District Court of New York. Roth's lawyers appealed the decision, claiming that the Comstock Act violated the First Amendment. The Supreme Court agreed to hear the case, and in its 6–3 decision, it ruled that "Obscenity is not within the area of constitutionally protected freedom of speech or press." It then described a test of obscenity based on "contemporary community standards." The last living justice presiding over this case was **William J. Brennan Jr.,** who passed away in 1997.

Mapp v. Ohio

In 1957, Cleveland police officers received a tip that a suspect in a recent local bombing was hiding out at the home of a woman named Dolly Mapp. Police went to the home and demanded entrance. When Mapp refused, the officers forced their way in. During their search they found pornographic materials and placed Mapp under arrest. Mapp was tried and found guilty, but her lawyers appealed on the grounds that her Fourth Amendment rights forbidding unreasonable searches and seizures had been violated. The Supreme Court of Ohio upheld her conviction, ruling that although the search was unlawful, Mapp's conviction resting on evidence from the search was still valid. The Supreme Court of the United States opted to hear the case, and in 1961 it held that evidence obtained in illegal searches and seizures cannot be used in criminal trials in state courts.

The last survivor of this Court was **William J. Brennan Jr.,** who died in 1997 at age 91. He voted with the majority.

New York Times v. Sullivan

In 1960, *The New York Times* ran a full-page ad alleging that the arrest of Martin Luther King Jr. for perjury in Montgomery, Alabama, was part of a campaign against his integration and civil rights efforts. Montgomery officials took offense to the ad, and Montgomery city commissioner L. B. Sullivan filed a libel action against *The New York Times* and the individuals who submitted the ad. An Alabama jury ruled in Sullivan's favor and awarded Sullivan $500,000. *The New York Times* appealed, and in 1964, the Supreme Court of the United States unanimously ruled that statements about public officials are protected from libelous actions except where "actual malice" is shown. The last member to survive from this Court was **Byron R. White,** who was 84 when he passed away in 2002.

Furman v. Georgia

In 1972, the Supreme Court ruled on a case brought by three death row inmates from Georgia and Texas. The inmates argued that the death penalty violated their Eighth Amendment rights against cruel and unusual punishment. In a 5–4 decision, the Supreme Court decided that the death penalty was not only cruel and unusual punishment, it also violated individuals' 14th Amendment rights because it was disproportionately meted out to the "poor and despised." This ruling led many states to rewrite their statutes relating to trial and sentencing procedures. The last justice involved in *Furman v. Georgia* to survive was **William H. Rehnquist,** who died in 2005 at age 80.

Regents of the University of California v. Bakke

Allan Bakke sued the University of California at Davis in 1974, claiming he was denied admission because he was white. His claim was based on the fact that the university's application process involved separating applicants into two pools for the 100 open spots. One pool was the regular pool, and 84 of the 100 spots were filled from this pool of applicants. The other pool was a special admissions pool for minority or disadvantaged applicants, and 16 of the 100 spots were filled from this pool.

All applicants with an undergraduate grade point average below 2.5 on a 4.0 scale were automatically rejected from the regular pool. The admissions committee then selected which remaining applicants would be granted an interview. Those applicants were then judged on many factors, including their interview performance, grade point averages, MCAT scores, and extracurricular activities. Each candidate's "benchmark score" was determined by these factors, and the 84 applicants with the highest scores were accepted to the program.

The applicants in the special admissions pool did not have to meet the grade point average requirement, nor were they compared with the applicants in the regular pool. Approximately 20 percent of the special admissions applicants were granted interviews, and after that the process was similar to the regular admissions process.

Bakke applied to the university in 1973 and again in 1974. After his second rejection, he filed suit. Bakke claimed his scores were higher than the applicants who were accepted through the special admissions process, and therefore the university was discrimating against him solely on the basis of his race, in violation of the 14th Amendment. After the Superior Court ruled in Bakke's favor, the university appealed, but the Supreme Court of California also ruled in Bakke's favor.

The Supreme Court of the United States heard the case in 1978. It ruled in Bakke's favor and declared racial quotas unconstitutional while at the same time stating that race could be considered as one of many factors in admissions decisions. The last of the *Regents of the University of California v. Bakke* justices to survive was **John Paul Stevens,** who was still on the Court in 2009 at age 89.

Hispanic History

❑ ❑ ❑ ❑

What happened on Clipperton Island?
Who was the last soldier who fought in the Mexican Revolution to survive?
Who were the great Mexican muralists?
All the answers are in this chapter.

Early 19th-Century South American Liberators

Argentine hero **José de San Martín** led the struggle against Spanish rule in South America. He died in 1850, the last of the five liberators of his era.

The following were his four contemporaries:

- Antonio José de Sucre (died 1830) helped liberate Peru.
- Simón Bolívar (died 1830) helped liberate Colombia.
- Francisco de Paula Santander (died 1840) helped liberate Colombia.
- Bernardo O'Higgins Riquelme (died 1842) helped liberate Chile.

Clipperton Island

Clipperton Island, an isolated Pacific island 700 miles southwest of Mexico, provided refuge for pirate John Clipperton in the 1700s and whaling ships in the 1800s. In 1897, ownership switched from France to Mexico; it went back to France in 1935. In 1914, approximately 100 people were living on the island when provisions from the mainland ceased because of the Mexican Revolution. Many of these people were dead by the following year, when the U.S. warship *Lexington* offered to evacuate the survivors. The Mexican governor refused, forcing the survivors to continue to fend for themselves.

By 1917, only one man remained alive on the island, lighthouse keeper Victoriano Álvarez. He had proclaimed himself the island's ruler, beating, raping, enslaving, and in some cases murdering the remaining women. On July 18, 1917, while searching for enemy

Germans, the USS *Yorktown* landed on Clipperton. The crew found only three women, eight children, and the body of Victoriano Álvarez, who had just been killed by one of the women.

In 1981, oceanographer Jacques Cousteau made the documentary *Clipperton: The Island Time Forgot*, bringing last survivor **Ramon Arnaud,** who was one of the children rescued in 1917, back to Clipperton Island, where he gave his account of Álvarez's killing.

Presidents During the Mexican Revolution

The Mexican Revolution lasted from the revolt against Porfirio Díaz in 1910 to the Álvaro Obregón presidency in 1921. Of the 14 men who occupied the presidency during this period, the last living was **Roque González Garza,** who served as president for five months in 1915. He died on November 12, 1962, at age 77.

Mexican Survivors Who Fought Pancho Villa

Teodoro Garcia died at age 110 in 1999. He was the last surviving soldier who fought in the Mexican Revolution (1910–20) against the forces of revolutionary leader Francisco "Pancho" Villa. Villa was assassinated in 1923 at age 45.

Zapata's Revolutionary Army

Mexican revolutionary leader Emiliano Zapata, a fighter for land redistribution, was assassinated in 1919 at the age of 39. **Emeterio Pantaleon,** Zapata's last surviving general, outlived him by almost 83 years, dying in 2002 at 105 years old. Pantaleon won 53 of his 55 battles during the Mexican Revolution.

Great Mexican Muralists

Many popular Mexican murals of the 1920s and '30s represented the artists' socialist political beliefs. The last living of these muralists was **David Alfaro Siqueiros,** who died in 1974.

Other popular Mexican mural artists of this period include:

- José Clemente Orozco (died 1949)
- Diego Rivera (died 1957)

Hispanic Actresses from the Golden Age of Hollywood

During the 1930s, '40s, and '50s, several actresses of Hispanic descent became well-known American movie stars. The last surviving actress is Puerto Rican-native **Rita Moreno,** who was born in 1931. A dancer and singer as well as an actress, she has won an Oscar, an Emmy, a Tony, and a Grammy.

Other popular Hispanic actresses from this period:

- Dolores del Río (died 1983)
- Katy Jurado (died 2002)

Hispanic Actors from the Golden Age of Hollywood

Of the handful of actors of Hispanic descent who became well-known movie stars, the last survivor was Mexican native **Ricardo Montalbán.** Winner of a Screen Actors Guild Life Achievement Award in 1994, Montalbán's many memorable roles included Mr. Roarke, the host of the *Fantasy Island* television series, and Khan, the villain of both the original *Star Trek* TV series and a subsequent movie. More recently, Montalbán played the grandfather role in the *Spy Kids* movies. He passed away on January 14, 2009, at age 88.

Other major male Hispanic actors of this era:

- Pedro Armendáriz (died 1963)
- Cantinflas (died 1993)
- César Romero (died January 1, 1994)
- Fernando Rey (died March 9, 1994)
- Gilbert Roland (died May 15, 1994)
- Anthony Quinn (died 2001)

Religion

❑ ❑ ❑ ❑

Who was the last surviving child of Muhammad?
Which Protestant Reformation leader lived the longest?
Which of the Jesuits involved in
the famous exorcism case
was the last to survive?
This chapter answers these questions and more!

Sons of Mattathias

As the Jews of Judea were being forced to accept Greek paganism, a man rose up in defiance: Mattathias. He and his five sons—Eleazar, John, Judas, Jonathan, and **Simon**—were known as the Maccabees. They fought throughout the country, gathering followers, destroying pagan altars, and forcing their enemies to flee. Simon, the last living of the five sons of Mattathias, was murdered around 135 B.C. The efforts of the Maccabees meant the resumption of Jewish control of Judea for another 80 years.

The 12 Apostles

John was the last of Jesus Christ's original 12 apostles. He is also the only one who is believed to have died of natural causes, passing away at about A.D. 100 at an estimated age of 90 to 100 years. Judas, the apostle who betrayed Christ, committed suicide, and the remaining ten apostles were most likely murdered between A.D. 33 and A.D. 67. John spent his last years in exile on the island of Patmos in the eastern Mediterranean, where he wrote the Book of Revelation, the last book of the New Testament.

Gospel Writers

The writers of the Bible's four gospels were Matthew, Mark, Luke, and **John.** Matthew and John were two of Jesus' 12 apostles, while Mark and Luke were associates of Apostle Paul. It is believed that Matthew, Mark, and John were of Jewish ancestry and that Luke was Greek. The last survivor was John, who died in about A.D. 100.

Children of Muhammad

Muhammad lived from about A.D. 570 to A.D. 632. **Fatima** (605–33) was his youngest daughter and last surviving child. Born in Mecca, Arabia, she married Ali, the fourth Muslim caliph. Fatima cared for Muhammad during his last illness and died soon after him. She was survived by two sons and two daughters.

Protestant Reformation Leaders

John Knox, leader of the Protestant Reformation in Scotland, was the last surviving of the religious movement's major leaders. He died in 1572 at around 57 to 67 years of age.

The following were other major leaders of the Protestant Reformation:

- Huldrych/Ulrich Zwingli (died 1531)
- Martin Luther (died 1546)
- Philipp Melanchthon (died 1560)
- John Calvin (died 1564)

John Calvin

Sikhism's Gurus

Of the more than 20 million people in the world who belong to the religion of Sikhism, the great majority live in the Indian province of Punjab. A monotheistic religion, it was founded by ten Gurus between 1469 and 1708. The last surviving of the original gurus was **Gobind Singh,** who died in 1708 at age 41.

First Quorum of the 12 Apostles

The Quorum of the 12 Apostles is a group that presides over the Church of Jesus Christ of Latter-day Saints after its president dies and until a new president is ordained. The last surviving member of the first quorum was mathematician **Orson Pratt.** His mission work took him across the Atlantic Ocean 16 times. Pratt died in 1881 at 70 years old.

Jesuits Involved in the Famous Exorcism Case

In 1973, William Peter Blatty's best-selling novel, *The Exorcist*, was made into a hit movie of the same name. It was based on an actual exorcism case in 1949 in the psychiatric wing at Alexian Brothers Hospital in St. Louis. The three Jesuit priests involved were William Bowdern, William Van Roo, and **Walter H. Halloran.** The last living of these, Father Halloran, died in 2005 at a Jesuit retirement home in suburban Milwaukee at age 83. In later years, he said he never came to a definite conclusion about the case—that is, whether it was a manifestation of supernatural evil or the result of psychosomatic illness.

Sons of Cheikh Ahmadou Bamba

Senegal native Cheikh Ahmadou Bamba was the founder of the Sufi Islam brotherhood. During the years of French colonization, he was exiled by French authorities because of his influential nonviolent campaign. He died at the age of 74 in 1927. Each year many people make a pilgrimage to his tomb.

Bamba's last surviving son was **Serigne Saliou Mbacke.** Head of the Mouride Brotherhood since 1990 and religious adviser to Senegal's president, Mbacke died on December 28, 2007, at age 92. He was succeeded by one of Bamba's grandsons.

Miscellaneous

❑ ❑ ❑ ❑

Read on to learn all about the grab bag of facts that conclude this book.

New Bedford Whalers

New Bedford, Massachusetts, supplanted Nantucket Island as the Yankee whaling industry's hub in the 1840s. Why? Sea access was simpler. Returning whaling ships (which had heavy cargo on board) had difficulty navigating the Nantucket Harbor sandbar. Perhaps more importantly, the rise of railroads made it logical to offload whale products on the mainland.

In the late 19th century, the New Bedford whaling industry began its own slow decline. When the 1849 Gold Rush came, many whalers relocated to San Francisco. The New Bedford industry encountered other problems, such as whale depletion, whale oil's gradual replacement by petroleum, and the inherent dangers of the trade. The schooner *John L. Manta* made New Bedford's last whaling voyage in 1925.

When the National Park Service interviewed people for an oral history project in 1999, it found **Antonio Lopes** to be the last living New Bedford whaler. Born in the Cape Verde Islands, Lopes had been on two six-month trips in the early 1920s. He passed away in 2000 at age 103.

East River Bridges

Henry Hornbostel, who worked on both the Williamsburg and Queensboro bridges, died in 1961 at age 94. He was the last living of the East River bridge designers.

The following are New York City's East River bridges and their designers:

- The Brooklyn Bridge, built from 1870 to 1883; designed by John Augustus Roebling (1806–69) and completed by his son, Washington Roebling (1837–1926)

- The Manhattan Bridge, completed in 1909; designed by Leon Moisseiff (1872–1943)
- The Williamsburg Bridge, completed in 1903; designed by Leffert L. Buck (1837–1909) and Henry Hornbostel (1867–1961)

Brooklyn Bridge

- The Queensboro Bridge, completed in 1909; designed by Gustav Lindenthal (1850–1935) and Henry Hornbostel (1867–1961)

Construction Difficulties

Understanding the construction challenges the East River bridges posed becomes easier when one understands the East River, which is a silt-bottomed tidal strait known for heavy maritime traffic and ferocious currents. John Roebling died of complications from a freak ferry accident during the Brooklyn Bridge's design phase. Dozens of workers were also killed before the bridges were complete.

In an attempt to rest the Brooklyn Bridge's piers on bedrock, engineers designed large, vertical, airtight concrete cylinders called *caissons.* These dangerous cement jars enabled workers to haul out the silt, but it was difficult to regulate the air pressure inside. Some workers died of "caisson disease" (aka "the bends," the bane of careless scuba divers) after sudden pressure changes. This affliction paralyzed Washington Roebling for life in 1872, but his talented wife, Emily Warren Roebling, supervised construction to completion.

Presidential Memorial Designers

The last designer of the three original Washington, D.C., presidential memorials was **John Russell Pope,** designer of the Jefferson Memorial, who died in 1937. The structure was dedicated in 1943, the 200th anniversary of the third president's birth.

The following individuals designed the other two original memorials:

- Robert Mills (1781–1855), designer of the Washington Monument
- Daniel Chester French (1850–1931), designer of the Lincoln Memorial

The United Nations Charter

Harold Stassen was known as the "Boy Governor" after his election to the Minnesota governorship at age 31. In 1943, he resigned to join the U.S. Navy. He served on the staff of Admiral William Halsey and reached the rank of captain by war's end.

During the Eisenhower administration, Stassen was a member of the National Security Council, director of the Foreign Operations Administration, and deputy representative of the United States to the United Nations Disarmament Commission. However, he will probably go down in history mostly for his role in the creation of the United Nations.

President Roosevelt appointed him a member of the 1945 San Francisco UN Charter Conference. In later years he repeatedly ran for the U.S. presidency, not so much because he had a chance of winning but rather to provide a vehicle for his views. At the time of his death on March 4, 2001, at age 93, he was the last living signatory of the United Nations Charter.

* * * *

In 1946, John D. Rockefeller Jr. donated land on Manhattan Island for the United Nations headquarters.

* * * *

The Taft-Hartley Act

Ohio Senator Robert Taft and New Jersey Representative **Fred Hartley** cosponsored the 1947 Taft-Hartley Act. Officially titled the Labor-Management Relations Act, it limited some of the pro-union features of the Wagner Act of 1935. The Taft-Hartley Act provided for the following stipulations:

- Closed union shops were now illegal.
- To form a union, a majority of employees would have to vote in favor of unionization.
- The president could, for reasons of national security, investigate and halt a strike.
- Jurisdictional strikes (those over competing unions or over use of nonunion work) and wildcat strikes (strikes without union officials' support) were now illegal.
- Unions couldn't contribute to political campaigns.

Taft-Hartley came about as a reaction to union gains during the FDR years and also because companies had the support of influential pro-business politicians (such as Robert Taft). Although President Truman vetoed Taft-Hartley, Congress overrode his veto. Taft (1889–1953), son of William Howard Taft, the 27th president of the United States, was a longtime U.S. senator and unsuccessful Republican presidential hopeful. Hartley, a 20-year veteran of the House of Representatives, survived Taft by 16 years, dying in 1969 at age 67. However, one key architect of the bill was Cincinnati attorney and Taft confidant Mack Swigert, who turned 101 in September 2008.

The "Hollywood Ten"

The last surviving member of the blacklisted film screenwriters, producers, and directors known as the Hollywood Ten was Oscar-winning screenwriter **Ring Lardner Jr.** The others were Alvah Bessie, Herbert Biberman, Lester Cole, Edward Dmytryk, John Howard Lawson, Albert Maltz, Sam Ornitz, Robert Adrian Scott, and Dalton Trumbo. In 1947, Lardner refused to answer the questions of the House Un-American Activities Committee and was sentenced to a year in prison. Like others of the Ten, Lardner continued to work in film by using various names to hide his identity. Many years later, the Writers Guild of America gave blacklisted writers credit for the film work they had done under other names. Lardner died on October 31, 2000, at age 85.

Namesakes of U.S. States

George Washington, who died in 1799, was the last survivor of the nine people after whom states of the United States have been named.

The following states were also named after real people:

- Virginia and West Virginia were named for Queen Elizabeth I, the "Virgin Queen" (1533–1603)
- Delaware was named for Thomas West, Baron De La Warr (1577–1618)
- North Carolina and South Carolina were named for King Charles I (1600–49)
- Maine and Maryland were named for Queen Henrietta Maria (1609–69), queen of Charles I and mother of kings Charles II and James II
- Pennsylvania was named for Admiral Sir William Penn, father of William Penn (1621–70)
- New York was named for James Stuart, Duke of York, and later King James II (1633–1701), the second son of Charles I
- Louisiana was named for King Louis XIV (1638–1715)
- Georgia was named for King George II (1683–1760)

Namesakes of U.S. State Capitals

Christopher Columbus

Of the 50 state capitals in the United States, 23 are named after people. These include two named after Christopher Columbus, two after Revolutionary War generals (Richard Montgomery, Francis Nash), and four after U.S. presidents (Jefferson, Madison, Jackson, and Lincoln). The last living state capital namesake was Quebec-born gold prospector **Joseph Juneau.** Cofounder of Juneau, Alaska, he was among the first men to discover gold in the Juneau area. Born in 1826, he passed away in March 1899.

Index

❑ ❑ ❑ ❑

D

E

F

G

H

S

Y

Z